K–12 CLASSROOM TEACHING

K–12 CLASSROOM TEACHING

A Primer for New Professionals

Fourth Edition

Andrea M. Guillaume

California State University, Fullerton

PEARSON

Boston   Columbus   Indianapolis   New York   San Francisco   Upper Saddle River
Amsterdam   Cape Town   Dubai   London   Madrid   Milan   Munich   Paris   Montreal   Toronto
Delhi   Mexico City   São Paulo   Sydney   Hong Kong   Seoul   Singapore   Taipei   Tokyo

Senior Acquisitions Editor: Kelly Villella Canton
Editorial Assistant: Annalea Manalili
Senior Marketing Manager: Darcy Betts
Production Editor: Paula Carroll
Editorial Production Service: S4Carlisle Publishing
Manufacturing Buyer: Megan Cochran
Electronic Composition: S4Carlisle Publishing
Interior Design: S4Carlisle Publishing
Photo Researcher: Kate Cebik
Cover Designer: Linda Knowles

Credits and acknowledgments borrowed from other sources and reproduced, with permission, in this textbook appear on appropriate page within text.

Library of Congress Cataloging-in-Publication Data
Guillaume, Andrea M.
  K-12 classroom teaching: a primer for new professionals/Andrea M. Guillaume.—4th ed.
    p. cm.
  ISBN 978-0-13-256549-3
 1. First year teachers—United States. 2. Teaching—United States. I. Title.
LB2844.1.N4G85 2012
371.102—dc22

2011003121

10 9 8 7 6 5 4 3 2 1   15 14 13 12 11

www.pearsonhighered.com

ISBN-10: 0-13-256549-8
ISBN-13: 978-0-13-256549-3

About the Author

Andrea Guillaume began her career in education as a public middle school teacher. She specializes in pedagogy, particularly in active teaching and content methods. At California State University, Fullerton, she teaches future and current teachers foundations, mathematics and science methods, and educational research. She also enjoys working with teachers new to their career in a local induction program. Andrea has written numerous texts and articles related to teaching. She cherishes every second she spends with her husband, two sons (Alex and Zach), and Black Labrador Lilah.

For Marnie, forever.

Brief Contents

Contents

Note: The pronouns *she, he, her,* and *his* are used variously throughout the text to represent either teacher or student.

Note: Every effort has been made to provide accurate and current Internet information in this book. However, the Internet and information posted on it are constantly changing, so it is inevitable that some of the Internet addresses listed in this textbook will change.

Preface

By learning you will teach; by teaching you will learn.

—Latin Proverb

K–12 Classroom Teaching: A Primer for New Professionals is a core text for elementary and secondary preservice teachers who are taking introduction to teaching courses, field experience courses, or general methods courses. It is also a quick but thorough core text for inservice teachers who are gaining certification at the same time they are beginning to teach. Instructors of specialized methods courses or foundations of education courses will find this primer a useful supplemental text.

K–12 Classroom Teaching presents useful, practical points of view that can provide meaning and direction behind new teachers' actions related to a number of central educational issues. It uses clear, reader-friendly language to concisely explore key aspects of classroom teaching, including 21st-century teaching and learning, strategies for learning about students and their families, educational stances, planning and assessment, inclusive and responsive instruction, instructional models and strategies, classroom management and discipline, and professional growth. Chapters include a balance of up-to-date discussions of educational issues, research findings, and practical advice. The selection and presentation of topics is guided by a conceptual approach that emphasizes the active nature of learning to teach.

Conceptual Approach

K–12 Classroom Teaching: A Primer for New Professionals is based on the premise that teaching is goal directed, interactional, and mindful of the local setting in its efforts to encourage learners' growth. Two core convictions are that classroom teaching is complex and that today's teachers face special difficulties given current demands and events at home and abroad. It takes the conceptual approach that in the face of these challenging conditions, teachers at their best are guided by:

- A commitment to understanding their particular students and placing students at the center of every decision.
- A clear sense of what they hope to accomplish.
- An understanding of the context and of what research shows to be effective.
- A set of professional knowledge and skills.
- A sense of ethics concerning what is right.
- A sense of responsibility to value and enhance the learning of every student.

Building these dispositions, commitments, and understandings is hard work, so this text approaches the process of learning to teach (and of learning in general) as an active, social one. Through its content and through its approach, the text encourages readers to reflect on past experience, to question assumptions, to consider multiple sources of information, and to commit to enacting well-defined notions of good practice that address learners' diverse needs and honor the dignity of the human experience.

Organization of the Text

Chapters are arranged topically, and content of later chapters draws from the work the reader accomplishes in earlier chapters.

- In Chapter 1, the text begins with an exploration of the distinct character of classroom teaching. Chapter 1 explores this character through six propositions of teaching that lay a foundation for the entire text through their content and their implications for each chapter's presentation-of information. These propositions include:
  1. Teaching looks easy . . . from the outside.
  2. Every teacher is part of a system.
  3. Teaching is goal driven.
  4. Teaching is more than telling.
  5. There is agreement on what teachers need to know and be able to do.
  6. Teachers can be effective and yet not just alike.

- Chapter 2 stresses the importance of understanding the philosophical bases found in educational practice and of developing one's own stance toward education. Subsequent chapters ask readers to use their stance to guide their decisions related to the chapters' content.
- Chapter 3 explores the growing range of strengths and needs exhibited by students in U.S. schools and urges new teachers to use knowledge of specific students and families as the starting point for their instructional decisions.
- Chapter 4 argues that, because students are the basis of our decisions, instruction must be inclusive and responsive to the very wide range of student needs and interests we find in every classroom. The chapter explores approaches that can respond to issues such as gender, special educational needs, and English acquisition.
- Chapter 5 addresses instructional planning both in the long range and in the short term. It guides teachers in making decisions about resources and student groupings and presents a variety of unit planning approaches and standards-based lesson planning.
- Chapter 6 introduces six pieces of general advice for instruction using the mnemonic device COME IN: **C**onnect, **O**rganize, **M**odel, **E**nrich, **I**nteract, and consider **N**ature and **N**eeds. The chapter argues that this advice can encourage rigorous learning through rich and purposeful instruction.
- Chapter 7 shares instructional models and strategies and discusses the strengths and potential drawbacks of models such as direct instruction and inquiry.
- Chapter 8 explores principles of assessment and offers a variety of assessment strategies in keeping with those principles. Special attention is given to current concerns about accountability and its focus on student achievement as required by the No Child Left Behind Act.
- Chapter 9 addresses classroom management. It focuses on the importance of productive relationships, structure, and proactive decision making.
- Chapter 10 focuses on classroom discipline and encouraging appropriate student behavior in ways that respect students, prevent misbehavior, and encourage self-control.
- Finally, Chapter 11 addresses issues of professional involvement and growth for new teachers.

Features of the Text

Readers and reviewers of earlier editions of *K–12 Classroom Teaching* commented positively on a variety of the text's characteristics, and those have been retained in the fourth edition. They include the text's condensed format, its readable style, its useful ideas, and its personal approach.

In keeping with the text's active approach to learning, a number of special features can also be found throughout the text.

Warm-Up Exercises. Because past experience influences present learning, chapters begin with warm-up activities that help readers access their thinking related to major points about to be explored.

Presentation of Information. Key concepts are presented in clear language. Figures are often used to present information in a succinct format.

Teaching Tips. Plentiful practical classroom suggestions are placed in boxes throughout each of the chapters. Readers find three types of tips: generic teaching tips, inclusive and responsive teaching tips, and 21st-century teaching and learning tips.

Words from Teachers. The voices of previous readers, now teachers, offer advice and writing samples that are presented in many chapters. Examples include advice for building community, encouraging student participation, structuring a productive learning environment, and pursuing financial literacy.

Parting Words. Rather than concluding with a traditional summary, chapters conclude with some final words of advice related to the issues at hand.

Web Sites. Web sites related to the chapter's content are provided. Web sites provide connections to professional organizations and instructionally related resources and materials.

Opportunities to Practice. Application exercises conclude each chapter. They are meant to extend readers' connections with the content in a variety of ways that directly relate to the world of the classroom.

Blank Forms. Opportunities to Practice exercises, along with many figures throughout the text, provide for structured practice and application of the chapters' key ideas. Examples include blank observation guides, lesson plan forms, and assessment and management plans.

New to this Edition

The fourth edition of *K–12 Classroom Teaching: A Primer for New Professionals* responds to the dynamic conditions teachers today face. A number of updates enhance the text:

- The research and literature base has been thoroughly updated, and hundreds of new citations have been added. Included are recent trends such as the Core Common Standards movement, the growing body of knowledge related to the No Child Left Behind Act, and the achievement and opportunity gaps for many groups of students.
- The seed of "starting with students" from earlier editions has blossomed into a conception of inclusive and responsive teaching that provides the underpinnings of the fourth edition. Inclusive and responsive teaching is introduced in Chapter 1 and explored in all chapters. Notable examples include a new chapter, Chapter 4, Providing Inclusive and Responsive Instruction and Chapter 10, Classroom Discipline: Encouraging Appropriate Behavior.
- The link between family and school has been tightened, including an expanded treatment of the research related to the importance of family-school connections in Chapter 3. Many strategies, such as home visits and surveys (Chapter 3), and partnership in student assessment (Chapter 8) are found throughout.
- A focus on the multifaceted demands of the 21st century is sharp in the fourth edition. Demands for the 21st century such as creativity, critical thinking, systems thinking, collaboration, and multiple literacies (like Information and Communication Technology—ICT—literacy) are thoroughly addressed throughout. Every chapter has 21st Century Teaching and Learning Tips and technology-rich examples that draw from Web 2.0 applications such as social networking and authoring tools. Each chapter—such as Chapters 7, 8, and 9—addresses 21st-century demands as it discusses the knowledge and skills required of teachers of today . . . and tomorrow. Chapter 11, for example, asks teachers to explore their fit with e-learning as they consider professional development beyond their credential.

- *Issues related to secondary teachers* (middle school, junior high school, and high school teachers) have been incorporated more directly. Research and perspectives addressing the special conditions faced by secondary students and teachers are incorporated throughout the text. Two examples include:
  - Research and suggestions related to working with gay, lesbian, bisexual, and transgender (GLBT) students and families (Chapter 4).
  - Research and practical suggestions related to classroom management and discipline for secondary students (Chapters 9 and 10).

Supplements

An electronic instructor's manual is available at www.pearsonhighered.com on the Instructor's Resource Center without cost to instructors using *K–12 Classroom Teaching: A Primer for New Professionals* as part of their courses. The comprehensive instructor's manual includes the following components:

Chapter overview and key outcomes. An at-a-glance preview of the chapter and a listing of some outcomes students should be able to demonstrate after reading the chapter.
Chapter outline and graphic organizer. Two different presentations of the chapter's key points.
PowerPoint presentations. Slides that present information related to the chapter content and can be used to spark classroom discussions.
Sample class activities. Activities that can be used to access readers' prior knowledge, connect the text's main points to their lives and practice, and extend their practice.
Test bank items. Assessment tasks and traditional test items.

Acknowledgments

I am grateful to my colleagues at California State University, Fullerton, and the surrounding schools for their expertise and assistance in the development of this edition.

- Thanks to Kim Case for her assistance in obtaining schedules from practicing teachers, and to Richard Kravitz and Susan Zack for those schedules. Thanks to Loretta for hers as well.
- Thanks to colleagues who are current and former students—Dionne Sincire, Robin Mackie, Philip Campos, Britni Hong, Brittany Even, and Dan Otter—for their willing contributions and insights into teaching and learning.
- Special thanks to Cynthia Gautreau for her expertise and generosity in reviewing the information related to technology throughout the text.

Thanks, too, to family members:

- My mom, LuAnn Berthel, who worked hard not to call or email until I was finished.
- My boys—husband and sons—for friendship, support, and all they teach me.

Finally, thanks to my colleagues in the wider profession of education for their perspectives and for the wisdom that continues to shape the evolution of this text.

- Thanks to those who reviewed the third edition and provided valuable insights and directions for development of the fourth edition. They are Brenda M. Davis, Randolph-Macon College; Michael F. Hawke, Tarleton State University; Elvira K. Katić, Ramapo College of New Jersey; Christine A. Mayfield, California State University, Fullerton; Marilyn Ruda, Hunter College; and Beth R. Walizer, Fort Hays State University. The text is stronger as a result of their critiques.
- I appreciate the support of Kelly Villella Canton. Her keen knowledge of the field helped shape this text.
- Thanks are in order, too, to the production team at Pearson. You've been terrific, Annalea Manalili and Paula Carroll.

K–12 CLASSROOM TEACHING

The Nature of Teaching

Before You Begin Reading

Learning is an active process. Your current beliefs, motivations, and goals will shape what you learn as you interact with this text. Before you read, complete the following chart. What are your core convictions about teaching right now? For example, do you believe teachers make all the difference in learning? Next, record your goals as an educator. Why have you selected teaching? What do you hope to accomplish? Learning is a process not only of adding to our knowledge stores, but of also modifying or discarding notions when necessary. Revise your work as you continue learning about your profession.

Warm-Up Exercise for the Nature of Teaching	
My Core Convictions about Teaching and Learning	My Goals as a Teacher

Children play school, spend many years as students in classrooms, and encounter countless media images of teachers. As a result, by the time we reach adulthood, it is tempting to believe that we know all there is to know about teaching. However, our earlier experiences with teaching may not provide accurate information that helps us to teach well. What is teaching? How is it different from other things people do? How does one teach well? The following six propositions help to distinguish teaching from other activities, combat common misconceptions about teaching, and guide us on the journey of learning to teach well.

1. Teaching looks easy . . . from the outside.
2. Every teacher is part of a system.
3. Teaching is goal driven.
4. Teaching is more than telling.
5. There is agreement on what teachers need to know and be able to do.
6. Teachers can be effective and yet not just alike.

Teaching Looks Easy . . . from the Outside

The prevailing perception is that teaching is simple. The movies suggest that nearly anyone can teach, and earning a teaching credential somehow doesn't sound as daunting as the sleepless nights of a medical school residency. Also, current accountability demands wrongly imply that raising student achievement should be a straightforward matter (Amrein & Berliner, 2002, 2003; Cochran-Smith, 2003; Rose, 2004). In reality, the relationships among factors like teaching, learning, and testing are often very complicated. "Success at learning requires a combination of circumstances well beyond the actions of a teacher" (Fenstermacher & Richardson, 2005, p. 191). Not until we examine the myriad of factors that influence student learning, and not until we step in front of a classroom ourselves, might we realize how difficult teaching can be. Perhaps it is for this reason that some student teachers and interns become temporarily disillusioned when they begin their field experiences (Goldstein, 2005).

Teaching looks easy from the outside

Source: Scott Cunningham/Merrill.

Teaching is difficult partly because classrooms are complex (Douglas, 2009; Doyle, 1986). First, teachers are required to serve in several roles. They need to serve as advocate (Kaplan, 2003), instructor, observer, evaluator, coach, activities director, supply master, tech support, and confidante, for instance. In their varied roles, teachers make many decisions about different kinds of issues. Teachers make hundreds of decisions per day (Danielson, 1996). They need to think about students' safety, their learning, and their other needs simultaneously, all while they also consider their own personal and professional issues.

> Exercise 2 in Opportunities to Practice at the close of this chapter presents a number of recently offered metaphors for the many roles of teachers. Take a look, and think about your own vision related to these roles.

Second, the number and rapidity of events make classrooms complex. Many things happen at once, they happen quickly, and they tend to overlap. Classroom teachers must make quick judgments without time to reflect or weigh the consequences of their actions. Third, although classrooms have common elements, every learning situation is different. Individual learners' experiences and needs affect the nature of the class. Students start the year in different places academically and socially, have different interests and preferences, and go home to different circumstances. The physical, **sociocultural,** and historical setting of the class varies as well. Consequently, as teachers and their students spend time together, they build a shared and unique history. Perhaps you have noticed this yourself if you and your classmates have laughed at an inside joke, one that only the people in your particular class could appreciate.

Good teaching is neither obvious nor simplistic.

—National Board for Professional Teaching Standards (2002)

A fourth way in which classrooms are complex is that, because people affect each other, the act of teaching is inherently uncertain (Helsing, 2007). It is difficult for even an experienced teacher to predict with certainty how a class will respond to a lesson. Classrooms are also unpredictable because as teachers we may pursue goals that are unclear, our base of authority may be in question, and we are usually unsure of the outcomes of our efforts, especially long-range outcomes (Jackson, 1986). Although the desire to touch the future is a strong draw for many teachers (Eisner, 2006), we are often left uncertain about the effects of our efforts. What happens to students after they leave us? What did they learn? Did they learn *because of us* or *in spite of us?* The Teaching Tip gives a quick strategy to discover what students learn from day to day.

Finally, teaching is complex because it reaches into time both before and after face-to-face interaction with students. It requires preparation, and it requires reflection and revision. As a result, many teachers feel like their work is never finished (Lindqvist & Nordänger, 2006). Because classrooms are complex, it takes *years* to master the craft of teaching (Berliner, 2004; Cuban, 2010). Both careful study and reflective experience are necessary.

Teaching Tip

EXIT CARDS

Use exit cards to quickly discover some things about what your students learn during your lessons. At the close of a lesson, period, or day, distribute index cards or slips of paper and ask students to respond to one or two brief prompts such as, "List one thing you learned today," "Solve for x," or "What question do you still have after today's lesson?" Students leave the cards in a container by the door as their ticket out. Study the cards quickly and start the next lesson by addressing the exit card results.

Do you remember the television commercial that hawks deodorant by warning "never let them see you sweat"? That commercial seems to capture the first aspect of teaching: Teaching looks easy . . . from the outside. Though public attention on teaching and on student performance is high, few people witness the day-to-day conditions under which teachers are expected to encourage learning and to manage the complexity of the classroom without a drop of perspiration. Further, classroom complexity is compounded because classrooms exist as part of a larger system.

Every Teacher Is Part of a System

No teacher is an island. Closing the classroom door does not seal away outside influences. Instead, a teacher serves at the center of a set of nested circles of influence, as shown in Figure 1.1. Imagine an archery target. You, the teacher, are in the bull's-eye, and the outermost ring contains society in the broadest sense. What happens in your society and in the world affects your classroom daily. Let's explore a couple societal expectations and influences that affect teachers and students—the demands of the *where* and the *when* of teaching and learning today.

Teachers and the Law

As a teacher, you are expected to act in ways that are consistent with the rules and goals of the place you live: your society. In addition to the rules that guide our actions as citizens, laws govern many aspects of your behavior and professional practice as a teacher. Many laws affecting teachers are summarized in Figure 1.2.

Figure 1.1 *Circles of influence that affect classroom teachers.*

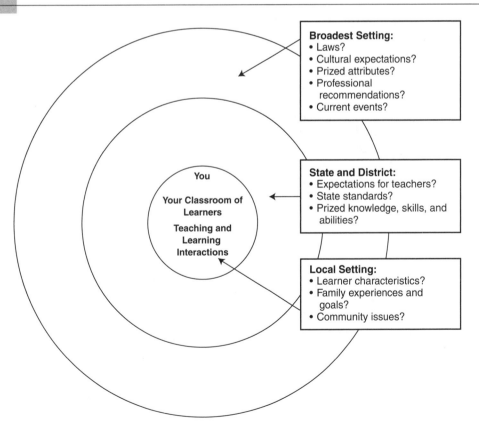

Figure 1.2   *Teachers and the law.*

1. *Public schools must not promote worship.* Schools may teach about religion if the intent is not to worship.

   If a public school allows some groups to meet there, it must provide equal access and allow religious-based groups (such as religious clubs) to meet there as well. The groups cannot be school sponsored (Alexander & Alexander, 2005).

   Students cannot be required to salute the flag if their religious convictions or matters of conscience (in some states) prohibit it (Fischer, Schimmel, & Kelly, 1999).

2. *Academic freedom has limits.* Education is a marketplace of ideas (Alexander & Alexander, 2005). Teachers are permitted to address controversial topics and use controversial methods if they are educationally defensible, appropriate for the students, and are not disruptive. School boards have authority to set curriculum and methods.

3. *Teachers' private activities must not impair their teaching effectiveness.* Although teachers hold the same rights as other citizens, their conduct is held to a higher standard. When teachers' private lives weaken their classroom effectiveness, it is possible that they may be dismissed. Sexual relationships with students are cause for dismissal (Fischer et al., 1999).

4. *Students have rights to due process.* Teachers' and schools' rules and procedures must be fair and reasonable, and justice must be administered even handedly. Due process is important for such issues as search and seizure, suspension, and expulsion (McCarthy, Cambron-McCabe, & Thomas, 1998). Families of students with disabilities have additional due process procedures related to special education services (Fischer et al., 1999).

5. *Teachers must not use academic penalties to punish behavior.* Students' academic grades cannot be lowered as a result of disciplinary infractions. Students must be allowed to make up work that accumulates during suspensions or other disciplinary periods (McCarthy et al., 1998).

6. *Corporal punishment must not be misused.* Fewer than half the states allow corporal—or physical—punishment (Underwood & Webb, 2006). In states where it is allowed, corporal punishment must be delivered while the teacher is not in a state of anger, it must fit the crime and the student's age and condition, and it must not lead to permanent injury or run the risk of such (McCarthy et al., 1998). Disciplinary actions that serve to humiliate a child may be illegal too.

7. *Teachers must protect children's safety.* Teachers must act in place of the parents (Alexander & Alexander, 2005), providing prudent, reasonable supervision to protect children from harm. They can be held negligent if they do not do so.

   Teachers and schools can protect children's safety by establishing and enforcing rules pertaining to safety and by providing prudent, reasonable care in their supervision (Fischer et al., 1999).

8. *Teachers must not slander or libel their students.* Teachers must say and write only things about students that they know objectively to be true. Even confidential files must not contain statements that demean a student's character, background, or home life. Statements should be based on relevant observable behavior (Fischer et al., 1999). Teachers must share information only with personnel who have a right to such information.

9. *Teachers must copy instructional materials in accordance with copyright laws.* The reproduction without the author's permission of copyrighted instructional materials, including print sources, visual images, videotapes, and computer software, is restricted to conditions of fair use. Examples of fair use are a single copy of a book chapter for a teacher's own use, or a copy of a poem. Teachers may not make copies to replace collected works, nor may they make copies of consumable materials. Teachers may not make copies of computer software, and they are greatly restricted in their use of videotape in the classroom (Fischer et al., 1999; McCarthy et al., 1998). Teachers should consider materials found on the World Wide Web to be copyright protected, unless the materials state that they are public domain (Underwood & Webb, 2006).

10. *Teachers must report suspected child abuse.* All states require teachers to report suspected physical or sexual abuse, and no state requires certainty, only reasonable cause to believe that abuse is present (Fischer et al., 1999). If the state requires teachers to report suspected abuse to an agency, then a teacher's report to a principal or district does not satisfy the agency requirement; the teacher must also report to the agency (Underwood & Webb, 2006).

11. *Teachers need to know the law.* Ignorance is no excuse.

12. *Teachers should be aware of emerging legal issues.* One is educational malpractice, which can be either instructional (wherein students fail to learn) or professional (wherein school personnel misdiagnose, provide improper placements, or misadvise students) (Underwood & Webb, 2006).

Source: Adapted from McDaniel (1979). Corroborated and updated with Alexander and Alexander (2005); Fischer, Schimmel, and Kelly (1999); McCarthy, Cambron-McCabe, and Thomas (1998); and Underwood and Webb (2006).

The most sweeping example of legislative action on classroom practice is the federal **No Child Left Behind (NCLB) Act of 2001.** A reauthorization of the Elementary and Secondary Education Act, NCLB was motivated by persistent disparities in student achievement—**achievement gaps**—between the performance of U.S. students overall and subgroups of the population such as minority students, students with disabilities, and students whose families face poverty. The act sought to improve **student achievement** and increase **school accountability** for that achievement. Its major requirements include:

- Development by all states of student content standards
- Annual assessment of students in grades 3 through 8 (and once in high school) to determine proficiency in mathematics and reading in line with content standards
- Measurement of all school districts for adequate yearly progress (AYP) and continuous improvement based on this AYP benchmark
- Meeting of AYP for each of nine student subgroups (based on factors such as ethnicity, physical disability, and poverty)
- Requirement for all schools to have **highly qualified teachers**

NCLB has changed our classrooms dramatically, and its effects are hotly debated. Some benefits include (Center on Education Policy, 2006):

- Concerted efforts to align content standards (goals), instruction, and assessment
- Better use of student assessment data to plan instruction and meet student needs
- Increased student achievement on state tests, including the achievement for students with disabilities (Aarons, 2009)

Some analyses (e.g., Lee, 2006), however, do not support a lessening of achievement differences. The **National Assessment of Education Progress,** or NAEP, assesses student progress across the fifty states. Study scores yourself at http://nces.ed.gov/nationsreportcard/. There you will see that, for 17-year-olds, reading and mathematics scores have not varied much; 2008 scores are just one or two points higher than 1973 scores (National Center for Education Statistics, 2009a). And approximately one-third of the nation's schools failed to make adequate yearly progress (AYP) in 2008–2009 (Center on Educational Policy, 2010).

Critics of NCLB condemn its assumptions (Rose, 2004), and many point to deleterious practices and effects associated with NCLB such as the following:

- The narrowing of the school curriculum, namely, to reading/language arts and mathematics (Berliner, 2009; Beveridge, 2010).
- A restriction of recess time, despite its cognitive, social, and health benefits (Pellegrini & Bohn, 2005).
- A lack of attention to students whose performance is perceived as less crucial for attaining targeted percentages of students deemed proficient. Such groups may include high-achieving students (Fordham Institute, 2008) and students whose performance is so low that they are unlikely to meet proficiency requirements, even with academic interventions (Booher-Jennings, 2006).
- "Gaming" practices wherein personnel focus on meeting achievement targets rather than on fostering student learning (Booher-Jennings, 2006; Rose, 2004).
- Lower teacher morale (Roller, n.d.), particularly in schools deemed high poverty (Byrd-Blake, Afolayan, Hunt, Fabunmi, Pryor, & Leander, 2010).

Current plans for the reauthorization of NCLB, among other things, attempt to address concerns such as sanctions-based growth models, equity gaps, the narrowed curriculum, and limits of current achievement tests (U.S. Department of Education, 2010). Through NCLB and other laws and expectations, society influences classrooms deeply.

Teaching and Learning in the 21st Century

The *when* of teaching—the historical context—also shapes classrooms. Current events change us. Imagine for a moment how different life is for Americans since the horrific events of September 11, 2001, or of the school-based acts of violence such as the 1999 Columbine shootings or the appalling 2007 shootings at Virginia Tech. Though rare, these events have shaped policies and procedures in schools, and they have affected the outlooks of many students and their families. We are a different people now.

Trends, too, matter. Your century—the 21st century—is one of globalization, regional economies, and connectivity. We have shifted from an industry-based society to an information-based one. Some telling examples of technology usage include such bits as:

- Americans have access to a trillion Web pages.
- Americans have 2 million televisions . . . in our bathrooms.
- During one month of his 2008 presidential campaign, Barack Obama earned $55 million . . . all on **social network services**.
- The social networking, microblogging service Twitter provided a key mechanism for mass protests in the disputed 2009 Iranian elections (*Economist*, 2009). Social media played perhaps even a larger role in the Egyptian unrest of 2011.

Indeed we live technology-soaked lives. Nearly three-quarters of people in the United States have access to the Internet at home (Internet World Statistics, 2010; U.S. Census Bureau, 2009). According to the *Economist* (2009), 93 percent of U.S. adults own cell phones, and the average teen sends 2,272 text messages per month. Not to be outdone, the average preschooler spends approximately fifty minutes on a home computer each day (Vandewater, Rideout, Wartella, Huang, Lee, & Shim, 2007). Today's students are thus often considered **digital natives** (Prensky 2001, 2005/2006) who have grown up wired.

The influence of technology in our society is indeed fierce and pervasive, and some foresee that the rate of change fueled by technology will continue to increase and result in an unpredictable future. Such a future requires that our students possess a broad range of flexible skills. For example, a national organization, the Partnership for 21st Century Skills (2009, p. 5) states, "People in the 21st century live in a technology and media-suffused environment, marked by various characteristics, including: 1) access to an abundance of information, 2) rapid changes in technology tools, and 3) the ability to collaborate and make individual contributions on an unprecedented scale. To be effective in the 21st century, citizens and workers must be able to exhibit a range of functional and critical thinking skills related to information, media and technology." See 21st Century Teaching and Learning Tip for more on 21st century outcomes.

21st Century Teaching and Learning Tip

21ST CENTURY LEARNING OUTCOMES

Some organizations have specified standards for 21st century learners. For one set, visit www.p21.org for the Partnership for 21st Cenzztury Learning's ideas about essential skills for the 21st century. Familiarize yourself with the framework, exploring the four major student outcomes:

1. Core subjects (such as mathematics) and 21st century themes (such as global awareness and health literacy)
2. Learning and innovation skills
3. Information, media, and technology skills
4. Life and career skills

According to the American Association of School Librarians' (2007, p. 3) *Standards for the 21st Century Learner*, "Learners use skills, resources, and tools to:

1. Inquire, think critically, and gain knowledge.
2. Draw conclusions, make informed decisions, apply knowledge to new situations, and create new knowledge.
3. Share knowledge and participate ethically and productively as members of our democratic society.
4. Pursue personal and aesthetic growth."

Visit these standards at the Association's Web site (ala.org)

Do schools have the technology tools to meet 21st century challenges? According to the National Center for Education Statistics (2010a):

- Approximately 100 percent of public schools have at least one computer with Internet access. In approximately one-third of the schools, that access is wireless.
- Nearly all (97%) schools have at least one instructional computer located in classrooms. The ratio of students to instructional computers with Internet access has dropped to 3.1 to 1.
- In most schools (93%), there is access to digital cameras or **interactive whiteboards** (73%).
- Public schools provide **handheld devices** infrequently to teachers (15%) and students (4%).

One-to-one laptop programs, where every student uses a laptop computer regularly, show potential for many positive outcomes (Holcomb, 2009). Some critics do, though, remain skeptical about expenses and effects of 1:1 computing (Cuban, 2006). Students are increasingly drawn to online instruction, which offers flexible scheduling and connects them with learners from all over the world. Even in 2005, 37 percent of U.S. school districts had students enrolled in technology-based distance education courses (National Center for Education Statistics, 2005). Clearly, the 21st century and its ubiquitous technology affect *who* we teach, *what* we teach, and *how* we teach today, with more change in sight.

Local Influences on Teaching Today

By moving toward the center of the target in Figure 1.1, you travel through rings that represent increasingly local and specific settings. The settings found in these rings often have narrower and more explicitly defined purposes and expectations. For example, states develop **content standards** across the curriculum, and these standards influence state and local **textbook adoptions,** professional development activities for teachers, and learning opportunities for students. Community conditions, traditions, and events provide more local influences.

People, too, offer a variety of local influences. One integral group of people is the family. Effective teachers respond to the values and dreams of the families they serve and make use of the resources offered by families and their communities (Gonzalez, Andrade, Civil, & Moll, 2001; Gonzalez, Moll, & Amanti, 2005). In fact, research consistently links effective family involvement programs with increased student achievement and other positive outcomes (e.g., Jeynes, 2005; Sheldon & Epstein, 2005). Others who affect new teachers include their colleagues, administrators, and the experienced educators—**mentors**—who supervise their growth and represent the interests and values of the profession.

Circles of Influence: Opportunities and Challenges

The relationships among circles of influence (Figure 1.1) are dynamic and often riddled with tension and dilemma. Throughout history, the interactions among rings have frequently been emotionally, culturally, and politically charged. Which influences should receive priority? How do we as teachers manage demands and priorities from different sources and levels, especially when they compete? What are the opportunities and constraints offered by the many sources of influence? Questions such as these require us to consider—and reconsider—carefully the role of schooling in our society.

Sources of influence in the various rings offer many opportunities: The United States is a wealthy nation and has an estimated literacy rate of 99 percent (Central Intelligence Agency, 2010). We are leaders in fields such as technology and medical innovations. These are potentially positive sources of influence. However, sources of influence also offer constraints. Although the United States is a wealthy nation, we find huge disparities in wealth and opportunities to learn. Berliner (2006) indicates that students who face poverty face more severe health issues, lower academic achievement, and diminished life chances. Kozol's work (1991, 2000, 2005) painfully documents the experiences of students who experience institutionalized racism in unsafe and woefully understocked urban schools. Students in many urban and less affluent suburban schools, Kozol reports, can expect funding rates half those of nearby affluent schools. Less-than-fully-qualified teachers still disproportionately inhabit high-poverty, high-minority schools (Akiba, LeTendre, & Scribner, 2010; National Comprehensive Center for Teacher Quality, 2009). Reports (e.g., Fordham Foundation, 2006) suggest that current reform efforts have done little to raise achievement for the students who need us most. Paige and Witty (2010), in that vein, argue that the Black-white achievement gap is the greatest civil rights issue of our time.

As another example of disparity, despite the prevalence of technology in our society at large, some of our students view each other across a **digital divide.** White students are more likely to use the Internet at home than are African-Americans or Latinos, and families with higher incomes and educational attainments are also more likely to use technology (U.S. Census Bureau, 2009). Latino immigrants are the least likely to have computer access (Fairlie, London, Rosner, & Pastor, 2006). The same divide exists for students who have physical disabilities.

Digital disparities are found in public schools as well. For example, a Florida study shows that students who attend low-socioeconomic schools have significantly less access to digital resources in every regard (Hohlfeld, Ritzhaupt, Barron, & Kemker, 2008). As a side note, technology and achievement gaps based on wealth and demographic factors occur across the globe, not just in the United States; try the search term "global digital divide." Still, even though the United States is a country rich with opportunities, patterns of inequity exist, and those patterns affect what happens in classrooms and in the lives of our students—in and out of school.

It may appear that the general direction of influence for the rings or sources of influence is inward: Each of the concentric layers present daunting circumstances as well opportunities that press teachers to act in certain ways and to accomplish certain ends. Fortunately, the schools and the people who work within them can push back. They can act to lessen inequities in order to improve life and learning. For instance, in a growing set of schools studied by Reeves (2003), 90% percent or more of the students are from ethnic minorities, 90 percent or more are eligible for free or reduced lunch, and 90 percent or more achieve high academic standards. Clearly poverty need not be linked to low academic achievement; committed, caring, ardent individuals make a measurable difference daily. In the case of the digital divide, schools often also serve as an equalizing factor by providing access to technology that may not be available in students' homes (DeBell & Chapman, 2006).

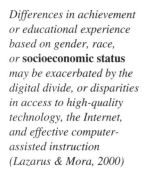

Differences in achievement or educational experience based on gender, race, or **socioeconomic status** *may be exacerbated by the digital divide, or disparities in access to high-quality technology, the Internet, and effective computer-assisted instruction (Lazarus & Mora, 2000)*

Source: Thinkstock.

Inclusive and Responsive Teaching Tip

DEMOCRATIC CLASSROOM PRACTICES

Democratic classrooms work toward three themes: liberty and freedom, justice and fairness, and equity and equal participation (Pryor, 2004). Try some of these ideas to build democratic classrooms:

- Have students help make the rules for classroom behavior via collaborative rule making (Effrat & Schimmel, 2003).
- Hold a compliments circle. Instruct students in how to give a compliment to a peer who recently did something that was helpful or noteworthy. Teach students, also, to receive compliments. Pass an item from speaker to listener. (I recently used a foam rock, and students started their compliments with, "You rock because . . .") Caution: Set up your circles to ensure that every person receives a compliment within one or two sessions. Do not allow compliments that focus on appearance or possessions.
- Use learning contracts or other self-selected learning plans to encourage students to direct their own study. Provide support along the way.
- Allow some choice in student homework.
- Allow students to conduct self-critiques of their work and resubmit after revision.
- Use learning activities where the expertise of every class member is necessary, regardless of students' status. For instance, you may give each member of a small group just one bit of information. Each group member must rely on the others' information to accomplish the goal.

Our students themselves also offer huge potential for shaping life within the classroom. A large body of literature on **democratic classrooms** and education for democratic purposes urges us to mold classrooms that reflect each student as a caring member of the class and society (e.g., Allen, 1999; Banks, 2009; Bomer & Bomer, 2001; Education Commission of the States, 2000; Fuhrman & Lazerson, 2005; Rush, 2006). In democratic classrooms, students learn to care for each other and participate in decision making as they take responsibility for their behavior and learning. Democratic practices are especially important in diverse classrooms because they equalize status differences that may arise given student differences. See Inclusive and Responsive Teaching Tip for some ideas for encouraging democratic processes.

Students' influence can extend beyond the classroom walls. For instance, Oakes and Rogers (2006) vigorously describe California students who *learn power* and reshape their woefully lacking public high schools by organizing and by working effectively with adult school leaders and community members. A similarly impressive effort is Voices of Youth in Chicago Education (VOYCE; voyceproject.org), where students conducted action research and created a report of recommendations to lower the nation's high school dropout rates (VOYCE, 2008). As students examine local conditions, challenge existing practices, and participate in **social action** or **service learning** projects (e.g., Allen, 2003; Darling-Hammond, French, & Garcia-Lopez, 2002), they shape their communities and their world.

In sum, as a teacher you are expected to teach not only toward your own ideals and aims but also toward the goals of the nested groups—rings on the target—to which you belong. A major theme of this text is that your teaching must start with the students; you must be *inclusive of* and *responsive to* your students and their families. You also have the responsibility to consider your outward influences as well. No doubt you will have opportunities to witness and manage tensions that result from the competing goals found in different rings. Part of your job will be to negotiate at least temporary solutions for the dilemmas found in competing goals. Take a few minutes to consider the goals and expectations of the circles of influence that envelop you. What influence do you hope to have in each of the rings? Try jotting your notes on Figure 1.1.

Teaching Is Goal Driven

Why are you here? Look back at your chart from the beginning of this chapter. Many teachers select education as a profession because of the desire to help "light the candle" or watch the "lightbulbs click on" as they help students learn. Others hope to help students realize the power of an education to improve life. If so, you are not alone; teaching is driven by the goal of student improvement. Students should come to know more; to know more deeply; or to have enhanced skills, abilities, or attitudes because of their time with you. Although certainly teachers are affected by their learners, and effective teachers all continue to grow over time, instructor improvement is not the universal goal of teaching. The goal of teaching is change for the learner. What changes are expected? Who creates the change? Which methods are used? The answers to these questions vary, but always we expect that learners will leave the setting different from when they entered it. Teachers strive for positive differences in learners' lives.

Teaching becomes complicated by the fact that teachers usually pursue many—and sometimes conflicting—goals. For instance, although a teacher may strive to help learners become more independent, she also needs to encourage order, and she may do so by praising conformity ("I like the way that Sung is sitting so nicely!"). Learners also pursue their own agendas. In a recent survey, fully one-third of the grade 3–12 respondents agreed with the statement, "I only do enough work to do as well as I need to get by in school" (MetLife, 2010). Here's another example of a student agenda, this one from my son Alex. When his first-grade teacher stepped into the hall for a brief conversation, Alex immediately seized the moment and leapt onto his chair. Fists and face raised to the sky, he screamed "Let's party!" In the face of many—sometimes competing—agendas, effective teachers are driven by the urgent goal of fostering change for the learners.

Do teachers in fact make a difference for learners? Research indicates that enhanced teacher preparation is associated with improved student learning (e.g., Darling-Hammond, 2000; Laczko-Kerr & Berliner, 2002, 2003), and research reported by Berliner (2004) finds that expert teachers have greater student achievement gains. Further, reviews of the literature (e.g., Bumgardner, 2010; U.S. Department of Education, 2003) present compelling evidence that individual teachers do, indeed, have a powerful effect on student learning. In a first-grade study, the teacher was *five times* more predictive of students' mathematics achievement than was family socioeconomic status (Croninger, Rice, Rathbun, & Nishio, 2007).

Teaching is goal driven: Effective teachers set high expectations for students and then *warmly demand* that students meet those expectations (Kleinfeld; 1975). *Warm demanders* build authentic relationships with their diverse students and then insist that they achieve (Bondy & Ross; 2008; Irvine & Fraser, 1998; Ross, Bondy, Gallingane, & Hambacher, 2008). Overall, you—the teacher—are the single most influential in-school contributor to student learning.

Teaching Is More than Telling

Part of the perception that teaching is easy stems from the mistaken notion that teaching and telling are the same thing: If a teacher *says it*, students will *know it*. Hear, if you will, that common though misguided teacher lament: "Come on, Class! We went *over* this!" Certainly a good lecture can be a powerful learning tool, but knowledge does not travel directly from the mouth of the teacher to the mind of the learner. Knowledge is constructed as learners filter and operate on new information using their own perspectives and experiences. Teachers need to help students connect new information to the known and to their own lives. Factors such as teachers' experience and expectations affect student learning, and so do many factors such as students' culture, physical characteristics, preferences, and prior experiences.

Because classrooms are interactive and dynamic, "teaching as telling" does not capitalize on the learners' goals or on the power of their experiences. It also does not draw directly from current theories on how children learn. Figure 1.3 summarizes current views on how people learn.

One trend that emerges from these views on how people learn is that learning seems not to be a simple matter of reception. Instead, it appears to be about active engagement, about questioning, and about facing misunderstandings and building better understandings by organizing information in meaningful ways (Bransford, 2000; Gagnon & Collay, 2001; Marlowe & Page, 1998; National Research Council, 2000). Teaching as purely telling also

Figure 1.3 *Influential views on how people learn.*

Behaviorist Approaches

- Hold that learning occurs continuously and can be intentional or unintentional.
- Focus on observable behaviors and shaping them through rewards and punishments, or consequences.
- Reinforcers include grades, praise, and tangible items. Punishment can take the form of time-outs, detentions, and names on the board for misbehavior.
- Theorists include Skinner (1971), and, more recently, Bandura.

Information Processing Approaches

- Focus on how information is selectively perceived, stored in memory, and retrieved.
- Liken the brain to a computer, a system with limited capacity that processes information according to logic and rules. Information is received through the senses and then is perceived by the mind. It enters short-term memory either from the process of sensation or from long-term memory. Concepts are stored through schemata (systems of linked concepts).
- Teachers should be systematic in their instruction to enhance learning. Some important activities are gaining students' attention, accessing background knowledge, focusing on organization of ideas, providing feedback, and supplying meaningful practice.
- Theorists include Gagne (1985) and Miller (Miller, 1956; Miller, Galanter, & Pribam, 1960).

Constructivist Approaches

- Focus on processes by which students *build* knowledge rather than *receive* it.
- Hold that we continually check new information against our mental rules in order to internalize and act on information.
- Purport that learning is social, and "disequilibration," or cognitively unsettling experiences, cause learners to reorganize cognition at higher levels.
- Students should confront their current thinking by actively testing and refining their ideas. Heterogeneous groups provide opportunities for students to challenge and support each other's thinking.
- Theorists and researchers include Bruner (1986), Driver (1989a, 1989b), Piaget (1952), and Vygotsky (1978).

Multiple Intelligence Theory

- Challenges the notion that intelligence is a single construct and suggests instead that people can be smart in many different ways.
- Holds that intelligences are many and currently include (1) logical or mathematical, (2) linguistic, (3) musical, (4) spatial, (5) bodily or kinesthetic, (6) interpersonal, (7) intrapersonal, and (8) naturalist intelligences.
- Urges schools and teachers to broaden the kinds of experiences offered to children.
- Practitioners find the theory powerful for questioning the assumption that a certain level of performance in one area is necessarily associated with a similar level of performance in another area.
- Developed by Howard Gardner, first in 1983, and explored more fully in recent works (including Gardner, 1999, 2006).

Brain-Based Research

- Draws from neuroscience and suggests that the brain functions holistically, processing many kinds of information (such as emotions and facts) at once.
- Holds that the search for meaning and pattern making is innate.
- School experiences should be directly guided by how the brain functions by providing numerous complex and concrete experiences that are rich in sensory stimulation and embedded within human contexts.
- Some writers (Bruer, 1997), including proponents (Jensen, 2000), caution against making large inferential leaps to classroom contexts. Research is new and limited.
- Popular proponents include Caine and Caine (1994; Caine, Caine, McClintic, & Klimek, 2005) and Jensen (2005).

Source: Barbara Schwartz/Merrill.

short-circuits learning by ignoring the large variety of strategies that teachers can use to help encourage growth. Skilled teachers have rich repertoires of **instructional strategies.** For example, research identifies teaching practices such as helping students to identify similarities and differences and to generate and test hypotheses as supporting student achievement (Marzano, Pickering, & Pollack, 2001).

Teachers can also foster learning by encouraging students to learn via texts, by themselves via experiences, and from each other through discussion and inquiry (Finkel, 2000).

Teaching is more than telling, too, because it involves listening (Mosher, 2001; Schultz, 2003). When people learn, they try to figure things out, to make sense of new information. One effective way to help learners understand things is to listen to their musings and questions. *Listening* is an important strategy that teachers can employ to slow down the presentation of new information, to give learners an opportunity to sort things out, and to help learners discover what they think. Finally, because teaching is interactional, listening is an informal assessment strategy; it gives us information about

 ## Teaching Tip

ACTIVE LISTENING

Try some of these ways to encourage active listening in your classroom—for you *and* the students.

- Use and teach listening behaviors such as SLANT: Sit up, Lean forward, Ask questions, Nod, Track the speaker.
- Use and teach active listening strategies such as paraphrasing: "So what I hear you saying is . . ."
- Wait a bit after asking a question, and again before responding. Teach students to do the same.
- Call on multiple students to comment on any one question. Require students to link their comments to the previous student's comments.
- Have students toss a ball made of something soft to each other as they comment. Only the person holding the ball speaks.
- If a student's comments go unheard, don't repeat the student's comments for those who were not listening. Instead say, "I know your peers want to hear that. Wait just a second until . . . Okay, try again."

the learners' reasoning that can be used to guide our instructional decisions. The Teaching Tip gives suggestions to help you—and your students—practice active listening. The fact that teaching is more than telling is reflected in the agreement on what teachers need to know and be able to do.

There Is Agreement on What Teachers Need to Know and Be able To Do

Despite the perception that most people who have attended school understand teaching, and although some individuals may appear to be "born teachers," there is a body of knowledge, attitudes, and skills that teachers can acquire. National and state panels codify the domains that teachers consider in their work. One of the most influential boards that has considered what it means to be an excellent teacher is the **National Board for Professional Teaching Standards** (NBPTS; see http://NBPTS.org). The NBPTS sets forth five propositions of effective practice, and these domains are assessed as experienced teachers pursue **National Board certification.** Domains of competence are assessed also for prospective and beginning teachers. Danielson's (1996) framework for teaching, for instance, explores domains of practice for new teachers and forms the basis for the content assessed by the Praxis examination Educational Testing Service (ETS). The ETS has further explored the domains of practice by surveying practicing teachers and administrators (Tannenbaum & Rosenfeld, 1997). Many states also publish their own standards for the teaching profession. Figure 1.4

Figure 1.4 *Domains of teacher expertise.*

Subject-Matter Knowledge	• Understanding human learning and the many factors (e.g., culture and context) that affect it • Holding rich, organized understanding of the content and how it is used • Using specialized knowledge to help students build accurate and deep understandings of the content
Planning	• Assessing and using students' background knowledge and incorporating it into instruction • Setting and communicating clear learning goals • Creating and selecting learning experiences appropriate for students and goals • Creating and selecting a rich variety of resources to enrich learning
Instruction	• Committing to students and their ability to learn • Providing instruction aligned with communicated goals • Building connections with previous learning • Making content understandable for all students • Teaching for meaning, critical thinking, problem solving, and creative thinking • Monitoring student responses and adjusting instruction
Assessment	• Creating or selecting assessment strategies consistent with learning goals and student needs • Measuring learning for groups and individuals • Using multiple measures to assess growth
Classroom Management and Discipline	• Creating safe climates that promote fairness, autonomy, and respect • Setting norms for social interaction • Establishing and maintaining standards of student behavior • Using routines, procedures, and time effectively
Professional Growth	• Modeling traits of an educated person • Reflecting on goals and practice • Building professional relationships • Working with families, communities, and the profession

synthesizes general conclusions about excellent teaching, drawn from the National Board for Professional Teaching Standards (2002), the **Praxis** domains (Educational Testing Service, 2002), and various state standards for teaching.

In general, effective teachers

- Create productive and humane learning environments.
- Understand their subject matter, human development, diversity, and learning.
- Use their knowledge to plan meaningful instruction.
- Teach in ways that help students learn deeply.
- Assess students' growth carefully and use results to modify their instruction.
- Engage in their profession by working with families, communities, and other educators to reflect on and improve teaching and learning.

Large bodies of research examine schooling practices, both to capture the experiences of teachers and learners and to determine promising teaching practices. Decades of research have provided some insights into how students and teachers make sense of the schooling experience, and this research provides many directions for practice (e.g., Berliner, 1984; Marzano, Pickering, & Pollock, 2001; Reynolds, 1992; Richardson, 2001; Stronge, 2002). This text distills past research and my own stance in urging you to become a successful teacher, an inclusive and responsive teacher. Figure 1.5 summarizes the vision of inclusive and responsive teaching developed throughout this text.

Figure 1.5 *Inclusive and responsive teaching.*

Inclusive and responsive teachers . . .

1. Pursue understanding and continuous learning

   - Recognize their own biases and the limits of their knowledge
   - Gather, analyze, and use data to replace assumptions and ignorance
   - Focus learning efforts on self, students, families, and the profession

2. Display attitudes and build relationships of acceptance, trust, support, and high expectations

   - Incorporate unfolding knowledge of students and families
   - View differences as normal
   - Build authentic relationships of warmth and trust
   - Set and communicate high expectations, pushing students to succeed
   - Do what it takes to support student success

3. Use inclusive and responsive instructional and assessment approaches

   - Incorporate unfolding understanding of students
   - Use a full range of resources to meet student needs
   - Use recognized approaches and strategies for meeting student needs
   - Include student choice and meaning-based approaches

4. Use inclusive and responsive management approaches

   - Maximize learning through a task-focused, structured environment
   - Focus on community building and authentic relationships
   - Employ democratic practices
   - Work toward self control

Figure 1.6 *Questionnaire for self-analysis of teaching.*

		Strongly Disagree			Strongly Agree
1.	I can explain how people learn.	1	2	3	4
2.	I know my subject matter.	1	2	3	4
3.	I can list some ways to find out who my students are and what they know.	1	2	3	4
4.	I can plan a lesson related to a content standard.	1	2	3	4
5.	I can demonstrate more than one instructional strategy or technique that helps make the content clear to students with varying needs.	1	2	3	4
6.	I can assess students' learning based on traditional tests and at least one other measure.	1	2	3	4
7.	I can modify my instruction based on what I discover about students' learning students treat.	1	2	3	4
8.	I know how to help each other and me respectfully during class.	1	2	3	4

The questionnaire in Figure 1.6 presents an entry-level self-assessment that you can use to consider your current knowledge and skills. Mark areas that may figure prominently in a plan for your professional growth. If you like, formulate questions to capture these areas and record goals on your chart from the beginning of the chapter. You may also wish to flip ahead to chapters that will address your questions.

Teachers Can Be Effective and Yet Not Just Alike

Although there are documented domains of teaching expertise, few prescriptions hold in every circumstance. Teaching is uncertain and interactional. Part of teaching well is using a combination of one's own talents, insights, skills, and professional judgments to encourage students' learning and development.

Cicero's sentiment underscores the personal and giving nature of teaching: When we teach, we offer gifts to our students—gifts that depend on our traits and triumphs as givers. Think back to two teachers who had a powerful effect on your learning. What were their gifts? If you make lists of strengths for those two teachers (Figure 1.7), you may find areas of overlap; the teachers probably shared some common strengths and abilities. These instructors probably also made unique contributions to your learning. Your lists should contain both personal attributes and professional skills, attitudes, and abilities.

When asked to consider their memorable teachers, my students often find commonalities such as genuine regard for the learner, high expectations for student achievement, and passion for the subject matter. However, the idiosyncratic contributions that their teachers offered are many. Some mention humor, others reserve. Some mention competitive learning activities, others mention collaborative ones. Teachers bring themselves and their abilities to their students. What do you bring to the classroom? Use Figure 1.8 to display your gifts.

> *W*hat better or greater gift can we offer the republic than to teach and to instruct our young?
>
> —*Cicero*

Figure 1.7 *Characteristics of effective teachers I have known.*

Personal Attributes	Professional Skills, Attributes, and Abilities
Teacher One: _____	
Teacher Two: _____	

Figure 1.8 *Personal characteristics that I bring to learners.*

My Personal Attributes	My Professional Skills and Abilities

Parting Words

Common misconceptions hold that teachers work toward a single set of unquestioned goals, usually by standing in front of a calm classroom and talking. Instead, this chapter suggests that teaching is a far more complicated act. It argues that teachers must encourage learner growth of many kinds while weighing often-competing demands and carefully considering their learners and the local context. Despite the complexity of teaching, we find some agreement in the literature about the kinds of things teachers should know and be able to do, and we know that there are many ways to practice the craft of teaching well. One place to start is by forming an educational philosophy, a personal stance toward teaching, as is encouraged in Chapter 2.

Between here and Chapter 2 you will find two end-of-chapter features. "Opportunities to Practice" asks you to apply what you know and to connect chapter ideas with your own thoughts and practice. "Web Sites" provides an opportunity for you to join a larger community conversation about teaching.

Opportunities to Practice

1. You know that good readers check their own comprehension. Without looking back through the text, jot down a list of important words from Chapter 1. Now compare your work with mine. Figure 1.9 is a **word cloud** of the text from Chapter 1. Compare your important words list with the cloud. Any surprises?

2. Teachers and researchers alike use metaphor as a tool to examine the nuances and varied roles of teaching. An Internet search using the linked terms "teacher as" and "metaphor" yielded the following recent analogies for what it means to teach. Place a checkmark near the ones that compel you. Use them to think about your own metaphors for teaching. You may elect to conduct your own Web search related to the metaphors that make you curious.

   Teacher as . . .
   ✔ Cultural broker
   ✔ Consciousness of the collective

   ✔ Container of anxiety
   ✔ DJ
   ✔ Executive
   ✔ Shaman
   ✔ Facilitator and authority
   ✔ Hero
   ✔ Leader
   ✔ Learner
   ✔ Rain dancer
   ✔ Archetype of spirit

3. Connect the work you did in Figures 1.1 and 1.6. In what ways have various sources of influence affected your perceived abilities as a teacher thus far? How might they influence your growth as a teacher in the future? Discuss the questionnaire in Figure 1.6 with a relatively new teacher

Figure 1.9 *Word cloud.*

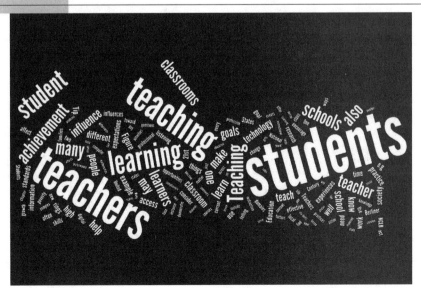

21st Century Teaching and Learning Tip

USING WORDLE TO CREATE WORD CLOUDS

I created the nature of teaching word cloud with a free **Web 2.0** application called Wordle (www.wordle.net). You and your students will no doubt find many uses for this easy-to-use, appealing application. Be sure to talk with your students about how design elements such as size, font, and color affect overall meaning.

and with an experienced one. You may wish to compare the value they place on the content of each question.

4. Visit MyLabSchool and select two contrasting lesson videos, perhaps two at different grade levels. As you view them, complete the chart below to consider how propositions of teaching play out in classroom interactions.

5. Go to one of the Web sites listed at the close of Chapter 1. First, find sources that influence what happens in classrooms. Add them to your work in Figure 1.1. Second, connect what you read on the Web sites with one or more of the six propositions of teaching. Talk with an experienced colleague about recent history related to that issue.

6. Interview a nonteacher about her views on effective teaching. Consider speaking with a parent, a student, or a professional who works outside of education and has little contact with students or schools. What do good teachers do? What do students wish teachers knew? How closely do your interviewee's insights match the propositions from the chapter?

	Lesson 1	Lesson 2
1. What are the contextual features that seem to shape the lesson? (example: age of student, geographic region, physical resources) (Teachers are part of a system.)		
2. What does the teacher appear to be trying to help the students learn? How is she or he communicating high expectations and holding students to them? (Teaching is goal-driven.)		
3. What strategies (other than "teaching as telling") does the teacher use to help the students learn? (Teaching is more than telling.)		
4. What is one individual—perhaps contrasting—strength that each teacher displays? (Teachers can be effective and yet not just alike.)		

Web Sites

http://www.ednews.org/
Education News.org. This site includes daily news related to education, updates on education law and policy, links to college and university newspapers, and links to education organizations.

http://www.ed.gov
The U.S. Department of Education. Provides information on legislative and policy issues such as the No Child Left Behind Act. The site has resources for students, parents, teachers, and administrators.

http://thegateway.org/
The Gateway to 21st Century Skills. This site is a consortium-run digital library that provides access to Internet-based instructional materials. Browse or search the catalog, or click on a term in the word cloud.

http://www.globalschoolnet.org/
Global SchoolNet is the original virtual meeting place for those interested in education to collaborate. Its goal is to improve 21st century learning through Web-based collaboration. Check the Projects Registry to find projects and partners.

http://www.servicelearning.org/
National Service-Learning Clearinghouse. A project of Learn and Serve America, the Clearinghouse includes national listservs and many service learning opportunities for students kindergarten through grade 12.

www.stateline.org
A public service funded by the Pew Charitable Trusts, Stateline.org publishes news and policy information every week day. Choose a state or choose a topic, such as "education" or "technology."

Although states are responsible for adopting their own academic content standards, professional organizations and other groups are influential in developing and recommending subject-area standards. A current state-led move seeks to develop a set of common core standards in mathematics and English language arts. States have the option of adopting these standards, and, at press time, most have. View the standards and learn more about the Common Core State Standards Initiative at http://www.corestandards.org/. Also view subject-based professional organizations and their recommendations by visiting the sites in the following chart.

Subject Area	Standards	Related Web Sites and Organizations	Subject Area	Standards	Related Web Sites and Organizations
Arts	National Standards for Arts Education, developed by the Consortium of National Arts Education Association	http://artsedge .kennedy-center.org/ kennedy-center.org/ ARTSEDGE: National Arts and Education Network	History and Social Science	Expectations of Excellence: Curriculum Standards for the Social Studies	http://www.socialstudies.org National Council for the Social Studies
English Language Arts	Standards for the English Language Arts	http://www.ncte.org National Council of Teachers of English http://www.reading.org International Reading Association	Mathematics	Principles and Standards for School Mathematics	http://www.nctm.org National Council of Teachers of Mathematics
Foreign Language	National Standards in Foreign Language Project	http://www.actfl.org American Council on the Teaching of Foreign Languages	Science	National Science Education Standards	http://www.nap.edu National Academies Press National Research Council
Health	Joint Committee on National Health Education Standards	http://www.aahperd.org American Alliance for Health, Physical Education, Recreation and Dance	Technology	National Educational Technology Standards for Students	http://www.iste.org International Society for Technology in Education

Note: For a concise history and summary of national standards across the curriculum, visit the Mid-continent Region Education and Learning site (http://www.mcrel.org/). Click on the "Compendium of Standards & Benchmarks" quick link.

Developing Your Stance Toward Education

Before You Begin Reading

Warm-Up Exercise for Developing Your Stance Toward Education

Below are six images of U.S. children. If you were these children's teacher, who would you like to help them become as adults? Your answer reflects your educational stance. Now study the captions. What privileges did these children have? What challenges did they face? How might knowing a bit more about them change your thinking about the education they should receive?

Child 1: Early 1860s. Tad Lincoln, son of President Abraham Lincoln, in Union Army Uniform. (http://www.loc.gov/exhibits/young/young-exhibit.html)

Child 2: 1909. (Called "Bologna") Tony Casale, 11 years old been selling 4 years. Sells until 10 P.M. sometimes. His paper boss told me the boy had shown him the marks on his arm where his father had bitten him for not selling more papers. He (the boy) said, "Drunken men say bad words to us." Hartford, Connecticut. (http://www.loc.gov/pictures/item/ncl2004000788/PP/)

Children 3: 1934: Mexican girls, San Antonio Texas. Part of Lomax collection of photographs depicting folk musicians, primarily in the southern United States and the Bahamas. (http://www.loc.gov/pictures/item/2007660002/)

Children 4: 1935. Pea picker's child. Two girls(?), head-and-shoulders portrait. Nipomo, California. (http://www.loc.gov/pictures/item/97515137/0)

Child 5: 1941. Adolescent boy dressed up for the Easter parade, Chicago, Illinois. (http://www.loc.gov/pictures/item/fsa1997015632/PP/)

Child 6: 1944. Children playing on the roof of the Lighthouse, an institution for the blind, at 111 East Fifty-ninth Street. New York, New York. (http://www.loc.gov/pictures/item/owi2001038554/PP/)

"Now in teaching, as in several other things, it does not matter what your philosophy is or is not. It matters more whether you have a philosophy or not. And it matters very much whether you try to live up to your philosophy or not. The only principles of teaching which I thoroughly dislike are those to which people pay only lip service."

—George Polya, *Mathematical Discovery*

Your philosophy, or stance, is a systematic, rational statement of your convictions about the ideals, purposes, and nature of education. It is your plan for teaching well. Bellamy and Goodlad (2008, p. 556) warn that the schools, "lack educational mission, both individually and collectively." In the opening quote, why does Polya so emphasize the importance of having a plan and of trying very hard to follow that plan? It's because if we do not have a plan, we may pursue the wrong goals, we might use methods that are unethical or unworthy, or we might judge our work by the wrong standards.

The importance of a plan has never been greater than it is today, when the context of accountability suggests to many (e.g., Keller & Bichelmeyer 2004) that the mission of our schools has shrunk to the pursuit of test scores. Many teachers (e.g., Starnes, 2010) seem to have a growing sense of unease, fearing that we are aiming toward the wrong things—or at least are limiting our sights—and thus lowering the quality of our teaching.

Quality teaching has two components: *good teaching* (that is, teaching that follows an appropriate plan with worthy aims and acceptable methods) and *successful teaching* (that is, effective teaching, or teaching that results in learning) (Fenstermacher & Richardson, 2005). Thus, to judge the quality of our teaching, we must look to student learning, yes, but not solely to student learning. We also have the responsibility to continuously reevaluate our work in terms of the quality of our plan, of goals we seek and the methods we employ. It is thus imperative that we teachers take guidance from a larger vision of what should be (Duffy, 1998). Here are six more reasons that it is critical that you dream big and develop a stance toward education today:

1. Inclusive and responsive teachers are guided by clear knowledge of their own perspectives and commitments. Your stance tells you who are you and what you are hoping to accomplish.
2. Teaching today can be overwhelming, especially for the novice. So many decisions need to be made. So many needs must be considered. A stance toward education provides a compass for decision making.
3. Classrooms are so busy, and pressure for teacher and student performance is so high, that it is easy to lose sight of the long-term goals and consequences of our actions. A stance can help you remember to maintain your focus on the big picture of what we hope our schools will accomplish and to reflect over your efforts.

As a teacher, you have the moral and ethical responsibility to say no when no is the right answer.

—Bobby Ann Starnes, 2010, p. 75.

21st Century Teaching and Learning Tip

MEDIA LITERACY: PHOTO ANALYSIS

The Before you Begin Reading exercise asked you to analyze visual media: Photos.

Media literacy is the ability to "access, analyze, evaluate and create messages in a variety of forms. . . . Media literacy builds an understanding of the role of media in society as well as essential skills of inquiry and self-expression necessary for citizens of a democracy" (Center for Media Literacy, 2007). There are many digital collections of images available to you and your students. The Library of Congress and the World Digital Library are examples. Also try search engines to locate images (http://images.google.com/, http://images.search.yahoo.com/, and http:/www.picsearch.com/ are examples). Check the sites for **fair use** rules. Teach your students to both comprehend images ("Who and what do you see?" "What do you know about the time period?") and to analyze them as well ("What is the message conveyed?" "How might others interpret this image differently?").

4. Mandates, such as for *what* we teach and *how* we teach it, are nothing until actual teachers implement them. Your choices for how you interpret mandates and how you enact them with your particular students each minute of the day make you powerful indeed (Elmore, 1979–1980; Web, 2002). Your vision of education provides you with guidance on how to breathe life into directives.

5. Having your own stance and understanding of the stances of others allows you to understand their perspectives and the kinds of criteria and evidence they accept. It can allow you to select the language you use in speaking about issues with someone who has a different stance.

6. Laws and policies have unintended consequences. Having a clear stance allows you to assess the unintended consequences that result (or not) from legislative and policy decisions. This can help you in determining whether the benefits of our decisions are worth the inadvertent costs.

In sum, your teaching efforts will be richer and more cohesive when shaped by a thoughtful stance toward education, and this chapter supports you in developing such a stance. First, let's explore one pervasive aspect of the complexity of classroom teaching that necessitates a clear vision: the curricula that schools purposefully pursue and accidentally achieve.

Three Curricula

The term **curriculum** may appear at first glance to be straightforward, but it is actually a multifaceted, multilayered notion. Eisner (1979) argues convincingly that schools teach three kinds of curricula:

1. The explicit curriculum
2. The implicit curriculum
3. The null curriculum

The **explicit curriculum** is the content intentionally selected and addressed through instruction. Examples include traditional subject areas such as reading, mathematics, and physical education. For **English learners,** English acquisition *and* content mastery are high priorities in the explicit curriculum. The explicit curriculum also includes skills or habits that teachers purposefully select and teach. Examples may include neatness, politeness, and cooperation. For some students with disabilities, the explicit curriculum might be a functional one where students learn self-care and life skills.

Content standards form the basis for many explicit curricula, including expectations for ICT (**information and communication technology**). For example, the International Society for Technology Education (ISTE, 2007) recommends six major technology outcomes for K–12 students:

1. *Creativity and Innovation:* Students demonstrate creative thinking, construct knowledge, and develop innovative products and processes using technology.

2. *Communication and Collaboration:* Students use digital media and environments to communicate and work collaboratively, including at a distance, to support individual learning and contribute to the learning of others.

3. *Research and Information Fluency:* Students apply digital tools to gather, evaluate, and use information.

4. *Critical Thinking, Problem Solving, and Decision Making:* Students use critical thinking skills to plan and conduct research, manage projects, solve problems, and make informed decisions using appropriate digital tools and resources.

5. *Digital Citizenship:* Students understand human, cultural, and societal issues related to technology and practice legal and ethical behavior.

6. *Technology Operations and Concepts:* Students demonstrate a sound understanding of technology concepts, systems, and operations.

What are these students learning through their interactions with their teacher?

Source: Courtesy of the Library of Congress
Anthony Magnacca/Merrill

Visit the National Education Technology Standards (NETS) at ISTE's Web site (www .iste.org) and read the outcomes for students at your grade level, then think about the school experiences that will lead students to the outcomes; the school experiences are the explicit curriculum.

In contrast to the explicit curriculum, the **implicit curriculum,** or hidden curriculum, is not purposefully selected. Rather, it includes the lessons taught tacitly through actions and through unconsidered consequences. Some say that the hidden curriculum is "caught" rather than "taught," and for this reason it tends to be highly memorable. Examples of the hidden curriculum may include competition and deference to authority. John Gatto, a New York Teacher of the Year, is a supporter of education, but a critic of compulsory schooling (1992, 2001). He captures his view of the hidden curriculum of U.S. schools with the lessons all teachers teach, including these two (1992) examples:

- *I teach confusion.* Everything I teach is out of context. I teach the un-relating of everything. I teach disconnections.
- *I teach emotional dependency.* By stars and red checks, smiles and frowns, prizes, honors and disgraces I teach kids to surrender their will to the predestined chain of command.

Do you agree with Gatto about the lessons we teach? Clearly few teachers would select these lessons as their explicit curriculum; rather, the hidden curriculum is often a set of *unintended consequences* that results from our conscious long-range decisions and our spur-of-the-moment choices. Although the hidden curriculum is sometimes in conflict with the explicit curriculum, there are positive aspects of the implicit curriculum as well. These include outcomes such as kindness, respect, and the notion that people believe in one's abilities to succeed.

One benefit of uncovering the hidden curriculum is that, once we expose it, we can determine the extent to which we are teaching the lessons we intend, and we can address the harmful lessons students may be learning with us. Additionally, many of our students may need our assistance in understanding the tacit rules of behavior transmitted through the implicit curriculum. As an inclusive and responsive teacher, you will need to help make what is "natural and normal" to some of your students (such as those whose home cultures match the school culture) is accessible to all of your students (Weinstein,

Inclusive and Responsive Teaching Tip

UNCOVERING SCHOOL CULTURE

Part of the implicit curriculum is what students learn via their school's culture. Teachers can begin to examine school culture by analyzing school documents, rules, ceremonies, rituals, and routines. Uncover school culture by examining questions such as the following (based on Wren, 1999):

- What are the messages of the school newspaper, student handbook, and yearbook?
- What are the messages of the documents available for faculty, students, families, and community members?

- What are the regular assemblies and competitions?
- What are the school-year opening and closing activities?
- What are the school's mascot, motto, colors, and other identifying symbols?
- What are the avenues for regular recognition for outstanding achievement?
- What are the school policies, and how well known and consistently enforced are they?
- Which students participate in which school activities?
- To what extent do different segments of the student population experience the culture in the same ways? In different ways?

Tomlinson-Clarke, & Curran, 2004). Begin by trying the Inclusive and Responsive Teaching Tip to analyze school culture.

As another example of making the implicit explicit, students (such as those with **Asperger's syndrome**) who struggle to understand social relationships can benefit from assistance in learning and using the rules by which people interact (Myles & Simpson, 2001; Tse, Strulovitch, Tagalakis, Meng, & Fombonne, 2007).

The third curriculum, the **null curriculum,** refers to what we learn because of the subject matter *not* taught. An example of what many students in the United States *don't* learn in school is a world language. In most U.S. schools, it is not mandatory to study a language other than English, and most of us who do so wait until junior high or high school. This is in contrast to the requirement in many countries (such as the European Union) that students study at least one other world language, usually beginning in the primary grades. From *not* learning another language, then, many Americans conclude that knowing English is enough.

Often, the force of history creates the null curriculum as it tramples one explicit curriculum into extinction and gives rise to new, more relevant content. For example, at her teacher's college, my grandmother was graded on her penmanship. Neither of my children learned to write in cursive. In high school, I learned to type; my children learned keyboarding. My children's children will learn a different skill set as the keyboard is increasingly replaced with input devices such as touch screens (Gartner, 2010), voice recognition (Rogers, 2006), eye tracking (Hadhazy, 2010), imaginary interfaces (Hadhazy, 2010), and brain wave control systems (Gaudin, 2009). Similarly, the childhoods of the six children in the chapter opener spanned about 100 years. Look at the technology in the backdrops in the photos. No doubt 1940's Child 5 learned about things that were vastly different from those that 1860's Child 1 could even imagine.

Eisner's three curricula, the explicit, implicit, and null, warn that every action a teacher takes—or does not take—can teach. Think about the powerful things you learned in school that were probably not recorded in your teachers' plan books. Even instantaneous decisions and fleeting behaviors convey our stance to our learners and to our communities, so a coherent stance will serve as a reminder to be intentional with words and actions. Let's begin the important work of developing your stance by considering a set of enduring questions of education.

> *A*s with all great teachers, his curriculum was an insignificant part of what he communicated. From him you didn't learn a subject but life. . . . Tolerance and justice, fearlessness and pride, reverence and pity are learned in a course on long division if the teacher has those qualities.
>
> —*William Alexander Percy*

Considering the Questions of Education

Philosophical questions are different from scientific questions. In science, we rely on *data* to answer questions about the *natural world*. But philosophy addresses questions about esoteric things like beauty, logic, ethics, morality, the nature of reality, and the character of knowledge. Such questions never go away; answering them just once isn't enough. In education, questions such as "Should education prepare students for particular roles in society or for personal enlightenment?" and "Is a classical curriculum adequate for today's students?" (Noddings, 1995) are deliberated daily. It's through deliberation that we plan, individually and as groups, how to best educate our young.

An especially useful set of questions regarding education was proposed by the ancient Greeks and captured by Dillon (1987). These questions, which parallel the concerns of the famous sixteenth-century philosopher John Comenius (Sadler, 1966), ask the following:

1. What is the good? Who is the good person living in the good society?
2. What is the purpose of education?
3. What should everyone learn? Why?
4. What is the nature of learning?
5. What is (excellent) teaching?
6. What does school do?

It may be helpful for you to study the answers to these perennial questions found in existing conceptions of education as you develop your own answers to them.

> *E*very science and every inquiry, and similarly every activity and pursuit, is thought to aim at some good.
>
> *—Aristotle*

Conceptions of Education Found in Practice

Education holds a special place in a democracy. In fact, Jefferson saw education as the foundation of a democracy; only well-informed citizens can be expected to govern themselves and throw off oppression. Indeed, the more educated people are, the more likely they are to participate in political and civic life and to be tolerant and equity minded (Kingston, Hubbard, Lapp, Schroeder, & Wilson, 2003).

Curriculum researchers have traced U.S. views toward education, finding that visions of education are fluid and responsive to the contexts of the people who create them while they simultaneously address the perennial struggles of education in a democracy (Kliebard, 2002; Tyack, 2003; Tyack & Cuban, 1995). Events such as the war on poverty and the race for space, for instance, influence the trajectory of the nation's views of the purpose of the schools and education.

> *T*he role of the teacher remains the highest calling of a free people. To the teacher, America entrusts her most precious resource, her children; and asks that they be prepared . . . to face the rigors of individual participation in a democratic society.
>
> *—Shirley Hufstedler*

For example, look again at Child 2 in the photos at the chapter's opening. As Tony sold his newspapers in the city, the United States was completing its transformation to an industrialized society. It struggled with massive urban population growth, and child labor was about to peak. Despite the fact that the National Child Labor Committee—which aggressively sought labor reform—was established five years prior to the date of this photo, boys 10 to 15 years old constituted one-quarter of the labor force (and girls 6 percent) (Child Labor Public Education Program, n.d.; Whaples, 2005). Meanwhile, in Chicago, John Dewey's progressive notions of education took hold in his newly formed Laboratory School and mirrored the progressive politics sweeping the nation. Tony lived in an era of social change—for children and for the nation at large.

Along with change over time, we also find similarities across stances; that is, stances can be grouped into families. Perhaps you have studied philosophies such as idealism, essentialism, and realism. Prakash and Waks (1985) provide another categorization of educational philosophies: the four broad families of conceptions of excellence shown in Figure 2.1 (technical, rational, personal, and social). As you study the figure, notice that each of the stances has distinct visions of what we should accomplish and how to go about accomplishing it.

The technical conception of education tends to be prevalent in K–12 public education, whereas the rational model tends to prevail in universities. The personal stance tends to occur more often in private, or independent, schools and in less traditional educational endeavors such as **unschooling.** However, some current powerful public school reform efforts hold personalization as the key (Darling-Hammond & Friedlaender, 2008; Wolk, 2010). In personalized schools, students play a role in planning their own curricula and teachers act more as advisors, helping students to educate themselves.

Figure 2.1 *Prakash and Waks's description of different conceptions of education.*

	What is the good?	What is the purpose of education?	What is learning?	What does the teacher do?
Technical	Efficiency Proficiency	To produce high achievement To adjust productive means to measurable ends	Memorizing Problem solving: applying facts to routines	Provides information for rote acquisition
Rational	Disciplined thinking Initiation Imagination	To transmit values by involving students in worthwhile activities Cognitive socialization of youth	Problem solving: higher-order creative and logical abilities Building complex schema	Presents ideas and concepts in a way that allows learners to see the structure of the subject Leads discussions and projects
Personal	Self-actualization (reaching individual potential)	To create opportunities so that individuals can develop along unique paths	Learning through own mistakes and experiences Introspection Being "centered" (in touch with self)	Acts as independent, aware individual Provides resources and space for exploration
Social	Individual development within the context of the common good Social responsibility	To provide skills for competence in civic life To teach the ability to identify and solve problems related to societal issues To foster the dispositions needed to take action	Interacting with a group Thinking beyond "I" to "we" Focusing on the disciplines only so far as they relate to relevant problems	Provides choices for group projects and actions Facilitates problem identification and solution Provides leadership

The social stance also has vocal proponents today. Bellamy and Goodlad (2008, p. 566) argue that the mission of the schools must include "providing students with the knowledge, skills, and dispositions to become fully engaged participants in a democratic society." Banks (2008) emphasizes that schools must prepare students for citizenship in a global age. One example of civic-minded practice is a student portfolio that explains the author's participation in the political process of the community (Glickman, 2009). Which stance is most prevalent in your area? Can you find exceptions to the technical conception?

What do these stances look like in individual teachers' ideas? Figure 2.2 gives brief phrases from two teachers' (Rae Ann and Jaime) conceptions of education. See if you can place Rae Anne's and Jaime's stances in one of the rows within Figure 2.1. They view their jobs as helping young people value each other and work well in groups. They see themselves as facilitators who will match their methods to students' needs and help students take an active stance in solving important problems. These positions are consistent with the social realm. Their stances are relatively conservative within the social school of thinking, however, because both Rae Anne and Jaime plan to teach core academic areas

| Figure 2.2 | *Excerpts from two teachers' philosophies.* |

	Rae Anne	Jaime
Who is the good person living in the good society?	Considers actions before committing them Lives harmoniously and gains knowledge from his or her surroundings in order to improve the present quality of life	Recognizes cultural differences and takes pride in diversity People work, socialize, mingle with kindness and respect Actively participates in the life of the community Passionately engages in the pursuit of knowledge
What is the purpose of education?	To create equal opportunities To provide the power to obtain one's goals and dreams To broaden one's thinking To build self-esteem and character	To draw from the lives of participants To encourage social development To provide the opportunity to discover individual passions To prepare participants for active engagement in the community To encourage lifelong learning
What should everyone learn?	That which will create citizens who can contribute new ideas and understanding to society Problem solving	Positive attitudes toward challenging subject matter Real-world applications of the subject matter That which will allow citizens to participate
What is the nature of learning?	Building on previous information through interaction Asking questions Understanding, not memorizing Varies by person: doing, observing, reading	Comparing new experiences with information from previous endeavors Trial and error Watching Examining physical representations Interacting in groups Fostered by safe environment
What is (excellent) teaching?	Reaches greatest number of students possible Is flexible and willing to change methods to enrich students' learning Creates many alternate plans Searches for new information and improvement as teacher	Holds passion for education and children Models actions and behaviors desired by the society Commits to reaching every student and meeting the needs of all Plans to incorporate different ways and rates of learning Respects the dignity of the learner Taps into background knowledge

as a focus and to infuse problem solving within the schooling context. Some more radical proponents of the social stance suggest that we use schools to reconstruct society. Had they fallen within the technical stance, Rae Anne and Jaime would have placed greater emphasis on mastery of basic skills and far less emphasis on group dynamics. As you examine the work of Jaime and Rae Anne, you may think about the consequences of the stances they hold. Prakash and Waks (1985) argue that there is no neutral philosophy. What are the benefits of the stance you see as most prevalent? What are the drawbacks? Who wins? Who loses?

The usefulness of examining current stances lies in the fact that stances expose very different answers to often-unexamined questions. We all say that we want what is best for the next generation and for the nation. Examining stances helps us to realize that "best" is a matter requiring much deliberation. Bringing about the "best" requires even more. Our stances are not disembodied ideals but rather important matters that play out daily, with great implications for the nation's children.

Developing Your Stance

Do you recall the saying, "The last one to see the water is the fish"? Answering the seemingly simple questions of education may put you in the position of the fish, exploring the world that has been your home and thus has many aspects that may be invisible to you. Considering the questions of education means exposing some of your tacit notions about how the world is and should be. It also entails considering the fact that there are alternatives to your perspectives.

To address these questions, think solely about your own ideas—no need to quote famous people. Write no more than a page to answer each of the questions, taken in order.

1. What is the good? Who is the good person living in the good society?
2. What is the purpose of education?
3. What should everyone learn? Why?
4. What is the nature of learning?
5. What is (excellent) teaching?
6. What does school do?

You may stumble a bit in interpreting the questions. Interpret them any way you like, as long as they guide you in discovering what you think and capturing convictions that are central for you. Do not be tempted to include a little of every way of thinking; for instance, some ideas from the technical conception and some from the social conception. If you did, elements would probably contradict each other and would not provide guidance when you need it.

After you compose a first draft, check your answers for consistency from question to question. Revise so that answers are coherent. Take out extra words. Read your answers aloud to yourself and then to a friend to be sure that your answers truly communicate your convictions. You will know when you have finished when not a word can be cut and when each reading convinces you more fully of the soundness of your stance. The Teaching Tip offers the long, if not somewhat macabre, view in considering whether you have gotten your stance right. Here are suggestions related to the questions to get you started on composing your stance.

Teaching Tip

A TEACHER'S EPITAPH

An epitaph is the inscription on a person's tomb, plaque, or gravestone, commemorating the life that passed. Epitaphs are typically brief and often wry. Poets often choose their own epitaphs, as do others. For example, Ludolph van Ceulen, the mathematician who dedicated his life to the task of calculating the value of pi to thirty-five places, had it inscribed on his headstone. Another mathematician, Paul Erdos, celebrated, "Finally I am becoming stupider no more." Enjoy some literary and historical epitaphs at http://web.cn.edu/kwheeler/epitaphs.html. Then write your own. Looking forward, what mark would you hope to leave on the world through your profession? Compose your own epitaph, and then attempt to live up to it.

What Is the Good? Who Is the Good Person Living in the Good Society?

As you consider the questions of "*What is the good? Who is the good person living in the good society?*" consider your own upbringing. If you were raised as part of the **dominant culture** in the United States, or if you interacted with people who were part of that culture, you no doubt were exposed to American core values. Some macro culture U.S. ideals include (Banks, 2005; Pai, Adler, & Shadiow, 2006):

- Equality of opportunities
- Achievement orientation (we should all try to achieve higher goals through hard work; successful people work hard and unsuccessful people do not)
- Individualism and its emphasis on self-reliance and originality (individual success is prized above that of the family, community, and nation)
- Future time orientation (saving for tomorrow)
- Orientation toward materialism and exploitation of the natural environment

These values are not universal; other cultures, including nondominant U.S. groups, often hold alternative values. Here are three tips to get you thinking about your own values and convictions regarding the good person in the good society:

1. Consider your own test of a "good" society. Many have said that a true test of society is how it treats its most vulnerable members. Do you agree? With a visual impairment, Child 6 in the chapter opening photographs spent time at the Lighthouse Institute in New York, 1944. The "house" had existed for three decades before Child 6 was photographed in the roof garden, much anticipated at its construction. President Taft laid the cornerstone (*New York Times*, 1911), and long before Child 6 played in the garden, personnel had opened a similar institution in France for soldiers blinded in World War I (*New York Times*, 1915). Personnel also had fought hard to have students with visual impairments permitted to enroll in New York public schools. Still, a common 1940's attitude toward people with disabilities was pity and a desire to isolate them from society (Adams, Bell, & Griffin, 2007). Child 6's president, Franklin Delano Roosevelt, hid his own physical disability so the public would not see it as a weakness. It was not until 1975 that all Americans were granted the right to a free and public education, provided to the extent possible with typically developing (or nondisabled) peers (Public Law 94-142: Education of All Handicapped Children Act). What responsibilities do you see the good society as having to each of its members?

2. Look back at your work in Figure 1.1. It encouraged you to consider the system within which you teach. What expectations does your society hold for you? To what extent do those shape your view of what is possible in society?

3. List no more than 10 core values or characteristics you think a good person or society *must* possess. It is tempting to make a much longer list, but that will be less useful in guiding your actions. Try making your own list, then compare it to the thinking of others. My recent Web search for "universal values" resulted in no less than 50 proposed values. Eleven recurring values were:

• Compassion	• Equality	• Freedom
• Honesty	• Respect	• Service
• Justice	• Responsibility	• Tolerance
• Peace	• Unity	

To what extent are *these* values *your* values? Are there some you would delete? Which must you add?

What Is the Purpose of Education?

In thinking about the *purpose of education,* consider carefully how it is that society brings its people to "the good." Look back at your list of values and convictions related to the good person and the good society. How is it that education serves as a vehicle to create "the good society"? Some focus on education as the full development of each individual citizen. Here's an excerpt of Martin Luther King, Jr.'s (1947) essay on the purpose of education, which he wrote as an undergraduate student:

> The function of education, therefore, is to teach one to think intensively and to think critically. . . . We must remember that intelligence is not enough. Intelligence plus character— that is the goal of true education.

Others assert that the purpose of education is to transmit the best of our society to the next generation. For example, English essayist Chesterton wrote, "Education is simply the soul of a society as it passes from one generation to another." Still others believe that, through education, we should transform society. What's your view? What can and should we accomplish through education?

Remember to think broadly about education. Education and school are not the same things. Think about all of the different mechanisms (such as family and religious organizations) that educate and how those might work in concert (or not) to fulfill the purpose of education.

What Should Everyone Learn? Why?

Considering *what everyone should learn and why* gives you an opportunity to think about the subject matter that is important enough for each person in the society to learn. As you consider subject matter, remember that what is considered "basic" in one part of the world or at one time in history may be superfluous in another. For example, look at Children 3 in the chapter opening photographs. These children danced during the Great Depression (1934) in San Antonio, Texas, a city hard hit by the mass migrations of people displaced by lack of work in U.S. cities and by "repatriations" of people of Mexican descent (McKay, 2010). Schools were segregated: black, white, and Hispanic (Orozco, 2002), and because of the Depression, many schools had closed or reduced their hours (Nelson, n.d.). Such dire conditions heighten the importance of careful decisions about what people should learn. Looking back, what content might have best helped all students (regardless of gender, race, or ethnicity) stretch toward becoming "the good person" and have a hand in contributing to or reshaping their society?

In your own stance, remember to think not just about what might be considered traditional content but issues of character, skills, values, and abilities as well. Theodore Roosevelt mused that, "to educate a man in mind and not in morale is to educate a menace to society." Be able to explain why people should learn what you suggest, and not something else. Remember, too, that "everyone" means *every* person; this question addresses the common core of learning to be mastered in the society. Here are five tips to get you thinking:

1. Look back at your list of values, characteristics, knowledge, and skills of the good person. Do you believe the good person is "born good"? Probably not entirely. Instead, he must attain (learn) at least some of those positive qualities. Look at your list of characteristics of the good person and good society and determine what knowledge, values, and skills people must learn in order to bring about the good. *That* is core subject matter.

2. Look beyond your own school experience; it is place-bound. What seems "basic" to you may not be basic at all in other schools or settings. Learning multiple languages, dance, a musical instrument, or geometry is considered basic in some places. Additionally, other countries tend to approach the "basics" differently than we do with mathematics serving as an example (Schmidt, Wang, & McKnight, 2005). Whereas the U.S. curriculum tends to focus repeatedly over the years on topics that we see as basic (such as arithmetic), high-achieving countries tend to focus on their basics in set grade levels and then move on to other subjects.

3. Look beyond your own school experience; it is time-bound. You may believe that knowledge is unchanging and should remain constant over time. That is a defensible position, one held by many others. An alternative perspective states that as our world changes, so must the knowledge and skills we must gain to find our place in it. John

Adams (1780) argued in a letter to his wife that, "I must study politics and war that my sons may have liberty to study mathematics and philosophy." A world that is constantly changing may require a changing core of knowledge for its citizens.

4. Avoid suggesting that "all" subject matter is important. First, it is impossible to learn everything that is known. Second, "all" would include a body of knowledge that is odious (white supremacy doctrine?) or is now proven false (phrenology?).

5. Recall that we educate hugely diverse groups of students in the United States, and that which should be accomplished by all is a matter of ongoing and heated consideration. We wrestle with tensions such as holding high expectations for each of our learners while we simultaneously attend to vast individual differences. For instance, should your **gifted** students achieve the same curriculum as your students with developmental delays? As you consider such tensions, it may help to list the subjects or outcomes that are important to you and then consider whether they could in fact be grouped into categories such as things "everyone learns," "some people learn," and "a few people learn."

In sum, think broadly about subject matter; it includes life's lessons in addition to school subjects. School is but one of our educative institutions, and defining what should be core requires you to think about all learners.

What Is the Nature of Learning?

The *nature of learning* includes the nature of knowledge, the nature of the learner, and the processes by which we learn.

As you regard the nature of knowledge, ask yourself: Is it unchanging or tentative? Is it objective, or is it constructed by people and thus inherently subjective? The branch of philosophy that examines the nature of knowledge is deemed *epistemology*. Your epistemological convictions will influence your decisions about both what you teach and how you teach it. For example, the conviction that scientific knowledge changes with evidence brings the obligation to teach students values such as a preference for evidence and skills such as the testing of hypotheses.

As you regard the nature of the learner, ask: Are people inherently bad? Inherently good? What are your convictions about people in general? Will they usually do the right thing, or must they have an external motivation to do so? Again, your convictions related to human nature will permeate your classroom decisions related to factors such as how you manage your classroom and interact with your students. For example, Kohn (2006) argues compellingly that most approaches to classroom discipline are predicated on pessimistic views of children, views that regard humans as power hungry, aggressive, and self-centered.

As you consider the nature of learning, ask: What are the processes by which *all* humans learn? How is that we take in information from the environment, make sense of it, and use it as our own? Within the larger framework of how humans learn, what are the relevant differences in learning preferences? One suggestion: It will not be useful for you to conclude that "everyone learns differently." If we can draw no common threads through human learning, your attempts to address students' needs will be random and most probably futile.

What Is (Excellent) Teaching?

You have begun to think about *excellent teaching* through your work in Chapter 1. That is, you have thought about how teaching is different from other endeavors, you have begun to examine the domains of professional expertise, and you have thought some about how excellent teachers might be different from each other. Perhaps these five sets of question will continue to fuel your thinking:

1. Is there a set of personal attributes required of excellent teachers? To what extent is an excellent teacher an example of "the good person"? What, if any, is the teacher's special obligation to serve as a role model of a good person? For example, must he employ all the 21st century skills that he expects his students to master?

2. To what extent is an excellent teacher an integral part of "the good society"? To what extent do teachers actively shape that society?

3. Is it enough for an excellent teacher to be a good person? To what extent do you agree that teachers know and can do things that represent a unique set of professional skills? What, then, are the professional knowledge, skills, and abilities that excellent teachers have?

4. How important is it that an excellent teacher is a good learner?

5. What are an excellent teacher's moral and ethical obligations?

What Does School Do?

As you consider this question, keep in mind that "school" is just one of the educative institutions in a society. Efforts such as **home schooling** and unschooling (Holt, 2004) indicate that schools are just one type of institution for education. "The social curriculum" includes vehicles such as the media, the family, and the neighborhood, and institutions such as religion and youth groups (Cortes, 2000). What unique contribution does schooling provide? Try these questions:

1. What *should* schools do? What should be our mission? Should we pursue student achievement in reading and mathematics as our sole aim?

2. What can be the school's role in bringing about the good society? Berliner (2006) argues that schools continue to be asked to solve huge public problems while we as a society ignore root causes, such as poverty, that contribute to differential student achievement.

Because you are preparing for a career spent in schools, it is important that you consider—and continue to reconsider—what those schools *do* and *can do*.

In closing, when you reflect on your answers to the six questions as a set, you will have developed for yourself a stance toward education that can be a useful guide in selecting your priorities and making professional decisions.

 ## Using Your Stance

Your stance should be reflected in your yearlong plans, in your lessons, and in your minute-by-minute interactions and decisions. Further, a conception of education offers *should* statements to direct you. Questions such as "What *should* we teach?" and "How *should* we group students?" are answered in terms of both philosophy and empirical evidence (Fenstermacher's and Richardson's *good* and *successful* teaching). Use what you know about findings from educational research to enrich your stance and guide your professional decisions.

Your stance can be a useful guide for short-term instructional decisions. I know a teacher who condenses her stance into a single sentence and then copies it onto an index card that she clips to her plan book. Before leaving school each evening, sometimes feeling harried and tired, she takes one last glance at that card. If she feels that she worked in some way toward the greater good listed in her stance, she goes home happy. My students find it useful, in fact, to condense their stances not into a single sentence but into a single word (see "Word Journal" in Guillaume, Yopp, & Yopp, 2007) and then to think about how that single word guides their actions daily. This year, some examples include *passion*, *care*, *cooperation*, *strive*, and *responsibility*. Another teacher I know shares his stance with his students via a poster and in words and occasionally asks them to provide anonymous written feedback on the extent to which he is living his vision. Check the Teaching Tip for some other ideas on using your stance in these days of accountability.

Use your stance to guide your long-term instructional decisions, too. As you work with your colleagues in committees that address topics such as long-term planning or

Teaching Tip

USING YOUR STANCE IN THE DAYS OF ACCOUNTABILITY

Try some tips for using your stance to remain true to your ideal in the days of educational accountability:

1. Regardless of the importance of test scores, helping our students learn and use social skills should remain a top priority as we educate competent and caring citizens of tomorrow (Garrett, 2006). Use your stance to help you focus on important social goals that must co-occur with academic goals. The National Association of School Psychologists (2002) places social skills into four helpful categories:
   - Survival skills (e.g., ignoring distractions and following directions)
   - Interpersonal skills (e.g., sharing, joining an activity)
   - Problem-solving skills (e.g., apologizing and accepting consequences)
   - Conflict resolution skills (e.g., dealing with teasing and peer pressure)
2. Consider state content mandates as a baseline rather than as the sole targets for what you are to teach. Good schools go beyond requirements to reach for a vision that exceeds the scope of narrow measures of learning (Keller & Bichelmeyer, 2004).
3. Use your stance as the organizing principle for your professional portfolio.
4. Post your stance-at-a-glance in your classroom. Before you shut off the lights at the end of the day, ask yourself for at least one example of how you enacted that stance in concrete ways. Set one goal for tomorrow.

assessment, continue to raise gentle questions related to the big picture of what you as a team (and we as a profession) should be pursuing. As your colleagues speak, listen for their convictions about the purpose of education. Look for common ground. Remind yourself that when you choose one course of action, you necessarily reject others. For instance, if you include primarily small-group projects, students have fewer experiences in working on skills as individuals. Make sure your choices are in line with achieving excellence in the long view.

Finally, revise your stance. You are an adult with many years of life experience, so your stance may not change radically over time. On the other hand, it may. Thoughtful teachers engage in frequent reflection on their experience and seek to improve their thinking as their thinking changes.

Parting Words

Today's demands upon teachers' attention are great. Time is short, lists of standards or outcomes to be mastered are long, and priorities sometimes conflict. Maintaining a clear sense of focus about what you consider central to your work as a teacher can help you decide at the close of a hectic day whether you have contributed to the world through your efforts as a teacher. Having a well-formulated educational stance can help you to shape your participation in the school policies, instructional practices, committees, and co-curricular duties that are part of your professional responsibilities.

With the completion of these first two chapters, you will have built a foundation for understanding the nature of teaching and your own vision of education. This foundation will come to life in each of the dimensions of your professional decision making: planning, instruction, assessment, management, and—as the following chapter shows— basing decisions on a solid understanding of your students.

Opportunities to Practice

1. Ask students with whom you work to help you find what is hidden: the implicit and null curriculum. Secondary students are often able to articulate their experience without much prompting. For example, one secondary student told me recently that, through his school's **tracking** practices, he has learned that some kids are valued as smarter than others by the school: different classes for different kids, better teachers for more advanced students. Younger students may respond to more specific questions such as, "How do you know whether you have done a good job at school? What behaviors do teachers like? What have you not learned in school that you would like to learn?" Do you find patterns in students' responses? Is the news good?

2. Four imaginary teachers (each with a different conception of education) are being interviewed. Label each teacher with the appropriate stance from Figure 2.1 technical, rational, personal, or social.

    a. In my classroom I try to include lots of . . .

    ABIGAIL: "opportunities for kids to choose their own activities. They need to be able to follow their own interests."

    BEN: "resources for kids to learn about current, real-life issues. Then they need experience in addressing those issues."

    CARA: "opportunities for kids to memorize important facts. These facts will help them all their lives!"

    DIEGO: "chances for kids to think like experts in the field, like artists or scientists, for example."

    b. You will know children are solving problems in my class when . . .

    ABIGAIL: "they have a clearer view of themselves and use that information to confront challenges. *That's* problem solving!"

    BEN: "they find something that is happening right now in the real world and I see them actually show the heart and courage to do something about it!"

    CARA: "children use their facts to solve more complex exercises. The lightbulbs just glow!"

    DIEGO: "children use their creativity and logic to solve classical problems or to create something new. You should see what they come up with!"

    c. Assessment of student learning . . .

    ABIGAIL: "too often interferes with individual students' dignity and sense of self."

    BEN: "is done in groups, with the criteria developed by the students."

    CARA: "is valid only when it is an objective measurement of children's accuracy."

    DIEGO: "should include student portfolios, in which students display their own style and approach to the subject matter."

    d. As a teacher, I try hard to . . .

    ABIGAIL: "place the learner at the center of all of my choices. If an activity does not meet my students' individual needs, we do not do it."

    BEN: "put my money where my mouth is. I show commitment to charitable causes."

    CARA: "make it fun for children to learn the skills from the book."

    DIEGO: "emphasize that the students and I embark on an exciting adventure together."

    e. My metaphor for teacher is "teacher as . . .

    ABIGAIL: 'a lens through which students can better know themselves.'"

    BEN: 'a spark who can ignite the fire of action for the common good.'"

    CARA: 'a factory leader who uses resources efficiently for the best product possible.'"

    DIEGO: 'a sage who helps students learn to judge performance.'"

    Were you drawn toward any one teacher's cluster of responses from the first exercise? These imaginary statements may provide specific examples to help you pin down your own stance toward education.

    Key: Technical: Cara; Rational: Diego; Personal: Abigail; Social: Ben.

3. Stretch your thinking by imagining the implications of different stances on some common issues in classroom teaching. Try to imagine how these different conceptions would play out for the elements listed in Figure 2.3. Note that your own stance provides the final entries in the table. Check back to your row in Figure 2.3 as you read subsequent chapters . . . you may already know the punch lines!

4. Analyze school mission statements, beginning with your own school's statement. Go online and check your site's Web site or **School Accountability Report Card (SARC).** Or, if you aren't assigned to a school yet, go to the Internet and locate some using the search term "school mission statements." Is it possible to place the statement in one of the families of educational thought from Chapter 2? Look for areas of agreement and disagreement with your own stance. Talk with experienced teachers about how mission statements are written and discuss issues such as group consensus, conceptual coherence, and enacting the mission statement.

5. The circumstances of classroom teaching sometimes present obstacles for enacting one's teaching stance. For instance, you may want students to be the ultimate judges of their work, but you are required to give standardized tests. Use Figure 2.4 to help structure your thinking and to consider how to address potential obstacles. Heads up: You will need this chart in Chapter 6.

Figure 2.3 *Daily implications of conceptions of education.*

	Common Learning Experiences	Prevalent Teaching Methods	Assessment Instruments	Homework Assignments	Expectations for Parents
Technical					
Rational					
Personal					
Social					
My own stance					

6. Create an alternative display of your stance, one that does not rely solely on linear text. Try one or more of these ideas:

   • A word cloud (try www.wordle.net)

   • An art piece such as a collage or painting

   • A digital story (try Microsoft's free Photo Story 3 for Windows at http://www.microsoft.com/windowsxp/ using/digitalphotography/photostory/default.mspx or use I-Movie for Macintosh)

   • A six-word memoir: "Won't teach how I was taught." Another: "I promise to never stop learning." (search "Teachers' six word memoirs" and try Smith Magazine's memoirs at http://www .smithmag.net/)

   • A podcast (see 21st Century Teaching and Learning Tip on page 39)

Figure 2.4   *Enacting my stance toward education.*

	My Convictions	Possible Obstacles	Strategies to Consider
A good society			
What education (and school) should do			
What everyone should learn			
How I should teach			

21st Century Teaching and Learning Tip

PODCASTING: YOUR STANCE AND YOUR STUDENTS

- Podcasting is a way of sharing audio and media files on the Web. Not a direct download, a podcast has a news feed that allows it to be catalogued through programs like iTunes or Podcast Alley. Podcasts typically have many episodes, like a weekly show. You can listen to or view podcasts through a portable digital media player or through your Web browser.
- A podcast might be a great way to communicate your stance with students, families, colleagues, and potential employers. Follow these three steps to create an audio podcast of your stance.
  1. Use a script and record your most important points, limiting your recording to a minute or two. Use a program like GarageBand for Macintosh or the free Audacity (www.http://audacity.sourceforge.net/).
  2. Save your recording file as an MP3 file.
  3. Publish your recording through a service such as the free Podomatic.
     For more specific directions, download Vincent's (2009) free, helpful podcasting guide for teachers and students.
- Students and teachers are finding great enjoyment in taking learning outside the classroom by listening to and creating their own podcasts for content area learning (e.g., Putman & Kingsley, 2009). See what's out there using directories such as http://www.podcastalley.com. Why not jump into podcasting with your 21st century students?

 ## Web Sites

http://www.ffst.hr/ENCYCLOPAEDIA/doku.php?id=welcome
Encyclopedia of Philosophy of Education. This site includes an alphabetic listing of philosophers of education and relevant works. It also includes links to other Web sites that treat philosophy.

http://tip.psychology.org/
Explorations in Learning & Instruction: The Theory into Practice Database. This site can help you think about your stance on what it means to learn by exploring 50 theories of learning and instruction.

http://cuip.net/jds/
The John Dewey Society. The society's mission is to "keep alive John Dewey's commitment to the use of critical and reflective intelligence in the search for solutions to crucial problems in education and culture." There are links to the society's journals, including online access to articles.

http://philosophyofeducation.org/
Philosophy of Education Society. This site includes information on the Philosophy of Education Society, provides access to its publications, and includes links to other organizations and resources addressing philosophy of education topics.

http://www.tolerance.org/
Tolerance.org. This Web site is a project of the Southern Poverty Law Center. If ideals such as tolerance, peace, or respect figure prominently in your stance, check this site's array of Web-based and free print materials to help you enact your principles.

Use the search words "My Philosophy of Education" to search and view thousands of philosophies of education students from around the nation . . . and beyond. For some inspirational video examples, use that same search term at YouTube.

Getting to Know Students and Families

3

Before You Begin Reading

Warm-Up Exercise for Getting to Know Students and Families

Engage in a bit of personal introspection by writing an "I am from" poem. There is only one simple rule: Each line must begin with the words "I am from." As you compose your poem, think about all the factors that make you who you are. You may wish to think about features such as your unique qualities, your values, your ethnic heritage, your family experiences, your spiritual identity, significant events, and about your favorites in life. There are no rules about length, rhyme, meter, or sharing it with an audience.

I Am From

Read it aloud. Now reflect on your poem. What new insights (if any) did you gain? Excerpts from some recently composed poems are found at the end of this chapter. As you read them over, look for themes: Who are we? What matters to us? Themes such as immigration experiences, ethnic and national identity, conflict, the importance of family regardless of its structure, and a sense of growth seem to speak clearly. *Now imagine a world where schools knew where we were from and embraced us.*

"The secret in education lies in respecting the student."

—Ralph Waldo Emerson

Your students' success depends on so many factors (Fenstermacher & Richardson, 2005). One is quality teaching. Second, students must extend willingness and effort to learn. Third, student success requires opportunity to learn. Your students need access to rigorous content, time, and resources to learn. Finally, student success requires a supportive surround, with factors such as caring families, peers, and effective social systems.

With so many things influencing success, it's clear that your journey ahead is not one to be taken lightly, nor is it one to be taken alone. It will require you to work closely with whole teams—students, families, colleagues, and communities—on your students' behalf. In fact, building and sustaining effective relationships lies at the core of successful teaching and learning. It is only when people know, respect, and trust each other that the task at hand—student success—can come sharply into focus.

Inclusive and responsive teachers strive to be effective team members and leaders. In inclusive classrooms, all students feel valued, cared for, and respected for who they are, regardless of their particular shortcomings and strengths (McLeskey, Rosenberg, & Westling, 2010). In *culturally responsive* classrooms, the cultural and other background experiences of all members are valued and connected to content and classroom life. Traditional ways of conducting classroom life are also reconsidered (Gay, 2002). An inclusive and responsive teacher communicates to students:

- I care about you.
- You belong.
- What you think matters.
- Differences are normal.
- Your educational needs will be met.
- I will push you to succeed.
- I will do what it takes to help you succeed.

Further, inclusive and responsive teachers communicate attitudes of openness and a commitment to continuous learning and understanding:

- Your experiences are valuable and valued.
- I know and understand some things about you, and I am committed to understanding better.
- We all have the responsibility to see things from others' viewpoints.
- There may be a better way of doing things, and we can figure it out together.

Inclusive and responsive teachers communicate similar messages to students' families.

This chapter supports you on your journey with the first steps of building good teams: getting to know your students and their families. It is organized in the following sections:

- The Generic U.S. Classroom
- Rough Terrain Ahead: Gaps and Inequities
- Will the Real U.S. Student Please Stand Up? Getting to Know Your Students and Families
- Working with Families

The Generic U.S. Classroom

Class sizes vary, but imagine that your class has twenty-eight students. Let's say your twenty-eight students represent the nation's student population at large. In your generic classroom of twenty-eight, you have

- Twenty-four students whose parents completed high school (National Center for Education Statistics, 2008a)
- Nineteen students who live in married-couple families and nine in other family structures (National Center for Education Statistics, 2009b)

- Eighteen students with broadband access to the Internet at home (U.S. Census Bureau, 2009)
- Twelve students who are racial or ethnic minorities (including six Hispanics, five African-Americans, and one Asian/Pacific Islander) (Your classroom doesn't have an American Indian or Alaskan Native; go two doors down to find one that does.) (National Center for Education Statistics, 2010b)
- Eight students eligible for free or reduced lunch (National Center for Education Statistics, 2009c)
- Six students living in poverty (U.S. Census Bureau, 2009)
- Six students who speak a language other than English at home (U.S. Census Bureau, 2008)
- Four students receiving special education services (with two having specific learning disabilities) (National Center for Education Statistics, 2009d; 2010c)
- Two students classified as gifted (National Center for Education Statistics, 2009e)

Are you looking forward to the richness and challenges such a group of students will bring? Sorry, but there is no generic U.S. classroom. Although these statistics represent students across the nation, they won't represent *your* classroom. Figures vary dramatically by region, state, and local area. For instance, all regions have increasing ethnic or racial diversity, but the numbers and patterns differ. In the West, "minority" student numbers exceed those of white students, with Hispanics predominating. In the South, African-American student numbers exceed those of Hispanics. Poverty rates and numbers of students living in large cities or rural areas vary widely, too. The patterns of distribution of students in schools affect the makeup of your actual classroom and can lead to inequities that present rough terrain as you pursue student success.

Rough Terrain Ahead: Gaps and Inequities

Many students and teachers alike face rough educational terrain in our schools. Figure 3.1 displays one such gap in student achievement, the gap based on parental education level. Recent research supports long-term findings in revealing the following inequities:

- Schools have become increasingly segregated, and that segregation leads to wider achievement gaps (Berends & Peñaloza, 2010).
- Blacks, Hispanics, and American Indian/Alaska Native students are more likely to attend high-poverty schools than are Asian/Pacific Islanders or whites. Whites are least likely. Limited English proficient students are also more likely to attend high-poverty schools (National Center for Education Statistics, 2010c). This despite international data indicating that all students tend to do better in higher-socioeconomic-status schools (Perry & McConney, 2010).
- Teachers without full certification, experience, or advanced degrees are more prevalent in high-poverty schools (National Center for Educational Statistics, 2010e).
- African-American students are overrepresented in special education programs (Blanchett, 2006) and underrepresented in gifted programs (Frye & Vogt, 2010).
- Students from poverty are more likely to be placed in lower tracks, have fewer opportunities to learn high-status knowledge (Oakes, 2005), and receive lower-quality instruction (e.g., Cummins, 2007; Watanabe, 2008).

Adding more bumps to the road, classroom structures reflect the interests of the dominant culture, sometimes making classrooms unfriendly places for students from cultures other than the dominant culture (Ladson-Billings, 2003; Nieto, 2004; Tyson, 2003). The gaps and inequities that present rough terrain in our pursuit of student success thus result from a combination of unequal schooling practices (Ladson-Billings, 2006) and larger societal disparities (Berliner, 2006). Vast changes at all levels will be necessary to pay off the "education debt," or significant educational inequities (Ladson-Billings, 2006), that have been accruing throughout our nation's history.

Figure 3.1   *Parental education level–based achievement gap: 17-year-olds' mathematics scores on the National Educational Assessment Program (NAEP) assessment, compared by parents' level of educational attainment.*

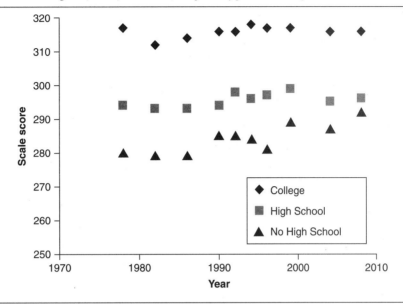

Source: National Educational Assessment Program, 2008a.

Note: Go to the NAEP Web site (nationsreportcard.gov) to view other gaps and results, including your state's results. Try comparing national results with your state test measures. Find your state test measures at your state's department of education site, typically on a page called "testing."

Source: Barbara Schwartz/Merrill

So what's the good news? The good news is that we, as individual teachers and as a profession, have the tools we need to navigate the tough road ahead. We have control over so many factors that contribute to student success. Schools make a difference. Many studies find that student success is far more a factor of high-quality opportunities at school than features such as race or family socioeconomic status (Croninger, Rice, Rathbun, & Nishio, 2007;

Figure 3.2   *Inclusive and cultural self-assessment.*

1. What are some of my favorite elements of my tangible culture? (art, food, clothing...) What are some aspects of my intangible culture? (Family rituals, dance, social knowledge)

2. How do I feel about working with students whose values and beliefs are different than mine? Do I have a color-blind philosophy?

3. Do I care if all of my students feel like they have a good relationship with me?

4. How do I work with students with different traditions and customs?

5. What stereotypes or biases do I have about people in other groups?

6. What are the sources of my perceptions?

7. How might these perceptions interfere with my teaching students well?

8. How much do I know about the cultures and histories of different groups? About my students physical and learning needs?

9. What do I need to do next to learn about groups and needs represented in my classroom?

Sources: Many questions are influenced by Ford (2005; 2010); Ford and Kea (2009); and Montgomery (2001)

Darling-Hammond, 2007; Schmidt & Cogan, 2009). Schools can—and many do—take an active role to ensure that students have quality and equitable opportunities to learn (Borman & Dowling, 2010; Muller, Riegle-Crumb, Schiller, Wilkinson, & Frank, 2010). The even better news is that the factor over which you have the most control—yourself— makes a huge difference. "The teacher remains the key" (Shulman, 1983, p. 504). Teachers contribute substantially not only students' learning outcomes but to their social and emotional development (Jennings & Greenberg, 2010). Beyond learning, students' *motivation* to learn is also directly influenced by the quality of their relationship with their teachers (Jennings & Greenberg, 2010; Lewis & Kim, 2008; Pawan, 2008). It all begins, as Emerson reminded us at the beginning of the chapter, with respect for the student.

Building warm, positive, and productive relationships with your students begins with getting to know them. However, inclusive and responsive teachers realize that their own cultural background and life experiences create the filters through which they see their students. For this reason, start getting to know your students by getting to know a bit more about yourself. Developing your stance (Chapter 2) and composing the "I am from" poem as a warm-up to this chapter may provide some insights, and you can try the questions suggested in Figure 3.2 to explore some of your own values and perceptions, including working with students who are different from you. If you are (as I am) one of the 83 percent of our nation's teachers who are white (National Center for Educational Statistics, 2009f), you might face the special challenge of cultural encapsulation, or a lack of identity related to your race given the pervasiveness of whiteness in our society (Dutro, Kazemi, Balf, & Lin, 2008; Weinstein, Tomlinson-Clarke, & Curran, 2004). Quick! From the blog *Stuff White People Like* (stuffwhitepeoplelike.com): What's number one on the list of stuff white people like? Coffee!

Will the Real U.S. Student Please Stand Up? Getting to Know Your Students and Families

Are you a European American who doesn't like coffee? A Latino or Latina who does? If so, you illustrate firsthand a bit of the complexity of identity and the problems of using categories to describe people. First, each of us is a product of many sources of identity, and those sources combine differently for each of us. Race or ethnicity, gender, sexual orientation, language, age, class, and more all coalesce in ways that make it impossible to describe any of us as members of solely one group. We each have commonalties that make us members of certain groups, but we also all have unique experiences that factor into who we are. Each of us is a dynamic product of the many painful and sweet experiences life has to offer.

Further, the "categories by which we classify people are constantly evolving, overlapping, mixing" (Weinstein, Tomlinson-Clarke, & Curran, 2004, p. 30) so that identity formation is a process without end and any description of culture can be no more than an "approximation of reality" (Gay, 2000, p. 12). Two examples include the categories of *English language learners* and *race and ethnicity*. The category "English language learner" sounds homogenous. It's composed of people who are working to master English, right? Yes, but English language learners can vary widely. They might include students from well-established linguistic groups such as Native American communities across the nation, French-speaking communities in the Northeast, or Spanish-speaking communities in the Southwest. You might also have English learners whose families are more recent arrivals. And within the group of recent arrivals, students may be literate in their home languages, or they may be new to school. Race and ethnicity provide another example of fuzzy categories. The number of individuals identifying themselves as members as more than one racial or ethnic group is on the rise, and the literature documents some of the complexities they face in schools as a result (e.g., Dutro, Kazemi, Balf, & Lin, 2008; Williams, 2009).

Thus, just as there is no generic classroom, there is no generic child. No child can serve as an ambassador for any culture, and we cannot rely on our assumptions or on our existing, limited knowledge of groups to know our particular students. There is no substitute for real information about the specific students before us. Inclusive and responsive teachers gather, analyze, and use data to make decisions that best serve their students. Learning about students and their families involves us in questioning our assumptions and gathering information that will direct us in our efforts to address student needs and foster success.

Questioning Assumptions

Ronald, one of my middle school students, was struggling with medical and home-life issues, so I made a special point to make personal contact with him during class each day, to look him in the eye and converse with him about his life. At a conference a few months into the school year, his mother told me that Ronald *hated* my daily conversations. The shock and discomfort I still feel in recounting Ronald's episode reflects the extent of my surprise in discovering what a horrible job I had done in discovering my student's actual needs and preferences. My assumptions about what I thought would be right for my student were deeply rooted and unquestioned: I *assumed* that my effort to engage him personally would be a good thing and that there was just one way to go about establishing contact: my way. In Ronald's experience, my efforts were anything *but* helpful. Thanks, Ronald, for teaching me an important lesson: question assumptions.

Inclusive and Responsive Teaching Tip

THINK: WHAT ELSE?

Try this: When you are tempted to draw a conclusion, list for yourself several alternative explanations for what you see. Try asking students to do the same. It can help them learn to take other perspectives and draw conclusions based on evidence.

Here is one for practice: One-third of your middle school students had no family members attend Open House.

One conclusion: They don't value education. What else? They forgot. What else? They work nights. What else? They work days, too. What else? They don't feel welcome at school. What else? Their student begged them not to go. What else?

Part of our human intelligence stems from our ability to draw inferences quickly from limited information. Although they allow us to make sense of the world, our inferences can also get us into trouble. When our inferences about others are based on limited information, we run the risk of making faulty and counterproductive decisions. Instead, we need to realize that our assumptions may be incorrect and replace them with accurate information.

Perhaps the best synonym for "inclusive and responsive teacher" is "learner." Rather than relying on assumptions, approach every situation as an opportunity to learn more about life for your students. See the Inclusive and Responsive Teaching Tip for an exercise to help you avoid assumptions.

Sometimes life's rapid pace does indeed require us to make assumptions. When those occasions present themselves, it is important that we draw the most helpful conclusions possible. As my colleague Pat Keig unfailingly urges, we can *make the polite assumption.* It is far more productive to assume the best about people than to assume the worst. Making the polite assumption opens doors for further collaboration; making negative assumptions closes them. Gathering accurate information about our students also allows us to serve them well.

Gathering Information About Students and Families

Inclusive and responsive teachers are committed to continuous learning, including efforts to increase our cultural competence, or knowledge about our students' heritage and culture (Brown, 2007; Gay, 2002). To do so, we commit to admitting that our own knowledge is necessarily limited and to observing quietly and asking, in gentle and respectful ways, questions that will help us learn. "I thought I could learn about [the students'] culture by just having them in my classroom, but I now realize that when they're in the classroom, they're experiencing my culture, not theirs," remarked a teacher struggling to get to know her sixth-graders (Frank, 1999, p. 20). To begin to understand your students, you will need to gather information about their lives both outside the classroom and within it.

Learning About Students' Lives   Getting to know our students requires us to step outside the classroom and learn about their lives (Grant & Sleeter, 1998). Kottler (1997) suggests that we teach as if we are anthropologists, focusing on people's cultural practices, on the knowledge base they share with others in their group that guides their thoughts, feelings, and actions. Kottler (p. 98) urges us to address a number of questions:

- How are my cultural values and biases getting in the way of honoring those among my students who are different from what I am used to?
- What is it that I do not know or understand about this child's background that might help me make sense of what is happening?
- What is it about where this student comes from that leads him or her to respond to others the way he or she does?
- How might I investigate further the customs of this child's family?

Ethnographers, one branch of anthropologists, use naturalistic methods such as observations and unstructured interviews to address questions such as those just noted. We can use these methods to gain insider information about our students' ways of living. See the Teaching Tip for methods to get to know students using the lens of an ethnographer.

Some teachers visit students and families at home to reach out and honor the places students live (Baeder, 2010; Faltis, 2001; Ginsberg, 2007). Home visits are an excellent means to learn more about students and families. Visits also shift the power balance in favor of the family, and they give teachers information they can use to bridge the school curriculum to students' lives. See Opportunity to Practice Exercise 1 at the close of this chapter if you're ready to try home visits. Attending community happenings such as holiday celebrations or sporting events also places you on the students' turf. For example, when my son Zachary was in first grade, his teacher came to watch one of his soccer

Teaching Tip

GETTING TO KNOW STUDENTS USING THE LENSES OF AN ETHNOGRAPHER

Frank (1999) suggests a number of helpful methods for getting to know students using the lenses of an ethnographer.

1. *Mapping:* Get a neighborhood map and pinpoint each student's home. Walk (or drive) to them all to physically see where each student lives.

2. *Observation:* Go to a location where students congregate after school. As unobtrusively as possible, watch how they interact. If it is appropriate and they invite you, join in their activities with the goal of learning about their lives.

3. *Interview:* Lead a conversation with a student or family member that follows the topics important to your interviewee. Ask a combination of "grand tour" (or big picture) questions and more specific questions about topics such as space, time, events, people, activities, and objects.

4. *Note taking and note making:* During observations and interviews, take two-column notes. In the left column, record your observations. In the right, record your inferences, or the meanings you derive from your evidence.

5. *Case study:* Gather data about one particular student from a variety of sources and in multiple settings. Analyze data from across sources to find patterns related to the student's perspectives and preferences.

games. Eleven years later, I saw her at a restaurant and was compelled to walk over and say, "Thanks again."

As you learn about families, it can be helpful to remind yourself: "If I don't know, I won't assume. I'll ask!" One thread of research suggests that teachers' assumptions about families are indeed sometimes faulty. For example, in one study, teachers in low-socioeconomic schools underestimated the technology available to families. As a result, they did not assign homework that involved computers (Warschauer, Knobel, & Stone, 2004). Had the teachers used a quick family survey (see the 21st Century Teaching and Learning Tip), they would have had data to combat their misperceptions and could have used homework opportunities to support the development of 21st-century skills.

Surveys are a quick and easy way to get information from your families. Near the beginning of the year, students and family members alike can provide information about students' general interests via attitude inventories, surveys, and brief questionnaires. The questionnaires may ask for information such as each student's preferred learning experiences, possible ongoing school-related struggles, and strategies for working successfully with the student. For instance, sample prompts for students include:

- If I were in charge of the world . . .
- What I appreciate about my family is . . .
- One thing I'm proud of is . . .
- One unfair thing is . . .
- If I could help someone in need, I would . . .
- I wish school . . .
- It helps me learn when . . .
- One thing I would like to learn at school is . . .
- In this class, I hope we never . . .
- I'd like you to know that . . .

Of family members, you might ask:

- Some of the things that make my child special include . . .
- Past teachers who did well with my child were successful by . . .
- A struggle my child has experienced in the past is . . .
- This year, I hope my child learns . . .
- The information or resources we could use at home are . . .

21st Century Teaching and Learning Tip

TECH SURVEY

Send home a brief survey to discover the kinds of technology use regularly. Or have older students complete it in class. Results will allow you to build home-school connections and provide support. Here is a brief excerpt of a sample survey.

Dear Families,

Sometimes families own or use machines that can help students and teachers do a better job. I can plan to help your students better if I know whether you use any of the following devices at home. Please place a mark by any devices you own or use frequently at home.

_____ Cell phone
_____ Digital camera (still __ video__)
_____ CD player
_____ DVD player
_____ Printer

_____ Desktop or lap top computer with Internet access
_____ Handheld device: _____
_____ MP3 or MP4 player
_____ Other (such as fax machine)

Do you have special expertise with some form of technology that you could contribute to our class? Does anyone else at your home? If so, please write your contact information and expertise here. Thanks!

Have respondents answer only those prompts with which they feel comfortable, and think about whether you need to provide your questions in a different format, such as a translated handout or an oral interview, to make them accessible.

You can also get to know about your students' lives through artifacts they bring in and display on a bulletin board, or that they share electronically. The 21st Century Learning Tip shares one strategy for building and sharing digital scrapbooks of student-selected materials.

The time and effort you expend in getting to know students and families will reap huge rewards in your ongoing relationships, your classroom management, and student learning. Here are some final suggestions for becoming acquainted with students and families beyond the classroom door.

- Visit the school's Web site and the Web site of the city in which the school is located. What are the local issues and priorities?
- Drive or walk through the community. Visit its places of business. Talk with shoppers. If you have a good relationship with a family in the community, ask for a guided tour.
- Meet with families and talk with them about their students. Ensure that the meeting times and places accommodate families' schedules and preferences. Some of these may work:
  - Meeting at school for breakfast, coffee or tea, or a potluck.
  - Meeting at sites in the community where families usually gather.
  - Meeting at a park for a back-to-school barbeque or picnic.

21st Century Teaching and Learning Tip

GETTING TO KNOW STUDENTS THROUGH DIGITAL PRESENTATIONS

There are many Web-based tools that allow students to safely post and share information about themselves with you and their classmates. For example, you might use a protected Google doc presentation with each student completing one slide, or students might try scrapblogging (scrapblog.com). Figure 3.3 shows a poster Zachary created using Glogster (free at edu.glogster.com) to share messages about himself. Remember that 75 percent of U.S. homes have ready access to the Internet. Rather than assuming your students don't have access, ask. If they don't have home access, provide alternative Internet access such as through the public library or your classroom computers. As a last resort, go low-tech with paper versions of students' self-presentations.

Figure 3.3 *Zach's Glogster (Created at www.glogster.com).*

"Everyone and everything that shows up in our life is a reflection of something that is happening inside of us."

- Search out and respect families' communication preferences. Find out which family member(s) have responsibility for the student, and ask which form of communication— such as school-door conversations, cell phone calls, or e-mails—they prefer. Be respectful about where you send messages and the number of messages you send. Also ask which language families prefer to use with school personnel. Get help from a translator as appropriate.
- Find out about families' goals for their students. Relationships are often based on shared goals, and inquiring into families' goals can build common ground.

Learning About Life at School   Students and family members can also provide information throughout the year to help you plan learning experiences in the classroom and at home. For example, some student teachers recently developed brief family surveys to determine how they could link science learning at school and home (Family Links). They delivered the survey in a manner that fit their class (e.g., translated or delivered by students). They (and their master teachers) were surprised at high response rates and by the families' enthusiasm about having their voices heard. Student teachers found a wide variety of family members willing to act as guest speakers on topics such as anthropology, electricity, and heart disease. The student teachers also were able to send home inexpensive materials for science experiences and to recommend high-quality Web sites based on families' feedback. One student teacher concluded:

> I want you to know that I was inspired to find ways to include parents who may not speak English. The language divide may prevent some teachers from trying to involve parents in science learning, but it was refreshing to see that there are ways to engage them and make family connections that transcend language.

Opportunity to Practice Exercise 2 invites you to try Family Links with your families. Many of the techniques noted for home and community use can be useful for getting to know students within the classroom context as well. You might map the classroom and observe students during breaks, for example. Also, the Inclusive and Responsive Teaching Tip gives a classroom observation procedure intended to surface facets of a single student's style and interactions. It may help you to gain information about a student whose particular strengths and struggles may otherwise go unnoticed. Keep your eyes open, too, for experienced teachers' methods of getting to know students. Some use lunch with the students, and many learn much about students by simply listening to their stories and perspectives (e.g., Thorson, 2003).

Inclusive and Responsive Teaching Tip

UNDERSTANDING A STUDENT THROUGH OBSERVATION

1. Select a student who does not immediately attract notice. This student may quietly pass the days without much demand for your attention.
2. Unobtrusively observe the student for a sustained period of time. Better yet, select varied times over the course of several days.
3. Take notes that describe the student's behavior:
   a. What does this student care about?
   b. Does this student show discomfort or fear? Of what?
   c. Does he have any skills or behaviors for avoiding notice?
   d. Does he initiate contact with peers? Which ones? How do they respond?
   e. How does he interact with the content? Is he on task? What evidence is there that he understands?
4. Analyze your observations:
   a. Would this student be learning more if he were more actively engaged?
   b. What forms of active engagement can you use that might show this student that you are teaching him as well as others?
   c. In what ways is this student exceptional?
   d. What could you do to get to know the student better?

Other techniques for gathering information include some of the assessment strategies addressed in Chapter 8. Examples include:

- Attitude surveys ("Please rank these class activities in order of your preference.")
- Interviews ("Bring in an object that represents your favorite pastime and be ready to tell us about it.")
- Journal entries ("What is the best thing that happened in class this week?")
- Drawings and diagrams ("Draw a picture of your face as you study biology.")

Surveys can be administered on paper, orally, or online. Examples of free online survey services include surveypirate (surveypirate.com), surveymonkey (surveymonkey.com), and zoomerang (zoomerang.com). Try your hand at an online survey in Opportunities to Practice Exercise 3. In summary, students and their families can provide unique information about students' strengths, needs, and accomplishments over time, within the classroom, and beyond.

Learning About Students' General Progress and Needs   You also need to get to know students academically. You might begin by checking on student records and past assessments. Look for information on students' reading levels, English language levels, and special needs. Who has an **Individualized Education Program (IEP)**? What special physical, emotional, social, and cognitive needs are present in your class? Once you discover your students' needs, educate yourself. How much do you know, for example, about childhood diabetes? About specific learning disabilities? Today's the day to start learning.

The amount of information available regarding students' progress can be overwhelming. Many school districts use data management systems. Another way to manage numeric data so that it is useful in your planning is to create a spreadsheet that lists current assessment information for each student. The benefit of a spreadsheet is that it can be easily re-sorted so that you can view students' scores in a variety of ways. For instance, you might sort by one variable (such as English language level) to form heterogeneous groups and another variable (such as reading level) to view the range of students' achievement. Imagine pasting re-sorted lists onto a clipboard to help you make student grouping and other planning decisions.

Learning Styles and Preferences   Many teachers find gathering information on students' **learning styles** appealing. A learning style is the combination of factors that together indicate how a person prefers to perceive information, interact with it, and respond to the learning environment. A familiar example divides learners' sensory modalities: visual, auditory, and kinesthetic. These divisions differentiate among students with preferences for learning by seeing, by hearing, and by doing.

Assessments of learning styles are usually made in one of two ways: student self-report or teacher observation. Common self-report measures are questionnaires that give agree/disagree statements such as, "I like to see models and make things" and "I like helping other people" (Gregory & Kuzmich, 2004, p. 33). Many free versions are available online, accessible through the search term "free learning style assessment." Be cautious in your selection, however, because most inventories are meant to be informal and have not been carefully validated.

There is another, more pressing reason to be cautious in assessing and using learning styles. The notion is that if instruction matches our learning styles, we learn better. However, research does not clearly support that notion. The link between learning-style-based instruction and student achievement is tenuous at best (Coffield, Moseley, Hall, & Ecclestone, 2004; Pashler, McDaniel, Rohrer, & Bjork, 2008). Some researchers are concerned that adherence to learning styles can actually perpetuate stereotypes and limited instructional practices (Scott, 2010). Still, assessing learning styles might spark some interesting conversations. Figure 3.4 suggests some ways to use learning styles thoughtfully in the classroom. In sum, there are many aspects of students and families that are important for you to learn about, and there are many tools at your disposal to achieve this objective. That information can help you work successfully with families.

Figure 3.4 *Using learning styles thoughtfully in the classroom.*

1. Create a "lexicon of learning" by teaching terms related to learning styles to open discussion about learning (Coffield et al., 2004).

2. Teach students to be aware of their own preferences, strengths, and struggles. Questions such as "What's easy for you?" "What's hard?" can help.

3. Students in control of their learning are powerful learners. Teach students to assess their goals, motivations, and learning strategies (Harrison, Andrews, & Saklofske, 2003). Also teach them to judge the environment and the demands of the task at hand.

4. Teach students learning strategies.

5. Flexible learners are powerful learners. Teach flexibility by providing both instructional "matches" and "mismatches" for students' learning preferences. Working within one's style is comfortable and easy, but working in a mismatch encourages stretching and building new life skills.

6. Gather ongoing assessment information and adjust instruction to students' progress. For eight excellent educators, teaching to learning styles meant teaching with a constant eye toward assessing learners' success in the moment and adjusting instruction based on that success (Haar, Hall, Schoepp, & Smith, 2002).

7. Use students' preferences as a starting point to re-envision practice. Studies of students with attention deficit hyperactivity disorder found a distinct preference for afternoon (rather than morning) learning (Brand et al., 2002). How might that information affect scheduling decisions?

8. Be careful not to make it simple! People are complicated. Rather than using learning styles as one more way to label students, and thus limit possibilities, use learning styles as another set of variables that add to human complexity.

 ## Working with Families

Strong family-school connections have incredible potential for fueling students' success. This section explores the research on family involvement and suggests things you can do to build bridges with families.

What We Know About Families and Schools

There is overwhelming evidence that family participation has positive effects on a number of student outcomes (Epstein, 2005; Henderson & Mapp, 2002; Jeynes, 2005; Sheldon & Epstein, 2005). Positive outcomes associated with family involvement include student attendance, social skills and adaptation to school, enrollment in higher-level curricular programs, and achievement. Family participation is twice as predictive of student success as is family socioeconomic status. Also, parental involvement can counteract factors such as poverty that have a negative effect on students.

However, not all families feel welcomed by schools, and most families want more and better information from schools (Civic Enterprises, 2008; Epstein, 2008; Quiocho & Daoud, 2006). Some discouraged teachers assume that parents—especially those of certain groups such as students of color—just do not care about their children's progress. Don't fall into that trap. Research indicates solidly that families in different ethnic groups *do care* about education and their students' success (e.g., Valencia & Block, 2002). In a recent survey of high school parents, all ethnic groups valued education, including the importance of college (Civic Enterprises, 2008). Similarly, in a recent nationwide survey, parents of all ethnic or racial groups reported participating in general school meetings and parent conferences at the same levels (National Center for Education Statistics, 2008b). It is essential, then, that schools and teachers—that's you!—take the initiative and reach out to build connections with families.

There are many strong examples of family-school partnerships (e.g., Black, 2010; Henderson, Mapp, Johnson, & Davies, 2007; Rodriguez-Brown, 2009). Common threads include:

1. Participants need to recognize that each of us is steeped in our own culture and values and be willing to explore those values and to accept that there are alternatives to them. This awareness allows each partner to be vigilant about remaining sensitive to others' perspectives. The greater the mismatch between a parent's experience and the culture of the school, the greater the likelihood that the parent will feel estranged from the schooling process, and the more trust and support in understanding this new culture the teacher may need to establish.

2. Partnerships need to be two-way and balanced. Both parties need to be seen as having valuable knowledge and perspectives. Effective family involvement programs begin with the assumption that parents are knowledgeable, influential people who have contributions to make to students and their education. According to Nieto (1996), strong parent programs hold parent empowerment as a main goal.

3. There is **mutual accommodation**, in that teachers seek to learn about students' communities and cultures and about how to communicate effectively with families. Parents new to the United States or the region may need teachers to serve as ambassadors, explaining aspects of the local education system such as expectations for family involvement (Rodriguez-Brown, 2009). This is especially important for family members participating in the IEP process (Sheehey, Ornelles, & Noonan, 2009). Schools that accommodate families "never say no" (Black, 2010). They partner with community organizations to meet family needs.

4. There are clear, frequent, and multifaceted attempts to communicate. The communication needs to be respectful, in the language of the home, and it needs to take many forms including both written and oral messages. Care must be taken not to offend families with requests that they may consider inappropriate (Davidman & Davidman, 1997). The 21st Century Teaching and Learning Tip includes gives Web 2.0 tools that can expand the range of how students, families, and teachers communicate.

5. Partnerships need to expand traditional options for family involvement. Epstein (2002, 2008) reminds us to broaden our views of family participation, which can exist through six kinds of activities:

- Parenting
- Communicating
- Volunteering
- Learning at home
- Decision making
- Collaborating with the community

Examples include literacy programs where parents join school-based writing clubs and units of study that incorporate the **funds of knowledge** of the community. Funds of knowledge are the rich understandings and networks of support that community members develop and use in daily life. In expanding participation options, special effort must be given to draw in parents who speak a language other than English and those who are bicultural (Olivos, 2006). Think, too, about other families who may need special effort on your part to participate. One group might be families who live in homeless shelters (MacGillivray, Ardell, & Curwen, 2010). For example, such families may have restrictions on their time for school involvement and homework completion.

21st Century Teaching and Learning Tip

COMMUNICATING THROUGH THE WEB

Try these free Web 2.0 tools to open more doors for communicating with students and families.

- Edmodo (edmodo.com): A social networking site for educational purposes. You can post homework, post document files, send messages to individuals and groups, and host discussions.
- Tokbox (tokbox.com): A free video chat tool that allows up to twenty people to video chat, with file sharing. You and your students can record video messages and send them via e-mail. Here's one way to introduce yourself to families!
- Fotobabble (fotobabble.com): A photo-sharing site that allows you to easily upload, voice narrate, and share photos. You, your students, and family members can share personally meaningful images, and you can extend content learning with images.

6. Partnerships need to grow over time, and as trust builds, teachers can provide suggestions for how parents may support their students' school success (Faltis, 2001).

Many successful partnerships now focus sharply on student achievement as well. Such efforts might provide opportunities for family participation in learning at home (as in the Family Links activity described earlier), might provide family members with information on how to support student achievement at home, or might focus on student-achievement conversations by studying data in teams at school (Epstein & Salinas, 2004; Henderson, Mapp, Johnson, & Davies, 2007).

Start Now to Involve Families

From the start, you can work toward effective family participation by encouraging family members to play an active role on the education team. Let parents know that you value their expertise about their children and that you can teach the student together much better than you could alone.

Act on your conviction that the world looks different from their perspective, and that you can benefit by learning about those perspectives. Here's an example. As a new and childless middle school teacher, I had little understanding of the stresses that my monthly book reports and 30-minute nightly homework assignments added to families, especially when compounded with students' assignments from other classes and the three or four weekly quizzes students took each Friday. The world looked very different later from my perspective as a parent of two teenagers. Research documents the stress that homework can bring to families (e.g., Solomon, Warrin, & Lewis, 2002). Further, it has questionable contributions to academic and nonacademic outcomes, particularly for students younger than high school age (Kohn, 2006). As a teacher, I wish I had challenged my own assumption that the homework I assigned unquestionably supported our learning goals. I wish I had invited families to sit and talk with their students about the content rather than assigning another page from the text. I wish I had asked a few more questions.

Use concrete strategies to welcome family input and to communicate openly. Capitalize on the power that "back-to-school night" and other formal meetings have to establish partnerships, especially since formal meetings are one of the most common avenues for family participation. The Teaching Tip gives a to-do list for back-to-school night; items on the list are meant to help you build bridges with families from the start (Guillaume, Yopp, & Twardos, 2006).

Use a variety of forms of communication as well. For instance, if appropriate, send a letter home during the first week of school asking families about students' experiences and families' hopes and wishes for their children's education. Call or send home a note, written in the home language, during the first month of school to share each student's success. Use a newsletter or Web site (see the 21st Century

Teaching Tip

BACK-TO-SCHOOL NIGHT TO-DO LIST

- Dress to convey respect.
- Use nonverbal communication that is welcoming and conveys your competence. Smile. Stand up. Don't put physical barriers between you and families.
- Tell why you are a teacher. Make sure your reasons include students.
- Explain the important things students will learn and be able to do as a result of this year.
- Show your passion for the subject matter.
- Show why your classroom is a good place to be.
- Build the family–school team.
- Address agenda topics required by your school.

Teaching and Learning tip) to keep families abreast of classroom events. Try e-mail·if that is appropriate, or establish telephone trees to spread information to each family. Sometimes standing in front of the school after dismissal allows teachers to talk with parents or other caregivers.

It is essential that you find different ways for families to be involved in education. For those who can volunteer in your classroom, arrange for activities such as small-group tutoring and materials preparation. Send projects home for parents to complete with their students. Try sending home literacy backpacks for younger students (Bright, 2006) or other projects that engage families. Include a range of involvement opportunities so that all families can experience success with their students. For example, parents may have the option of (a) listening to their student recount an event from the day or (b) participating in an interview about family experiences related to the day's story.

Additionally, Jeynes (2010) reminds us to expand our view of "family participation." Some of the more subtle aspects of parental involvement may be among the most effective in supporting student achievement. He recommends that we educate parents that their high expectations and clear communication without a doubt affect student achievement. Next we should help parents to act on those subtle aspects of parental involvement.

Establishing effective partnerships is long, hard work. Despite your best efforts, you may occasionally grumble about an obstinate parent. Sometimes the job may feel more difficult because of actively engaged parents. If you find yourself in this situation, it may help to remember that parents are experts on their students. Most have

21st Century Teaching and Learning Tip

USING THE WEB TO STAY IN TOUCH

The Web is nearly ubiquitous. Use it to stay in contact with your families.

- If your district or school uses online systems to maintain and share grades with families, keep your information up to date. Include homework information and individual comments on student progress.
- Determine whether your district houses faculty Web pages. If so, create one and keep it current.
- Use a free Web page tool to create your page. Examples are wix (wix.com) and google sites.
- If your school or district doesn't host an e-mail system, try www.gaggle.net for safe e-mail for students and their parents.

See a sample teacher blog entry, Maestra Manifesto, at the chapter's close. It is composed by sixth-grade teacher Dionne Sincire.

SAMPLE TEACHER BLOG: MAESTRA MANIFESTO (FROM P. 55)

Sixth-grade teacher Dionne Sincire keeps families and the community up-to-date on students' impressive accomplishments in her district-sponsored blog, Maestra Manifesto. Dionne is committed to 21st-century learning skills including creativity and innovation, which involve thinking creatively, working creatively with others, and implementing innovations (Partnership for 21st Century Skills, 2009), as shown in a recent blog entry. For example, (https://cal2.fsd .k12.ca.us/users/dionne_sincire/weblog/cfdef/Creativity_and_Arts_Center.html). Dionne and her students share a group grid drawing they did of their choice of the decade's cultural icon, Michael Jackson. The entry shares links to the art show at which the work was displayed, links to local press coverage, and student writing that captures what students learned through the project, which took them across the curriculum in meaningful ways.

spent years tending these young lives. They know some things about their students that teachers may never understand. They also have a right to make some choices about what they perceive as best for their students. Work to separate your own feelings from a parent's emotional demands. Whether or not you agree with the course of action suggested by the parent, consider the possibility that the parent is motivated by his or her ideas of what is best for the student. Welcome input and retain your stance as an instructional leader. Figure 3.5 shares some strategies for communicating effectively with family members.

Another motivation to consider is that parents' egos and protection defenses can be deeply involved. For many parents, nurturing a child is an act without comparison. Many of us discover the depths of love when we become parents. That deep love—and some ego—can color the way parents interact with teachers and other professionals. Please be gentle with parents who defend their children in the face of a perceived threat or criticism or who live through the accomplishments of their children.

Parenting can be stressful, and some students are more difficult to parent than others (Dyson, 2010). If you feel frustrated when it appears that parents are falling short of your expectations, it can be helpful to make the polite assumption. Instead of assuming that family members do not care about their child or they would ensure that daily homework is completed, think about what other things might account for the fact that homework is not getting finished: Does the parent perceive that the student needs to take sole responsibility?

Does he view it as outside the scope of his authority so that it would be an affront to your professionalism if he were to step in? Is there a tough softball schedule? Is the student caring for younger siblings? When you assume that families do not care, you close the door on your chances of working with them on behalf of the student. Assume the best.

Figure 3.5	*Suggestions for communicating the family members.*

1. Set a warm and supportive tone for your conversation.	
Establish yourself as an authority figure.	Use genuine concern for students and your expert knowledge base to build trust with families. You may be new, but you are a professional.
	Be certain that the care you feel for each of your students is reflected in your words and actions.
Use nonverbal communication.	Communicate your concern for students by choosing a collegial location for conferences (not, for instance, you behind an imposing desk). Share your care and enthusiasm in your handshake, your posture, and your facial expression.
Celebrate and suffer.	Appreciate—don't evaluate—families' successes and struggles with their children. It's hard work to be a parent. Remember, your work with the students stops every day. Families are in for the long haul.
Actively listen.	Use body language to indicate that you are fully attentive.
	Paraphrase your understanding of what parents say. Show that you understand the parents' concerns.
Keep things positive. Use laughter.	Keep the tone of your conference hopeful and assertive: This is an effective team! Express shared commitment and communicate your sense of certainty that together you and the family can help the student. Use humor appropriately to keep a sense of perspective.

2. State your concerns fairly and without evoking defensiveness.	
Use a strength refresher.	Begin with a statement of the student's tremendous strengths. Use that as a context for what you can work on next. We can all improve.
Use *I*-messages to communicate your concerns.	You can lessen parents' defensiveness by not placing blame. Not: "*You* aren't checking that homework is done" but "When Joey does not complete homework, *I* worry that he won't master these fundamental concepts."
Address the behavior, not the person.	Talk in specific terms about what you see the student doing and saying. Then talk about the consequences. Steer clear of phrases that label. Provide specific evidence, including work samples and grade-book marks, to illustrate the student's strengths and struggles.

3. Work on addressing issues as a team.	
Ask for family insights.	Draw on families' considerable years of experience: "What has been effective in the past?" Talk frankly about what seems effective and ineffective in your own efforts.
Establish clear expectations.	Give parents clear guidelines of things they can do to help. Share professional literature. Give lists of suggestions. Especially if parents are feeling ineffective, you'll need to give concrete suggestions for things to try. Remember, you need a license to be a teacher, but parents typically have no training for their role. We all can use some friendly suggestions, especially when shared by someone we trust and respect.
Offer choices and respect decisions.	Suggest for parents some specific options for strategies to help their students. When parents make a choice, respect it instead of suggesting others.
Follow through.	Do what you say you'll do. Check to see that the parents do the same. If they don't, talk about changing the system to make it more manageable for them.
Talk about addressing issues in many ways and on different levels.	Discuss possible motivations for misbehavior. For example, are things going well for the student at home? In Scouts? In day care? Make a plan to address issues in the short run and in the longer range. Be certain the plan includes both home and school aspects.

(Continued)

Figure 3.5   *Suggestions for communicating the family members. (Continued)*

---

4. Avoid ugliness.

Model emotional control.	Even if parents express emotions inappropriately, you need to remain calm and professional.
	If parents have difficulty collecting themselves, use a supportive statement that recognizes their right to feel strongly.
	You may want to suggest that you talk another time.
	Do the same if you are no longer in control:"I care so much about this issue that I'm having trouble remaining calm.I'd like to excuse myself. We can talk again tomorrow evening."
Use anger shields.	Occasionally parents become so emotional that they can no longer behave with the best interests of their children in mind.
	Don't talk to a parent who angrily interrupts your instruction.Instead suggest that the parent stop by the office and make an appointment to see you after school or during your conference period.
	If a conference takes a hostile turn, stand up and excuse yourself:"Isee you care deeply about your student. However, this conversation is no longer professional.I'll be glad to talk to you at another time when the principal is able to join us."

Parting Words

If we are to teach students well, we must make genuine efforts to understand their strengths, needs, perspectives, and experiences. We must also establish effective partnerships with their families. Some core suggestions for working with families include:

1. Draw on their broad and long history with their children.
2. Remember that parental ego and protection defenses can be deeply involved in parenthood.
3. Make the most helpful assumptions possible.
4. Include families as essential team members. Use inclusive language and plan for solutions together.
5. Provide different ways for families to be involved.

Remember the powerful role you play in forming effective home–school teams and in leading learning. Teachers who think that they *can* make a difference *do*.

Opportunities to Practice

1. Home visits are a powerful way to build bridges. Try just one visit to get started. Here's a checklist.

   ✔ Clear the visit with your administration or university.

   ✔ Research at least one website on home visits (try "teacher home visits" as your search term). Or, read at least one article on home visits (Baeder, 2010, and Ginsberg, 2007, are excellent).

   ✔ Establish a purpose for the visit. Common purposes include: establishing rapport and communication,

   learning about family strengths, and learning about student interests and concerns.

   ✔ Schedule the visit. Use the phone, e-mail, or a note, depending on family preferences.

   ✔ Arrange for a translator if necessary.

   ✔ Limit your visit to 30 minutes. Consider bringing something to share with the family, but let them lead the visit. Take notes of their concerns and desires.

2. Create, administer, and analyze a family survey regarding an upcoming unit. Then build a Family Links choice sheet based on your results.

   Sample Survey Questions

   a. We would enjoy having our student bring home science activities to share with us.

   b. We would enjoy receiving information about incorporating science activities into our family life (i.e., places to visit, projects, online activities).

   c. We have frequent access to the Internet.

   Sample Elementary Family Link Activities for a Unit on Weather (Families chose 3 items from a longer list)

   a. Look online and record the weather conditions of two different locations for one day. Practice math skills and have your student find the difference between the two temperatures and analyze the results.

   b. Writing Together: Reminisce with your student about a time the weather played a role in a family experience or vacation. Write a story and draw a picture to recapture this memory.

   c. Take Home Bag: Use the thermometer and cup in this bag. Take the temperature of a glass of water at room temperature. Then put it in the sun or under a lamp. Let it sit for a while and then take the temperature again. The sun warming the oceans makes a big difference in our weather!

3. Use one of the tools, tips, or activities in the chapter and share your results with a peer.

4. Create a free survey and try it with friends or students. Figure 3.6 is a sample created using Doodle. (www.doodle.com)

5. Remember that most students with identified special needs spend at least half their day in the general education classroom. Spend some time learning about the IEP process and special education services by trying one or more of these ideas:

   a. Find the IEP form your district uses and ask to see a sample.

   b. If this is not possible, go online and use the search term "sample IEP." Try narrowing the search by also adding the name of your state, district, or county. You will see that the IEP components are very similar, despite some local differences.

   c. Shadow a special education specialist for a day.

   d. Ask if you can attend an IEP, 504, or BIPS meeting. If you are a student teacher, you are often considered part of the professional team for whom meeting attendance is appropriate, but family (and staff) permission is important.

   Collect materials such as agendas and samples and take careful notes to document your discoveries. Compare your findings with those of a peer who might be working in a different setting.

6. Delpit (1995) finds that schools may devalue students' home language and thus decrease students' commitment to school. If your home language was not English and you attended an English-speaking school, compare your experiences to Delpit's finding. Otherwise, interview a person who spoke a language in addition to English as a young student. Analyze your school's culture in terms of the acceptance of languages other than English.

Figure 3.6 *Sample student survey (created at www.doodle.com).*

"I Am From"
(excerpts of poems by prospective teachers)

I am from New Jersey, Florida, Germany, and Samoa.
I am from California, China, Singapore, Thailand, and
  Australia.
I am from divorces, an immigrant, and a soldier.
I am from opposing forces, wild horses, and fires that
  continue to smolder.
I am from two brutal brothers who helped me to grow.
I am from a single mother, always off to work she'd go.
I am from both good and bad, a fair mix of the two.
I am from . . . hmm I'll need to think more before I'm
  truly through.

—Joseph DeLuca

I am from life's experiences of laughter, pain, and joy.
I am from an Italian, Japanese, German, and
  Czechoslovakian heritage.
I am from the era of the bubble gum, punk, pop music,
  and fluorescent colors.
I am from a mind that yearns and seeks for knowledge.
I am from a universe where mere existence intrigues
  my soul to treasure every breath I take.

—Jennifer Junio

I am from a family that prepares meals from recipes
  brought to America in steamer trunks.
I am from a dysfunctional family that keeps the dark
  issues private.
I am from this same family; we cling to our strengths
  and display them proudly.
I am from this family. It is mine.

—Julie Clark

I am from a salvaged home where all is bright on the
  outside and has been saved on the inside.
I am from a land where no word can speak without a
  beckon, and where no answer can but agree.
I am from a rejection of the self to acceptance of the
  reflection in the mirror.
I am from many places, but headed for only one place.

—Janny Kim

I am from my faith that guides me.
I am from the mother inside me.
I am from the land of the Hispanic.
I am from a coast of diversity.
I am from the love that changed me.
I am from the education that fills me.
I am from the family who cares for me.
I am from the God who made me.

—Trista Matthews

All excerpts used with permission.

 Web Sites

http://www.csos.jhu.edu/p2000/center.htm
  Center on School, Family, and Community Partnership.
  The Center encourages schools and communities to work
  to together organize and sustain programs for family and
  community involvement. Check the Success Stories for
  inspiration for local action, and see Teachers Involving
  Parents in Schoolwork (TIPS) for interactive homework.

http:// www.hfrp.org/family-involvement/projects
  Family-Schools Partnership Project at Harvard University.
  This site includes research and resources such as teaching
  cases to help families and schools work together.

http://www.teachervision.fen.com/education-and-parents/
    resource/3730.html
  The Teacher Parent Collaboration section of Teacher
  Vision Web site offers practical suggestions for working
  with parents, including questionnaires and handouts that
  can be used for parent education.

http://www.census.gov/
  U.S. Census Bureau. An incredible wealth of demographic
  information about the United States and its people. A quick
  start: In the site's search line (or in Quick Facts), type
  your city or county. You'll get quick facts about people,
  businesses, and geography, and you can compare your
  locale to the nation's statistics.

http://www.chadd.org
  Children and Adults with Attention Deficit/Hyperactivity
  Disorder. This organization provides information and assistance
  related to ADHD. Especially useful is the link to its National
  Resource Center on ADHD, which includes information for
  families and teachers to help children with ADHD.

http://www.cec.sped.org
  Council for Exceptional Children. Try the "Teaching &
  Learning Center" in this international professional
  organization's site. Some resources are restricted for
  members only.

http://www.ldonline.org

LDOnline is an educational program service of public television station WETA in Washington, D.C. This site touts itself as the world's leading Web site on learning disabilities. It includes numerous helpful and easy-to-find resources for teachers and parents relating to learning disabilities and ADHD.

http://www.nabe.org

National Association for Bilingual Education. This organization is one of a kind at the national level. It includes links to its state affiliates and research and other resources related to bilingual education.

http://www.nagc.org/

National Associate for Gifted Children. Check contacts for gifted education in your state at "Gifted by State," and view the many informative resources at the "educators" tab.

http://www.nameorg.org

National Association for Multicultural Education. Join the listserv or check out the Resource Center.

http://www.ld.org

National Center for Learning Disabilities. This site gives factual information and policy and advocacy information concerning learning disabilities. There are early childhood, K–8, and high school sections that provide helpful information for people with learning disabilities and their teachers. For example, teens can learn tips for getting organized and building social skills.

http://www.ncela.gwu.edu/

National Clearinghouse for English Language Acquisition & Language Instructional Education Programs. This site shares information about language instruction educational programs for English learners. You can ask an expert your questions and visit links that will be of interest to you and your students. Start with the tabs for "resources about" and "practice."

http://www2.ed.gov/about/offices/list/oela/index.html

Office of English Language Acquisition, Language Enhancement, and Academic Achievement for Limited English Proficient Students (OELA). This site contains information on federal and state initiatives for English learners. It has helpful resources and links for parents and teachers.

Providing Inclusive and Responsive Instruction

4

Before You Begin

Congratulations! You got the job! A photo of your classroom is below. Study the photo as you think about the range of needs and interests your students are likely to present. Quick! What are the five most important things you need to check or do right now to ensure that your room is accessible and inclusive of each of your students?

PhotosToGo

The Top Five Things I Need to Check or Do to Make My Room Accessible and Inclusive

1. Talk to the students about other things other than school work
2. Make sure there is engaging information for the lessons
3. That they have some knowledge of the subjects that will be covered
4. Accomadate and modify for certain students
5. Create a safe place

Hints: Think about factors like students' physical abilities, cultures (home and pop), interests, academic needs, English language levels, and about your technology priorities.

"*D*emocracy is a small hard core of common agreement, surrounded by a rich variety of individual differences."

—James B. Conant

The rich variety of individual differences that are central to who we are as a people are alive in our classrooms, and our responsibility as educators is to embrace our students and their differences while we encourage each to flourish in a strong community. Thus, responsive instruction involves *mutual accommodation* (Nieto, 1996). Students must meet exacting standards, adjust to the culture of schooling, and become participating members of our democracy (Goodlad, 1997). However, teachers and schools must also adjust; we must accommodate students' perspectives, cultures, and needs to help them succeed. We must continually ask ourselves, "What can I do better to help this student learn?" and "How can I learn more to foster success?"

Chapter 3 addressed the importance of and strategies for getting to know your individual students and their families and for beginning to build relationships and a classroom community. This chapter introduces you to a variety of student needs and characteristics and gives nine general approaches for meeting the diverse needs of students in our classrooms. Although presented individually, the approaches are often used in concert (e.g., Walker-Dalhouse et al., 2009). The approaches are:

1. Treat students as individuals
2. Plan for all students with universal design
3. Differentiate instruction
4. Use varied student groupings
5. Address students' special educational needs
   - Accommodate and modify
   - Use response to intervention
6. Shelter English instruction for English language learners
7. Challenge advanced and gifted learners
8. Foster gender equity
9. Create safe spaces

Treat Students as Individuals

The foundation for providing responsive instruction lies in treating students as individuals. Though this may seem obvious, some teachers proudly proclaim that their goal is to *treat everyone the same*. Such a desire is found in the color-blind perspective (Schofield, 2005), whereby educators aim to treat students as if their group affiliations (such as race) and prior experiences have no instructional implication. One danger in treating the students the same, according to Grant (1995), lies in the fact that it does not enhance students' learning about themselves as members of many groups. Grant (p. 10) urges: "The individual diversity and humanness that each and every student brings to school must be accepted and affirmed. Those who tend to see (or want to see) every group, and every member of that group, as the same, miss or deny the beauty of human diversity and variety."

Although all students deserve high expectations and deserve to be treated fairly and with respect, different students need different things. Treating each student the same can be inherently unfair. Nonetheless, teachers' emphasis on sameness often translates to their classroom practice. In many general education classrooms, students are indeed treated *the same*. According to Cole (1995, p. 12), "Instead of being presented in a variety of modes, instruction in U.S. schools tends to be abstract, barren of application, overly sequential, and redundant." Fortunately, schools are beginning to combat overstandardization with attempts to personalize education. For instance, in New Jersey, middle and high schools students develop individual learning plans based on ongoing assessments of their strengths, needs, and preferences (Hu, 2010).

There are many ways you can treat students as individuals in your classroom. You can see students for their strengths and incorporate their interests in your lessons. You can use democratic classroom management, a variety of instructional strategies, an enriched learning environment, and student choice, all based on ongoing assessments of each student's progress. To meet the needs of your students, you must accomplish both big things that take much time (for instance, developing a range of assignments and activities for a single outcome, learning new instructional strategies, setting long-range goals, or changing your interactional style for particular students) and smaller things that can be implemented quickly (for instance, shortening homework assignments for those who take more time or moving a student toward a helpful peer). Universal Design is one approach that can help you provide instruction that is responsive to your students as individuals.

Plan for All Students with Universal Design

Universal Design for Learning (UDL) seeks to provide instruction that is built from the start—rather than modified later—to address varying needs, interests, and preferences. It arose from an interest in accessibility in architecture (see Pisha & Coyne, 2001). Rather than designing a house that must later be modified to meet the needs of occupants (perhaps by cutting curbs, widening doorways, adding grab bars, or adjusting counter heights), Universal Design suggests that the house be designed *from the ground up* to address the needs of a variety of people who might live there. Ramps, for instance, would not only help people using wheelchairs, but would also help those pushing strollers, using walkers, or carrying heavy or bulky items. So it is with Universal Design for learning: Instruction should be planned *from the ground up* to meet a variety of learning needs such as English acquisition, giftedness, emotional or behavioral difficulties, differences in motivation, and learning or physical disabilities. New technologies often play a central role in Universal Design. As you plan your units and lessons, Universal Design (Center for Applied Special Technology [CAST], 2010) recommends that you accomplish three tasks by providing *multiple means of . . .*

- *Representation*—To help students transform information into usable knowledge, we must provide options for how ideas are represented. We must include information in a variety of formats so that it is perceptible to all students (for example, we might need to provide printed text, digital text, and audio recordings of a work). We must provide information in a variety of forms (such as vocabulary terms, graphs, images), and we must ensure the clarity of that information. Finally, we need to provide options to ensure comprehension.
- *Action and Expression*—To allow students to demonstrate what they know, we need to provide options regarding physical movement and expression and for students' use of executive functions such as goal setting and progress monitoring.
- *Engagement*—We need to use a variety of options in how we build student interest, support students' ongoing effort and persistence, and for regulating their own learning.

Teaching Every Student on CAST's Web site (http://www.cast.org/teachingeverystudent/) provides UDL resources and model lessons that use the principles of Universal Design. The principles of Universal Design provide an important criterion by which you judge the quality of your instruction: How well do your lessons provide information in accessible ways that foster comprehension, encourage each of your students to engage in instruction, acquire information, and express what they know? A related approach is differentiated instruction.

Differentiate Instruction

Differentiated instruction helps you address your students' different levels of readiness, interests, and learning profiles. Key elements of differentiated instruction are a sharp focus on essential learning, student choice, flexibility, and ongoing assessment. Research on the effectiveness of differentiated instruction is in its early stages, but available evidence suggests that differentiated instruction can be effective for encouraging success across the student spectra (Huebner, 2010).

Differentiation begins when teachers gather information about their students' readiness (current progress), interests, and learning profiles. Next, according to Tomlinson (2001), teachers use that information to differentiate their plans in response to information about students in three ways:

- Content—*what* students learn or how we give them *access* to it
- Process—the *activities* students pursue to *make sense of*, or process, the content
- Product—the longer-term endeavors students create to *display* their learning

Here are some recent examples of how teachers have differentiated instruction for these three categories.

Content

- *Spread (Rock, Gregg, Ellis, & Gable, 2008):* To determine the extent to which they need to differentiate learning goals, teachers examine the *spread* of student achievement on a given assessment: How far is it between the top and bottom scores? How does the rest of the distribution fall out?
- *Reading Choices (Knowles, 2009):* Students have plentiful opportunities to read widely from good literature of their choice and document their reading on a log.
- *Levels of Support (Kelley & Clausen-Grace, 2009):* Teachers observe students to determine what level and kind of support they will need. For independent reading, for example, teachers observe students to place them on the independent reading continuum (from fake readers to book worms) and provide differential support to stretch all readers. Fake readers, for instance, need close monitoring and special assistance in selecting interesting books.
- *Running Assignments (Nunley, 2006):* Students pursue ongoing assignments of their choice during independent work times throughout the semester. An example is an inquiry into a topic of the student's choosing.

Process

- *Input Choices:* Students explore information using varied sources such as different kinds of text, expert interviews (face-to-face or through tools such as chat, e-mail, or discussion boards), audio recordings, and multimedia recordings.
- *Blogs (Colombo & Colombo, 2007):* To expand learning time outside of the classroom, teachers create content-based blogs that contain rich resources like video and audio files and strategy instruction. Students with different needs focus on the parts of the blogs that meet their immediate needs. For example, a reader who struggles might listen to an audio file of the teacher describing strategies for reading the textbook. There are plenty of free audiobooks online; Story Nory (http://storynory.com/) has examples for younger students, and Open Culture (http://www.openculture.com/freeaudiobooks) has many works of classic literature.
- *Choice Boards (Anderson, 2007):* Students receive individual listings of learning options and select from among them. Only the teacher knows that options vary by students based on readiness.

Product

- *Product Option Contracts (Anderson, 2007):* Students select from a list of options or suggest their own product, give their choice of individual or group work, and state their timeline on a contract submitted for teacher approval.
- *Varied Technologies (Painter, 2009):* Students select the tools by which they will create their products. Examples include multimedia programs, publishing software,

Figure 4.1   *Sample questions to guide planning for differentiated instruction.*

	Readiness	Profile	Interest
Content	• Same or different learning objectives? • Primary language or English?	• Together or alone? • Which intelligences?	• How can choice be built into the learning goals? • What student choices in materials?
Process	• Which instructional strategies? (Read Chapter 7). • Which small-group activities? Individual assignments?	• Auditory or visual? • More structured or more open? • Together or alone?	• How to build new skills based on students' favored skills? • What choices in activities?
Product	• How to apply or extend basic ideas? • Same criteria or different? • How to support strugglers and push advanced learners?	• Variety of formats? • Which skills to teach to support product development?	• What choices in products? • What real-world interests can provide a context for product development?

paint/draw programs, cartoon programs (e.g., Go Animate and ToonDo), and word processing programs.

• *Culturally Sensitive Assessments (Thousand, Villa, & Nevin, 2007):* Students can show what they know in a style that is comfortable for them. Examples include translated tests, instructional conversations, and other alternatives to paper/pencil assessments.

Figure 4.1 draws from Tomlinson's ideas to provide a grid with questions that can guide your planning as you think about differentiating instruction.

There is no single approach to differentiated instruction, but a general procedure might include steps such as these:

1. Assess students' interests and current understandings of upcoming content.
2. Select learning outcomes based on assessment data. Remember that students study the same curriculum; to the extent possible, the content standards provide a minimum—not maximum—expectation.
3. Plan learning activities that address the outcomes and provide student choice based on interest. Students pursue activities only for content they have not yet mastered.
4. Use **flexible groupings** such as partners and small groups based on a variety of criteria as appropriate for student interest and content outcomes.

 Teaching Tip

DIFFERENTIATED INSTRUCTION QUICK START

Ready to jump into differentiated instruction? An easy way to begin is to provide a couple options for students' independent work after a lesson (Nunley, 2006). Example: "Your choice: (a) Complete the worksheet, (b) Use a class computer to create a graphic organizer using Cacoo (cacoo.com/) and upload it to our website, or (c) Write 10 questions and answers about the content. We'll use these for review."

5. Use formative assessment frequently to gather information on student success and adjust activities and outcomes. Analyze summative (final) assessment results in light of essential understandings.

Differentiated instruction utilizes a variety of grouping structures, an important aspect of responsive instruction.

Use Varied Student Groupings

You have a number of choices to make as you decide how to group your students for instruction. Some common student groupings include:

- *Whole class:* All students receive the same lesson from the teacher, at the same time. During work time, all students work on the same task.
- *Small group:* Students work with a few other students, often in groups with three to five members. All groups may have the same task, or each group may receive different instruction or tasks. Groups can be homogeneous (that is, similar to each other based on a selected variable such as interest or achievement level) or heterogeneous (that is, composed of members who are different from each other on the selected variable). Groups can also be randomly formed and can be teacher or student selected.
- *Partners:* Students work in groups of two. Just like small groups, partners can be formed heterogeneously, homogeneously, or randomly. Partners can also be selected by the teacher or by students. Tutoring (the same or across grades) is a special version of partner work.
- *Individuals:* Students receive one-on-one instruction from the teacher or work on tasks that are different from those of their neighbors.

Grouping Decisions

Grouping decisions are not simple. Answers to the question, "*Who* should learn what with *whom*?" are hotly debated. For example, it took federal legislation to ensure that students with special needs are educated with their typically developing peers. Oakes (2005) documents impoverished expectations and opportunities for high school students placed in lower academic tracks. In fact, many schools are now "detracking" in an effort to promote equity and close the achievement gap (e.g., Burris, 2010). According to Fordham Institute (2008), the scores of high-achieving students stagnated after NCLB as teachers focus on bringing lower-achieving students up to par. Do gifted students, then, have a right to be placed in homogeneous classes to receive more instructional attention, an advanced curriculum, and a quicker pace?

Which grouping patterns should you employ? Your stance regarding the good society and the purpose of education clearly will provide some guidance. So can research. Small-group instruction tends to be effective for many students (Lou et al., 1996), but static ability-based groups, such as primary-grade reading groups, tend to provide poorer opportunities for students in lower groups (e.g., Chorzempa & Graham, 2006). If you do use ability grouping, to maximize effectiveness, be sure that your groups:

- Are based on assessment of specific performance related to the content to be mastered rather than on a single static measure of perceived student ability.
- Are flexible rather than long-standing. That is, groups should be dissolved and re-formed as needs change.
- Address a narrow range of student need (e.g., a specific skill, procedure, or interest) rather than a general perceived level.
- Provide opportunities to work with a variety of peers over time (Caldwell & Ford, 2002).

In general, the research suggests that *grouping* alone does not cause positive effects: *Instruction* does. Positive effects of grouping on achievement are strongest when teachers are trained in using small-group instruction and when they vary their content and instruction based on their groups. Thus, a variety of strategies can be effective, and a combination of whole-group and small-group configurations supports student learning. Figure 4.2 provides some factors for you to consider as you plan to group students.

Mixing It Up with Student Groups

Gregory and Kuzmich (2004) provide a helpful suggestion regarding student groups: TAPS. During each unit, give students opportunities to work in the *t*otal group, *a*lone, in *p*artners, and in *s*mall groups. In the total group, you may present information or model a procedure. Alone, students may complete journal entries or self-assess. In pairs, students

---

Figure 4.2   *Things to think about as you make grouping decisions.*

Configuration	Possible Benefits	Possible Drawbacks	Use It When . . .
Whole class Examples: • Introducing a new concept • Read-aloud • Whole-class discussion	• Can build a store of shared experience • Can make management easier • Can allow teacher to focus preparation time on one lesson instead of several • Can maximize teacher-directed instructional time	• Can be difficult to meet full range of student needs • Can decrease student interaction • Can decrease opportunities for student choice	• Students all have necessary and equivalent background knowledge • The objective is appropriate for all students • All students can understand and benefit from the same instruction
Small groups Examples • Cooperative learning activities (see Chapter 7) • Literature circles • Group projects	• Can free up time for teacher to work with struggling students • Can provide flexibility for the teacher in modifying objectives, pace, and activities based on student needs • Can enhance opportunities for student interaction	• Can require preparation of several lessons, sets of material, or activities • Can complicate management • Can decrease student accountability • Students need to be taught to work together	• You want students to interact • Your goals include social ones • Students can enhance each other's learning • There is a range of needs or interest related to the objective
Partners Examples: • Partner reading • Peer tutoring	• Can maximize student interaction • Can enhance motivation	• Can decrease student accountability • Can decrease time on task • Students need to be taught to work together	• You want students to talk • Your goals include social ones • Students can further each other's learning
Individuals Examples: • Reteaching a missed concept • Targeting a skill important for one student	• Can pinpoint instruction for highly specific needs • Can provide valid and specific assessement information	• Can decrease overall instructional time with the teacher • Can decrease accountability for others	• Students have highly specific needs

might conduct Internet research or peer edit. In small groups, students might brainstorm or solve a problem.

So, as you plan your groups, think about what students like, what they know—based on assessment data of a variety of types—and what they need related both to your goals and specific content objectives. Set the groups in a variety of ways, including student selection, random grouping, and teacher selection. Ensuring that students have opportunities to work regularly with different peers provides them with opportunities to gain social skills and can equalize inevitable differences in power and status. Guillaume, Yopp, and Yopp (2007) suggest a variety of random grouping strategies, including:

- Numbering off (1, 2, 3, 1, 2, 3, . . .)
- Having students find a partner with the same number of siblings (or birth month, etc.)
- Distributing picture postcards, cut in half, one half per student, and then having students find the other half of theirs
- Distributing playing cards and then having students meet with peers who have the same number and color (for partners), or same number (for groups of four), or same suit (for larger groups)
- Having students sign up for partners and then meeting with those partners during different times of the lesson

Grouping students effectively means matching your students with your goals through a variety of structures.

Address Students' Special Educational Needs

Varied student groupings and approaches such as Universal Design and differentiated instruction will help you meet student needs across the whole spectrum. Some of your students will, additionally, have needs that are addressed by more formalized guidelines, those related to special education services. Let's examine some student statistics and laws before approaching two major approaches for addressing special needs.

Some Statistics and Laws Related to Students with Identified Needs

In 2008, approximately 6.6 million students in U.S. schools received special education services (13% of all students; National Center for Education Statistics, 2010c). "Students with disabilities" are one of the student subgroups that must make adequate yearly progress under NCLB. State data, such as those for California in Figure 4.3, reveal that we have considerable work to do to ameliorate the achievement gap between students with disabilities and those without.

IDEA specifies thirteen categories of special education services; the two most prevalent categories account for the majority of students receiving services. Most students receiving special education services (39%) have specific learning disabilities. Students with specific learning disabilities have adequate cognitive functioning, learn some skills well, and struggle in one or more others. The majority of students with learning disabilities face severe literacy problems. "Speech and language impairments" is the second most prevalent category, comprised of 22 percent of those students with special needs. Other categories (such as health impairments and autism) constitute 10 percent or fewer of students receiving special services.

A number of federal laws govern the services students with disabilities receive. The **Individuals with Disabilities Education Improvement Act (IDEA)** is perhaps the most important. Established in 1975 as Public Law 94–142, this legislation sought to ensure that all children receive appropriate educational services—regardless of their disabilities. Read the law and see related resources at http://idea.ed.gov/.

Under IDEA, students with identified special needs have the right to a **free appropriate public education** in the **least restrictive environment.** As a result, students with disabilities have the right to an education that is tailored to their specific needs, and these students are to be educated, to the maximum extent possible, with their peers without

Figure 4.3 *Achievement gap for California English language arts student achievement based on students' disability status.*

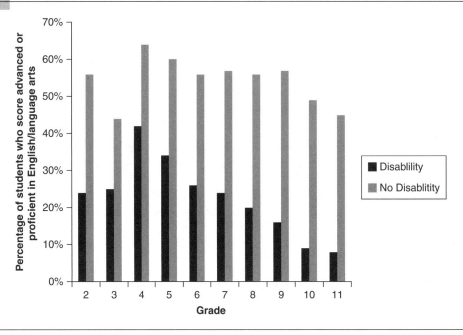

source: 2009 California Standards Test Scores. Scores given at http://star.cde.ca.gov/star2009/

disabilities. Indeed, in 2007, almost all (96%) of students with disabilities were served in typical schools, and of those, most (78%) spent at least 40 percent of their day in a **general education** setting (National Center for Education Statistics, 2009b). Only when the general education classroom does not provide an appropriate setting are other more restrictive settings, such as a special day class or special school, considered.

Today we emphasize **inclusion,** or the education of students with disabilities in the general education classroom. Our commitment to inclusiveness should be reflected in the language we use to refer to our students. The Inclusive and Responsive Teaching Tip gives advice for putting the person first.

IDEA also mandates the development and implementation of **Individualized Education Programs (IEPs)** for all students with special needs. IEPs are plans. These plans must specify annual goals, and staff and family members must meet regularly to discuss the student's progress. In addition to IDEA, two other federal laws notably address the education of students with disabilities:

- Section 504 of the Veterans' Rehabilitation Act of 1973: This law prohibits exclusion (based solely on handicaps) of people with disabilities from participating in federally funded programs and activities. Section 504 covers any condition that interferes with learning. Conditions such as attention deficit hyperactivity disorder, asthma, depression, or diabetes might generate 504 plans, which mandate instructional modifications.

Inclusive and Responsive Teaching Tip

PUT THE PERSON FIRST

When speaking and thinking about students, put the person first. For example say, "I am thinking of my student with ADHD," not "She's my ADHD student." Putting the exceptionality second staves off the tendency to define a person entirely in terms of a single exceptionality, and it emphasizes the "having" of a condition rather than the "being" of one. Heads up: Some people reject person-first terminology because they perceive their condition (such as autism or blindness) as a valued, central part of their identity. Not sure? Take the lead from your students and families.

- Hughes Bill: This bill addresses students with behavioral problems. Before students can be referred for special education services for behavior disorders, they must receive an assessment in their natural environment and, based on the results of the assessment, a **behavior intervention plan (BIP)** that details positive behavioral supports must be developed and implemented.

Serving Students with Special Needs

As achievement gap data (Figure 4.3) suggest, vigilant attention to your students with special needs is essential. You will act as a part of a team of family members, advocates they may enlist, and professionals who work together to meet students' educational needs. A resource specialist, educational psychologist, speech therapist, occupational therapist, and administrator may be among those on the team. You will need to check students' records carefully to ensure that you are implementing their mandated plans, and you will need to monitor your instruction and students' responses to ensure that you are helping them move forward.

At times you will work with students who struggle but have not been identified as having special needs. They might have persistent trouble learning, communicating, or interacting with you or the other students. If you suspect that a student has special needs that have not yet been identified, make careful observations, document those observations, collect student work samples, speak with specialists at your site, keep close contact with the family, and find out about referral processes such as *Student Intervention Teams* or *Student Study Teams* at your school. Throughout this process, continue to adjust your instruction to the student's benefit. **Accommodations** and **modifications** allow you to proactively address individual student needs.

Accommodate and Modify

"A truly inclusive school reflects a democratic philosophy whereby all students are valued, *educators normalize differences* . . . and the school culture reflects an ethic of caring and community" (Baglieri & Knopf, 2004, p. 525; emphasis added). Indeed, a core principle of inclusive classrooms is that all members see differences as normal. Inclusive teachers help students realize that nobody is perfect (in the traditional sense), and our imperfections contribute to who we are, adding richness to the ways we perceive and interact with our world.

Along this line, none of us has a disability, and all of us do. The construct of disability is not one that lies within the individual. Rather it is defined by context, by the interactions between the individual and the environment (Broderick, Mehta-Parekh, & Reid, 2005). For instance, the fact that Zach uses some pretty impressive unconventional spelling mattered very much in second grade as he was learning to read and write; it matters far less now as he completes high school with its emphasis on strong thinking and argumentation (and as he employs spell check). The context and tools determined whether Zach's spelling eccentricities interfered with his success. *Accommodations* and *modifications* help us incorporate students' inevitable differences through environments and instruction that allow students to work to potential. Accommodations and modifications have been shown to increase student academic engagement and decrease teacher's time spent on classroom management (Lee, Wehmeyer, Soukup, & Palmer, 2010).

Accommodations make room for the abilities and needs of your students without substantially altering what they are expected to learn. Accommodations change the way students are presented with information or display their learning. Depending on student needs, you might make accommodations to the physical environment, ways you present information, materials students use, or conditions under which students display their knowledge. Examples include modified furniture, a preview of the lesson (in English or in the student's native language), textbooks with large print, a weekly homework log signed by a family member, and an oral (rather than written) test. *Accommodations* change conditions without much altering expected outcomes.

On the other hand, *modifications* substantially alter what students are expected to learn. Modifications may require that students use materials at a different instructional level or that they be evaluated according to different performance criteria. For individual students, cutting a spelling list in half, allowing the use of a calculator on an assessment, and providing a word bank for use during a test are examples of modifications. Modifications are typically made for students with significant disabilities, such as severe developmental delay or traumatic brain injury. We know that students come to us with a variety of needs. It is your responsibility to search out the technological aids that can help each of your students to achieve to full potential.

Use Assistive Technology to Accommodate and Modify

Assistive technology (sometimes called assistive and adaptive technology) addresses students' physical and cognitive needs. Broadly, assistive technology includes any invention that enhances the performance of people with disabilities. A wheelchair is an example. In terms of computers, assistive technology includes both hardware and software that support student performance. Assistive technology encompasses input devices—devices that allow users to feed information more easily into the computer—and output devices—devices that communicate the users' meaning in alternate forms. A few examples of assistive input devices include:

- Alternative keyboards (including those with larger or smaller keys, reconfigured keys, or keyboards made for one hand)
- Touch screens
- Sip and puff systems (activated when the user inhales or exhales)
- Electronic pointing devices (which allow the user to move the mouse on screen by use of a means other than the hands, such as eye movements)

Output devices include mechanisms such as:

- Braille embossers (which allow users with visual impairments to print from the computer)
- Screen magnifiers (to enlarge the screen display)
- Text-to-speech or speech synthesizers (so that users with reading or visual difficulties can hear what is presented on the screen; these also provide users without oral communication a voice)

Assistive software also includes any program that enhances a person's ability to perform. Consider how spell checkers, calculators, and text magnification functions can help each of us at times. See the 21st Century Teaching and Learning Tip for accessibility features in software applications.

Audio downloads of novels or other text materials can be useful to support the comprehension of students who struggle with text or would benefit from repeated readings. Many text-to-speech programs are available, some for free, on the web. Cell phone videos might allow students to view a peer's performance multiple times as they learn to emulate that performance. Because you are responsible for student learning, you need to assess student needs carefully, then search out and implement technologies that meet those needs.

Required accommodations and modifications are listed on students' IEPs and other educational plans. By now, though, you will have no doubt concluded that teachers have a professional

---

21st Century Teaching and Learning Tip

USING ACCESSIBILITY FEATURES

Common applications like word processing programs and spreadsheets usually contain many functions designed to enhance productivity in the face of special needs. Accessibility features make the software more useful to people with needs such as lower vision or limited dexterity. Macros (shortcuts for sequences of keystrokes or mouse clicks), keyboard shortcuts, and customized toolbars are examples. In your word processing program or other application, search "help" for "accessibility" for more.

Student using assistive technology device

Robin Nelson/PhotoEdit

responsibility to account for all learners' instructional needs, regardless of legally mandated plans. Driven by the goal of powerful learning for all, you will no doubt look for opportunities to make room for student needs whether or not students have formal plans on file.

Use Response to Intervention

With the 2004 reauthorization of IDEA came a change in how learning disabilities can be identified and addressed. Previously, students were identified after assessment results showed a discrepancy between their intelligence and their academic performance. As a result, most learning disabilities were identified in grade 3 or later, after students had already experienced academic failure. IDEA allows for this discrepancy model's continued use, and the majority of states still allow for it (Zirkel & Thomas, 2010).

But now schools are also allowed to use a different model for assessing and instructing students with learning disabilities: **response to intervention (RTI).** To be identified as having a learning disability, students must show nonresponsiveness to systematic instruction. This change shifts the focus from determining eligibility to providing intense instruction for struggling students and making early identification as necessary so that all students can be well served *before* they start to fail and so that students are not misidentified as qualifying for special education merely as a result of poor instruction (Fuchs & Fuchs, 2005). Basic tenets of RTI are these:

1. *Careful Screening:* Rigorous assessments are used to determine all students' initial needs.
2. *Tiered Interventions:* Students receive increasingly intense, well-researched instructional interventions when they do not respond to interventions at lower tiers.
3. *Student Assessment:* Student progress is frequently and systematically monitored through careful assessments. Assessment data are used to maintain, decrease, or increase the instructional interventions (Griffiths, VanDerHeyden, Parson, & Burns, 2006).

In RTI, all students are screened and receive rigorous instruction in the general education setting (that's Tier One). If assessments show that they do not respond to (succeed with) that instruction, students move to Tier Two, which serves a smaller number of students and provides more intense intervention. Some schools use a three-tiered model;

Figure 4.4 *Response to intervention.*

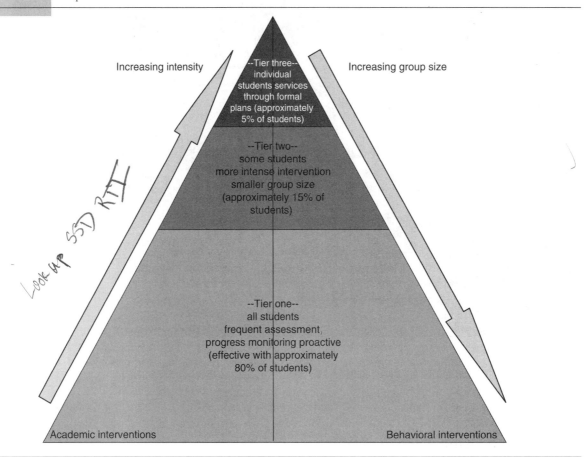

Increasing intensity

Increasing group size

--Tier three--
individual
students services
through formal
plans (approximately
5% of students)

--Tier two--
some students
more intense intervention
smaller group size
(approximately 15% of
students)

--Tier one--
all students
frequent assessment,
progress monitoring proactive
(effective with approximately
80% of students)

Academic interventions

Behavioral interventions

others use four or five tiers. A very small number of students is served by the most intense tiers. Response to intervention is commonly used in reading instruction—where most students with learning disabilities struggle—and it is also used to address student behavior. Figure 4.4 gives a common depiction of RTI.

Local districts pursue their own RTI models, and they are at different stages in doing so. Schools that have implemented RTI for a number of years are beginning to report gains in student learning and large drops in special education referrals (e.g., Butler, 2010). Vaughn et al. (2010) obtained small positive effects for RTI for middle school students, but RTI brings to secondary schools special issues that affect feasibility and success. In junior high and high schools, it can be difficult to implement rigorous, differentiated instruction at Tier One (Brozo, 2009), scheduling is difficult, and many students experience low motivation to learn, after experiencing years of difficulty in schools (Fuchs, Fuchs, & Compton, 2010). In sum, RTI as an approach to preventing learning disabilities and supporting student success is evolving and is part of a multipronged approach to meet special educational needs. Students who are acquiring English need a different set of approaches.

Shelter English Instruction for English Language Learners

Linguistic diversity has always been a part of our U.S. heritage. Did you know that nearly 400 languages are spoken in the United States, including dozens of indigenous languages (Modern Language Association, 2010)? In terms of numbers of speakers, Spanish takes second place to English, and Chinese third (Modern Language

Association, 2010). In 2007, approximately 21 percent of U.S. children spoke a language other than English at home (National Center for Education Statistics, 2010g). Although all states have English learners, the prevalence of speakers of languages other than English tend to be highest in the West and lowest in the South and parts of the Midwest (U.S. Census Bureau, 2008).

Language Acquisition

Your English learners—also called English language learners or limited English proficient students—have a difficult job: They must simultaneously master challenging academic content standards as they acquire a new language (English). Additionally, it is important that students work to maintain their primary language. Multilingual skills are recognized as important resources (Bilingual Education Act of 1994), and fluency in the home language boosts fluency and academic achievement in English (Karathanos, 2009; Krashen, 1997; Thomas & Collier, 2001).

Although conversational aspects of a language often develop in just a couple years, it takes at least five years—often longer—for a student to develop a second language (WongFillmore & Snow, 2000). Students' acquisition of English will depend on factors such as their level of literacy in their home language and their previous school experiences, but all students pass through a number of predictable stages in acquiring a language (summarized by Holmes, Rutledge, & Gauthier, 2009):

- *Stage 1*—Pre-Production: Students actively take in the sounds and structure of the new language.
- *Stage 2*—Early Production: Student utterances are short.
- *Stage 3*—Speech Emergence: Confidence and language skills increase. Vocabulary is still limited.
- *Stage 4*—Intermediate Fluency: Students can read with fluency; decontextualized, academic language presents challenges.
- *Stage 5*—Advanced Fluency: Students' language complexity and vocabulary approximate that of native speakers.

You will know students' language levels through a variety of mechanisms including classroom observations and analysis of their writing samples. Also, under NCLB, English learners' language proficiency is assessed annually, and you will receive score reports that give your students' progress in reading, writing, listening, and speaking. All of these assessment results will help you provide instruction that fosters your students' language acquisition and content learning.

Teaching English Learners

The civil rights case *Lau v. Nichols* (1974) expanded the rights of English learners in the United States by finding that linguistically appropriate modifications must be made so that English learners are not denied equal education opportunities. English learners are now educated in a variety of settings, such as **bilingual education programs,** pullout programs, and mainstream English settings. State law and local policies dictate these decisions. Some states such as Arizona, California, and Massachusetts require instructions to be primarily in English through structured immersion. Check the directives for your state and district on your state department of education's Web site.

Achievement and opportunity gap data (e.g., Abedi & Herman, 2010) indicate just how much work we and our English learners have ahead of us. In the classroom, educational efforts typically focus on two goals: English language acquisition and content mastery. The regular classroom teacher often is primarily responsible for both. Other specialists may assist, particularly in the case of English language development. An approach called sheltered English instruction helps English learners build content knowledge despite limited English proficiency.

Sheltered English Instruction

To make content accessible for English learners, we modify lessons by lightening the cognitive, cultural, linguistic, and learning loads that can present barriers (Meyer, 2000). The use of Universal Design and differentiated instruction addresses this goal. So does sheltered instruction. **Sheltered instruction** attempts to provide "a refuge from the linguistic demands of mainstream instruction" (Echevarria & Graves, 1998, p. 54) and is called by various names in different regions, including *content ESL* (English as a second language), *ESL content*, and *specially designed academic instruction in English* (SDAIE). It addresses grade-level curriculum standards but makes content accessible by embedding instruction into meaningful contexts and a supportive learning environment. Each of the strategies you employ will be based on your knowledge of student needs given their language development levels. Experts generally agree on methods of sheltered instruction (Center for Research on Education, Diversity & Excellence, 2002; Cummins, 1981; Echevarria, Vogt, & Short, 2004; Fillmore, 1982; Gersten, Baker, Shanahan, Linan-Thompson, Collins, & Scarcella, 2007; Hill & Flynn, 2006; Holmes, Rutledge, & Gauthier, 2009; Janzen, 2008; Krashen, 1981; Meyer, 2000; Swain, 1985; Thomas & Collier, 2001). They are:

1. *Supportive Environment.* In a supportive environment, students' cultures, home languages, and background experiences are seen as assets from which students can draw rather than as deficits that detract from their English acquisition. The teacher respects preferences for communication styles that may differ from her own. Examples include discourse patterns and rules on interrupting, eye contact, and turn taking. The environment provides a context where people feel comfortable experimenting with language and asking questions about it. The teacher minimizes direct correction and shapes accurate English through modeling and provides frequent positive reinforcement for students' legitimate successes.

2. *Focused Content.* Teachers focus instruction on the acquisition of three kinds of English: social English (such as that required by informal conversation), academic English (which is more sophisticated and complex and requires more time to develop), and subject-specific language that is used exclusively within particular content areas (including specialized terms such as "sextant" and "velocity"). Each lesson's content objectives focus on just a few carefully selected main ideas. Content objectives must be rigorous and reflect grade-level expectations. A small handful of key content-related vocabulary terms are explicitly developed during each lesson.

3. *Embedded Content.* Teachers should embed instruction within meaningful contexts where language is used for a purpose and connected to wider experiences. The acts of explaining something to a younger child or of writing a letter to a peer are examples of potentially meaningful contexts. Teachers set a context for new information by explicitly tying it to past learning and to students' previous experiences and background knowledge, gained at home and in the community.

4. *Comprehensible Input.* Language can be made more understandable by modifying it (text and speech), guiding understanding, and scaffolding. Teachers may provide recorded versions of class material (such as tape recordings, audio files, and podcasts) so that students can preview material and revisit it multiple times. Teachers may also provide outlines of the text, rewrite important passages in simpler language, highlight it, provide graphic organizers, or use alternate readings (such as text materials provided in students' primary language). To make their speech more accessible, teachers may focus on **caretaker speech,** which mimics the language caretakers provide for charges by focusing on communication rather than on form. Examples of speech modifications include speech appropriate for students' proficiency level and slower but still natural speech.

5. *Increased Interaction.* English learners need plentiful opportunities to interact with peers and with their teacher to make purposeful use of the language. A variety of grouping structures, such as pairs and small groups chosen in different ways such as matching or contrasting language levels, interest, and random groupings are used.

21st Century Teaching and Learning Tip

USING THE INTERNET AS A LANGUAGE LEARNING TOOL

At school or at home, the Internet provides great opportunities for hearing native speakers, revisiting content, learning new vocabulary, and using English. Try some of these tools:

- *Video quizzes:* You and your students can create multiple-choice questions to accompany your choice of YouTube videos at ESL Video (eslvideo.com).
- *Language podcasts:* You and your students can record and post podcasts or audio files. Audicity (http://audacity.sourceforge.net/) is a free and easy audio recorder. Search for "language podcasts" for many free podcasts designed for English learners.
- *Vocabulary flashcards:* You and your students can develop e-flashcards for targeted vocabulary. Quizlet (quizlet.com) lets you save and share your cards on the Web, and it has some effective teaching tools (like games) to make practice more engaging.
- *Language games:* Sites like Digital Dialects (http://www.digitaldialects .com/index.htm) have free games for learning and practicing a number of target languages. Make your own games at classtools.net.
- *Conversing using Voice Over Internet Protocol:* Tools like Skype or Google Talk allow students to practice English in relaxed settings.
- *And one more for fun:* Voki (www.voki.com). Students create avatars, record their voices conveying a brief message in the target language, and share. You can require certain vocabulary and sentence complexity. Students typically rehearse their recordings several times, giving purposeful opportunities for language practice, and the audience is real, heightening motivation. Here's a screen shot of a Voki: My dog Lila using descriptive language to convey the mountain scene behind her.

Teaching Tip

VOCAB CARDS

Before your lesson write three to five key terms on large cards. Give students their own smaller copies. Use these cards in a variety of ways for introducing, developing, and practicing new words. For example, begin a lesson by asking students to nominate their favorite words, or the most and least familiar words. Have them predict the word(s) that will be most important during the lesson. At their seats, ask partners to pick a card they know something about and tell their neighbor what they know. During the lesson, have students practice saying the words aloud and developing meanings in multiple ways such as drawing pictures on the backs of cards. To close the lesson, revisit students' predictions, say the words again, and use each in a sentence. Practice these words on a different day, using the cards in engaging ways. For instance, ask students to pick two cards whose words are related, or unrelated. Ask them to give examples or use them in sentences (after Spencer & Guillaume, 2009).

For example, partners might together select, study, read, and question each other on a content text (Ogle & Correa-Kovtun, 2010). The teacher is included as a participant in interactions and monitors and guides students' collaborations and use of language. The vocab cards presented in Teaching Tip can be used to encourage student conversations that include content vocabulary. The room is arranged to facilitate conversation, and the students talk as much—or more—than the teacher does to rehearse the content and practice English.

6. *Emphasis on Higher-Level Thinking.* Sheltered instruction focuses on nudging English learners to use higher-level thinking through activities such as adhering to challenging content standards; using questions that ask students to interpret and

analyze ideas; providing activities that encourage students to see the whole picture related to the content in addition to its smaller parts; and requiring students to use the text and other evidence to support their opinions. Expectations must remain high (Parish et al., 2006).

Sheltered instruction is most effective with students who are beyond the earliest stages of English acquisition, although it is still better than unsupported immersion into a mainstream English language class for fostering student success. Even the best-sheltered instruction reduces the achievement gap between English-only students and English learners only by half (Thomas & Collier, 2001). Although it is a relatively easy thing to suggest effective practices, it is quite another to put them into practice each day in ways that respond to specific students and their varied profiles. There are no "three easy steps," no magic answers to provide instruction that responds to culturally and linguistically diverse students (Bartolome, 1994). Doing so is a difficult undertaking that requires ongoing assessment, strategic teaching, sustained effort, and a constant commitment to learning. It is often an uncertain enterprise in which participants give focused attention to respecting each other's cultures and perspectives, negotiate meaning, and find their way together.

Challenge Gifted and Advanced Learners

A student might qualify for special education services in reading, but have great mathematical talent. Gardner (2006) reminds us that there are many ways to be smart. Indeed, each of our students has gifts. However, a small segment of the population is designated as "gifted" and receives services based on that classification. In 2006, more than 3 million students in U.S. elementary and secondary schools were classified as gifted (6.7%; National Center for Education Statistics, 2009c).

Defining Giftedness and Identifying Gifted Learners

Definitions of giftedness vary, and states have different criteria and policies for determining eligibility. In general, gifted or talented students show performance high above that of their age mates in intellectual, creative, artistic, or other endeavors. Gifted students are diverse, but many are problem solvers who benefit from addressing open-ended and complex problems, often related to their own interests. Many are considered to be emotionally and academically intense (Manning, 2006). Teachers who think life would be easy if their room were full of gifted students are often mistaken. In addition to their incredible gifts, advanced learners may also face a number of issues that affect classroom performance. According to Manning, classroom issues that may stem from giftedness include problematic work habits and a heightened sensitivity to others. In one study, highly gifted boys and boys with learning disabilities were alike in their classroom behavior (Shaywitz et al., 2001). Once again we are reminded that no one classification explains a person fully and that all students have needs that can stretch their teachers' skills.

Decisions about how best to serve gifted students are often heated. Examine some of the issues by reviewing the National Association for Gifted Children's (http://www.nagc .org) standards for exemplary gifted programs. Check with your school site to determine the arrangements within which students classified as gifted are served. Some districts have magnet schools for gifted students. Additionally, many schools have self-contained gifted classes. Others have **Gifted and Talented Education** (GATE) clusters within larger classes. Gifted students also frequently attend general education classes and visit resource programs or receive all of their education within their regular classroom.

Check for the referral process for identifying gifted students at your location. Although the identification process should include more than one screening device (Smutny, 2003), it often begins with a parent request or observations by the classroom teacher. When you suspect that a student may be gifted, observe the student carefully and ask questions such as, Does the student learn rapidly and possess a large store of information? Does the student exhibit originality in written or oral expression? Does the student use materials in extremely creative ways? Does the student contribute to class discussions with unique and insightful perspectives? As you observe students, be sure that you are watching all for signs of giftedness, including those exhibited by students who might be less visible than others, such as students with disabilities, students who belong to ethnic or racial minorities, and students who are acquiring English.

Meeting the Needs of Advanced and Gifted Learners

Responsive instruction entails not only providing instruction that makes content accessible but also pushing students to their limits to grasp content that is as deep and as rich as their current capacities will allow. Advanced learners often require substantial modifications to the general curriculum to ensure that they, too, find new meaning each day at school. Advanced learners include those classified as gifted and those who are intensely interested in or performing at high levels for particular content areas.

Many teachers find that meeting the needs of advanced learners can be more of a challenge than meeting the needs of struggling students because gifted learners often enter a grade or class knowing significant amounts of the content, move beyond grade-level content standards, and sometimes bring strong independent approaches to their learning goals and choices. They ask tough questions, too. Yet our responsibility to ensure that students working at advanced levels make substantial academic progress is the same as our responsibility to the rest of our students. Gifted students' needs to learn and develop will not be met by correcting spelling tests for us, tutoring peers for most of the day, or completing additional worksheets on the same topic.

Approaches such as Universal Design, RTI (Rollins, Mursky, Shah-Coltrane, & Johnsen, 2009), and differentiated instruction (Manning, Stanford, & Reeves, 2010) provide useful frameworks for addressing the needs of advanced learners. Inquiry-based learning experiences (see Chapter 7) are often appropriate as well. Additional strategies you may try include acceleration, **curriculum compacting,** and modification of the depth and complexity of instruction.

Acceleration In acceleration, students are moved to other settings to receive instruction at their level. A junior high school student may, for example, take mathematics at the high school or a nearby college. Or they may work with materials from higher grade levels within their regular classroom.

Curriculum Compacting In curriculum compacting, all students are given a preassessment such as a written test to determine which content in an upcoming unit they have already mastered. Students receive instruction with the rest of the class for nonmastered objectives and spend the rest of their instructional time pursuing projects and independent work that is more appropriate for their needs (Reis & Renzulli, 1995). Strategies that replace classroom instruction during curriculum compacting may include acceleration, community service projects, independent research, and enrichment activities. Systematic assessment of students' entry knowledge is essential for compacting to be effective.

Depth and Complexity Advanced learners can also address the same topics as their peers, but in greater depth or complexity (California Department of Education & California Association for the Gifted, 1994). Many school districts are pursuing depth and complexity to meet gifted needs in GATE programs. To alter the *depth* of the content students might:

- Pursue the tools and language used by specialists in the content.
- Go into greater detail.
- Look for patterns related to the content, such as trends over time.
- Study the underlying structure of the content.
- Examine ethical considerations related to the content.
- Pursue unanswered questions.

Interactions with a variety of materials and people can help address students' learning needs

Source: Scott Cunningham/Merrill.

To study the content in greater *complexity,* students might examine relationships within the content, or relationships between the content and a different entity. They might also examine different points of view related to the content. Alterations of depth and complexity can be accomplished by mechanisms such as learning or interest centers (for an example, see Wilkins, Wilkins, & Oliver, 2006), differentiated assignments, student contracts, and small-group projects.

Foster Gender Equity

Gender continues to be a variable of interest the world round. U.S. figures show, for example, noted disparities related to gender:

- Females, equally trained, continue to earn less than men (about 73%; Pay Scale, 2010).
- Females pursue high-status science, technology, engineering, mathematics (STEM) schooling and careers at lower rates, and progressively fewer pursue advanced STEM degrees. Figures are particularly pronounced in physics, chemistry, and engineering and for women of color (De Welde, Laursen, & Thiry, n.d).
- Males are incarcerated at rates 100 times greater than those of females (Prison Policy Initiative, 2005).
- Males' suicide rates are four times that of women (suicide.org, n.d.).
- Males now constitute a minority of college students (U.S. Census Bureau, 2010).
- Males drop out of school more often than do females (Greene & Winters, 2006).
- Males comprise the majority of students receiving special education services (Tyre, 2008).
- As measured by grades and test scores, female achievement typically equals or exceeds that of males. For example, the gender gap in reading achievement starts early and is persistent, with 17-year-old females outscoring their male peers by 11 points on the National Assessment of Educational Progress (NAEP, 2008b).
- Boys are referred for discipline issues more frequently than girls (Kaufman et al., 2010) and experience more conflict with and distance from their teachers (Koepke & Harkins, 2008).

Such differential outcomes seem to be a result of combined effects of factors such as biology, culture, the media, and society. Schools, too, contribute to some differences. In subtle ways, despite efforts to be fair, schools treat male and female children differently in ways that limit members of both groups. For example, some research indicates that teachers have gender-related beliefs about classroom discipline (Erden & Wolfgang, 2004), and based on gender, we tend to praise students to hold different standards for behavior and participation.

Initial concerns about gender equity grew out of alarm over ways that schools were shortchanging girls (Wellesley College Center for Research on Women, 1992). Indeed, strategic efforts are still required as we strive to help girls remain engaged in science-related studies and perceive a full range of options for advanced studies.

Inclusive and Responsive Teaching Tip

STRATEGIES FOR ACHIEVING GENDER EQUITY

1. Study your classroom to assess your own gender biases. Check the physical environment, activities, student feedback, and classroom management to ensure that student opportunities are not limited by gender.

2. Encourage students to take risks and set goals. This helps students to take ownership over goals and see them as achievable. Focus on progress goals (not solely performance goals) to encourage intrinsic motivation. Include intermediate and long-term goals.

3. Help students value their successes and learn from mistakes. Classroom activities should encourage legitimate success, but not 100 percent of the time. Students need to be challenged.

4. Keep expectations for learning high and send positive messages. Refrain from sending the message that you do not expect success from some students or that certain kinds of failure are acceptable based on gender. Avoid excessive praise for substandard performance.

5. Provide good feedback. Good feedback (a) focuses students on the relevant aspects of the problem, (b) gives information about outcomes *and* processes, (c) challenges incorrect conclusions, and (d) corrects students' flawed self-assessments.

6. Encourage appropriate attributions. Help students explain success and failure by linking performance with effort, encouraging internal explanations for success, and emphasizing specific and temporary explanations for failure. Help students focus on making choices and exercising control.

7. Challenge stereotypes. In neutral settings, ask students to think about common stereotypes. Address stereotypes found in the media. Model gender-fair language and behavior. Value both typically masculine and typically feminine perspectives and activities, and value a fuller range of what constitutes "masculine" and "feminine."

8. Use groups flexibly. Encourage children to work well within a variety of settings. Vary group compositions frequently, perhaps including single-gender groupings as one learning option. Monitor students' interactions and intervene for support.

9. Teach the null curriculum. Include readings and other activities that address the varied contributions of men and women in nonstereotypical ways.

To these gender concerns we add apprehension regarding differences that seem to place males at a disadvantage. Some experts argue that schools have become unfriendly places for boys (Mulvey, 2010; Tyre, 2008). They cite explanations such as a more adult-driven society with fewer unstructured play opportunities for children, the accelerating curriculum (difficult for some boys, who tend to mature later), declining opportunities for physical activity in school, and schools' push for skills that may not come as easily to some boys (such as organization, neatness, and collaboration).

Schools are responding to gender differences with a variety of approaches. There is much interest in single-sex schools, for example, and the research gives "mild to moderate" support for such schools on a variety of student outcomes (Mael, Alonso, Gibson, Rogers, & Smith, 2005). Horgan's (1995) strategies remain fresh for today's classrooms, adapted in the Inclusive and Responsive Teaching Tip. To these, we may add the following promising paractices:

- Encourage mentoring experiences.
- Provide opportunities for physical movement and action.
- Provide opportunities for both collaboration and competition.
- Expand the reading options available. Nonfiction materials, books with adventure or danger, materials with interesting text features (such as graphics), series of beloved characters, and books by favored authors are good bets for boys (Farris, Werderich, Nelson, & Fuhler, 2009).

As with all student needs and characteristics, it is important not to rely on stereotypical images based on gender—what *boys* or *girls* are like. When it comes to gender, the areas of overlap in performance and preference are far greater than the regions of difference (Campbell & Storo, 1994). As is the case with other student characteristics and needs, gender provides you the opportunity to:

1. Build an understanding of the research and consider that what happens for some groups of students may also relate to your students' experiences.
2. Gather varied data to understand your actual students and their preferences.

3. Communicate high expectations for all and push them to broaden their expectations for the range of options life experience, schooling, and career options available to them.

4. Expand the range of classroom options available in your classroom, providing for some student choice in terms of content, activities, and independent activities. Examples include physical movement, noise level, competitive and cooperative structures, and mode of communication.

Creating inclusive classrooms also entails ensuring that all students feel safe to learn.

Create Safe Spaces

Issues facing gay, lesbian, bisexual, and transgender (GLBT) students and their families are increasingly the focus of national conversations. In the last century, we have moved from the perceived dangers of homosexual teachers to the risks schools present for GLBT students (Griffin, & Ouelett, 2003). GLBT students face a school environment than is more hostile than for the general school population. The National School Climate Study reveals that general negative comments ("That's so gay!" "Fag!") are common and widely tolerated, and in some cases are perpetrated by teachers (GLSEN, 2009). In that study, students perceived that teachers' interventions to stop such language were infrequent. GLBT middle school students were more vulnerable than high school students in many respects. GLBT students also historically report an increased threat of bullying and physical violence at school, sometimes to the point of skipping school for their perceived safety (Safe Schools Coalition of Washington, 1999; GLSEN 2009). Further, GLBT parents noted hearing negative remarks or feeling excluded from schooling activities more than did the general population (Kosciw, & Diaz, 2008).

In such a climate, it's not difficult to understand why some students would have concerns about physical and emotional safety that might take precedence over academic concerns. Many teachers are hesitant to raise or respond to students' questions, comments, or issues related to sexual orientation or gender expression, but teachers and schools are essential for creating safe spaces—inclusive spaces—for all of our students.

GLSEN (2009) gives suggestions for creating safe spaces for student who are GLBT or are members of GLBT families. Check your biases and educate yourself on issues related to sexual orientation. What are the issues at your site? Serve as an ally for students. Ensure that they know that you are a safe person who advocates for all students; be a role model of acceptance. Use inclusive language (such as "partner"). Respond to anti-GLBT language. Let it be known that harassment is not tolerated, and hold students accountable for their behavior. Overall, we teachers need to question assumptions, educate ourselves, listen, be ready to advocate for our students, and seek out resources that can allow all students to feel safe and included at school.

Parting Words

Each of these nine approaches for providing responsive instruction—and others—will require deep and sustained inquiry and practice. I introduce them here for two reasons. First, I hope to help you build an initial awareness and an emerging repertoire of strategies to use now, in your early days as a professional. More important, I hope to help you build an inclusive mindset. Your students' learning needs related to sexual orientation, gender, giftedness, exceptionality, language, or culture are not layered upon those of their "regular" needs. You build instruction from the ground up that addresses the variety of needs possessed by each of your students and encourages each of them to strive forward in their growth as individuals.

Opportunities to Practice

1. Inclusive and responsive teachers pursue understanding and continued growth. Choose one approach for inclusive and responsive teaching addressed in this chapter where you judge your knowledge to be limited. Examples include sheltering instruction and meeting the needs of students identified as gifted. The Web sites from this chapter and from Chapter 3 provide some suggested resources.

2. Use Figure 4.5 to complete a scavenger hunt for resources at your site. Tell people it is for an assignment but take careful notes for later.

Figure 4.5 *Site scavenger hunt: Inclusive and responsive teaching resources.*

At your site, find someone who…	
1. Can point you to translation services and procedures	Name: Service or procedure:
2. Teaches students with identified needs who are taught in the general education setting for at least a portion of the day	Name: Location or contact information: Teaching responsibility:
3. Has expertise or responsibility for teaching students identified as advanced or gifted	Name: Location or contact information: Expertise:
4. Differentiates instruction regularly	Name: Location or contact information: One sample strategy:
5. Has certification or expertise in working successfully with English learners	Name: Location or contact information: One piece of advice:
6. Has a great reputation for including families	Name: Location or contact information: One piece of advice:
At your site, find materials that . . .	
7. Use assistive technology or general technology	Equipment: or Location:
8. Provide challenges for eager learners or to increase depth or complexity	Materials: Location:
9. Help you arrange the learning space for students who need fewer distractions	Materials: Location:
At your site, find services that . . .	
10. Help you meet the needs of families with limited income	Services: Accessing the services:
11. Help students who are working on clear speech	Services: Accessing the services:
12. [Pick a need based on your students] Need:	Services: Accessing the services:

3. Play with one of the tech tools recommended throughout the chapter, perhaps in the 21st Century Teaching and Learning Tips.

4. Make a set of vocab cards (see the Teaching Tip) for an upcoming lesson, or for ten terms that are found in the content standards for your discipline.

5. Interview an experienced teacher at your site regarding response to intervention. Is it being implemented at your site? What model is in place? Is there current evidence of effectiveness? How can you learn more? How can you contribute?

 Web Sites

http://www.rti4success.org/
National Center on Response to Intervention. The Center's mission is to provide assistance in implementing research-based models of RTI. The library is a great place to start.

http://iris.peabody.vanderbilt.edu
The IRIS Center. Special Education Resources for Inclusion, Scientifically-Validated and Evidence-Based Instructional

Strategies. This site is rich with tutorials and resources for many kinds of special education needs.

http://www.glsen.org/
Gay, Lesbian and Straight Education Network. The network is focused on ensuring safe schools for all students. Check Research and the Educator Resources under Tools and Tips. The Safe Space Tool Kit is a great place to start.

Planning for Instruction

Before You Begin Reading

As an adult who has experienced some success in navigating through life and its opportunities, you already know a bit about planning. Before you read Chapter 5, think about your own life and how you have planned for it thus far. Jot down some first-impression notes in response to these questions.

Warm-Up Exercise for Planning

1. When do you plan? (*Hints*: Think small and large. Do you plan on a daily basis? Do you plan for the distant future?)

2. What format do you use to capture your plans? (*Hints*: Do you use to-do lists? Do you build flow charts? Do you store plans in your memory?)

3. What do you notice about your efforts to plan? (*Hints*: How do plans help? How do you respond to changes?)

4. How do you know when you have accomplished your goals?

As you read Chapter 5, compare what you know about planning in the broader sense to classroom planning. Points of similarity may include, for instance, that teachers plan at different levels and use their plans to ensure that they meet goals and maintain focus on priorities?

"Cheshire Puss . . . Would you tell me, please, which way I ought to go from here?"

"That depends a good deal on where you want to get to," said the Cat.

"I don't much care where—" said Alice.

"Then it doesn't matter which way you go," said the Cat.

—Lewis Carroll, *Alice's Adventures in Wonderland*

This chapter will help you devise plans to increase the likelihood that you and your students end up where you want to be. It has six major points:

1. Planning today is shaped by our context of accountability and drive to provide high-quality learning opportunities for all students.
2. Planning starts with the students.
3. Plans are driven by what we want to accomplish, by our goals.
4. Plans should include thoughtful use of instructional resources.
5. Long-term planning usually precedes short-term planning; it provides a structure for daily events.
6. Short-term planning, or lesson planning, arranges activities in logical ways for daily instruction.

Planning Today

Planning today is shaped by our context. We live in a culture of standards-based accountability. Central to education reform efforts that began in the 1980s was the development and implementation of rigorous statements of expectations for student learning: content standards or **student performance standards.** Content standards tell what students are expected to know and be able to do and performance standards tell how they will show it.

The Basics of Standards-Based Instruction

In **standards-based instruction,** the educational community first develops content standards and operationalizes them through performance standards. Next, educators develop or select tools to assess student mastery of those standards. Common assessment tools are paper/pencil tests and teacher observation. After checking students' entry-level performance related to the standard, educators plan instruction to bring about student mastery of the standard. They develop or select materials that will help teachers guide students toward mastery. Next, teachers present information and check students' progress along the way. Then students are assessed for mastery of the standard. Finally, educators analyze results and determine the next course of action: Do they move on or provide further development on the standard at hand? A critical attribute of standards-based instruction is that all elements are in alignment: the goals, the resources, the instruction, and the assessment.

The Promise and Pitfalls of Standards-Based Instruction

You enter the profession of education at a time when we as a community have wrestled for years with standards-based accountability. Standards initially were seen as the key to raising our expectations for what all students should learn, a critical step in raising student achievement. Standards' partner, assessment, would be used to hold students and schools accountable for mastery of those expectations. Two key lessons learned along the way are these:

*   *There is considerable variation across the 50 states in terms of the <u>content</u> students are expected to learn, <u>when</u> they are expected to learn it, and the <u>criteria</u> by which students are judged as having mastered it* (Center for the Study of Mathematics Curriculum, 2006; Schmidt & Cogan, 2009). This is one reason that efforts to develop voluntary national standards are now afoot (see http://www.corestandards.org/ for the Common Core State Standards Inititative).
*   *Setting rigorous content standards is not the same as achieving them.* Time, resources, and opportunity to learn are all required for the mastery of rigorous content standards, and those quantities have not been equitably distributed (Oakes & Rogers, 2006). In some instances, students have taken educational inequities to the courts, noting that if all students are to meet the same standards, they must receive the same resources to do so (e.g., *Williams v. State of California*; see Powers, 2004).

Content standards have opened the educational conversation about what students should learn, how and when they should learn it, and how their learning should be measured. These conversations address many deep and persistent dilemmas of schooling in a diverse society. For instance, should we aim for personalization rather than standardization (Noddings, 2010)? Should we aim for developmental appropriateness or the same standard for all (Rettig, McCullough, Santos, & Watson, 2004)? Perhaps the most important insight gained is that standards can, at their best, serve as powerful tools to help us focus purposefully on our students. Our journey has led us to the point that standards are now accepted as part of the educational landscape and are viewed as important for educational improvement (National Research Council, 2008). Expanding high-quality learning opportunities to meet rigorous and appropriate standards is a next step in our journey as inclusive and responsive teachers.

All Means All

Planning today means meeting an increasingly broad range of student needs and warmly demanding that all students meet high expectations. Inclusive and responsive teachers aim to consider students' perspectives, current experiences, and needs and abilities and to push all students unfailingly forward in their learning and development. Your students' learning is too important a responsibility to abdicate to others, such as textbook publishers, software developers, or the teacher next door, and careful planning is necessary for helping your students learn and grow as much as possible during the short time they will spend in your classroom.

Planning Starts with the Students

You have a responsibility to base your instructional decisions—what, when, and how you will teach—on a firm foundation of knowledge regarding who your students are and what they need. In fact, the major criterion for your planning decisions should be access to powerful learning for each of your students.

Effective planning begins with gathering and analyzing a variety of kinds of information related to your students. When you plan instruction that draws from what students already know and can do, from their strengths and needs, and from their interests and perspectives, your lessons are far more likely to result in powerful learning for each individual and for the classroom community. Chapter 3 introduced several factors related to students as individuals and as members of groups that can be useful to you as you plan. It included gathering holistic information from families and students and information about students' general progress and needs. Examples include a review of existing records (such as IEPs and levels of English acquisition) and use of interviews and general surveys.

Planning also includes **preassessment** of students' content-specific needs and interests. **Formative assessment,** or assessment that guides instruction (see Chapter 8 for more), allows you to discover what students know, believe, or can do prior to your instruction. Caution! Some teachers, feeling pressed for time, skip the formative assessment stage of planning. Don't be tempted to skip early assessments! Formative assessment is consistently linked with student achievement (Marzano, 2007). Some strategies to gather formative information include brief pretests, informal conversations, self-checks, and journal entries. Figure 5.1 shows two teachers' use of audience response systems to gather, record, and analyze formative assessment data at the click of the students' button. Gregory and Kuzmich (2004) suggest that teachers use rapid preassessments to discover what students know. Examples are homework assignments and group problems, as in these sample tasks:

- In a primary-grade mathematics lesson before a unit on quadrilaterals, small groups of students attack a nonroutine problem, "How many squares are on a checkerboard?" Their teacher observes and takes notes on the concepts they possess, the processes they employ to solve the problem, and the gaps in their reasoning that may be present.

Figure 5.1   *Audience response systems for formative assessment.*

After the prompt was displayed on the screen, students sent their responses to the teachers' computer via handheld devices, informally called clickers. This figure shows students' displayed responses. In 5.1A, the high school teacher held a subsequent discussion based on students' opinions. In 5.1B, the fourth-grade teacher used students' data—most students (70%) were incorrect—to plan his geology lesson. Although many audience response systems exist, these teachers used Turning Point (through Turning Technologies).

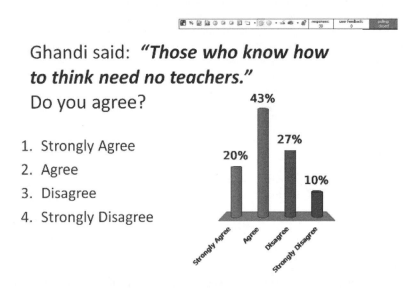

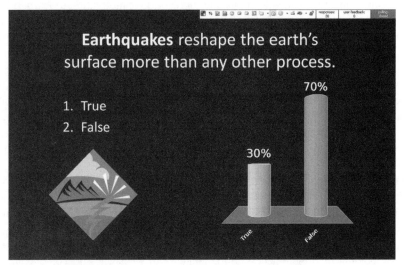

Drawing by Annie Fuller

- For a junior high science homework assignment, students analyze the errors in a hypothetical student's explanation for an observed phenomenon. The prompt reads: "Martin predicts that the water level in a container will rise as the ice it holds melts. Where does Martin's thinking go wrong?" Students discuss their analyses before submitting them.

When conducted far enough in advance, such assessments yield information that can shape instructional planning in productive ways so that you neither duplicate what students already know nor take too big a step beyond their current understandings.

Teaching Tip

INTEREST INVENTORIES

Try writing brief surveys to assess students' interests for upcoming units of study. Here is an example from a history class.

Interest Rating: What Do You Want to Learn about U.S. Social Issues?

We will be learning about some of the issues faced by people in the United States during the late 1800s. Here are some of the social issues we will study. I want to know which issues are most interesting to you. Some of your assignments will be based on your interests. Number your choices from 1 to 5. Number 1 should be the item that is most interesting to you, and number 5 should be the item that is least interesting to you.

Treatment of minorities
Child labor
Growth of cities
Problems faced by immigrants

Other. Tell me more:

You might have family members or know other people who could help us understand these issues. If so, list their names and how they might help.

In addition to students' *content knowledge* related to the topic, you should also consider their *interests*. By considering the facets of the content of most interest to the students, you can connect to their own goals and increase their motivation to learn. Your observations of the free reading books students choose and the activities they pursue will provide some information about their interests. Additionally, you can try using simple inventories directly related to your upcoming instruction. For example, as part of their course on U.S. History Studies since 1877, Texas high school students study social changes in the United States from 1877 to 1898. To plan his unit, one teacher might distribute an interest inventory, excerpted in the Teaching Tip. The teacher plans to have all students read the textbook, but students will, based on survey results, form interest groups to read other materials and complete independent assignments, too. Also, the teacher plans to have students share their issue-specific knowledge later in mixed groups so that the class draws some broader generalizations about U.S. history.

Chapter 4 introduced you to principles of Universal Design, differentiated instruction, and accommodations and modifications. Such approaches should be at the forefront of your thinking as you plan daily: To what extent do your lessons meet the wide range of learning needs? How will you accommodate your students with physical disabilities? How will you push your advanced learners? How do you help struggling readers improve their skills while simultaneously helping them gain access to the content? In what ways do you encourage language development for your English learners?

As the next step in planning instruction for diverse student needs, this chapter helps you plan in ways that consider students' specific profiles to design clear and appropriate goals, to use an expansive variety of resources, and to develop and organize your instruction in the long and short term. Understanding your students helps shape the next phase of planning: goal setting.

Goals Drive Planning

As the Cheshire cat reminds Alice, if we do not have a goal in mind, it does not much matter how we spend our time. But you and your students have places to go! You need a clear set of goals to guide you.

Kinds of Goals

What are our overall goals for our students? What kinds of knowledge or skills do we want them to possess? Our visions and concerns shape our goals for what students should know and become. For instance, the Partnership for 21st Century Skills presents the rainbow found in Figure 5.2 to encompass the broad range of outcomes they deem essential for today's students. Note that the outcomes encompass not only core subject matter knowledge but also skills deemed necessary for life today and tomorrow. The pool beneath the rainbow represents the support systems necessary to affect the broad outcomes found in the rainbow.

Standards are one influence on our goals for student learning. Look again at your stance toward education (see Chapter 2). It provides another, probably spanning far beyond the traditional content delineated in your state's content standards. Your greatest hopes for your students, your goals, are probably related to their attitudes and actions. Are you interested in your students exhibiting persistence? Exercising objectivity? Taking responsibility? Employing empathy? Communicating effectively? These interests show up on many teachers' lists of goals. For instance, there is increasing interest in the goal of **emotional intelligence** (Csikszentmihalyi & Csikszentmihalyi, 2006; Goleman, 1995, 1998). Emotional intelligence allows us to do such things as identify and manage our emotions, empathize with others, and persist in the presence of frustration. Emotional intelligence is highly prized as effective teamwork becomes increasingly important. The Partnership for 21st Century Skills (2004), for example, lists life skills such as

- Flexibility (adapting to varied roles, jobs responsibilities, schedules and context in a climate of ambiguity and changing priorities)
- Time and goal management (setting goals, prioritizing, and balancing short- and long-term goals, managing resources)
- Effective interaction (knowing when to listen and when to speak; conducting oneself in a professional manner)
- Intercultural communication (respecting cultural differences and working effectively with a range of people)

Educated people not only *know* things, they also *feel* things and *can do* things. Theorists have, for this reason, divided the world of educational goals into three domains:

Figure 5.2   *Partnership for 21st Century Learning's rainbow of student outcomes.*

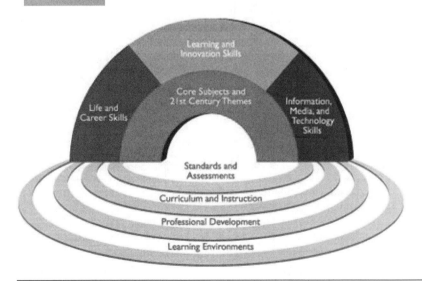

Partnership for 21st Century Skills (2004) http://www.p21.org/index.php?option=com_content&task=view&id=254&Itemid=119 Used with permission.

the cognitive, the affective, and the psychomotor domains. Figure 5.3 presents commonly used taxonomies—or classification systems—for each of these domains. Note that in each taxonomy, the first entry is the simplest and requires the least from the learner. Higher levels place increasing demands on the learner. The more complex levels require that the learner draw on the lower levels, and each level contributes to a fuller understanding, appreciation, or performance. The value of these taxonomies is that they remind us of two things. First, we teach more than just cognitive information. We need to specify goals related to different kinds of learning. Second, within each of the areas we teach, there are levels of understanding and action. Teachers need to provide opportunities for mastery across many levels. Students need to process information in increasingly deep and complex ways and to respond to their worlds via sophisticated thoughts, feelings, and actions.

The most widely discussed taxonomy in schools is Bloom's taxonomy for the cognitive domain. A variety of levels is typically represented in state standards, and teachers are expected to help students work at all levels of Bloom's taxonomy, not just at the rote recall level. Examine, for instance, a sampling of Ohio's mathematics standards for grades 11–12 (Ohio Department of Education, 2001; emphasis added):

- Develop an *understanding* of properties of and representations for addition and multiplication of vectors and matrices.
- *Apply* various measurement scales to describe phenomena and solve problems.
- *Analyze* functions by investigating rates of change, zeroes, asymptotes, and local and global behavior.
- *Create* . . . tabular and graphical displays of data, using appropriate tools, including spreadsheets and graphing calculators.

Take some time to carefully study the levels of Bloom's taxonomy and work with them until they become part of your vocabulary and practice. Opportunity to Practice Exercise 6 at the end of the chapter can get you started. As you work with the levels of Bloom's taxonomy, you may uncover some of the common criticisms of it. The levels are probably not linear.

Figure 5.3   *Taxonomies for the domains of learning.*

Domain	Levels
Cognitive Domain Thinking	Knowledge: recall Comprehension: show understanding Application: use knowledge in a new setting Analysis: identify logical errors; differentiate Synthesis: make something new Evaluation: form judgments; make decisions (Bloom, Englehart, Hill, Furst, & Krathwohl, 1956)
Affective Domain Feeling	Receiving: be aware of certain stimuli Responding: react to stimuli when asked Valuing: act on a belief when not asked to do so Organization: commit to a set of values Characterization: display behaviors that are all consistent with one's set of beliefs (Krathwohl, Bloom, & Masia, 1964)
Psychomotor Domain Doing	Imitation: repeat an action after observing a model Manipulation: perform an action without a model Precision: perform a refined action without a model or directions Articulation: sequence and perform a series of acts with control, timing, and speed Naturalization: perform actions that are now routine and spontaneous (Harrow, 1969)

Figure 5.4   *Revised levels of the cognitive taxonomy.*

Original Level and Order	Revised Level and Order
Knowledge	Remember
Comprehension	Understand
Application	Apply
Analysis	Analyze
Synthesis	Evaluate
Evaluation	Create

For example, synthesis may not always be predicated on analysis (Marlowe & Page, 1998). As a result, Anderson and colleagues (Anderson, 2005; Anderson et al., 2001) revised the taxonomy. In the revised version of Bloom's taxonomy, two of the cognitive processes have been reordered, and their labels, originally nouns, have been replaced with verbs, as shown in Figure 5.4.

Additionally, the revised taxonomy recognizes the multidimensional nature of knowledge that can be possessed at each cognitive process level: the factual, conceptual, procedural, and metacognitive dimensions. Anderson et al. (2001, p. 29) define each dimension of knowledge as follows:

- *Factual:* The basic elements students must know to be acquainted with a discipline or solve problems within it
- *Conceptual:* The interrelationships among the basic elements within a larger structure that enable them to function together
- *Procedural:* How to do something, methods of inquiry, and criteria for using skills, algorithms techniques, and methods
- *Metacognitive:* Knowledge of cognition in general as well as awareness and knowledge of one's own cognition

The revised taxonomy is presented as a table, with the cognitive process level serving as column headings and the above four dimensions serving as row headings. Both the original and the revised taxonomy serve an important function: to remind teachers to provide both a solid core of basic knowledge and opportunities to act on that knowledge in more sophisticated ways. Teachers also find that the revised Bloom's taxonomy can serve as a useful tool to help them differentiate their tasks for a broad range of student needs (Noble, 2004).

Goals, then, can fall into a number of domains, including cognitive, affective, and psychomotor. The educational outcomes teachers set also vary in terms of specificity.

Goals versus Objectives

Outcomes that are broad or general are typically termed *goals.* Goals drive our long-term planning. General goals encompass more specific and detailed statements. Deemed *objectives*, these specific statements guide daily instruction. Thus, objectives can be considered to be the intermediate steps students must master before their end goal is achieved. See if you can sort the statements from Figure 5.5 into goals and objectives.

Notice that the goal statements are lofty pursuits that are not yet operationalized, or put into a form that specifies students' exact actions. The specific objective statements in Figure 5.5 will help students build toward an understanding of the larger goals. Notice that though the statements in Figure 5.5 differ in terms of specificity, they are alike in a very important way: Both goals and objectives are worded in terms of what the student should be able to do. Teaching is goal driven. As you examine national and state content standards, you will note that they also are phrased in terms of student outcomes. This keeps the focus

Figure 5.5   *Goal or objective.*

Set One: Mathematics
1. Given paper and pencil, students will add two-digit numbers with 90% accuracy.
2. Students will improve their computation skills.

Set Two: Science
1. Without reference materials, students will draw a diagram of the water cycle and describe how humans can affect the cycle at two points at least.
2. Students will use scientific principles to make decisions in their own lives.

on students and their learning. As an example, here is a draft core common standard for fifth-grade language arts in the area of writing:

> Conduct short research projects that use several sources to build knowledge through investigation of different aspects of a topic. (Common Core State Standards Initiative, 2010)

A few objectives to help students reach this standard might include:

1. The learner will be able to locate different types of sources related to a topic.
2. The learner will be able to synthesize information from more than one source.
3. The learner will be able to compose a one-page report that conveys new knowledge (conclusions) from information from more than one source.

Teachers develop and implement hundreds of objectives, and the lesson-planning portion of this chapter will help you to write instructional objectives. Your objectives, though, will be shaped by your broader vision of what needs to be accomplished, by your set of goals.

Determining Goals

Professional teachers are charged with making important decisions: What should be taught? To whom? When? These decisions need to be guided by your consideration of the larger system. To develop your classroom goals for the term or year, you need to examine various sources. Recall the bull's eye of sources of influence from Chapter 1 (Figure 1.1). As you write a set of goals for student learning, consider the following suggestions, alone if necessary but in a group with other teachers if possible. For some suggestions, the perspectives of other stakeholders such as family members will enrich your thinking. These tips apply to a set of overarching goals for the year or term, and many apply to the goals you'll develop as you plan specific units too.

- Think again about broad contexts. What are the larger issues facing your students and families? Your state? For example, how are subgroups of students such as students of color, students with special needs, and students who are acquiring English succeeding in school? (Examining test results for your state, district, and local school can provide some insights.) What are the community priorities?
- Analyze information about your students. What do they know now? How do they learn? What would they like to learn? What are their interests and plans? What support will they need from you as they master challenging standards?
- Review your stance. What are your hopes for students? Check your school's mission statement as well.
- Review content standards. Spend some time studying the content expectations to which you and your students will be held. Merely glancing over them will not provide the deep understanding you need. Many teachers find it helpful to work together to examine connections across subject areas and to look for common core concepts such as "change" or "structure" (Hurt, 2003). Be sure to include 21st-century learning

skills as well. How can you incorporate, for example, communication and collaboration? Critical thinking and problem solving?

- Consider content standards in light of your students. Will you need to differentiate your goals based on students' progress, needs, and interests? For example, will some of your students require a set of intermediate goals to address missing knowledge? Will some need goals that take them far beyond grade-level expectations? Which students need English language development goals? What are the goals specified in IEPs and other individualized plans?
- Check grade-level articulation. What are students expected to learn in the year or years before your grade? What will their teachers in future grades expect them to know?
- Examine your materials. What goals are identified in your adopted curricular materials such as your textbooks? How do they align with your standards?

Jot down information from each of these sources. Look for areas of overlap and areas where goals seem dissimilar. Use a critical eye: Whose perspective is left out of your list of goals? Could a different set of goals be used to improve existing practice? Talk with experienced teachers and other colleagues. Prioritize the goals. You will keep these goals in mind as you develop your long-term plans, develop your daily schedule, and plan individual lessons. For example, if you hold goals that focus on intercultural commnunication, you may need to structure your schedule to include projects with investigations into other cultures. If empathy and community connections arose as essential, you may plan a service learning project that includes collaborating with a local retirement home.

Planning to Use Instructional Resources

Once you have set goals, the world is your oyster. Look around you and determine which materials and resources are most likely to foster students' learning and development toward goals. Based on what you have discovered about your students' prior experiences, interests, abilities, and needs—and based on the high expectations you place upon students to master content—search out the resources that will push all of your students forward. A vast array of tools is available to help you and your students reach your goals.

Textbooks

Most teachers start with adopted materials such as textbooks as they make their planning decisions. In fact, many schools mandate their use, in some cases their *strict* use. Textbooks provide a reasonable starting point because they are composed by teams of experts, are subjected to extensive reviews, are field tested, and undergo periodic revision. Textbooks can be effective supports for student learning (Elsaleh, 2010; Wakefield, 2006). Too, many students and districts find that plentiful online materials for textbooks make them more interactive and supportive (Sunkin, 2010).

However, a long history of controversies surrounds textbooks and their shortcomings. Some authors argue that texts are boring, bland, or dumbed-down (Dorrell & Busch, 2000; R. Jones, 2000; Ravitch 2003a, 2003b). Textbooks may not address standards well (O'Shea, 2005) or follow research-driven recommendations for learning. For example, Brenner and Hiebert (2010) found that, despite the fact that teachers are required to follow their core reading textbooks closely, major texts included just a fraction of the number of words that third-graders should read per day to improve as readers. Through their analyses, authors have also found that many textbooks include content inaccuracies (Levy, 2000; Loewen, 1996; Jehlen, 2000) and biases such as class privilege (Dutro, 2009).

For these reasons, it is important to study texts carefully, render your own well-supported decisions, and use textbooks judiciously. Start by examining your goals, objectives, and related standards, and then study the text for its relation to those targets. Examine the accuracy and completeness of the text, and search out possible biases. Determine the extent to which

21st Century Teaching and Learning Tip

CHECKING THE LEVEL OF TEXT MATERIALS

You can more easily match text to students if you know the reading level of the text. Word processing programs often now report one or more different text ratings as part of the "tools" package. One measure of the text's difficulty is its Lexile rating. A Lexile measure is based on two factors: sentence length and word frequency. You can search the Lexile Web site (http://www.lexile.com) for books already rated, and you can get Lexile ratings of your own materials. Try using the analyzer on the Lexile Web site, or see if your word processing program has "Lexile" as a tool. As another use, some teachers complete Lexile ratings of students' writing to help them track changes over time. Readability depends on many factors (such as student interest and the conceptual abstractness and developmental appropriateness of the text), so readability formulas offer just one more piece of information, or a starting point, to match texts to students.

the reading level of the text matches your students' current abilities (the Teaching Tip, Checking the Level of Text Materials, gave an idea for matching students with text). Then think about ways to use the text in support of your goals.

It will be important for you to determine the amount of judgment local policy allows you to exercise in deciding how you will use textbooks. Ask the person in charge how closely you are expected to adhere to text materials. Are you required to "stick to the text"? If the answer is yes, ask a few more questions. What does it mean in your district to "stick to the text"? It can mean very different things, ranging from "use each of the activities exactly as written in the teacher's edition" to "teach to the text's objectives using your choice of activities (text and other) that will encourage learning best for your particular students." In making decisions about using texts, I encourage you to exercise your professional judgment to the fullest extent allowed so that you can provide responsive instruction. For situations in which teachers are granted wide latitude, Dunn (2000) offers suggestions for strategic use of textbooks. She suggests using the textbook as

- A framework to find key ideas.
- A source of questions and possible activities.
- Background reading and reference.
- The basis for cooperative learning activities.

As you consider using your text, remember to use it as just one of many resources that can help students accomplish their aims. Supplement textbooks with other rich resources.

Rich Instructional Resources

Plan your instruction to include rich resources such as primary sources, manipulatives, realia, a variety of sources of print, software, maps and globes, outside speakers, family members, and multimedia. Using rich resources serves many purposes. First, it increases your opportunities to include materials that build a learning environment that incorporates students' worlds. Second, it helps students learn to think the way experts in the field think. Social scientists, for example, know how to interpret primary sources, conduct and analyze oral interviews, and use maps. Third, using a variety of materials ensures that students with different needs can gain access to the information. Students who struggle with reading, for instance, are placed at a disadvantage if instruction is entirely text-based (Frey, Fisher, & Moore, 2005). Also, rich source materials deepen student learning by inciting student interest and curiosity, by making the content more accessible and memorable, by helping students connect with the content, by allowing them to more effectively comprehend and practice the material, and by grounding it more fully in the real-world context within which the content will be used. Although gathering rich resources takes some thought and time, it need not necessarily require a large budget. The Teaching Tip gives some ideas for securing resources when budgets are tight.

Include technological resources in your instructional planning, both in lesson presentations and for 21st-century learning goals. Many schools have projection systems so

Teaching Tip

FINDING RESOURCES WHEN MONEY IS SCARCE

Resources do not need to be expensive to be useful. Imaginative teachers use strategies such as the following to obtain resources to enrich their plans.

- Talk with your parent-teacher organization. Many grant small amounts of money for instructional materials.
- Look for grants. Contact district personnel to scout out opportunities to fund promising projects.
- Get corporate support. Businesses near you will welcome the opportunity to serve the local community by donating supplies. You can also electronically register for donations from organizations around the world. See dozens of sites for donations at the American Federation of Teachers' database (http://www.aft.org/yourwork/tools4teachers/fundingdatabase/), for example, or try Donors Choose (www.donorschoose.org).
- When you purchase materials, tell businesses that you are a teacher. Many businesses offer discount programs for teachers. Others provide materials at drastically reduced prices, or at cost.
- Ask families. Send a note home (translated as necessary) asking for supplies. Do not assume that families will not contribute simply because they have low incomes. Many teachers who work with families of limited means find that families contribute generously. Throwaways such as paper tubes, plastic grocery sacks, and cardboard may become treasures in your room.
- Visit thrift shops. I bought a whole class set of white men's dress shirts to use as lab coats for $2.00 a shirt.
- Use your scouts to visit garage sales. Tell family and friends what you need (board games for your game center? uncommon musical instruments?) and put them on the lookout. Give them a tough budget: 50 cents for a puzzle?
- Encourage your students to raise funds as a class. Some classes run recycling programs and use the proceeds to fund field trips or social action projects. Check school polices on fund-raising first.
- Head to the public or university library. You can check out books, or you can stock your classroom library by attending libraries' book sales, where books are often sold for pennies.
- Borrow. Many organizations have lending libraries of materials that stretch far beyond texts. Check your local museums and state agencies. Or go national. The National Gallery of Art (http://www.nga.gov), for example, will ship loaner recordings and art samples free of charge.
- Use free Web-based materials. Search, for example, for free e books for teachers as students.
- Share. Work with other teachers in your department or at your grade level to make the best of scarce resources.

teachers can display presentations and other files. Use the Internet's vast array of resources to enhance your lesson presentations. An endless collection of video clips, webcam feeds, multimedia files, still photographs, and the like is literally at your fingertips and waiting to

21st Century Teaching and Learning Tip

USING DIGITAL FILES IN LESSONS

- Use digital images that you or your students take, or find them on the Web through an image search. Fliker (Fliker.com) is a popular photo-sharing site.
- Use your own audio or video files or find them on the Web through sources like YouTube (youtube.com) and TeacherTube (teachertube.com).
- Can't access video sites at school? Use a conversion site like Zamzar (zamzar.com) or KeepVid (keepvid.com) to download and save files so you can play them anytime, without Internet access.
- Remember to check and follow copyright rules. In general, teachers can use small amounts of information for educational purposes. When in doubt, ask for permission.

enhance student learning. See the 21st Century Teaching and Learning Tip for some ideas for using digital files in your lessons.

Whenever you can, have students use technology to work toward information and communication technology standards in addition to their content work. If you don't have local technology standards, you can rely on ISTE's student standards (ISTE, 2007). For example, as you plan, ask yourself what resources and opportunities are available to help students work toward goals like using technology systems better and using digital tools to gather, use, and evaluate information.

To stretch toward ICT goals, find out what resources are available for you and your students. Most U.S. schools do have some equipment (recall Chapter 1 statistics). Most classrooms have desktop or laptop computers with Internet connections. Many teachers also augment the effectiveness of their computers by adding equipment such as cameras for videoconferencing, measurement instruments for collecting science data, and assistive technologies to increase access for students with physical disabilities. Internet access opens the world of Web-based learning (check out the longstanding Web quest page http://webquest.org/index.php) and **social media** for student learning. Social media such as blogs, wikis, social bookmarking and networking, and virtual worlds democratize learning by allowing all to become content producers who share and interact with information and other producers.

Many schools have interactive whiteboards (IWBs). Research on IWBs is fairly new, and it's mixed. IWBs can support student motivation, engagement, thinking and achievement (Lopez, 2010; Metiri Group, 2006; Torff & Tirotta, 2010), but effects are small and uneven. For example, in the research reviewed by Marzano (2009), in one-quarter of the studies, IWB classrooms did worse than those without IWBs. As a result, some educators judge IWBs as unworthy of their required substantial investment (Johnson & Hirsch, 2010; Meeks, 2009). To maximize IWB effectiveness, Marzano (2009) suggests our use of them should:

- Present information in logically organized bits during well-paced lessons.
- Ensure visual information supports main content points.
- Use results from voting systems as part of the lessons, not ignore results.
- Use reinforcers (like virtual applause audio files) judiciously and focus on why responses are correct.

Research (e.g., Kulik & Kulik, 1991; Metiri Group, 2006) indicates that technology *can* support teacher effectiveness and student learning outcomes such as achievement, social development, and attitude toward the subject matter. The extent to which technology *does* facilitate teaching and learning rests largely in the care taken by the teacher to consider purposes carefully and to implement technology as a tool effectively. Technology presents us with tools; the expense of the tool matters, and it's the skill of the teacher who holds the tool that typically makes the difference. Be sure to use the tools you select in ways that enhance student engagement in the content and in the process of learning.

You have a responsibility to be aggressive in your search for tools that can promote students' development, content mastery, and 21st-century learning. If you work at a site with limited resources, remember the responsibilities that schools have to help bridge the digital divide and other gaps. You'll need to be proactive. Look around. Check storage rooms for older computers. See if families might donate their older equipment. I have a friend who, realizing the classroom potential of a **document camera**, found an old but serviceable one on eBay for $20. Another teacher, without classroom computers or classroom volunteers, brings in her personal laptop computer and uses PowerPoint presentations she has narrated to lead physical movement centers for her kindergartners. Responsive teachers do what it takes for student success.

In summary, early in your planning, consider the full range of resources available to you and your students. Figure 5.6 can be used to brainstorm the kinds of resources relevant to particular lessons or units. Note that some resources may occur in more than one row, which is fine for brainstorming. Use these resources in your long-range and short-term planning.

Figure 5.6   *Brainstorming instructional resources.*

Lesson Unit or Topic:	
Standard or Essential Question:	
Types of Resources	Brainstorming: List ideas for this type of resource (Possible sources? Actual titles?)
Techno Tools • What technological resources should you demonstrate? • Which tools should students use? (Think: productivity tools, research tools, communication tools) • How can technology help meet diverse needs? (e.g., assistive technology, primary language support, support for struggling readers)	
Text Materials • Textbook sections • Variety of types of print (newspapers, books, charts, manuals, letters, etc.) • Print in the students' environment • Print in students' home language • Student-created text	
Visual Images • Think about photographs, video clips, works of art, etc. • List potential Web sites or search terms	
Language of the Discipline • What tools do experts use? • Consider a variety of measurement tools, software applications, artistic media, data gathering strategies such as interviews, calculators, etc.	
Field Experiences • What expertise might family members have? Example: interviews about historical events or current experiences with the world at large • Which community members could contribute? • What sites could you use for visits to make the world your classroom? • Which contacts with faraway people may help?	

Many teachers bring coherence to their long-term plans by planning collaboratively.

Annie Fuller

Long-Range Planning

Although teachers plan differently, one reasonable approach is to move from the broadest level of planning down to the most specific. Long-range planning entails using your knowledge of your students, potential resources, and set of goals to map out the year (or term) and set out a structure for weekly and daily activities. It also includes unit planning. The Teaching Tip gives some advice for long-range planning.

Yearlong Planning

With knowledge about your students and your overarching goals in mind, study your content standards for every area you teach. Then, because you teach as part of a system, ask whether there is a **pacing guide** for your grade level or subject area. The pacing guide will give you direction about which standards to teach when, and it will make suggestions about the materials to use to address those standards. A pacing guide, though, is no excuse for you not to become well versed in the curricular goals your students are to attain. Only through careful study of your standards will you be able to teach in thoughtful ways that meaningfully connect ideas over time and to students' worlds.

If there is no pacing guide, create a curriculum map for the term or year. To do so, some teachers photocopy standards onto colored paper (one color per content area, such as "technology" and "language arts"). They cut apart the slips and group them logically.

Teaching Tip

ADVICE FOR LONG-RANGE PLANNING

1. Base your planning on student assessment data.
2. Be sure that your decisions about how to use instructional time reflect your goals and priorities.
3. Remember that most lessons and units can take about twice as long as expected, unless we are very careful with time.
4. Worry less about "covering" the material than about "uncovering" it.

Others use spreadsheets for this task. Electronic copies of your standards, downloaded from your state department of education Web site, can start you on your way. As you examine standards, look for underlying concepts that might capture enduring ideas and serve as glue to hold a variety of standards together. Hurt (2003, p. xv) lists helpful questions that can guide you in studying state standards:

1. What is so important about this standard that students should know?
2. What is within, beyond, beneath, and behind standards that makes them so important?
3. How can I use this standard to teach students about something that is more durable?
4. How can I use standards to help students transfer learning to other facets of their lives and to the world around them?

Where to start if you teach multiple subjects? Many teachers find it helpful to use social studies or science as a starting point and then progress to the other subject areas. Note that this process asks you to integrate content. Integration can create powerful learning by tying standards to real-life contexts or tapping into deep understandings about life's central or enduring ideas. However, not all standards can be integrated meaningfully. Let "stand-alone" standards remain separate from your grouping and plan to address them through other structures such as opening exercises or mini-units during the year or term.

Once standards are grouped logically, they can be sequenced over the year. As you decide how much time to devote to each area of study over the year, examine a school calendar for months, scheduled breaks, and local traditions. You may choose to glue to a large chart those colored strips you have organized so carefully in the preceding step.

Although your textbook may play a central role in determining what to teach when, examine your texts only after you have studied your standards carefully. Begin reviewing the text by examining the **scope and sequence** (a chart that gives a suggested layout for the term) and other information in the **teacher's editions** to determine the units or standards that are treated in good depth in your adopted materials and those that will need additional support. This will also help you locate possible extraneous material that does not support your content standards. Use the brainstorming chart (Figure 5.6) to consider rich resources to supplement or replace the text. Think, too, about whether certain units make more sense at certain times of the year as you decide when to teach each topic. Fit your topics into the school calendar by becoming more specific in your planning: Move to unit planning.

Unit Planning

Glance through a teacher's edition and you will see that authors arrange instruction in units. A **unit** is a set of related lessons that address a single topic, theme, or skill. For example, a literature unit might address a particular book or genre. A social studies unit might address a particular group of people or a time in history. A math unit might include a single skill area such as measurement. Units range in length from just a few lessons (perhaps a week in length) to many lessons (perhaps 2 months). Four to six weeks tends to be a typical length for instructional units.

There are several approaches to planning units. Here are three that allow you to address your goals while maintaining flexibility in developing (or selecting) and sequencing learning activities: backward planning, the "big idea" approach, and thematic instruction. The first format is increasingly popular as teachers plan units to meet content standards. It is called **backward planning** or backward design (Wiggins & McTighe, 2005). This model begins with the conviction that a student's performance is key to determining what the student knows. First, the teacher identifies what students should know and be able to do at the unit's end. Second, the teacher considers what evidence the students would need to provide for the teacher to determine that they have mastered the content. After the end performance is clearly in mind, the teacher develops activities to help students prepare for the performance. To use backward planning you might:

1. Select content standards or outcomes for mastery.
2. Unify these outcomes through a theme, an issue, or a "big idea."

3. Compose an **essential question** that, if answered, would demonstrate students' deep thinking about the content. Develop supporting unit questions as well.

4. Determine performance that you would accept as evidence that the students have mastered the content. Consider multiple measures as appropriate.

5. Develop **rubrics,** with the students if possible, or other measures to assess each performance. (Rubrics and other assessments are addressed in Chapter 8.)

6. Select activities that lead students toward mastery.

7. Review and revise until each component of the unit supports the others.

The power of the backward-planning model is that it turns the "teach my favorite activities" approach on its head and instead focuses on providing instruction that will help students meet the end goal.

A second unit planning format is recommended by experts in content areas such as social studies (Ellis, 1998; Savage & Armstrong, 2000) and science (Gega & Peters, 2002). We will call it the **"big idea" approach.**

1. Begin by determining the major ideas related to the content. Major ideas, or generalizations, are statements that connect facts and concepts. For example, "tree" is a concept, or a class of ideas with identifiable attributes. "Some trees lose their leaves" is a fact. "Trees and other organisms respond to environmental stimuli" is a generalization. It is a more inclusive statement that relates several concepts and has greater explanatory power. A sample generalization in social studies is, "All human societies change." In analyzing your content standards during yearlong planning, you probably identified these generalizations. You can also find them in teacher's editions, often under the heading "Chapter Concepts." Chapters typically include three to four big ideas.

2. Once you find generalizations, write standards-based objectives and then locate activities that can help your students learn the generalizations. In selecting activities, you may draw from your texts and from other sources such as literature, current events, and **trade books** (which are any nontextbook books, including literature and teaching materials devoted to particular topical areas, typically housed in curriculum libraries or offered for sale at teacher supply stores). An earlier section of this chapter urged you to consider an abundance of resources in your planning, and Chapter 6 will reinforce the importance of rich learning experiences that will lead to student mastery of important generalizations. Examples of enriching experiences include field trips, guest speakers, and **multimedia projects** (Green & Brown, 2002).

3. Then arrange the activities for daily instruction. Good instruction builds bridges between the students' lives and the content. You can plan lessons that begin with a "bridge" to take students from their lives into the content via an engaging question, demonstration, or other activity.

Note that, on their way to learning content generalizations, students will learn facts and concepts that should slowly coalesce to form larger understandings. It is indeed important to teach facts and specific information. The big idea method of unit planning ensures that facts build into larger, more coherent structures of understanding.

Another strength of this planning approach is that your focus on big ideas will ease decisions about which daily activities to cut or extend. Most teachers feel pressed for time. Using the big idea method of unit planning, you can drop activities that are less likely to help students build understanding of key concepts and spend more time on productive learning experiences.

A third popular approach to unit planning is **thematic instruction.** Many teachers find that integrating their content through themes allows them to address content standards efficiently and in ways that are interesting to students. Instead of being based solely on core ideas related to particular subject matters, thematic units are interdisciplinary, with learning activities emanating from the theme (Kovalik & Olsen; 2001; Pappas, Kiefer, & Levstik, 2006; Roberts & Kellough, 2008; Ronis, 2008). Thematic units can be helpful because they present content holistically, as it might appear in life, rather than as discrete entities. Further, thematic units hold the promise of helping students with high-incidence disabilities, whose educational experience may be fragmented as a result of receiving instruction in a variety of settings, to experience content in ways that transfer across subject areas and into real-life settings (Gardner, Wissick, Schweder, & Canter, 2003). These authors suggest that thematic units, particularly when they are enhanced with technology, help students with disabilities to gain and practice lifelong learning skills by using tools that can assist them throughout and beyond their school career.

Themes lie at the core of thematic units. Examples of themes include, for young students, *homes,* and for older students, *discoveries* or *interdependence.* Concepts from different subject areas are surfaced and linked through the use of the theme. Also, thematic units usually include choices for students, allowing students to select at least some of the learning experiences in the unit. The elements of choice and group discussion can develop a sense of ownership and community as students learn together and share their results. Pappas et al. (2006) suggest the following steps for planning thematic units:

1. *Select a theme.* The theme needs to be broad enough to encompass information from many subject areas but not so broad that meaningful connections are lost. Keep your larger goals and students' interests in mind.
2. *Create a planning web.* Brainstorm to create a web—a semantic map—that explores the many instances in which the theme arises. Figure 5.7 gives an abbreviated version of a planning web. Notice that it does not include mention of traditional subject areas such as mathematics or history; it should break away from traditional compartmentalized thinking. As you web, you will note connections among ideas

Figure 5.7 *Sample planning web.*

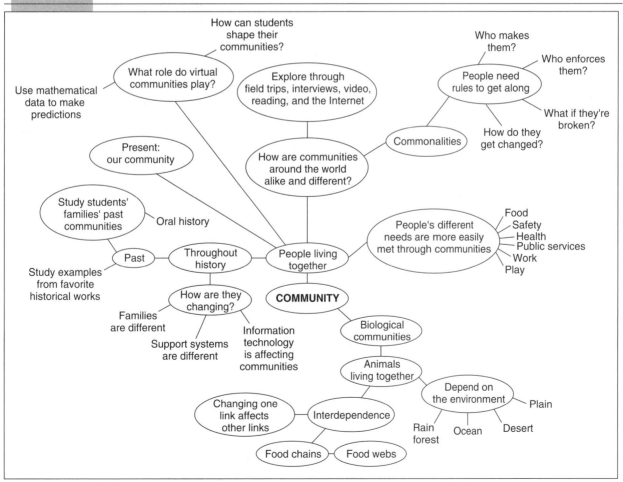

and can begin to categorize your ideas into groups. Jot down your ideas for resources, including books, technological materials, concrete materials, and community resources as you web.

3. *Select resources.* This chapter and Chapter 6 argue that teachers should create rich learning environments. As you plan, aim to provide a wealth of resources. Include the arts, literature, other print sources, tangible materials, technology, and community resources; flip ahead to Figure 6.4 (p. 126) for other ideas.

4. *Plan activities.* Choose or create activities that address the theme, utilize rich resources, and encourage students' progress toward learning goals. Remember to include opportunities for students to choose their learning activities.

Next, teachers organize their classrooms for instruction and implement their units. It is also important to consider plans for assessment.

Experts in multicultural studies advocate thematic approaches to planning because such approaches allow teachers and students to dissolve the traditional subject-matter distinctions in favor of content organizations that revolve around topics seen as immediately valuable and powerful. By restructuring the boundaries of curriculum, we may open our classrooms to more democratic and inclusive study.

How do you plan? Some teachers use index cards so they can rearrange activities as necessary. Some keep their plans in a loose-leaf notebook so that it is easy to insert other materials. Others create templates and word process their plans so that they can easily copy/paste information such as content standards into their plans. Others use fee-based Web-based programs such as Taskstream or OnCourse to author, store, and share their plans. PlanBook Edu (planbookedu.com) has a free lesson planning tool that saves your plans to the Web. Experiment and see which strategy works best for you.

In his book on ethnic studies, James Banks (2005) presents a unit-planning approach that has both an interdisciplinary focus, as does thematic planning, and a focus on key generalizations, as does the big idea approach. This approach allows students to gain information through many diverse examples to build universal, cross-disciplinary generalizations related to such multicultural education topics as ethnicity, socialization, intercultural communication, and power. Banks argues that this planning approach allows learners to gain the knowledge and multiple perspectives required for participation in their increasingly diverse world. Further, Banks and others remind us that the decisions a teacher makes, including decisions about curricular planning, are not purely technical. The ways in which we arrange our content and instruction—across the year, in units, and in weekly and daily schedules—mirror our visions of what we want for our students.

Weekly and Daily Schedules

Once you have determined a broad view of what should happen when, devise a schedule of daily and weekly events. A well-designed garden provides an analogy for a thoughtful weekly classroom schedule. According to Benzel (1997) every garden needs plants to serve as "bones," "binders," and "bursts." Bones, permanent and sturdy, provide the structure for the garden. Trees may serve as the bones, for example. Binders connect elements of the garden so that they relate smoothly to each other. Binders might be shrubs and large perennial plants. Bursts infuse the garden with color and excitement—think colorful flowers. In weekly planning for teaching, time structures provide the bones, routines and recurring events provide the binders, and engaging lessons provide the bursts.

Figure 5.8 shows two experienced teachers' classroom schedules, fourth and fifth grade at the same school, bones only. Notice that both Richard and Susie have devised structured, stable time schedules to ensure that they use their time well and to provide students with a sense of predictability and direction. Both teachers include similar subject areas, and they have devoted substantial instructional time to the language arts. You can see structured use of family volunteers. You also see that the school works to provide a balanced curriculum and uses specialists in technology, physical education, and the arts. Because all teachers at the site utilize the specialists, neither Richard nor Susie is free to choose the times for these subjects.

Figure 5.8 *Two teachers' daily schedules.*

Richard's Class (fourth grade)	Susie's Class (fifth grade)
7:50–8:00 Opening • Bell work • Attendance • Lunch count • Flag salute • Homework check	7:50–8:05 Opening • Opening exercises • Homework collection (with parent helpers)
8:00–9:40 Math • Warm-up • Homework correction • Math instruction	8:05–8:45 P.E. or Music • (alternating days: T, Th and W, F) 8:45–9:45 Math
9:45–10:07 Recess	
10:07–12:20 Language Arts	10:07–12:20 Language Arts
• Journal writing • Small reading groups and guided practice, follow-up activities • Grammar lessons • Writing instruction • Read-aloud • Silent reading • Vocabulary • Spelling	(We sometimes fit in a social studies or science reading or writing activity here if needed.)
12:20–1:05 Lunch	
1:05–2:00 Social Studies and Science	1:05–2:00 Social Studies or Science (alternating days)
2:00–2:10 Closing • Write in homework agendas • Cleanup	2:00–2:10 Agendas and cleanup
Special Notes: • Computer lab: T 10:20–11:05 • Music: T and Th 8:45–9:25 (don't forget instruments) • Library: Th 10:15–10:45 and as time permits • P.E.: Th 1:25–2:10 and F 8:00–8:45 (need appropriate shoes)	Special Notes for Language Arts Time (10:07–12:20): • GATE reading group with librarian on T (30 min) • GATE computers on W with parent volunteers (30 min) • Parent volunteers help with language arts T and Th • Computers on Th (45 minutes)
2:10 Dismissal	

Binders are found in the routines and recurring events of these scheduled time periods. For instance, during the opening in Richard's classroom, students know they will complete "bell work" (brief review assignments that commence when the morning bell rings) and check their homework. These activities can provide a personal and academic focus for the remainder of the day's work. Another example of a binder can be seen during the closing activities, where both teachers have students write in their agendas. Bursts are the engaging activities that happen during the day during content-area instruction. Examples include hands-on investigations in science and projects during social studies.

Bones, binders, and bursts apply to teachers in departmentalized secondary schools who work within the confines of a tight bell schedule as well. They just compress their usage of bones, binders, and bursts to serve them well during a 55-minute period. Figure 5.9 shows how Loretta, a junior high teacher, structures her time over a day and a week for one period near the beginning of her year.

Figure 5.9	*A junior high Language Arts teacher's schedule.*

	Monday	Tuesday	Wednesday	Thursday	Friday
Daily Schedule Period 5 8th-grade sheltered English (excerpt from plan book)	• Topic introduction • Vocabulary from literature • Language skill • Test-taking skill	• Literature connected to vocabulary • Practice language skill	• Literature connected to vocabulary • Practice language skill	• Literature connected to vocabulary • Practice language skill	• Test on vocabulary or language skill
Bones	• Six-period day, with periods 50 minutes in length. • Rotating schedule. Periods stay in order, but the first one of the day rotates through Periods 1–6. • Period 1 has five extra minutes for pledge, anthem, announcements. • No rainy day schedule. Lunch is 30 minutes long and cannot be shortened. • No assembly schedule (assemblies not held).				
Binders	• *Attendance:* Call roll. Students must answer with the phrase of the day. "I did/did not do my homework." "I like my English teacher." This is quick oral language practice. • *Opener:* Students do Daily Written Language (correct errors in passages placed on overhead transparency) and get materials ready before attendance has been taken. • *Closure:* Examples: "Tell your partner two things you learned about sonnets." "Share with someone the next step you need to take in writing your persuasive essay." • *Nightly homework:* Practice skills for Friday's test.				
Notes on Planning and Instruction (Bursts)	• *Major planning documents:* —District curriculum guide, based on California content standards —Drawn from language handbook (teacher's edition of text) —Overview schedule that lists writing activities, literature, test items to be mastered, and skills. • *Instructional methods:* Using direct instruction. Sharing pictures or photographs, reading poetry aloud, acting out vocabulary words, partner reading of literature selection, cooperative learning activities, student drawings of vocabulary words, creating flash cards with terms. • *To Do:* There is no coordination of topic or skill between the four items on the overview schedule and curriculum guide. Students might read a story about persuasion during the trimester when they are writing response to literature essays, but not during the trimester when they are writing persuasive essays. My grade-level team wants to work to coordinate these elements in the future.				

Lesson Planning

A lesson is a relatively brief instructional sequence that focuses on one or a few instructional objectives. When students master the objectives from one lesson, they are a step closer to building more complex ideas, attitudes, and actions related to the overall unit and to your guiding goals. Although lessons vary from 10 minutes to a week in length, depending on the content and on the age and sophistication of the students, lessons typically last less than an hour. The distinguishing characteristics of a lesson are that

1. It uses a set, logical structure.
2. Activities relate to each other and aim toward exploring ideas or skills related to a very limited set of objectives.

Although objectives take on different forms (e.g., Gronlund, 2004), a commonly used version is the behavioral objective (Mager, 1997). A behavioral objective is a specific statement about how students will be different at a lesson's close in terms of their knowledge, skills, attitudes, or abilities. Especially in your early days as a teacher, behavioral objectives can push you to focus on students and outcomes: What should students be able to do after your lessons?

Although many new teachers initially find that writing good objectives is time consuming and may feel artificial, repeated practice streamlines the time required and sharpens their instruction. It is worth the time. Objectives will clarify for you exactly what you want students to know, which increases the chance that students will learn it. Without objectives, plans tend to become mere scripts of what teachers do during lessons. The Teaching Tip gives advice for writing objectives.

Writing Objectives

Look again at the following objectives, found earlier in Figure 5.5:

1. Given paper and pencil, students will add two-digit numbers with 90 percent accuracy.
2. Without reference materials, students will draw a diagram of the water cycle and describe how humans can affect the cycle at two points at least.

These objectives have the three components typically specified for behavioral objectives (Popham & Baker, 1970): **behavior, conditions,** and **criteria,** described in Figure 5.10. For more examples of instructional objectives, examine your teacher's editions and other curricular materials. Check to see that each objective includes the three typically identified components of a behavioral objective.

Figure 5.10 *Components of a behavioral objective.*

- *Behavior:* What, specifically, should you see the students do as a result of your instruction? (What is the students' observable action on mastery?) In the first objective above, students will add. In the second, they will draw and describe.

- *Conditions:* Under what conditions should students perform? (Are there limits on time? What materials may they use?) The conditions of performance are found at the beginning of each of the objectives listed. You can imagine how the conditions would change based on both the students' characteristics and the teacher's expectations for appropriate performance.

- *Criteria:* How well should students perform? (How many? How fast? With what degree of accuracy?) Above the first objective gives a percentage rate for acceptable performance, and the second sets a minimal number of discussion points. You will need to think carefully about the kind and level of criteria that are appropriate for your students because your definition of success will influence the decisions you make as you plan instruction.

Teaching Tip

WRITING BEHAVIORAL OBJECTIVES

1. Be sure to focus on the intended *outcome* of the lesson, not on what students will do *throughout* the lesson.
2. Focus on the skill or concept involved, not the technique you will use to measure performance. (Why, for instance, have students "complete page 43"?) If you do not state the main intent, your objectives may appear trivial (Mager, 1997).
3. If the outcomes you seek are covert, add an indicator such as "circle" or "list."
4. List only the criteria and conditions that you will actually use. For conditions, think about what students may use—or not use—to demonstrate understanding, and think about real-world conditions in which they will need to use their knowledge. For criteria, if you will not check to see that all students attain 90 percent accuracy, do not list it in your objectives.

Despite their potential to focus attention on student learning, behavioral objectives are criticized on several grounds. They are criticized, for instance, as being too driven by the teacher and as being so mechanistic that little room is left for spontaneous learning. Opinion is divided in terms of how carefully teachers should compose and adhere to objectives. Mager (1997) instructs teachers to focus on observable behaviors. Gronlund (2004) does not. Many teachers elect to include only the observable behavior, leaving the conditions and criteria implicit. I adopted this approach in a fossil lesson I taught to second-graders (see Figure 5.12). Until you develop skill at writing objectives and using them to guide your teaching, you probably need to write full behavioral objectives. That way, if you decide to use shorthand objectives later, your choices will be based upon a full understanding of what is implied in the objective, even if it is not stated. As you become more comfortable with planning, select the format that is most useful for you in encouraging student learning. Once you are clear on what you intend for students to learn, you are ready to make decisions about structuring your lessons.

Lesson Structure

Lessons are composed of activities that are joined meaningfully into a regular structure that addresses the objective(s). Although there are many helpful planning formats, lesson formats share similar components. Every lesson has three sections: *open, body,* and *close.*

The *open* sets the stage for the lesson to come. The lesson probably begins with a "hook" that catches students' attention or a "bridge" that allows students to travel from their own worlds into the topic of the lesson. It is common to state the objective in student-friendly language and give a purpose for the lesson. The teacher might also state behavioral standards for the lesson; such standards tell the students in clear terms how they are expected to behave during the lesson. During the body, students develop concepts related to the objective. To close, the teacher and students consolidate and extend what they learned. They might bridge back out from the content to their lives outside of class. Figure 5.11 offers some options that may help you as you think about structuring your lessons according to the open-body-close format.

The fossil lesson (shown in Figure 5.12) demonstrates some of these activities in its open-body-close format. Perhaps as you review the lesson, alternative ways of opening, developing, and closing the lesson come to mind. Also, I taught this lesson in a room with little technology available. Think how technology might be used to enhance the lesson and differentiate learning experiences. The fossil lesson illustrates elements common to most lesson plans.

Elements of a Lesson Plan

In addition to structuring each of your lessons to include an opening, a development phase, and a closure, you should include in your plans information that will keep you organized

Figure 5.11   *Activities for different lesson stages.*

	Activities for Different Stages of the Lesson Sequence: Open, Body, Close
Open	1. Capture the students' attention: Share a real object, or try using a story, a picture, a book, a video clip, or a song. 2. Present a problem. (Challenge students to solve the problem through the lesson.) 3. Provide warm-up or review exercises to engage students. 4. Elicit students' prior knowledge, experience, or opinions about the content. 5. State your objectives. 6. Preview the lesson. 7. Give your expectations for students' behavior. 8. State the purpose of what they will learn.
Body	1. Present information verbally and through graphic representations. 2. Point out critical attributes, examples, and counter-examples. 3. Model. (Described in Chapter 6.) 4. Read. 5. Discuss. 6. Use hands-on materials. 7. Work in cooperative groups to solve a problem. 8. Make charts and graphs. 9. Use your questions and those of students to explore the content. 10. Do research at the library or on the World Wide Web. 11. Use computer-assisted instruction. 12. Check on students' understanding. Adjust instruction based on their responses.
Close	1. Restate the objective. 2. Gather individual lesson pieces into a coherent whole. 3. Draw conclusions. 4. Summarize what was learned. 5. Give a brief quiz to assess understanding. 6. Ask students to state something they learned. 7. Revisit prior knowledge charts or graphs from the lesson's opening. Revise to reflect new information. 8. Show students how the learning applies to real life, or ask students to make the connections. 9. Ask what students would like to study next, or record their unanswered questions. 10. Write in journals. 11. Connect this lesson to the next by describing the problem to be solved or idea to be explored for tomorrow. 12. Hold a gallery tour (described in Figure 6.6) for students to appreciate each others' work.

and that will help you communicate your intentions to yourself during teaching and to others who may wish to follow your instruction. Although you will find a great variety in lesson plans, six elements commonly included in lesson plans include the following:

1. *Housekeeping Details:* Include contextual information about the students (such as their English language proficiency, reading levels, and behavioral needs) to ensure that you are providing inclusive and responsive instruction, include information about the materials you will require, and address other contextual information that may affect the lesson.
2. *Concept, Generalization, or Skill:* Remind yourself of the "big idea" you are working toward. Individual lessons should add up to bigger things. You may elect to phrase the larger learning in terms of an essential question. Include target vocabulary terms as well, keeping the number of terms fewer than five.
3. *Objectives:* State the intended outcomes of your lesson using an observable student behavior, the conditions for performance, and the criteria for success. List the

Figure 5.12 *Fossil lesson.*

Lesson Plan: How Fossils Are Made

Subjects:	Science and Reading
Grade:	Second (7-year-olds)
Students:	20 children; all English speakers, some readers
Time:	1 hour 35 minutes

Objectives

1. Students will describe the process by which fossils are made in nature.
2. Students will summarize text by sharing two important points from their reading of self-selected portions of a nonfiction text on fossils.
3. Students will explain how the mock fossils they create are the same as and different from real fossils.

Procedure

Reading Portion (35 minutes)

1. Open: On the rug: Complete a five-item opinionnaire on fossils to find out what children know. (In an opinionnaire, respondents mark their agreement with statements such as "Real fossils are made in factories.") Encourage discussion of each item to get kids talking. (8 minutes)
2. Body: Pair up the children (more accomplished readers with newer readers) and pass out multiple copies of the fossil book. Read the introduction together. Glance at the table of contents. Encourage them to read the table of contents to choose the sections that interest them. Draw upon surprises from the opinionnaire. (5 minutes)
3. Release them to partner read anywhere they like in the room. Those who wish to stay and listen to the teacher read may stay and read along. (10 minutes)
4. Back at the rug discuss something surprising that the children learned by reading. Draw from students' ideas to explain the process by which fossils are made. Use illustrations from text as support. (8 minutes)

Science Portion (1 hour)

1. On the rug: Show real fossils. Contrast them with a sample fossil made from plaster of paris.
2. Have students make their own mock fossils. Model procedure, then students work as individuals:
   a) Pass out and soften plasticine (non-hardening) clay.
   b) Release students back to their tables to select items for imprinting: shells, leaves, plastic dinosaurs (already placed at tables).
   c) When ready, have students go to back of room on hard floor to mix their own plaster of paris, pour carefully onto plasticine mold.
   d) When dry, remove fossils.
3. Close: (May need to follow lunch recess.) Reread the text, compare the process and types of real fossils with class's mock fossils.
4. Assign homework: "Tell someone at home what you know about fossils. Use yours as an example."

Assessment: Students describe the fossil-making process, referring to texts and mock fossils.

relevant content standards. The typical lesson includes one to three objectives. Don't forget the cognitive, affective, and psychomotor domains.

4. *Procedure:* Use the open-body-close format to structure what you will do during each step of the lesson. Primarily use general descriptions of what you will say and do. For important points, or when the content is difficult or new for you, include scripted quotations. Include enough detail so that a substitute teacher could pick up

your plan and teach from it, but work on limiting the text. Think of the procedure as a *to-do list* that you can glance at quickly to remind yourself of what comes next.

Include information about student groupings (remember TAPS—*t*otal group *a*lone, *p*artners, *s*mall groups), the activities different individuals or groups may engage in, and about accommodations and modifications. Include time estimates for good time management and to help you develop realistic expectations for how much time the activities might take.

5. *Assessment:* Include a plan for how you will assess student learning in terms of the objectives and incidental learnings. Consider how you will assess your teaching as well. Note that objectives, activities, and assessments must all align.

6. *Differentiation:* Include any final notes on special considerations you need to take to attend to students' needs and interests as appropriate for this lesson.

Figure 5.13 gives a lesson plan format that can be used in many situations. The fossils lesson followed this format, as do lessons in future chapters. As you review these lessons, you may also notice that I tend to plan in fine detail. I am convinced that careful planning enhances teaching, so I encourage you to take great care in preparing good lessons for your students. The more specific and careful your individual lesson plans are, the more confident you can feel in front of the students, the more you will be able to focus on students' learning rather than on your own words and behaviors, and the more quickly you will learn from experience and be able to streamline your planning. So planning in detail is one "do" for lesson planning.

Lesson planning can be daunting for beginners. Perhaps some "do's and don'ts" may prove useful. When planning lessons, Don't . . .

1. Reinvent the wheel. Begin with existing materials—of what teachers have already tried—and check your resources. Modify based upon your own stance, students, and standards. Lesson plans are yours for the taking. Your adopted text probably has good ideas. Select from its many ideas those activities that meet the needs and interests of your particular students and that are directly related to your objectives and standards. If you are required to follow the textbook with little variation, study the text to analyze the quality of its activities. You can tweak it just a bit, as necessary, to ensure that you provide well-structured lessons that are appropriate for your students. At the very least, ensure that you can provide a solid rationale for each instructional move you make.

   The Internet is a rich source of lessons as well. Try using a search engine to search for "lesson plans" related to your topic at your selected grade level. A few likely sources are listed in the Web sites section at the chapter's close. The 21st Century Teaching and Learning Tip gives criteria for selecting high-quality lessons from the thousands that reside on the Web. Even if you are inspired by a lesson from the Web, make sure you adapt it to meet your students and standards.

2. Let materials make your important decisions. Planning is not the same as finding worksheets to fill the time until lunch, or glossing over lessons so that you can finish the book by June.

3. Be intimidated if the content is new to you. Check out some books and hit the Internet to study the information you will be teaching. All teachers should expect to continue to improve their subject-matter knowledge.

4. Be lured by the promise of "fun." Student engagement is important (critical in fact), but not everything that is fun encourages student learning.

Do . . .

1. Focus on thorough and rigorous treatment of the content. Most teachers feel as if they are pushed along by the hands of the clock. Rather than simply mentioning topics without exploring them in depth, consider cutting out topics that do not reflect key standards or that you cannot fully explore. Devote your planning efforts to encouraging lasting and meaningful learning.

Figure 5.13 *Lesson plan format.*

Lesson Plan

Students: 30, all english speakers, all readers, High School Juniors

Time: Four class periods, maybe five

Materials: Books, handouts,

Concepts/skills: Understanding the foundation of the United States, the roots of the foundations and before the constitution

Objectives: SWBAT:
- Know where majority of the ideas of the founding fathers came from
- Say what the government form was before the constitution
- Knows about the problems that would arise from the foundations

Open: Founding of the colonies 3   (Time: 1 – 1½ periods)
French Indian war
Influence for the founding Fathers
Start Rev. War   video "To late apologize"

Assign Homework of Outline/Read chapters that correspond to unit

Body: Finish Rev. War   (Time: 1 – 1½ periods)
Start on the Government of the colonies/States
watch video

Discuss chapters

Close: Finish Government   (Time: 1 – 1½ periods)
Start into after constitutional
Ratification

Assessment: Quiz/Test at end, collect outlines

Differentiation:

21st Century Teaching and Learning Tip

JUDGING THE QUALITY OF LESSONS FROM THE INTERNET

- Start your search with highly reliable sources such as professional organizations like the National Council of Teachers of Mathematics, the International Reading Association, and the National Council of Social Studies. Also check university- and state-based sites.
- When you find a lesson, look for its match with your content standards. Be sure to go beyond a surface-level match and aim for the bigger, transferable ideas.
- Select lessons that address more than one set of standards. For example, lessons can address social outcomes, technological outcomes, and English language development standards as they simultaneously address standards from another content area.
- Look for components of effective instruction (more to come in Chapter 6). For instance, lessons should connect with students' prior knowledge and encourage student interaction.
- Look for rigor and depth. Songs that have students memorize algorithms (such as "Please Excuse My Dear Aunt Sally" for the order of operations) may be catchy, but they do not encourage conceptual understanding; they don't teach the *why*, or transferable learning.
- Remember, a worksheet printed from the Internet is not inherently better than a worksheet torn from a workbook.

2. Plan with a partner or team. Experience and a rich supply of ideas help.
3. Anticipate students' varying responses. Develop alternate plans to address the things that may possibly go wrong.
4. Rehearse, especially if it is the first time you have taught the lesson or if you have a tough audience.
5. Prepare your materials so you are ready to go. Have your materials at your fingertips so that you feel calm and prepared as you begin your lesson.
6. Be prepared to scrap your lesson if you need to rethink it or pursue some other path that is likely to lead to significant learning. This applies even if you are being formally observed.

Parting Words

One of the reasons that teaching is more difficult than the uninitiated might expect is that so much time is spent outside of instructional hours preparing effective learning experiences. There are no shortcuts to good planning. Even teachers who are handed scripted materials and are asked to follow the text closely need to bring students and content together through careful planning. The more time and thought you devote to considering what your particular students need to learn and how you can help them learn it, the more likely they are to succeed.

Teaching is goal directed. This chapter was intended to help you think about structuring experiences likely to result in learning, and Chapter 6 gives advice on breathing life into your plans through your instruction.

Opportunities to Practice

1. Connect. Join a social network for teachers. A great place to start: Classroom 2.0 (classroom20.com). Browse the "groups" listed. See if the Classroom 2.0 Beginners group, or some other group, is the group for you. By the way, Classroom 2.0 is a network created on Ning, an online platform where people create their own social networks.

2. Pick a content area and grade level of interest to you. Compare national standards for that area and level with your state's standards. How close is the match?

3. Pick a single content standard. Write an essential question for it. List some objectives. List a large variety of resources that could be explored in conjunction with it.

4. The taxonomies of educational objectives (cognitive, affective, and psychomotor domains) are useful in helping teachers to broaden their scope during planning. However, the domains have been criticized in their application to classrooms. Think about a classroom instance where you learned something that you value greatly. Analyze that experience in terms of the domains of objectives:

   • Which domain or domains were primarily involved?

   • Which levels of understanding or performance were required?

   • What, if anything, can you conclude about the classroom use of educational taxonomies?

5. Examine an existing unit that is touted as having a multicultural emphasis. Use Banks's (2005) levels of planning (from Figure 5.14) to determine the extent to which the unit can help students develop a knowledge base and view issues meaningfully from multiple perspectives. In terms of its depth of treatment, how representative is the unit you selected of other approaches that claim to be multicultural? Which level of multicultural curricular planning do you see at your site? Is that good or bad?

6. Practice Bloom's taxonomy by identifying the level of each of the following general teacher statements. Then try writing your own statement at each of the levels.

   a. Did the main character make a good choice? Why or why not?

   b. Organize the story into parts and give a good title for each part.

   c. Tell about some people in real life who have the same problems as the person in the story.

   d. Name the characters in the story.

   e. Tell the story in your own words.

   f. Make a painting or construction to represent the main characters in the story.

   Key: a: Evaluate, b: Analyze, c: Apply, d: Remember, e: Understand, f: Create.

7. Write behavioral objectives for some of the following skills and concepts or choose some concepts from your upcoming lessons.

   • Composing a five-sentence paragraph
   • Identifying plot structure in a narrative story
   • Troubleshooting a computer glitch
   • Forming letters in cursive
   • Explaining causes and effects of an important historical event
   • Solving challenging story problems in mathematics
   • Creating a device that throws marbles at least 5 feet
   • Serving a volleyball
   • Responding to a piece of music
   • Analyzing the use of color in a painting
   • Balancing chemical equations
   • Doing a cartwheel

Analyze your objectives to be certain that each has

   • An observable verb (an action the students will take to demonstrate mastery). Underline the verb.
   • Conditions for performance of the observable action. Circle the conditions.
   • Criteria for acceptable performance. [Bracket] the criteria.

Figure 5.14 *Banks's (2005) levels of integration for multicultural content.*

Level 1: The Contributions Approach
• The mainstream perspective remains unchallenged.
• Study focuses on discrete elements that various cultures have contributed to the mainstream culture: their heroes and holidays.

Level 2: The Additive Approach
• Deeper content is introduced to the curriculum, but the structure of the curriculum remains unchanged.
• Books, readings, or lessons are added to existing materials.

Level 3: The Transformative Approach
• This approach shifts the assumption that there is one mainstream perspective and infuses the perspectives of several groups to enable students to view themes and issues from several perspectives.
• The structure of the curriculum is changed.

Level 4: The Social Action Approach
• Learning activities not only allow students to analyze issues from many perspectives but also require them to commit to personal social action related to those issues.

Explain your work to a devoted friend.

8. Try sketching out a lesson plan for a video recorded or observed lesson segment.

- Write behavioral objectives to guide the lesson. Write one for both the cognitive and affective domains.

- What materials are required?

- Write a brief open-body-close lesson plan for the lesson. Write a "close" that is logical based on what you see in the video.

- How will you know whether students have mastered the objectives?

9. Plan a lesson using the open-body-close format. Use the form in Figure 5.13. Choose some objectives for your own students or rewrite one of the plans presented in this chapter. Use this format for other plans that you teach in your own classroom as well. For extra credit, plan this lesson with a peer. Note the benefits of collaborative planning.

 Web Sites

http://www.coe.uga.edu/epltt/bloom.htm
Bloom's Taxonomy: Original and Revised. This site explores the original Bloom's taxonomy and the revised version. It includes links to other resources.

http://www.cast.org/research/udl/index.html
Home page for CAST, the Center for Applied Special Technology. This site includes rich resources for Universal Design for learning, including teaching modules and model lessons.

http://www.curriki.org/
Curriki. You can find free education resources here, and you can publish your own.

http://iris.peabody.vanderbilt.edu/
Home of the IRIS (IDEA and Research for Inclusive Settings) Center in the Peabody College of Education at Vanderbilt University. Click on "resources" and explore plentiful information on special education, including accommodations. Browse by topic or try the learning modules.

http://www.eduref.org/Virtual/Lessons/
The Educator's Reference Desk. This site allows you to search more than 2,000 lesson plans by grade level and subject.

http://www.free.ed.gov/
Federal resources for excellence in education. This site links your resources from a number of federal agencies. Check out the image collections.

http://www.merlot.org
Multimedia Educational Resource for Learning and Online Teaching (MERLOT). This site contains a searchable collection of peer-reviewed online learning materials. Go to "education" and browse.

http://teachnet.com/
Teachnet's goal is to link teachers and allow them to share resources. It includes lesson plans and links, power tools, and a forum for sharing your work. Be forewarned of plentiful advertisements.

Use search terms to search the Internet for additional information on selected topics, such as:

accommodations and modifications
backward planning (sample units are found on many sites)
differentiated instruction
interactive whiteboard (or, if you have an interactive board, search by your brand. For instance, Promethean Planet (prometheanplanet.com) has many resources for Promethean's active board, and Smart (smarttech.com) has them for the Smartboard.
lesson plans (you can list grade level and topic in an advanced search)
revised Bloom's taxonomy
thematic instruction

Advice on Instruction: COME IN

6

Before You Begin Reading

Take your pick of Exercise A or B, or, if you like, do both.

Warm-Up Exercise A	Warm-Up Exercise B
Think back to Chapter 1, which presented six propositions for the nature of teaching. How many propositions can you remember? Write as many as you can; then refer back to Chapter 1 to complete the list and check your work.	Think back to an instance when you, with the help of a coach or mentor, learned a new physical skill. Examples include sports and crafts. Make a list of the things that your coach or mentor did that were helpful. What made the coaching successful or unsuccessful?
The Nature of Teaching 1. Teaching looks 2. 3. 4. 5. 6.	Physical skill: Things that helped me to learn the skill: Things that interfered with my success:
Good for you for taking the time to review and write! The six points you just reviewed provide the foundation for the advice you will find in this chapter. For instance, because that teaching is goal directed, I suggest that you be organized when you teach. As you read, think about how these six propositions about teaching are reflected in the chapter's suggestions.	Now generalize. Mark the points on your list that seem to provide advice for classroom teaching. Keep them in mind as you read this chapter's advice on instruction. (Thanks to Charlotte Danielson at Educational Testing Service for this exercise.)

"Voyager, there are no bridges, one builds them as one walks."

—Gloria Evangelina Anzaldua

Perhaps teachers' most vital role is to serve as bridge builders with their students, helping them to construct meaning and forge connections to create their places in the world. We do so through our instruction. *Through our instruction, we help students reach for high expectations. We convey to students that they are capable learners whose perspectives matter. We provide goal-driven, organized opportunities to help all students engage deeply in working with new information, building connections, and formulating and testing theories about the world.*

Our instruction must be driven by a sense of urgency about what we must accomplish in the very short time we are allotted. It must be driven by our genuine regard for our students, by our unfailing belief in their potential, and by our passion for the subject matter and its transformative power (Bowman, 2007; Delpit, 2006; Schussler, 2009). Challenge motivates learning and a sense of pride in our accomplishments presents true motivation to learn (Bowman, 2007). Our instruction must create meaningful challenges—challenges that students believe they can meet—and assistance in meeting those challenges. As you strive to provide excellent instruction, consider:

- *Your Inclusive and Responsive Mindset:* Your instruction starts with your understanding of your students, places them at the center of your decisions, and provides flexible opportunities to meet learning goals. It builds bridges of relevance between home, school, community experience (Ford, 2010) and helps students challenge today's inequities and shortcomings (Delpit, 2006).
- *Your Stance:* Your instruction is guided by your notions of your place in the big picture of education, what you believe about humans and how they learn, what you know to be true about what you need to accomplish, and how you should accomplish it.
- *Goals:* Your instruction is driven by student learning goals such as specific content standards and more general outcomes such as 21st-century learning goals. For example, your instruction will push students toward critical and creative thinking, successful collaboration, and technology literacy.
- *Research on Teaching and Learning:* Your instruction incorporates what we know from the research about human development and learning and about effective teaching.

This chapter helps you make decisions about instruction by exploring six pieces of advice for instruction. Together, these six pieces of advice invite you to help your students . . . COME IN.

1. **C**onnect.
2. **O**rganize your instruction.
3. **M**odel.
4. **E**nrich.
5. **I**nteract.
6. Consider human **n**ature and student **n**eeds.

Connect

Human learning is biologically and socially an endeavor to form connections. Thus, one of our central instructional responsibilities is to *connect* and to help students form connections. As instructors, we form connections with and among people, we help students connect ideas, and connect their ideas with the real world and action. The rationale for each of these connections is made here. Figure 6.1 assists you and your students in making these varied connections.

Connecting People

"All of us yearn for a sense of relatedness or belonging, a feeling of being connected to others" (Kohn, 1999, p. 21). The first people with whom teachers must connect are their students. Authentic, caring, and respectful relationships lie at the heart of teaching and

Figure 6.1   *Tips for "Connect"*

Connecting People	• See Ideas for Encouraging Interaction and Active Participation (Figure 6.6), numbers 2, 5, 18–24, 29, and 31. • Contact students before school to welcome them. • Learn students' names the first day. Encourage them to learn each others' names. • Make participants' culture a part of classroom life and the curriculum. • Give students a space in the room to display items that are important to them. • Share appropriate information about yourself that reveals your love of learning, your willingness to make mistakes, and your eagerness to apply the content. • Laugh—and cry—with your students. Tell your own stories and listen to theirs.
Connecting to prior knowledge and experience	• Try Figure 6.6, Ideas for Encouraging Interaction and Active Participation. See numbers 4–6, 12, 18–20, 22, 24, 28, and 29.
Connecting with the outside world and its important ideas	• Use problem-based learning (Chapter 7). • Use strategies that place the content in a real context. One example is analyzing news stories. • Show how information has been important to real people in different times and in different ways.
Connecting to action	• Use action projects that allow students to apply their learning. Examples include letter-writing campaigns and community improvement projects. • Have students share what they know with other audiences, such as families, other students, or the community. • Try simulations and role play. • Use guest speakers.

learning. Students who report connections with their teachers report better attitudes toward education and school, and they have positive school experiences (Markow & Martin, 2005). The relationships you forge with families also offer connections that strengthen your instruction. Chapter 3 presented strategies for connecting with your students and families by getting to know their cultures, interests, and needs through strategies like home visits, surveys, and conversations. Incorporate this knowledge into your instruction and continue to build on it.

You must also help classroom participants to connect with each other. Helping students to form a cohesive group encourages a safe environment, and it can help students learn important lessons about working as members of a group. Additionally, learning strategies that require students to work together are effective in supporting academic achievement (Bowen, 2000; Hall & Stegila, 2003; Johnson & Johnson, 1999; Maheady, Michielli-Pendl, Mallette, & Harper, 2002; Marzano et al., 2001), language development (Center for Research on Education, Diversity & Excellence, 2002; Faltis, 2001), and social and emotional growth (Goleman, 1998).

There are plenty of strategies for building a sense of community in a classroom. Most important, teachers must model respect, revealing genuine interest in students as people, and they need to encourage students to do the same for each other. If one student ridicules another, the teacher's lesson of the day must necessarily shift to address expectations for how community members are to treat each other. Efforts to build community should incorporate students' individual cultures and work to build a shared culture. Several engaging techniques can foster a sense of community, as follows:

1. *Share expectations:* Hold a discussion, perhaps preceded by a journal writing session, of what class members expect from each other. What can students expect from their teacher? How do they expect to be treated by their peers?

Shutterstock

When classroom members form a cohesive community, they can support each other in learning.

2. *Use activities that help students get to know each other:* Choose from among many published activities that allow students to learn about each other. In an activity called "Trading Places" (Silberman, 1996), students write a favorite (e.g., book, place, song) on a sticky note, place the note on their shirts, and circulate to discuss each other's ideas. They negotiate trades of sticky notes based on self-selected criteria.

3. *Develop an outward symbol or sign to signify a sense of group identity:* Create a work of art, a name, a handshake, a logo, or other identification that signals your cohesion as a class. For instance, based on student Jodi's advice from her great-grandmother, my class recently decided on its motto: "Be good. And if you can't be good . . . be careful."[1]

4. Build a class wiki (e.g., Google presentation) and have students take a digital photo to represent some interest or value and upload it to the presentation.

Kagan (2000) similarly gives many games that can help build a sense of team spirit in noncompetitive and enjoyable ways. In "Smile If You Love Me," one student (Cupid) stands in the center of the circle, makes faces, and uses motions, words, and sounds to make another person smile. When people in the circle smile, they join the center of the circle as Cupids.

Technology, too, provides plenty of opportunities to increase connections among people within and beyond the classroom walls. We can harness students' connections via mechanisms such as blogs, social networking, and discussion boards to share perspectives and ideas, that can equalize students' social power. As a tongue-in-cheek usage of the familiar elementary technique of awarding good behavior with stars on a chart, for example, my graduate students recently created a virtual "star chart" using a wiki and gave themselves and each other stars for appreciated efforts and achievements (Figure 6.2).

Connecting Ideas

Helping students to connect ideas involves two components: connecting to prior knowledge and connecting ideas across contexts.

Connecting to Prior Knowledge and Experience   Learners have experiences and ways of thinking that strongly influence what they will learn and how they will learn it. Research reviewed by Marzano (2004) shows a high positive correlation between what

---

[1]Used with the permission of Jodi Elmore.

| Figure 6.2 | *Wiki star chart.* |

Here are E-cohort members earning gold stars. You might know something I don't. Add a gold star (yours or a peer's) and tell how the owner earned it. (Remember to hit "edit" to add to this page.)

Your name	Your star	How you earned it	Who stuck it to the chart	Who seconds that emotion?
Ashley	★	Skype scholar	Sarah	
Andrea	★	Supremely supportive	Belinda	Sarah, Sammy
Belinda	★	An excellent counselor	Maria	Sarah
Sarah	★	Vocabulary expert	Laurel	Warren
Ana	★	Wrote and received my first grant!	Ana	Belinda

students know about the content when they walk in your door and what they will know when they leave. Let's test this with a popular exercise. What does this sentence mean? *The notes were sour because the seam split.* You know each individual word in the sentence, but for most people, the words are not combined in a way that makes sense. However, if you know that the topic is *bagpipes,* then the meaning of the sentence becomes clearer. Your comprehension depends on your background knowledge.

Research also indicates that the background experiences we all have sometimes run contrary to established fact and accurate explanations of the world. These alternative or growing conceptions can be difficult to change (Driver, 1981; Marzano, Pickering, & Pollock, 2001; National Research Council, 2000).

Thus, it is critical that you help students find out what they bring to the current learning situation, revise it as necessary, and link it to the new information. Formative assessments (from Chapter 5) such as pretests and sample problems serve this purpose. So do strategies such as knowledge charts and clinical interviews. Chapter 8, Student Assessment, gives additional strategies that can be of use to you as you make it a point to include preassessment to guide instruction.

We help students link the new to the known through our **scaffolds**, our efforts to support students' developing constructions of the subject matter. In introducing new content, we should select analogies, metaphors, and experiences that are familiar to students and thus allow them to connect to school knowledge (Delpit, 2006). In one study, teachers' knowledge of cultural scaffolds was limited in comparison to the many other scaffolds they used to help English learners acquire content (Pawan, 2008). Once again we see the importance of understanding students' worlds; it helps us help students bridge the new to the known.

Connecting Ideas Across Contexts   What did you have for dinner last Friday? You probably can't answer that question immediately. To recall that information, you probably ask yourself a series of questions perhaps beginning with one like, "What was I doing last weekend?" You can probably retrieve your menu once you trace back the related links.

This exercise argues for how information is stored in our brains—not as isolated bits but as networks of related ideas. To increase the likelihood that information is retained, can be recalled, and is useful in a variety of settings, then, we can help students strengthen the networks in which information is situated. As bridge builders, you and your students can consider questions such as: "How does this concept apply in another subject area?" "Where in history do we see this notion?" and "Is this term's usage in the current context related to its usage in another field?" We need to be explicit in our efforts to help students connect their ideas and use them across contexts.

Connecting to the Outside World and Its Important Ideas

In connecting to the outside world, teachers provide students with authentic settings for using and developing their academic content. Reality-based approaches provide students with opportunities to enhance their skills at analyzing problems, gathering and summarizing important information, solving problems, and reflecting on their solutions (Cole, 1995). Examples of real-world connections include problem-based learning (Chapter 7); reading primary sources such as historical documents and the newspaper; beginning lessons by presenting photographs or realistic problems; and inviting guest speakers such as scientists, writers, or elected representatives into the classroom. Digital storytelling is another (see the 21st Century Teaching and Learning Tip). In digital storytelling, students create multimedia stories that place the content in context. Students studying the Great Depression, for instance, might capture the narratives of family members who remember it. Connecting to the real world heightens students' sense of relevance and enhances motivation to learn, perhaps especially important for your disengaged learners (Kajder, 2006; Schussler, 2009).

Authentic experiences are linked most closely to the settings in which students will use their new understanding. Important ideas are the ones worth having. For Duckworth (1996), the essence of intellectual development is the formation of connections or, in her terms, "the having of wonderful ideas." Wonderful ideas

> need not necessarily look wonderful to the outside world. I see no difference in kind between wonderful ideas that many other people have already had, and wonderful ideas that nobody has yet happened upon. That is, the nature of creative intellectual acts remains the same, whether it is an infant who for the first time marks the connection between seeing things and reaching for them . . . or a musician who invents a harmonic sequence. . . . In each case, *new connections are being made among things already mastered.* The more we help children to have their wonderful ideas and to feel good about themselves for having them, the more likely it is that they will some day happen upon wonderful ideas that no one else has happened upon before. (p. 14; emphasis added)

Connecting to Action

Your long view of learners is probably related to students' future behavior patterns and decision-making abilities. What we teach children, from kindergarten on, should connect to the ways we want them to act now and as adults. They deserve immediate opportunities to

---

21st Century Teaching and Learning Tip

DIGITAL STORIES

Digital stories are short (e.g., 2 minutes) multimedia productions that include visual images accompanied by a musical soundtrack and a narration, usually from a piece of personal writing. They tell the lives of everyday people. Digital storytelling is catching on as a way to empower youth while building both literacy and technological competence. Look at your unit plans and decide how you can include digital storytelling as one option for an upcoming assignment. Then look around you for available tools: What cameras are available? What software is available for sound editing? For now, simplify the project to use what you and your students have available, perhaps using widely available presentation software with still images and narration. Get more information at sites like the University of Houston (digitalstorytelling.coe.uh.edu/) and the Center for Digital Story Telling (storycenter.org/). Students are also recording cross-generational stories to connect with grandparents and preserve their personal histories. University of Maryland, Baltimore County, has one such project (http://www.umbc.edu/oit/newmedia/studio/digitalstories/index.html).

Teachers and students engaging in service learning, community action project

Thinkstock

act on what they learn. Social action projects can serve as a powerful mechanism to shape schools and communities into more humane and inclusive institutions (e.g., Banks, 1997; Bomer & Bomer, 2001; Nieto, 2004). Another chance for students to take action is through service learning, wherein they test and apply their content learning by serving the community (Allen, 2003). Examples include encouraging voter registration, teaching or tutoring younger students, and planning community gardens.

Organize Your Instruction

Effective instruction involves a high degree of organization. When you organize content, time, and materials thoughtfully, you maximize student learning time. Teachers who waste little instructional time and ensure that students are engaged affect student achievement positively (Miller & Hall, 2009). You need to be organized on more than one level: You need to organize content within and across individual lessons, and you need to organize times and tasks within the larger teaching environment.

Organizing Content

Information processing theory reminds us that the human brain *chunks* information into manageable pieces (Miller, 1956). Think back to Exercise B at the beginning of this chapter, where you were invited to think about what a good coach does well. One often-cited coaching skill is the ability to break a complicated task (for instance, sailing, golfing, or driving a manual-transmission car) down into smaller, more easily mastered skills. As does a coach, you need to analyze the content you are teaching. It needs to be broken into chunks before it can be presented in your classroom. What size should the chunks be? What shape? In which order should you present them?

The importance of scaffolding (introduced on p. 120 as part of connecting to prior knowledge) also will drive your decisions about how to organize content. Scaffolds allow us to "prop up" our students, giving them just enough support to succeed until they can succeed independently. We organize instruction to gradually withdraw assistance as students demonstrate increasing mastery. Because students vary, you will need to provide more scaffolding for some, less for others, and different sorts of support for still others.

21st Century Teaching and Learning Tip

INTERACTIVE GRAPHIC ORGANIZERS

Graphic organizers aren't just teacher tools. They can help students organize information as they build a number of 21st-century learning skills such as systems thinking, problem solving, logical reasoning and creative thinking. Plenty of free interactive graphic organizers and mapping tools are found online at sites like these:

- Holt (http://my.hrw.com/nsmedia/intgos/html/igo.htm)
- Read Write Think (http://www.readwritethink.org/classroom-resources/student-interactives/)
- Lexicon (http://www.lexiconsys.com/graphic_organizer.html)
- Bubbl.us (http://bubbl.us/)
- DropMind (http://web.dropmind.com/)
- Free Mind (http://sourceforge.net/projects/freemind/). For older students; download is required.
- Wise Mapping (http://www.wisemapping.com/). Sign in is required.
- Mind Node (http://www.mindnode.com/). For Mac.

Many of these sites allow for collaborative editing. Be sure to preview the sites before using them with students to ensure that you are ready to troubleshoot. Find more organizers using a search term like "interactive graphic organizers" or "interactive mind maps."

The manner in which you organize the content depends on your knowledge of the students, the amount of time you have with them, and your knowledge of the content itself. Before you teach, ensure that you have a firm grasp of the major concepts you will be teaching and that you understand the relationships among these ideas. Check your understanding by constructing a diagram or other visual representation of your knowledge. One example is a **concept map,** which relates ideas in a hierarchical structure. Figure 6.9, found in Opportunities to Practice Exercise 3 at the close of this chapter, is a concept map of this entire text. Try the free trial version of popular concept mapping programs, Inspiration and Kidspiration, at http://inspiration.com.

Being able to organize your ideas into a one-page diagram helps you discover the main points and supporting details so you can structure instruction and arrange your time appropriately. Additionally, using **graphic organizers,** diagrams, and other nonlinguistic representations of the text supports student achievement (Marzano et al., 2001). See the 21st Century Teaching and Learning Tip for more on graphic organizers.

By presenting information in particular ways, your curriculum materials will also provide clues for content organization. Often textbooks follow predictable structures in presenting content. Some typical patterns for the structure of text are suggested in Figure 6.3.

Also think about the organization that would best suit your purposes, even if it differs from the organization used in your curricular materials. Your learners' developmental levels provide one clue in organizing instruction. A general rule of thumb is that the less experience

Figure 6.3 *Some organizational patterns of content.*

Organizational Pattern	Example
Time sequence	Historical events presented chronologically
General principles to specific examples	Scientific laws and then real-world examples of them
Specific examples to general principles	Letters of the alphabet as examples of vowels or consonants
Topical	Aspects of family life within a culture: recreation, food, and work
Cause and effect	Historical events and new laws they inspired
Compare and contrast	Plants and animals
Problem and solution	An enigma and then its solution

learners have with the content, the smaller the chunks of content need to be. For example, kindergartners, who tend to have fewer background experiences from which to draw, need consistently smaller pieces of content. So do teenagers when exposed to complex information with which they have limited experience. Age and other elements such as the students' capacity to learn and language proficiency affect the amount of experience students have with the content and hence the size of the chunks of information their teachers present.

The most common mistake novice teachers make when organizing content is to include too much information (too many chunks) in a single lesson. I also made that mistake when I taught a reading and science lesson to second graders, as I described in Chapter 5. You read my plan (Figure 5.13) for the hour-and-a-half lesson. I planned to guide the children through some reading experiences and then have them make their own fossils to build an understanding of how fossils are made. Upon reflection, I overestimated second-graders' experience with text and could improve the lesson by breaking the reading portion of the lesson into even smaller chunks spread over more time.

Organizing Times and Tasks

The content that you so thoughtfully arrange within individual lessons is placed in a framework of how activities will flow over the course of the day, a daily structure (recall Chapter 5's discussion of planning). When you are ready to teach, make certain that the class understands and accepts the organizational scheme you have devised. Even if you teach from great lesson plans, your learners may leave dazed unless you provide clues about the organization of content and activities—or they may leave indifferent if they perceive that they had no input into the agenda. Learners deserve both an overall sense of where the day is headed and clues to let them know where they are on the day's map. The Inclusive and Responsive Teaching Tip provides some techniques for building and sharing your organizational plan.

As you teach, events will conspire to encourage stalls and side trips. Because classrooms are crowded, busy places, it is easy for plans to be forestalled. Students, for instance, may raise interesting questions or bring up points that warrant exploration. Instances like these—**teachable moments**—are not found explicitly listed in the daily plan book, but they present wonderful opportunities for learning. One difficult aspect of your job will be to decide which moments to pursue because of their rich promise and which opportunities may not be worth the time invested. That decision is not always easy, and not all students will perceive your adherence to or diversion from the plan with the same optimism.

When the situation arises in my classroom, I sometimes tell students "You are raising important issues! We can certainly explore them now. We will need to modify our agenda to make room for it by deleting *X*. Shall we?" Use your professional judgment, and refer back to contents standards and your stance toward education and its important goals, as you decide which paths to pursue. The point is to remain intentional. Keep your goals in mind.

Inclusive and Responsive Teaching Tip

TECHNIQUES FOR BUILDING AND SHARING YOUR ORGANIZATIONAL PLAN

- Ask students for their expectations at the beginning of a class (e.g., "What do you hope to learn this year?").
- Include an overview to the course, the year, or the upcoming unit on your Web site. Include your regular schedule, too.
- Write a daily agenda on the board. Try allowing learners to provide input by adding, deleting, or rearranging items.
- Provide a graphic organizer that shows how your instruction will be organized.

- Briefly tell students what will happen during the lesson.
- Preview the lesson's major points.
- If you intend to lecture, provide a note-taking form that helps student organize the information.
- During the lesson, use internal summaries and transition sentences so that students see when you are switching to a different point or activity.
- Refer back to your agenda or chart as the lessons progresses.
- Draw each lesson to closure. Try summarizing by asking students to share an important point or ask for input for the next agenda.

Teaching Tip

GIVING CLEAR DIRECTIONS

Ensuring that your directions to students are crystal clear will help you and your students remain organized and productive. When giving directions, remember the following:

1. Limit your directions to no more than three steps.
2. Use more than one form of input: Say your directions aloud, post them on the board, and model them. For older students, using just two forms of input may suffice.
3. Hold up your fingers to count steps as you state your directions: "The *first* thing you will do is . . ." Be certain that, for older students, you use natural phrasing and do not overemphasize the gesture.
4. Check for understanding of the directions before you release students to work: "What is the first thing you will do?" Reteach until students demonstrate understanding.
5. No matter the age of the learner, give your directions immediately before you want students to follow them. Students may forget what to do if you give directions and then talk about something else before releasing them.

You will no doubt discover that the clearer you are in your priorities and the more organized you are, the less time gets wasted. This is especially true with giving directions. If your directions are clear and students know just what to do, they can jump in and get to work. If directions are disorganized and unclear, your students will waste time and materials, and you will waste your time and energy reteaching individuals who have made a mess or wandered off course. The Teaching Tip suggests advice for giving clear directions.

It is also easy to lose track of time. If we were to list Murphy's Laws of Classroom Teaching, at the head of the list might be "Things always take longer than expected." Keep one eye on the clock and maintain your sense of urgency for all that needs to be accomplished. Use students' time well.

Model

In life outside the classroom walls, we often learn by example, by being shown how to conduct ourselves. Modeling, or showing students how to carry out a skill, is a powerful instructional strategy (Cole, 1995). For instance, students taught ICT skills through a modeling approach maintain higher computer self-efficacy than those taught without modeling (Moos & Azevedo, 2009). Figure 6.4 gives some examples of modeling.

Teaching Tip

TIPS FOR EFFECTIVE MODELING

1. As you plan, think about the most important elements of the skill or process you will model. List them you draw students' attention to **critical attributes** and remember that in many cases students' performances need not match yours. Their efforts may be both different from yours *and* good.
2. Verbalize your decisions; talk about what you are thinking and doing. This models **metacognition** and shows that we understand and have control over our thinking.
3. Provide plenty of good examples, including student models. Point out when the examples are different from each other and say what they have in common that makes them good. Showing different examples—**multiple embodiments**—helps students focus on the criteria for a successful performance.
4. If the behavior is complex, model sections of it and slow down your performance.
5. Model desired behaviors more than once. The less familiar students are with the skill, the more careful repetitions they need to see.
6. As students emulate your performance, observe carefully and provide specific feedback.

Figure 6.4   *Four examples of teacher modeling.*

Concepts and Skills	Modeling
Tying shoelaces	• Mr. Alvarez positions himself on the rug so his six kindergartners can see clearly. • He demonstrates each step of tying a bow, exaggerating and slowing his motions to make the steps obvious. • He asks the students to verbalize the procedure with him as he ties several times before handing each student a shoe to tie while he watches.
Cooperating with peers	• Having assigned his fourth graders to work in pairs, Mr. Pease reviews his expectations for partner work: "Partners support each other by reaching decisions together. Partners help each other when they get stuck." • He invites a student to the front of the room to play the role of his work partner. • The partners show the class how to compromise to reach decisions and how to use helpful words to get unstuck. • Mr. Pease reminds the class: "Here's what cooperation *looks like,* and here is what it *sounds like.*" • Now his students have some specific advice and behaviors to help them work together.
Writing a persuasive essay	• On a projected computer display in her seventh-grade class, Ms. Simon shows and reads aloud two examples of good persuasive essays. • She shares the criteria for effective persuasive writing and states that she will use those criteria to write her own essay. • She talks through her decisions about selecting a topic and its supporting points. • As she expresses her decisions, she writes a couple of drafts on the projected computer screen. • She and the students check to see whether the essays meet the criteria for good persuasive writing. • She e-mails her final essay to students or posts it on the class Web site, for students' later reference.
Solving a challenging word problem in math	• Miss Thompson reads the problem aloud to her ninth graders, varying her intonation as she reads critical components of the problem. • Using the **think aloud** strategy, she summarizes her understanding of the problem, discusses what she needs to know, and reacts to the problem to show her stance as a problem solver: "This one looks tough, but I have solved similar problems!" • She attacks the problem on the whiteboard, sharing her decisions for trying certain strategies. When her strategies do not bring immediate success, she shows students how to move forward by trying new approaches. • When she reaches a solution, she shares the joy she finds in persisting and solving a challenging problem.

To model, think about what you want students to learn, show them how to do it, watch them try it, and give them feedback on their performance. Modeling is effective for learners of all ages, and it is appropriate in every subject area. Modeling is important for helping students learn behaviors, such as using manners and showing consideration, as well as for helping them master content-area outcomes. When you model, try some of the suggestions in the Teaching Tip.

Digital technology greatly expands our ability to supply good instructional models for our students. A document camera, for example, allows the students to view in very good detail the teacher's modeling (see photo). Or students may view, for example, video clips that demonstrate how to sign the alphabet or change an oil filter. Multimedia clips of a performance are helpful because they can be magnified, played at variable speeds, and repeated endlessly as necessary. As they learn social skills, students with autism are benefitting from software that models emotions in the human face (Tanaka et al., 1010;

Paola uses the document camera to model an art project for her second-graders. The screen behind her shows, greatly enlarged, the art materials on top of a guided drawing she just modeled. Placing the camera in front of the class allows Paola to face her students as she uses the camera.

Tardif, Laine, Rodriguez, & Gepner, 2007). Software that models native pronunciation of a language (English or other target languages) is helpful because the computerized model never tires of being asked to repeat a phrase. Electronic models, then, can help you differentiate your instruction by allowing students who need particular kinds of help to view models targeted to their needs.

Additionally, technology allows us to more easily capture and share appropriate *student* models, or work samples. Ask for the permission of students (and families, as appropriate) to create and keep electronic copies of their work to serve as models for future students. Sample work created by other students tends to be very well received; such models show students what is possible by someone in their peer group. Also, *electronic* student models are especially helpful because they are easy to store, take up little space, do not fall apart over time, and—if shared on the Web or distributed to students—can be viewed by many students repeatedly and simultaneously. If you use electronic models, take precautions to ensure that students submit their own work by structuring the assignment carefully and by providing a variety of models that are different from each other and are still of high quality. Also, students may need to be reminded that any new technological tool takes time and patience to master.

Finally, through their modeling, teachers teach more than content-area skills, behaviors, and knowledge. Good and Brophy (1987) make the important point that through their modeling, teachers shape a healthy group climate, convey an interest in the students as people, and teach ideas about good listening and communication habits. Through teacher modeling, students learn to socialize as members of groups, to gain rational control over their own behaviors, and to respect others. Teacher modeling, then, is an important socializing force that helps teachers induce students toward the good.

Enrich

Because teachers are responsible for presenting a great deal of information to large groups of students in relatively brief periods of time, classrooms tend to ring with auditory input, or teacher talk. Listening is an efficient learning strategy for many students much of the time, but it does have at least six drawbacks:

1. People process information at different rates.
2. Because speech comes in a stream, listeners may not be able to separate main points and discern the supporting points.

3. It can be difficult for students to contribute to a lecture, change its pace, or connect with its content.

4. People learn differently (Gardner, 1993).

5. Students may have insufficient experience with the language of instruction or with the content to comprehend it solely by hearing it. Meaningful instruction for students acquiring English is most often embedded in realistic and rich contexts, as you will recall from Chapter 4 (Center for Research on Education, Diversity & Excellence, 2002; Echevarria, Vogt, & Short, 2004; Hill & Flynn, 2006; Krashen, 1981; Swain, 1985; Thomas & Collier, 2001).

6. Recent work in human learning suggests that varied stimulation is essential for brain development. The more varied and frequent the stimulation the brain receives, the more complex its development (Kovalik & Olsen, 2001; National Research Council, 2000).

For all of these reasons, teachers need to enrich the learning environment by providing rich input. Indeed, in a study of mathematics and science instruction, Wenglinsky (2000) found that hands-on lessons and higher-order thinking tasks resulted in higher student achievement. Think about powerful learning experiences you have had in life. Potent learning experiences tend to be full of sensations: new sights and sounds, textures and smells. We hear beautiful words and ideas that make us reconsider what we know. We try new things that just the day before seemed beyond our capabilities.

Classroom learning should mirror the most powerful kinds of learning from our outside lives. How well do our lectures, worksheets, spelling lists, and pages of math exercises live up to that challenge? How inclusive and responsive are such frontal, paper-based approaches? How well do they help our students build bridges between their home worlds and the school world?

As you teach, remember to fill students' lives with authentic—rich and real—opportunities to learn. Focus on meaning. Fill the classroom with sensations from students' own cultures. Give students a chance to see and try new things, to hear the music and speech of faraway places, to experience the struggles of those fighting for independence, to touch the moist skin of the amphibians they study, to read and hear the words of people who have shaped history. Figure 6.5 gives some ideas for enriching the learning environment.

*L*ife is amazing, and a teacher had better prepare himself to be a medium for that amazement.

—*Edward Blishen*

Rich environment foster deeper learning.

Annie Fuller

Figure 6.5   *Ideas for enriching the learning environment.*

Look for a variety of ways to present the content and for varied representations of it.

- *Meaning:* Focus on conceptual understanding, not just rote learning. Provide authentic experiences in the content areas.

- *Many kinds of print:* Fill your room with books of different genres. Include, too, other kinds of print such as posters, recipes, student-generated work, letters, and signs (Schifini, 1994). Include text in students' primary language.

- *Picture files:* Start clipping and saving pictures to support your instruction. Pictures can be used for concept sorts or to encourage small-group discussion. Old magazines and calendars are a good place to start. Many images can be downloaded and printed as well.

- *Realia:* Find real objects to provide examples of what you read and study.

- *Works of art:* Reproductions of great works are available in teaching materials and at libraries. They can set the stage for the study of concepts from the content areas.

- *Newspapers and current periodicals:* Look in the news for examples of what you are studying. Encourage your students to do the same.

- *Technology:* Help your students access information around the world through the Internet. See the Web sites at the close of this chapter for resources that can bring the world into your room.

- *Living things:* Instead of assigning only worksheets to study insects, bring in mealworms from the pet store. Create a worm garden in an aquarium. Grow mold.

- *Music:* Many students love to sing, and nearly all love to listen. Find recordings to support your study of history and culture. Try compact discs. Make instruments in science to study sound. Dance.

- *Food:* Try foods from different places or that illustrate different scientific or mathematical applications. Make butter as an example of a physical change. When students study about George Washington, bring in George's favorite breakfast: hoe cakes and tea.

- *Real tools:* Have your students *seen* the simple tools they read about in science? Bring in wedges, screws, and pulleys. Encourage students to hunt for them also. Bring in a computer or toaster beyond repair, cut off the plug, and let the students take it apart.

- *Models:* Use physical models to provide opportunities to study hard-to-reach phenomena such as atoms, planets, rockets, or the human heart.

- *Graphic organizers:* Provide visual displays of your information (Bromley, Irwin-De Vitis, & Modlo, 1995). Try Venn diagrams to compare and contrast. Make an outline that students view before they read.

- *Guest speakers and visitors:* Bring in family members and other guests. Do you know someone who has seen war? Volunteered? Marched in a protest? Named a star? Escaped persecution? Written a book? Played professional sports? Learners' lives are enriched when they meet people with great accomplishments.

- *Field trips:* Be certain to prepare your students for the trip by building connections between their studies and what they will be experiencing in the field. List their questions before you go. Consider whether it would be appropriate for your students to record information during the trip. When you return, process the field trip by focusing on what students saw, heard, and learned. Find out if they have answered their questions. Connect questions to past and future study. Even a 10-minute walk can provide abundant learning experiences (Russell, 1990).

Given their digital nature, electronic resources can easily be used to enrich whole-class instruction or to differentiate instruction. For example, in preparation to read one of William Shakespeare's plays, a high school English class divides into computer-based stations to listen to an audio file of a portion of the work in English or a home language, examine maps of Elizabethan England, work with an interactive timeline of world events during the period, view period art, read Shakespeare's biography, or research world events that influenced the work. The teacher decides whether to assign students, based on need, to particular stations. For instance, students who may struggle in reading the play may benefit from listening to a performance of the play first. Alternatively, the teacher may allow students to follow their interests in selecting stations. Popular stations may be duplicated so that more than one computer is dedicated to them.

Will providing enriched experiences take more of your preparation time than would photocopying a worksheet page? Almost certainly so. You can minimize your time investment by saving your collections, by inviting students to bring in materials, and by utilizing the expertise of community members and colleagues. On the other hand, do worksheets and book activities have their place in the classroom? Almost certainly so. You will need to balance the kinds of activities and input you provide, checking to see that you select a variety of activities that promote meaningful learning. Your efforts to provide rich input will pay off. Remember that you are a window to the world for your students.

Interact

In his classic study of U.S. classrooms, Goodlad (1984) witnessed the predominance of "frontal practices," where teachers stood in front of the room, presenting information and briskly quizzing students on factual content. Thirty years later, it appears that teachers are still talking.

In one study, teachers talked *eight times* more than their students did (National Center for Education Statistics, 2003). Similarly, in a British study, teachers made 75 percent of the classroom discourse moves (Smith, Hardman, Wall, & Mroz, 2004). When students *do* talk, their utterances tend to be short and dependent on the teachers' narrow requests for information. This is discouraging for all students, but the news gets worse. Students placed in low groups or tracks have poorer opportunities to interact with content (see Chorzempa and Graham's 2006 study of primary reading groups and Oakes's 2005 study of high schools). Additionally, the whole-class instruction that predominates in K–12 general education classrooms cuts opportunities for students with learning disabilities (Vaughn et al., 2001). Thus, exactly those students who need *enriched* opportunities to develop content and language mastery through interaction actually are granted *fewer*. The Inclusive and Responsive Teaching Tip gives one easy way to spread the participation.

Interaction is a critical component of good instruction for all students. Teaching is more than telling. Interaction allows students to build social skills, to refine their thinking, to consider alternative perspectives, to practice using language, and to provide ongoing assessment information for their teachers. As a result, teaching must be interactional; students must be active participants. Let's address three particular aspects of interaction here:

- Active participation and progress monitoring
- Structured interaction for language development
- Physical movement during classroom instruction

Active Participation: Engagement and Progress Monitoring

Active participation strategies are the teachers' explicit efforts to ensure that all students overtly engage in the lesson's activities. Figure 6.6 gives a list of thirty-one low-tech ideas for encouraging active participation. Some strategies are best for checking content mastery and others for sharing students' perspectives. Mastery strategies are listed first in each section.

Inclusive and Responsive Teaching Tip

SHARE THE WEALTH

When you feel obliged to ask a question, try this: Ask the question. Then say, "No matter what the first answer is, I'm going to call on four more hands." Wait a few seconds, then call on four in a row. This strategy can increase student participation for both convergent and divergent questions. Pair students who may need support constructing a verbal response. If you like, you can have students turn to a neighbor and discuss before asking for a show of hands.

| **Figure 6.6** | *Active participation strategies: thirty-one ideas for encouraging interaction and active participation.* |

Give prompts to discover what students know, think, feel, have experienced, and wonder.

	Teacher–Student Interactions
"Tell Me"	1. *Choral response:* When questions have convergent, brief answers, all students respond at once instead of one at a time. Teacher records and discusses items with muddy responses. 2. *Whip:* Everyone shares a brief response (word, phrase, or sentence) to a topic or question. Contributions move from one student to the next with no teacher intervention. Students are allowed to "pass." 3. *Stand to share:* All stand when they have developed a response to a question such as, "What was an important point in the chapter?" One person shares aloud, and all with the same or similar responses sit. Sharing continues until all are sitting (Kagan, 1994). 4. *Opinionnaire:* All respond privately to a set of statements related to the current topic, such as, "Efforts to clone humans are wrong." Responses can be formed as agree or disagree or as numbers that indicate degrees of agreement. Teacher leads a discussion to elicit students' responses. 5. *Share a story:* Teacher elicits students' stories related to the topic. If there are many stories, students can tell their stories to smaller groups or to partners. For instance, "I have told you a story about crickets in my apartment. I would like to hear a true cricket story that you may have." 6. *Student questions* (Dillon, 1988): Teacher provides time for students to formulate their questions about a topic. He might record them for discussion and study. For example, "We will be studying space. I have always wondered why stars twinkle. What do you wonder about space?"
"Show Me"	7. *Flash cards:* Individually or in groups students hold up color-coded or other flash cards in response to teacher's or peers' mastery questions. For example, teacher asks questions about the federal government, and students hold up red for legislative, yellow for executive, or blue for judicial. Students can also ask the questions. 8. *Hand signals:* Students hold up numbers of fingers to respond to mastery questions (e.g., "How many sides on a triangle?"). Other gestures can also be used. For instance, "I will watch while you draw a triangle in the air." 9. *Whiteboards:* Students record responses on individual boards, then show teacher or peers. Some examples include spelling words, cursive letter formation, French vocabulary, and brief math exercises. 10. *Letter and number tiles:* Students have sets of ceramic, magnetic, or tag board tiles displaying letters of the alphabet or digits 0 through 9. They display their tiles in response to tasks from the teacher or peers. For instance, "Build an even number that is greater than 50." Or: "Round 5,723.86 to the tenths place. I will come around and check your tiles." 11. *Comprehension check:* Students complete brief quizzes, written by teacher or pulled from existing materials, at the beginning or end of class. Students check their own work and analyze what they need help with before passing their papers to teacher. 12. *Quick write:* Students respond in writing to a prompt. For example, "Before we read this chapter, please take a minute and write about a time when you felt powerless." Quick writes can spur discussion and allow all students to express feelings or experiences in writing, even if they choose not to share aloud. Quick writes are not graded. 13. *Fuzzy points:* Near the end of a lesson, students anonymously record their fuzzy points, the concepts about which they are still unsure. Teacher collects and analyzes them for the next time.

(continued)

Figure 6.6	Active participation strategies (Continued)

	Student–Student Interactions
"Tell Each Other" (Be sure to process these activities. Come together as a class and briefly share. Discuss findings.)	14. *Peer coach:* In pairs, students take turns serving as coach and coachee. Coach observes coachee solve a problem and provides praise and suggestions. Roles switch. Teacher circulates to check for accuracy and social skills (Kagan, 1994).
	15. *Student-led recitation:* Students prepare written comprehension and challenge questions over course and reading material. They sit in a circle and take turns asking, answering, and evaluating each others' questions and responses (Dillon, 1988).
	16. *Numbered heads together:* In small groups, students number off. Teacher (or a peer) asks a question, and group members put their heads together to discuss. Teacher calls on one number to respond for each group (Kagan, 1994).
	17. *Toss the ball:* Students give a response to a factual or opinion question and toss a Koosh ball, Nerf ball, or other soft ball, to a peer, who becomes the next to answer or question.
	18. *Talk to your partner:* Students turn and discuss with a nearby partner. For instance, "Tell your partner about an animal you know with protective coloration."
	19. *Peer interview:* Students ask their partners questions about their experiences with a certain topic.
	20. *Values line up:* Present a prompt that is likely to elicit a wide range of responses. For instance, "To help the environment, families should own only one car." Have students numerically rate their agreement with the statement and then line up in order of their numerical ratings, 1 to 10. Split the line in half and pair students with extreme scores (1 goes to 10). Instruct them to give their responses and rationales and then to paraphrase each other's points of view. Draw conclusions as a class once students are again seated.
	21. *Scavenger hunt:* Prepare a scavenger hunt form that encourages discussion of students' varied backgrounds and knowledge. Allow students to circulate and record the names of peers who fit certain criteria. For instance, "Find someone who has seen a famous monument." You can also make the prompts content oriented. Students might be required to find the match for their chemical symbol, for instance.
"Show Each Other" (Process these activities, too.)	22. *Group chart:* In groups, students draw diagrams or charts to illustrate the content. Charts are displayed for class review and comparison.
	23. *Group problem:* Each member of a small group is given a vital piece of information necessary to solve a problem. Only when students share their information can they solve the problem together.
	24. *Snowballs:* Invite students to record their questions or perceptions on a sheet of paper. Then have them crumple the sheets into wads and, on your signal, toss them across the room. After the chaos subsides, students open the wad nearest them and respond to the question or add their own perspective in writing. Toss and respond a few times so that students can read a variety of perspectives. Process by asking for themes or questions that need to be addressed.
	25. *Student quiz:* Students develop written quizzes to check their peers' mastery. They check the content before handing papers to teacher. As an option, students can complete quizzes in groups.
	26. *Follow the leader:* One partner gives oral directions as the other partner tries to draw, make, or build a construction that fits the leader's description. Roles switch. Teacher leads discussion about effective communication.
	27. *Sorts:* In small groups, students sort objects (such as leaves or small tools) or ideas (recorded on cards such as elements on the periodic table). In open sorts, students choose but do not reveal their criteria for sorting. Peers discern the criteria by observing groups. In closed sorts, students follow the grouping criteria given by the teacher or a peer. Older students can use multistage classifications; younger students may group by one attribute only.

| Figure 6.6 | *Active participation strategies (Continued)* |

28. *Brainstorming and fact-storming:* Students in groups record as many ideas as they can generate related to a topic or solutions to a problem. Praise is given for fluency (number of ideas) and flexibility (variety of ideas). In fact-storming, students record as many relevant facts as they can. Facts can be grouped and labeled, or they can be placed on a chart for future revisions and additions.

29. *Partner journals:* Students can be paired anonymously or with friends. They respond to classroom activities and content by writing to each other. Teacher chooses whether to collect and review journals.

30. *Blackboard blitz:* During small-group work, representatives from each group simultaneously record their group's best ideas on the board. All students can view each others' ideas, and work continues while students write on the board (Kagan, 1994).

31. *Gallery tour:* Upon completion of individual or group projects, students place their projects on desks and tour the room to view other works. Students can respond to each other's works on sticky notes or on a response sheet for the author.

Some of these active participation suggestions have high-tech twins. For example, the student response systems shared in Figure 5.1 offer a digital alternative to opinionnaires (#4) and flashcards (#7). Students use their own wireless devices (Demski, 2010) or special hardware to send data to their teachers' computer, which quickly analyzes responses and projects results. Too, some teachers are now experimenting with Twitter, running back channels during lessons that allow students to anonymously make brief comments and ask questions during the lesson (Kennedy, 2009; Young, 2009). Some secondary teachers are using Web-based programs, some with free versions (such as polleverywhere.com) that use texting for audience responses. High or low tech, as you select active participation strategies, remember that you need to use a variety of strategies, and those you select should be consistent with your goals, your learners' needs, and your personal stance toward teaching.

Active participation strategies support participation and academic success. They break the traditional pattern of the teacher doing most of the talking while students either listen quietly or respond, one at a time, to the teacher's numerous questions. For instance, when students use response cards (or flash cards, #7 in Figure 6.6) rather than hand raising, instances of misbehavior decrease and participation and achievement increase significantly for students both with and without disabilities (George, 2010; Horn, 2010; Munro & Stephenson, 2009; Randolph, 2007). The Inclusive and Responsive Teaching Tip shares an active participation strategy that can balance the power scales for students who need more opportunities to be viewed as competent: Audience Plants (Guillaume, Yopp, & Yopp, 2007).

Active participation strategies also provide for progress monitoring. They provide informal assessment opportunities so that you can determine whether and what students understand and provide instructive feedback. Feedback is one of the most important activities teachers can employ to improve student learning (Northwest Regional Educational Laboratory, 2005). To be effective, feedback must relate directly to students' responses and provide specific suggestions. See the Teaching Tip. Such feedback corrects misunderstandings and reinforces learning. Active participation strategies provide a perfect opportunity to provide timely, specific feedback. Imagine how much more powerful active participation strategies can be than are the traditional queries, "Does anyone have a question? Anyone *not* get it?"

Inclusive and Responsive Teaching Tip

AUDIENCE PLANTS

1. Before the lesson, select brief content that can be shared by a student. You might select a question you want someone to ask or short answers you want someone to give.
2. If your students read, give them the content on paper along with a plea for secrecy.
3. Select one to three students and speak with them quietly before the lesson, teaching them the cue for when during the lesson they should share information. Tell them that they should use their best acting skills so that people don't know they are plants.
4. During the lesson, give the cue (for instance, ask, "What questions do you have?", scratch your nose, or ask the cue question).
5. Allow your audience plants to share their information.
6. There is often a strong positive reaction from the audience to the content shared by their peers. Decide whether you will share your strategy with the class.

Here's an example. Before Phil Campos taught his fifth-grade social studies lesson, he surreptitiously took the intermediate English learners outside and taught them their lines. They rehearsed, and on cue during the lesson, they shared their information smoothly. Phil noticed that after this lesson, his audience plants spoke spontaneously more often and demonstrated more confidence. Their English-only peers initiated more conversation with them as well.

Phil Campos

Teaching Tip

PROVIDING EFFECTIVE FEEDBACK (FROM HATTIE & TIMPERLEY, 2007)

Effective feedback allows learners to close the gap between their current performance and the goal. Provide feedback that will help students answer all three questions: "Where am I going?" "How am I going?" and "What's next?" (Think: *feed up*, *feed back*, and *feed forward*.) Praise, along with extrinsic rewards and punishment, is the least effective form of feedback. Instead, focus your feedback on ensuring that students have accurate information about their performance related to the task, about the necessary processes for completing the task, and about their self-regulation efforts to accomplish the task.

Structured Interaction for Language Development

Your students who are English learners rely on you to build opportunities for structured interactions that support their language development. Instruction for English learners must have an especially clear focus on the use of English to meet the dual goals of language and content objectives, as a reminder from Chapter 4. In addition to comprehensible input, your instruction must include opportunities to produce spoken and written English—to produce comprehensible output. By structuring interactions carefully, you help students work toward the triple goals of English acquisition, content mastery, and social growth. Figure 6.7 builds on those priorities by providing checkpoints for structured interactions for English learners.

In a sense, *every* student is an English learner. Every K–12 student should have structured opportunities to gain more powerful control over the English language, including the content-specific discourse considered "the language of the discipline." Students practice and refine their language through multiple opportunities to use it. Also, language provides a powerful vehicle for supporting content mastery. Meaningful opportunities to engage in elaborated, higher-level, subject-based conversations promote learning (Brophy, 1997). For these reasons, as you select strategies and plan and implement your lessons, ensure that you build in opportunities for students to use language frequently and purposefully. Review Figure 6.6 for supports for you in this goal by providing a variety of strategies to increase student interaction and talk. Be sure to vary the size of groups in which students interact and vary the partners regularly.

Figure 6.7	*Structuring interaction for English learners: checkpoints for sheltering instruction.*

Supportive environment	☐ Reflects and values students' cultures and community norms ☐ Encourages language experimentation ☐ Fosters motivation (downplays explicit or negative corrections and reinforces progress)
Content focused	☐ Grade-level content standards ☐ Literacy objectives in reading, writing, listening, and speaking ☐ Develops social, academic, and specialized English ☐ Focuses on a limited number of key ideas ☐ Develops key vocabulary terms systematically
Context embedded	☐ Purposeful use of language ☐ Meaningful to students ☐ Ties to students' prior knowledge and experience ☐ Plentiful use of objects and activities that provide context (realia—or real items—props, images, recordings, and demonstrations)
Comprehensible input	☐ Modified text (simplified, alternate forms) ☐ Modified speech (caretaker speech: enunciation, slower rate, matches students' level, repetition) ☐ Use of primary language for support ☐ Guides instruction (clear directions, checks for understanding, reviews, opportunities to practice) ☐ Scaffolding (appropriate support)
Increased interaction	☐ Includes teacher–student content-driven conversations ☐ Includes student–student content-driven conversations ☐ Room is arranged for interaction ☐ Various groupings (pairs, small groups) ☐ Maximizes student talk ☐ All participants foster language use (wait time, elongated responses)
Emphasis on higher-level thinking	☐ Challenging content expectations ☐ Higher-level tasks such as evaluation and analysis ☐ Teach strategies for powerful learning

Physical Movement during Classroom Instruction

Student engagement in lessons is clearly associated with student achievement (Marzano, 2007), and when energy lags, students, so does engagement. Physical movement during content instruction is one way to increase energy and engagement. Physical movement gives students an opportunity to interact with a variety of peers, to increase blood and oxygen flow to the brain (Corbin, 2008; Jensen, 2005), and to refocus during subsequent periods of sitting. Additionally, it provides students who need higher levels of physical activity to channel their energy toward content learning.

There are many simple ways to provide productive physical activity in service of student learning during your lessons, no matter the subject. From Figure 6.6 you can use stand to share, values line up, scavenger hunts, and gallery tours. Here are five more, some from Marzano (2007):

1. *Stand and Stretch:* After 10 or 15 minutes of lecture, ask students to stand and stretch. Challenge them with a flexibility test if you like.
2. *Physical Representations:* Ask students to stand and use their bodies—independently or in small teams—to represent concepts such as letters of the alphabet, angles of different measures, or abstract concepts such as *communalism*.
3. *Eye Contact Partners:* To process information, ask students to make eye contact with a peer across the room. At a signal, ask them to meet with their peer, papers

in hand, and discuss their notes, work a problem together, develop three questions about your content, or raise two plausible objections to the conclusions you drew.

4. *Appointment Partners:* Before the lesson, have students travel the room with an appointment sheet, signing up two or three partners for an hour lesson. Stop periodically during the lesson and have students meet with their appointment partners to discuss the content.

5. *Vote with Your Feet:* Have students express opinions by moving to specified areas in the room at your signal. For example, "If you think *climate change* is the most pressing issue we face, you'll come stand near the bookcase. If you think *disease* is the most pressing issue, . . ." Allow students to discuss responses with people in their area before sharing with the group and listening to alternative opinions.

Consider Human Nature and Student Needs

Finally, when we start with the students, our instruction reflects students' current physical and emotional states, and it should reflect an understanding of human nature. What you know about how humans learn and behave should be reflected in your teaching. For example, we know that people are more likely to engage in activity if they are motivated to do so. Glasser (1986) states that humans have five motivations. These include the need to be safe, belong, acquire power, be free, and have fun. Your instruction will be more successful if you ensure that those needs are met.

Other examples abound. For instance, we know that people have limited ability to take in new information and that they need opportunities to process—to think about—what they hear. As a result, you will need to vary your activities within a single lesson. We know, too, that people tend to protect themselves from public displays of ignorance; they tend to avoid intellectual risks in large groups. For that reason, you will create an environment where risk taking is the norm and students feel free to express their questions and wonderful ideas. Using strategies such as partner discussion instead of whole-class discussion can lower students' perceptions of personal risk. Another critical human need is the need to be treated as an individual deserving dignity and respect. Each of your lessons

Teaching Tip

OPENERS

Because of the **primacy effect,** people tend to remember the first things they hear and see. Make your first minutes count! Start your day or your lesson with an opener that catches students' attention and draws them into the content. Here are some samples.

- "In your small groups, make a list of four events that group members' families celebrate or honor. Each group's family must be represented. Write each event on a sentence strip and come place them on the board." (The lesson that follows is on ritual as an aspect of culture.)
- "Here's a picture of my dog. In your group, estimate how many teeth a dog has." (Or use some photos of student's pets. The lesson that follows is on digestion, which starts in the mouth.)
- "Use this string to shape an outline of Peru. We'll compare in two minutes." (The lesson that follows is on South American geography.)
- "Read these headlines about the Bay of Pigs and pick the one that is false." (The lesson that follows is on President Kennedy's foreign policy.)
- "Every generation has its protest songs. Who can name one? Now listen to this one and discuss: What are they protesting?" (The lesson that follows is on the First Amendment.)

In addition to being memorable, openers allow you make curricular links, practice past concepts, and address standards or topics that might not otherwise fit.

Head's up: There is a **recency effect,** too. People also tend to remember the *last* thing they hear. What does this tell you about how you close your lesson and day?

should incorporate human nature in order to propel learning. The Teaching Tip includes a concrete example of how you can capitalize on how human memory works by starting your lessons with a bang.

We must also recognize that at different times in their lives, humans vary predictably: They change, or develop, over time. You will need to carefully observe your students to note their current levels of physical, emotional, and cognitive development. Watch their physical skills, the ways they interpret problems, the ways they play or talk together on the school grounds, and listen to the issues they consider important. From your readings, observations, and conversations, your understanding of your students will become richer and more reliable explanations of human development.

Your instruction will not only need to take into account students' current levels of functioning, but it will also need to propel students' growth toward sophisticated ways of thinking, moving, and acting. To encourage development, teachers can provide varied experiences in rich physical and social environments and encourage students to confront their current understandings and ways of thinking and acting.

Digital technology presents resources that, when used wisely and evaluated carefully, can help teachers capture human nature and address highly specific needs. In terms of human nature, students tend to find new technologies to be motivating. Good software addresses human needs such as the need for feedback on performance, the desire to explore and test ideas, and the benefits of multimodal presentations. Given the popularity of computer gaming and its ability to motivate many people, for instance, experts in a number of fields are currently seeking ways to harness the power of video games to teach critical thinking in the schools (Federation of American Scientists, 2006). Thus, computer-based technology at its best presents content in ways that students find motivating and that are consistent with their developmental abilities.

Computer-based technology also provides avenues to more easily address a variety of student needs (Wahl & Duffield, 2005). Teacher-created Web pages, for instance, can differentiate instruction by providing assignments that differ in terms of their levels, interests, opportunities for interaction, and products (Cunningham & Billingsley, 2003). Technology can also provide strategies to address specific needs such as behavioral disorders and has good potential—when teachers plan carefully—to help students with moderate to severe disabilities find success in inclusive settings (Downing & Eichinger, 2003).

Finally, considering human needs and nature entails you looking beyond students' similarities and facing again the fact that each of your students comes to you with a unique constellation of characteristics, with an idiosyncratic set of strengths and issues. You must value all students and the contributions they will make to your life and work. When asked what you teach, perhaps your first response will be, "I teach *people*."

Parting Words

This chapter recognizes again the incredible power of a teacher to affect student success. It is through our instruction, the first paragraph of the chapter argued, that we help students reach for high expectations (ours and theirs) through goal-driven, organized opportunities to help them all engage deeply in the content and develop as individuals and communities. The six pieces of advice Connect, Organize, Model, Enrich, Interact, and consider Needs and nature (COME IN) can take you and your students a great distance as bridge builders constructing meaning and finding places in the world.

Opportunities to Practice

1. Use the form in Figure 6.8 to analyze a lesson. You have two choices:

   - Analyze a peer's lesson or one from your master teacher or mentor.

   - Analyze one of your own plans, perhaps one you wrote as you studied Chapter 5.

Figure 6.8   *Lesson analysis: COME IN.*

Advice	Evidence
Connect	To prior knowledge: To important ideas or the real world: To action: Participants:
Organize	Content: Time and activities:
Model	Draw attention to critical attributes: Use appropriate number and pace of repetitions:
Enrich	Provide rich experiences:
Interact	Strategies for active participation (verbal? written?): Sheltering instruction: Progress monitoring:
Nature and Needs	Human nature: Developmental needs:

2. Take another look at the fossils lesson in Figure 5.13. Use the lesson analysis in Figure 6.8 to analyze whether, during the lesson, I followed my own advice. Record any evidence you find and then draw a conclusion for each of the six pieces of advice.

3. Implement and practice one or more aspects of COME IN through mini-lessons. Try the following examples to get you started:

   • Create a semantic map or some other graphic organizer for a piece of text that either you or your students will read in the coming days. Use paper and pencil or one of the tools found in the 21st Century Teaching and Learning Tip, (p. 123). A concept map of this text, found in Figure 6.9 offers an example.

   • Write a daily agenda and share it with your class. Invite students' reactions and modifications.

   • Write and give a set of directions for how you want students to spend the first 5 minutes in your classroom each day. Use the advice for directions given in Teaching Tip, p. 125.

   • Model a new behavior, either for your students or for a willing friend. Select a skill or technique that is unfamiliar to your audience and, after modeling the skill, ask for feedback on which elements of your modeling were most successful.

   • Plan to use one active participation strategy (Figure 6.6) in an upcoming lesson. If you are not currently teaching, select a strategy from Figure 6.6 that could have been used during a lesson you recently experienced as a student.

   • Add one resource to your classroom materials. Consider adding to your picture file, or find or construct a model for a concept that is difficult to learn. Create a bookmarking site to collect your resource Web sites into one location. Try PortaPortal (www.portaportal.com).

   • Commit to opening an upcoming lesson with an activity that accesses students' prior knowledge. Seek to value different cultural experiences that students share. If you are not teaching now, have a conversation with a friend about an aspect of your friend's life with which you are unfamiliar. Remember to protect your friend's dignity and to appreciate what you learn.

   • Watch young students play either at recess or during unstructured class time. What is the range of differences you note in their physical development? Their social

Figure 6.9   *Concept map of K–12 classroom teaching textbook.*

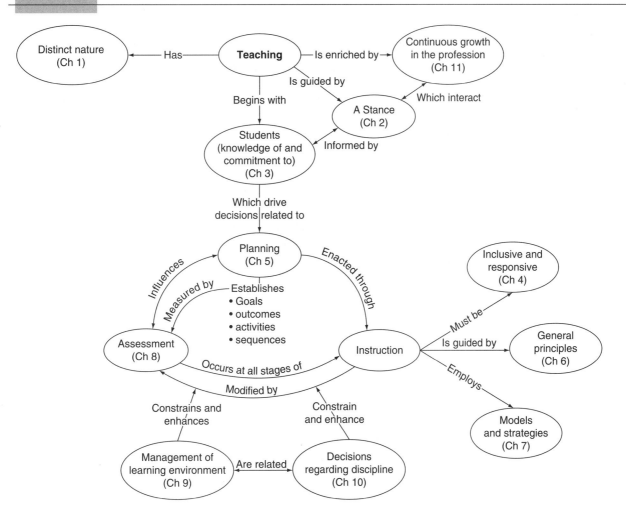

development? Their reasoning? How could you improve
your instruction by using this specific information?
If you are not teaching, try observing people at a
playground or other public place. What conclusions can
you reach about physical, social, and moral functioning?

4. Write a letter or presentation for families that describes
your principles of instruction. How will you teach
their children? Why have you chosen those principles?
Share your letter or notes with a colleague and then, if
appropriate, with the families of your students.

 Web Sites

http://jc-schools.net/
*Jefferson County Schools. Click on "Teachers" and look at
the Quick Links. The PowerPoint collection alone is worth
the trip. See the online science resources as well.*

http://www.historychannel.com
*The History Channel. Listen to historic speeches such as
Martin Luther King's "I have a dream" speech and Amelia
Earhart's discussion of the future of women in flying. I can
imagine starting class each day with "This day in History."*

http://www.loc.gov
*Library of Congress. An incredible source for American and
world history and culture.*

http://www.exploratorium.edu
*Museum of Science, Art, and Human Perception. An award-
winning site, this one will appeal to students and includes
many resources for educators. I enjoyed the mouse stem cell
video at the "Digital Library" and the "10 cool sites."*

http://www.funbrain.com
*Fun Brain. Go to the Teachers Center to find games that
provide good practice across the subjects, primarily for
elementary content. Otherwise, play online Sudoku, the only
way that wretched game should be played.*

http://nga.gov
*National Gallery of Art. Take a look at the online education
programs, NGA Kids, and the loan programs. The gallery
will send you loan materials through the U.S. mail. I have
tried it; it works!*

http://www.nationalgeographic.com
*National Geographic Society. The world at the click of a
mouse! Go to the site index for a listing of resources.*

http://enlvm.usu.edu/ma/nav/index.jsp
*National Library of Virtual Manipulatives. This site
gives mathematics manipulatives-based activities across
the math strands and grade levels. Excellent challenge
problems are provided to use in a center for early finishers
or for differentiating instruction. Good for the interactive
whiteboard, too.*

http://learning.blogs.nytimes.com/
*The Learning Network: Teaching and Learning with the
New York Times. This site includes rich resources for
teachers and learners based on the content of the* New York
Times. *Interactive activities abound.*

http://teach-nology.com/
*TeAchnology. This site is a Web portal that offers free
resources, links, and support tools to support educators in
teaching with technology. Many resources are free,
but access to some is limited to members.*

http://www.si.edu
*Smithsonian Institute. Rich resources for teachers and
students. Take a look at the ideas for podcasting.*

http://www.world-newspapers.com
*World Newspapers. This site gives news from English-
language newspapers around the world. See what they think
in Benin and Bangladesh. Picture having your students
contrast different—and international—perspectives on the
same event.*

http://epals.com
*ePals Global Community. Find e-pals for your students from
among 200 countries, or sign up to participate in digital
projects that link them with learners from around the world.*

Instructional Models and Strategies

7

Before You Begin Reading

Your prior experience with instructional models and strategies will influence what you learn from this chapter. Before you read, check your familiarity with some of Chapter 7's models and strategies by completing the following chart. Use your results to focus your efforts as you read, and check your ideas against those presented in the chapter.

Warm-Up Exercise for Instructional Models and Strategies		
Model or strategy	**Rate your level of familiarity***	**List bulleted phrases that come to mind when you think of this model or strategy.**
1. Classroom questions	1 2 3 4	
2. Direct instruction	1 2 3 4	
3. Inquiry	1 2 3 4	
4. Cooperative learning	1 2 3 4	

1 = I have no idea; 4 = I am a pro at using this strategy or model.

"Look for your choices, pick the best one, then go with it."

—Pat Riley

You have so many choices as you pick instructional models and teaching strategies to pursue student learning goals. For any lesson, how will you choose the best approach? First, consider your students. Be sure to select models and strategies that build from their strengths, engage them, and keep the content accessible to them (Grant & Sleeter, 1998; Horgan, 1995). Second, consider your goals: Overall, who are you helping students to become, and what are the logical steps to get there? There is much current interest in preparing students for this—their century—the 21st century. What sort of skills will they need to succeed in this digital, highly connected world? A review of works related to 21st-century learning yields some differences, but there are many common threads (American Association of School Librarians, 2007; Partnership for 21st Century Skills, 2009; Resnick, 2010; Sheridan-Rabideau, 2010; Tullis, 2010; Westby, 2010). In a nutshell, 21st-century success includes:

- Problem solving, decision making, and critical thinking (basing conclusions on evidence)
- Creative thinking (innovation and aesthetics)
- Collaboration (dispositions and skills for working openly and flexibly with diverse groups as both a member and a leader)
- Multiliteracies (analyzing and utilizing several symbol systems for creating and conveying meaning, including for example digital, visual, and language literacies)
- Skills for inquiring to generate new knowledge
- Dispositions for continued growth (including personal responsibility and accountability, self-assessment, and the will and desire to learn in many contexts)

Notice that this list makes different sorts of demands on students. It requires them to *know things* (like facts and language), *do things* (like inquire and use hardware and software), and *feel things* (like empathy and responsibility). Choose your instructional models and strategies so that students work toward this broad set of outcomes, moving every day closer to the competencies that will make them successful contributors to their world.

This chapter presents seven instructional models—or cohesive systems for engaging students in the content—that can serve as the basis for your instructional repertoire. But first it addresses two essential tools that cross any instructional model: information and communication technology (ICT) tools and questioning as a strategy.

Information and Communication Technology Tools

Technology, with its realistic contexts and capacity for providing engaging and reflective activity, is a perfect fit with the nature of human learning as contextual, active, social, and reflective (Driscoll, 2002). Technology resources provide a set of tools that can enrich any of the instructional models we choose and simultaneously assist students in gaining digital literacy.

Although no instructional model *requires* use of ICT, some include more prevalent use of technology. **Problem-based learning** is one example because technology can provide a multitude of resources quickly and can aid data management and analysis. **Simulations** are a second example; think of the ubiquity of virtual worlds in students' gaming lives today, and consider technology's prevalence in simulation trainings for professions such as space, flight, health care, law enforcement, and the military. ICT in simulations allows the user to virtually manipulate time, resources, and other variables without having to experience real consequences.

Computer-based simulations are becoming more prevalent in classrooms, too (e.g., O'Toole & Dunn, 2008; Peterson, 2010). Animal dissection is an example. For ethical, cost, and other reasons, some teachers and students select virtual dissections over traditional

21st Century Teaching and Learning

SOME SUPPORTS FOR INSTRUCTIONAL ICT

- American Libraries Association's Top 25 Web sites for Teaching and Learning http://www.ala.org/ala/mgrps/divs/aasl/ guidelinesandstandards/bestlist/bestwebsitestop25.cfm
- Curriki (Free, open-source materials for teachers) http://www.curriki.org/xwiki/bin/view/Main/WebHome
- Free Technology for Teachers http://www.freetech4teachers.com/
- Webquest.org http://webquest.org/index.php
- Partnership for 21st Century Skills (view the many Web-based resources associated with each learning outcome) http://www.p21.org/index.php?option=com_content&task=view&id=254&Itemid=119
- Google: Try some of the Google products such as Google Earth (http://www.google.com/earth/) for mapping experiences, Google Ocean (http://earth.google.com/ocean/) to explore the depths, and Google Art Project (http://www.googleartproject .com/) to explore museums once you're back on dry land. Try their tools like Blogger too.

animal dissections. Visit http://froguts.com and try out the frog demo as an example of virtual dissection. Despite their flaws (Allchin, 2005), evaluations of computer-based dissections indicate that students who engage in virtual dissections can learn at rates that are at least comparable to those who engage in traditional dissections (e.g., Maloney, 2002; Predavec, 2001).

Although the use of ICT figures more prominently in some instructional models than others, ICT serves as a useful tool for any instructional model you choose. For example, during a differentiated cooperative learning lesson, you might provide text at different levels (recall the Teaching Tip for leveling text, p. 96) or text that is read aloud by the computer for students with different needs. Or, in leading an inquiry lesson, you might make extensive use of the many Web 2.0 tools that present terrific options for fostering student inquiry (Berger, 2010). In short, ICT can allow you to present information engagingly and effectively, it can foster student research, it can facilitate interaction and communication (Hamm & Adams, 2002; Schultz-Zander, Buchter, & Dalmer, 2002), and it can expand the array of products students create.

Recall the Digital Divide? We have a responsibility to our students to ensure that schools level the ICT playing field so that all students build the knowledge and skills that will allow them to be powerful digital citizens. No matter the instructional model you employ, be sure to study the ICT standards relevant to your students and employ available technologies to enhance instruction and learning. See the 21st Century Teaching and Learning tip for a few useful Web sites to support you in this quest.

Questions in the Classroom

Let's say you close your eyes and are transported to a different place. How could you know, with your eyes still closed, that you are now in a K–12 classroom? Listen for talk. Hear it? And now listen for questions. Hear them? "Yes" to both means you're probably in a classroom.

The world over, classrooms are full of questions, and researchers devote much time to examining classroom questions. Why this fascination with questions? Questions are assumed to link with answers. Indeed, Aristotle postulated that knowledge itself exists in question-answer propositions: Without a question, there is no knowledge; and by generating and addressing a question to find its answer, we create knowledge. Because a major purpose of schooling is the transmission or generation of knowledge, then, questions abound. Here are six things we know from the decades of research about classroom questions:

1. *Teachers ask many, many questions.* In fact, in one estimate teachers spend one-third to one-half of their day asking questions (Black, 2001). Further, the many questions teachers ask are often not used to their best instructional advantage (e.g., Becker, 2000; Wimer, Ridenour, Thomas, & Place, 2001).

2. *Students ask very few questions* (Dillon, 1988a). Dillon (1990) reviewed elementary and secondary school studies and found that each pupil asks an average of only one question per month. Students in lower-track classrooms ask even fewer questions (Nystrand, Wu, Gamoran, Zeiser, & Long, 2003).

3. *Teachers ask questions for a variety of purposes,* such as to check for understanding, prompt thinking, maintain lesson flow, hold student attention, and punish misbehavior.

4. *Classroom questioning exchanges are typically rapid and follow a predictable pattern* (Cazden, 1986; Dillon, 1990; Good & Brophy, 1987). In the typical sequence, known as the IRE pattern, the teacher *initiates* a question, one student *responds*, and then the teacher *evaluates* the response. A new question from the teacher usually follows.

5. *Students receive different questions based on teachers' perceptions of them.* For instance, students who are perceived as of low academic ability get more factually based questions and receive less time to answer them (Cotton, 2001). A sizable group of students have zero questioning interactions in class, and a small group of "target students" (typically white males) receive a disproportionate amount of the teacher's attention in questioning (Walsch & Sattes, 2005).

6. *Research has not clearly linked the type or level of a question to the type or level of the response* (Cotton, 2001; Dillon, 1988b; Good & Brophy, 1987). Therefore, teachers cannot assume that asking higher-level questions will necessarily prompt higher-level responses-responses, or the reverse.

From this research, we can conclude that it is *teachers'* questions we hear most often in the classroom, and those questions are not always used productively. Instead, questions/ answer sessions often focus on lower-level exchanges that seek to reinforce teacher/student power differentials and a transmission model of learning. Although we use questioning with the best of intentions—to foster learning—then, we sometimes have the opposite effect. Recall the 21st-century emphasis on building the skills and dispositions of inquiry. And recall Aristotle's notion of knowledge: question + answer = knowledge. These conclusions help us reconsider classroom questioning and the environment in which it takes place. Rather than creating classrooms of *gentle inquisition*, we should strive to create contexts for grand conversations (Eeds & Wells, 1989). Teachers must create cultures where questioning occurs *with* students rather than *to* them. In such cultures, teachers foster student motivation and engagement, and they inspire and energize student learning (Caram & Davis, 2005). Figure 7.1 presents promising strategies improving our classroom questions.

Perhaps the most powerful way we can improve questioning in our classrooms is to foster students' questioning skills. Not only is the ability to inquire a life skill, current content standards demand it. For example, in California, science investigation standard for all grades, K–12, begins with: "Scientific progress is made by asking meaningful questions and conducting careful investigations. . . . Students should develop their own questions and perform investigations" (California Department of Education, 1998, p. 8). Research also supports the power of *student questions* as mechanisms that help students read with a purpose and comprehend (Taboada, & Guthrie, 2006), pursue meaningful investigations, and learn in deep and connected ways (Becker, 2000; Chin & Brown, 2000; Costa, Caldeira, Gallastegui, & Otero, 2000; Middlecamp & Nickel, 2000; Orsborn, Patrick, Dixon, & Moore, 1995; Sternberg, 1994; vanZee, Iwasyk, Kurose, Simpson, & Wild, 2001). Teachers can encourage students' questions by providing time and opportunities to ask them and by using specific strategies to support students' question formation and pursuit. More suggestions are found in the Responsive and Inclusive Teaching Tip.

Selecting Instructional Models

Look back to your work in the Before You Begin Reading section of this chapter. How many models and strategies were familiar to you? Teachers tend to teach the way they were taught. It is tempting to select strategies that feel comfortable and familiar, but part of good teaching involves taking risks and trying ideas that may, at least initially, fall beyond the

---

Figure 7.1	*Promising practices for teachers' questions.*

1. Create and maintain a culture that welcomes questions.
   - Encourage dialogue through nonverbal communication like a positive tone, nods, and smiles and by treating students' responses seriously (Caram & Davis, 2005).
   - Create a forum for student questions. An "I wonder" graffiti board hung in my middle school classroom. Students listed questions that intrigued them, and we discussed them weekly.
   - Respond with genuine enthusiasm when questions arise.
2. Plan your questions carefully.
   - Prepare your questions in advance to enhance students' opportunities to learn (Blosser, 1990; Lenski, 2001; Marzano, Pickering, & Pollock, 2001).
   - Think about your purposes for asking questions and what you will do with the results.
   - Ask authentic questions (Nystrand, et al., 2003).
3. Ask your questions equitably.
   - Ask all students to tell a partner an answer and then ask for volunteers.
   - Spread the wealth: Invite several students to answer the same question.
   - Use a random responder generator (like cards with students' names on them).
4. Slow down the pace of interaction.
   - Give students at least 3–5 seconds of wait time after you ask a question and again before you respond. This increases the length and quality of student response (Rowe, 1986; Stahl, 1984; Tobin, 1987).
   - Invite students to respond to each other's points. Teach stems such as "I have had a different experience" and "I have a point that builds on what X just said."
5. Consider *not* asking a question. Use the four S alternatives to questions instead (Dillon 1988b).
   - *Statements:* Say what you think, or reflect on what the student thinks.
   - *Student questions:* Encourage a single student to ask a question about a puzzling circumstance, or invite the class to phrase the question.
   - *Signals:* Use gestures of brief utterances ("mmm!") to refrain from taking control of the discourse.
   - *Silence:* Say nothing for a few seconds to allow others to join in (Orsborn et al., 1995).
6. Check the quality of your questioning practices.
   - Audio record your teaching and analyze it. Olson (2008) recommends listening for both the initial questions you ask and the subsequent interactions.
   - Analyze the patterns in student responses as well. Are levels of interaction equitable across student subgroups?

---

*B*ut habit rules the unreflective herd.

—*William Wordsworth*

realm of comfort. Several factors weigh into the choice of instructional model including your students and your goals (discussed earlier), the research, and the context.

No Child Left Behind requires the use of research-based instructional methods. Slavin (2003) explains "scientifically based research" studies as those that employ experimental or quasi-experimental designs with random assignment, if possible. Put simply, studies implement an instructional product or method with one randomly selected set of students then compare their progress with those of students who received a different treatment. Researchers use statistical methods to test the likelihood that differences in the groups' scores might arise by chance. Those differences that are highly unlikely are deemed "statistically significant." The federal government has established the What Works Clearinghouse to serve as a "trusted source of scientific evidence of what works in education." You can visit it at http://ies.ed.gov/ncee/wwc/. Empirical studies, then, can help you select your strategies by answering questions such as "How well has this strategy worked with other groups?" and "What happened when it was employed?"

Studies can support teachers in steering clear of untested innovations and provide evidence for schools to use as they justify their programs that receive federal funding (Slavin, 2003). They can give information about how strategies have worked with other

Inclusive and Responsive Teaching Tip

PRACTICES TO ENCOURAGE STUDENT QUESTIONS

- Use a question mailbox. Allow students to submit off-topic questions. Review the questions after class and decide whether to answer a question with the individual student or in front of class. Simms-Smith and Sterling (2006) report that this strategy helped them build solid relationships with their students and families and fostered students' inquiry.
- Teach students to ask themselves comprehension questions about what they read. This raises comprehension (Rosenshine, Meister, & Chapman, 1996).
- Require students to write "ignorance questions" (Carroll, 2001). Ignorance questions are those content-related questions to which students don't have answers. Carroll assigns ignorance questions, and they are discussed in class. Later, students contribute exam questions as well.

- Pause every 10 minutes or so during a lecture. Ask students to review and consolidate their notes. Ask small groups to think about three questions that are significant about what they are learning and to think about what makes the questions significant. Ask some to share (Donohue-Smith, 2006).
- Require students to compose and ask questions as part of their presentations, like book talks. Fishbaugh's (2008) students asked peers questions such as "deep connections" questions and "think outside the box" questions. They improved in their questioning skills over time, partly by using a rubric to analyze their own questions.
- Prompt student questions with a scenario. Middlecamp and Nickel (2005) provide their science students with a scenario and, in groups, have students devise lists of questions they should ask before taking any action. Using an intriguing object or photo to begin a lesson can serve the same purpose.

students whose characteristics and developmental levels are similar to those of your students. For instance, there is support in the research to indicate that students with low achievement (Baker, Gersten, & Lee, 2002) and learning disabilities (Swanson, 2001; Swanson & Sachse-Lee, 2000) can benefit from **direct instruction,** a strategy presented later in the chapter.

Although the effectiveness of many strategies is documented through research that links the teaching strategy with student outcomes such as increased academic achievement (e.g., Marzano et al., 2001), in general, research does not point to any one "best" instructional strategy. For instance, in comparing the practices of teachers judged highly effective in encouraging mathematics achievement and those who were not, researchers found no discrete set of practices that was held in common by the effective teachers (Smith, Hardman, Wall, & Mroz, 2004). Research is clearer in providing information related to questions such as "Under what conditions is this strategy useful?" and "For whom?"

Deductive and Inductive Strategies

One useful distinction among strategies is the point at which the major concept, skill, or understanding is stated during the lesson. Lessons that state the concept or understanding early in the lesson are deemed *deductive*. Using **deductive strategies,** the teacher states the concept or major learning promptly and then provides practice on that concept throughout the remainder of the lesson. Deductive strategies reason from the general to the specific: They present general rules, then specific examples. **Inductive strategies** do the reverse. In an inductive, or discovery, lesson the teacher provides specific data and guides students toward discerning a general rule or rules from those data. The major concept, skill, or understanding in an inductive lesson is not explicitly stated until later in the lesson, and students usually state it.

*D*eductive Strategies:
general rule → specific examples
Inductive Strategies:
specific examples → general rule

You will want to master both deductive and inductive strategies because each can address different needs and foster different kinds of student skills and attitudes. Both have been found to be effective in increasing student achievement (Marzano et al., 2001); deductive and inductive reasoning skills are both important (Partnership for 21st Century Learning, 2007). How often you use each of the contrasting strategies will depend on your own convictions about education, your learners, and the particular setting within which you find yourself.

A Sampling of Instructional Models

The remainder of this chapter presents seven instructional approaches:

1. Direct instruction
2. Inquiry training
3. Concept attainment
4. Learning cycle
5. Concept formation
6. Unguided inquiry
7. Cooperative learning

Each is presented first through a description, then a listing of lesson stages using the open-body-close format, next an example, and finally a discussion of strengths and criticisms.

Please note that the examples are meant to be streamlined so that you can quickly and clearly focus on the critical attributes of the strategy. The teachers in the sample lessons should all have conducted a good deal of work that is not evident in the brief description of their lessons. Namely, they should have studied their content and the standards and determined important ideas. They should have preassessed students to determine appropriate objectives based on their grade-level standards. They should have grouped students based on a selection of relevant concerns such as student interest, English language level, learning profile, and special needs. They should have built instruction from the ground up (remember Universal Design?) to meet these various needs. Some of the lessons include technology, and all employ the advice for instruction presented in Chapter 6 (COME IN). Note that most lessons have plentiful opportunities for students to interact and develop academic language, and most of the examples include context-embedded settings for the students to work with important ideas in realistic ways, thus sheltering instruction for English learners and attempting to enhance motivation for all students. Each of the lessons includes one or two hints on how the teacher differentiated instruction to meet student needs; these hints are meant to remind you that a myriad of instructional decisions come into play during any single lesson and that instructional strategies are employed in the context of these many decisions.

Direct Instruction

The direct instruction model is one of the most widely used and helpful deductive strategies. Direct instruction, sometimes called "explicit instruction," allows teachers to impart information or skills straightforwardly to their students and to help students master strategies for learning. The direct instruction format is flexible, and because one of the teacher's primary responsibilities is to present information, it fills a vital need in most classrooms. Particularly in today's climate, when most teachers feel pressure to help students master standards in an efficient manner, direct instruction is popular.

Description of the Direct Instruction Model In a directed lesson, the teacher systematically presents information related to an objective and carefully guides students' participation to ensure mastery. The emphasis is on efficient teacher presentation and eventual student command of a convergent set of objectives. Control over information or skills initially resides with the teacher, who relinquishes control as students first practice under the teacher's supervision and then eventually demonstrate independent mastery.

Stages of the Direct Instruction Model There are a few versions of direct instruction. In the seven-step model (Hunter, 1982), the directed lesson begins with the teacher's statement of his expectations for student behavior throughout the lesson. For example, the teacher may remind his students: "I need to see you sitting up straight and staying in your seats throughout this lesson." That statement of expectations is missing from the five-step version of the direct instruction model, but its reduced number of steps may make the five-step model easier to integrate into daily planning.

| Figure 7.2 | *Stages of the direct instruction model.* |

Open	1. *Anticipatory set*
	   a. Focus: Briefly gain the students' attention.
	   b. Objective: State the lesson's objective in student-friendly language.
	   c. Purpose: Tell students why this objective is important.

Body	2. *Input*
	
	Provide clear information related to the objective. One or more of the following may be appropriate:
	  • Present definitions.
	  • Share critical attributes.
	  • Give examples and nonexamples.
	  • Model.
	  • Check for understanding, usually through active participation devices.
	
	3. *Guided practice*
	
	Allow students to practice the objective under your supervision.
	
	Circulate to provide feedback to all learners. Employ praise–prompt–leave, wherein you give specific praise related to a student's effort, provide directions about what to improve, and then leave to check another student.

Close	4. *Closure* Observe all students performing the objective without your assistance. A performance, a brief test, or an active participation device (recall Figure 6.6) can help you check mastery. 5. *Independent practice* Have students practice the newly acquired objective on their own, often as homework or during individual work time. (Note: Some versions of the direct instruction model place independent practice before closure; however, that arrangement does not allow teachers to assess mastery before students practice alone.)

In the direct instruction lesson, the teacher provides a set for learning, gives focused input, helps the students practice, ensures that they mastered the objective, and then encourages them to practice on their own. As you read through the five stages of the model, found in Figure 7.2, remember that the model provides a mere blueprint for structuring lessons. Some teachers think of the stages as options from which they can choose, so not every lesson contains all five (or seven) steps. The length of a lesson can vary so that it may take a number of sessions to complete all of the stages. Also, through a teacher's ongoing assessment of student performance, he may decide to employ some back-and-forth movement between the lesson stages. For instance, students' performance during guided practice may indicate the need for further input rather than a move forward to closure. The steps of the direct instruction model are generic, so many teachers use this lesson format throughout the day.

A Sample Directed Lesson   Figure 7.3 presents a brief example that presents a skill, cursive letter formation.

Strengths and Criticisms of Direct Instruction   Research generally supports the effectiveness of direct instruction. In a meta-analysis reviewing more than 350 sources on direct instruction, Adams and Engelman (1996) found that direct instruction was highly effective in supporting student achievement. Slavin (1997) similarly found some forms of direct instruction to be effective in teaching basic skills, primarily in elementary-grade reading and mathematics. Baker, Gersten, and Lee (2002) also found explicit instruction effective for supporting mathematics acheivement for students with low achievement.

Immediate and specific feedback is an important part of guided practice.

Source: Scott Cunningham/Merrill.

The strength of direct instruction lies in the fact that it is carefully sequenced to provide key information, to lead the students in supervised practice, and then to finally release them for independent work after they demonstrate mastery of the content. Direct instruction provides an efficient mechanism to address one central purpose of education: to pass information and skills from one generation to the next. Direct instruction shows that even when a teacher is primarily sharing information, she can do so much more systematically than by just telling. She can carefully steer students toward control over new information or skills.

It is perhaps not surprising that direct, explicit teaching is now highly prevalent across the nation, given current interests in students' acquisition of basic literacy and mathematics skills. Also, direct instruction is comfortable for many new teachers because most directed lessons follow a predictable path, and the teacher retains control over most decisions during the lesson. Further, direct instruction exemplifies some of the principles of instruction from Chapter 6: It is highly organized, it makes use of modeling, and it is interactive.

One criticism of direct instruction offered by some (e.g., Coles, 2000) is that direct instruction's focus on the transmission of information or skills is too narrow. Because it is fully deductive, with the teacher presenting important concepts and students then practicing them, direct instruction is sometimes criticized as encouraging student passivity. The teacher retains primary control over the content, over the pace of delivery, and over selection of learning activities. Students have limited choices and control in a directed lesson. Also, direct instruction may not connect to the life of the learner or use enriched resources as readily as other instructional strategies might. It may also decrease student motivation to learn (as described by Flowers, Hancock, & Joyner, 2000).

Finally, despite its potential power, some of the research documenting the effects of direct instruction offers mixed results. This is the case in the use of directed teaching in literacy instruction today. Although some studies support the effectiveness of direct instruction (e.g., Din, 2000; Yu & Rachor, 2000), not every study does (e.g., MacIver & Kemper, 2002; St. John, Manset, Chung, & Worthington, 2001).

Figure 7.3	*A sample direct instruction lesson.*

Objective:	Third-grade students will correctly form the lowercase letter *t* in cursive.
Anticipatory set (Open)	1. Focus: "Watch me write a few words in cursive on the board and see if you can determine what thye all have in common." "You are right! They all have the cursive letter *t*."
	2. Objective: "By the time you leave for lunch, each of you will be able to write *t* in cursive."
	3. Purpose: "*T* is important because it will help with lots of other letters we will be learning to write in cursive, Learning to write *t* will make your cursive job easier. Besides, we cannot spell *Natalie* or *Xochitl* without *t*!"
Input (Body)	4. Model: "Watch me as I form the letter *t* on the board," (Teacher describes his actions as he forms five is on the board.)
	5. Critical attribute: "Notice that the vertical part of *t* is closed, not like *t*. Also notice that I cross the *t* from left to right."
	6. Check for understanding: Teacher draws incorrect *t*s and correct ones. He allows students to exclaim, "No! No!" or "Yes!" as he models, checking whether students are aware of the critical characteristics of the letter. "You seem ready to try your own *t*s! Let's go!"
Guided practice	7. Students use wipe boards with dry erase markers to make *t*s. The teacher selected these materials instead of pencils because he has a student with weak grip strength. Students like wipe boards better anyway.
	• Teacher criculates and checks each student's progress. "Raymond, you are holding your pencil just right! Remember that *t* doesn't have a loop. Close it up. I will be back to check on you soon."
	• Teacher has a pen with an adaptive grip ready if his student needs it.
Closure (Close)	8. "I have seen many excellent *t*s! We will do one more for the record. Please take out a piece of scratch paper. Write your name at the top and then form your best *t* for me. Make three or four *t*s if you like!" (Teacher can collect and check the slips later or circulate now and mark them as correct.)
Independent practice	9. If the students do not demonstrate mastery during closure, teacher will provide additional instruction. If the objective is mastered, teacher tells students "Aha! Remarkable *t*s! Please practice your *t*s on the whiteboard or in the salt box during center time today."

Given its strengths and weaknesses, when, if at all, will you use direct instruction? Direct instruction may be helpful when (1) it is important that all students master the same objectives to a similar degree, (2) you are interested in efficient use of time, (3) it may not be safe for students to discover concepts, and (4) students start from similar background experiences.

As a practical indicator of when it may be appropriate to use direct instruction, watch for telltale signs. When you have the urge to begin a lesson with the words "Please open to page 42" and then march your students straight through some exercises, please think *direct instruction*. Your students will almost certainly have a higher chance of success if you teach to the text's objective but structure your lesson using stages of the directed lesson. The Teaching Tip will help you use direct instruction during lessons and other times too.

Teaching Tip

DIRECT INSTRUCTION QUICK START

Often you need to teach a skill on the spot. For example, two students need to know how to set the low hurdles before a track meet. Don't just *show* them. Use *direct instruction* to make sure they've got it. After a few tries, you will internalize the method and be able to use it naturally even without a lesson plan. Use this flow:

✔ I do it.
✔ I check that you understand.
✔ We do it.
✔ You show me.
✔ You've got it! You do it.

Inductive Teaching

Inductive teaching presents a stark contrast to direct instruction. Through inductive methods, students create or discover important ideas by interacting with concrete materials or other data sources and their peers. When students analyze a poem, look for patterns in population distributions, or discover the identity of a mystery powder, they inquire.

Instead of stating the learning explicitly at the beginning of the lesson, during inductive lessons, the teacher guides students to interact with data, materials, and each other so that they discover the ideas. Additionally, whereas direct instruction focuses primarily on the *product,* or outcome, to be gained, inductive strategies also focus on the *processes* by which knowledge is formed. Reviewing state and national student content standards in science and social studies demonstrates that students literate in these subject matters not only have mastery of a body of information, they also can use the methods by which scientists and social scientists build knowledge. They can formulate questions, address their questions through appropriate methodologies, collect information, analyze it, and draw appropriate conclusions. Students learn these processes by using them, and inductive instruction provides an appropriate vehicle. The Teaching Tip provides an example of an inductive strategy, photo analysis, that can be used quickly and helps students to inquire into what they see.

Inductive methods can be convergent or divergent in nature. In convergent, or guided, approaches students are expected to discover or infer a single concept or generalization. In divergent, or unguided, approaches, the number of concepts or generalizations to be formed is greater.

Although many inductive approaches exist, unfortunately, most of us have had limited experience with inductive instruction as students. This chapter presents a variety of inductive strategies. The first three are highly convergent, and the last two are less so.

The art of teaching is the art of assisting discovery.

—*Mark Van Doren*

Teaching Tip

INQUIRY QUICK START

Use inquiry in your openers to start your day or lesson and hook those curious minds. One inquiry quick start is photo analysis (Guillaume, Yopp, & Yopp, 2007). Try it:

1. Find an intriguing photo that represents a current event or your content. Use one from home, the newspaper, your textbook, or the Internet. Try searching "photo of the day" or "photo in the news."
2. Display the image for the students.
3. Ask students to make careful observations of it: "What do you notice? What is in this quadrant?"
4. Ask students to make inferences about the photo: "When was it taken? Who are the people? What's the story?"
5. Tie it to your lesson. Come back to it at the end of the lesson and allow students to revise their inferences.

Inquiry Training

Suchman's (1962) inquiry training assists students in asking questions that help them move from the observation of facts to the development of theories. This strategy's power resides both in the way that it capitalizes on students' natural curiosity—the need to know—and in the fact that it puts students in the questioner's seat. Usually students in classrooms are expected to *answer* the questions, not to *ask* them. Asking a question can propel learning.

Description of the Inquiry Training Model   In an inquiry training lesson, the teacher presents a phenomenon, called a discrepant event, that piques curiosity. In a *discrepant event,* there is a mismatch between what students expect to happen, based on prior experience, and what actually does happen. For instance, a teacher may drop two full,

Students analyze data and draw conclusions through inductive instruction.

Source: Barbara Schwartz/Merrill.

An unusual artifact can spark students' curiosity and provide a discrepant event to begin a lesson.

Source: Parvin/Texas Memorial Museum/Pearson Education-Corporate Digital Archive.

unopened cans of soda into an aquarium. Students look puzzled when one floats and the other sinks (the floater is a diet drink, lacking sugar, which adds to the other can's density). For a discrepant event, I once filled a half-liter clear water bottle with water and baby oil. Although both liquids were clear, when students dropped food color into the bottle, the dye fell through the oil and dispersed in the water that rested in the bottom half of the bottle. A sample discrepant event in language arts might be a poem with no capitalization or punctuation. In social studies, it might be an unusual cultural artifact.

After presenting the discrepant event or stimulus, the teacher invites students to ask yes–no questions to develop explanations for what they observe. Through their questions, students develop and test causal connections to explain the discrepant event.

| Figure 7.4 | *Stages of the inquiry training model.* |

Open	1. Present a discrepant event or puzzling situation.
	2. Describe the procedure: Students are to form explanations for what they see by asking questions that you can answer with yes or no.
Body	3. Allow for questions that *verify* what events and conditions students observe. Forestall causal questions until the next stage.
	4. Allow for questions that allow children to *identify relevant variables* and *test their hypotheses.*
Close	5. Guide students to state the explanations they have formulated.
	6. Prompt students to analyze their inquiry strategy.

Suchman developed his model for science instruction, but as long as a teacher can locate relevant discrepant events or stimuli, inquiry training can be used across subject areas. It is useful for students of many ages, though younger children and English learners need extra support in formulating yes–no questions.

Stages of the Inquiry Training Model Figure 7.4 lists the stages of Suchman's inquiry training, moving through the presentation of the discrepant event through two stages of questioning: verification and hypothesis-testing questioning. As you read over the stages of inquiry training, please bear in mind that inquiry training is more than a guessing game. If a student states the correct explanation early on, resist the temptation to scold the student for "giving away" the answer. Treat the student's proposed explanation as yet another tentative explanation that needs to be verified through empirical testing. The social atmosphere is important; encourage students to listen to each other.

A Sample Inquiry Training Lesson Figure 7.5 relates an inquiry training lesson I have used with enthusiastic students of a variety of ages.

Concept Attainment

Recall that inductive teaching methods foster students' ability to discern patterns, impose structure, and discover important ideas by working with concrete data. The ability to categorize information is central to these processes of discovery. Categorization, or grouping items into classes, serves a number of important functions: It reduces the complexity of our environments, it helps us identify individual objects, it makes learning more efficient, it helps us make decisions without the need for testing every object's properties, and it allows us to relate and order classes of events (Bruner, Goodnow, & Austin, 1960). Further, Bruner et al. note that our understanding of the world is not purely objective. Our systems for processing new information are shaped by the ways of thinking in which we are immersed: "The categories in terms of which man sorts out and responds to the world around him reflect deeply the culture into which he is born. . . . His personal history comes to reflect the traditions and thought-ways of his culture, for the events that make it up are filtered through the categorical systems he has learned" (p. 10). The concept attainment model (Bruner et al., 1960) makes categorization schemes explicit and guides students to consider information conceptually toward the aim of categorizing information meaningfully.

Description of the Concept Attainment Model One object at a time, students observe a set of objects or examples, each deemed by their teacher as belonging—or not belonging—to a particular set. As the teacher presents more examples, students make hypotheses about the rule for grouping. They test their hypotheses on additional objects,

Figure 7.5	*A sample inquiry training lesson.*

Objectives:	Fifth-grade students will state the necessary components of an electric circuit. Students will demonstrate the ability to test cause–effect relationships by asking relevant yes–no questions (Guillaume, Yopp, & Yopp, 1996).

Open	Preview for English learners
	• Before the lesson, teacher calls her English learners to the side of the room and allows them to handle two toy chicks that chirp only when a circuit is completed by simultaneously touching both terminals on their feet to an electrical conductor, such as skin or metal.
	• She shows them a written sign, "What makes the chick chirp?" and reads it aloud as she points and uses facial expressions to support her message.
	• The three students who share a language talk among themselves excitedly in Spanish. Her one Chinese student works with her, asking for terms and trying things out.
	1. To open the lesson: Teacher presents the toy chick to the class.
	   • The terminals are two metal rings embedded in the toy's feet.
	   • Students chatter and express curiosity about the toy.
	2. Teacher states the task: "Your job is to ask me questions that I can answer with yes or no so that you can determine what makes the chick chirp."

Body	3. Students ask questions to verify what they see and interpret as the problem.
	   • Sample questions include "Is there a battery in the chick?" and "Are you flipping a switch to make it chirp?"
	   • She allows students to discuss their questions in partner pairs, providing specific support to her English learners who will benefit from talking with each other before speaking to the class, and for her students who need more time to process ideas.
	   • When students ask questions that test causal relationships ("Are you completing an electric circuit?"), teacher asks them to save those questions for a few minutes.
	   • When children ask questions that cannot be answered with yes or no, teacher asks them to rephrase, enlisting help from peers as necessary.
	   • For newer English learners, the teacher takes their utterances and rephrases them, into yes/no questions. She points to the written version of question as well.
	   • A family volunteer in the class records the students' questions on the board for all to see.
	4. Teacher asks for questions that move into the phase of identifying relevant variables and exploring hypotheses about cause–effect relationships.
	   • For instance, "Does it have anything to do with the heat in your hand?"
	   • When students hypothesize about the materials necessary to complete the circuit, teacher responds with actions: She places the chick on metal, then wood, and finally glass so that students can see the answers to their questions.

Close	5. Teacher directs students to talk in groups about their explanations. She requires each group member (including English learners) to make a contribution, even briefly. She entertains new questions that arise from group discussions.
	6. In their groups, students write an explanation for the chirping chick on sentence strips.
	   • They post and examine the explanations: An electrical circuit requires a power source, a conductor, and in this case a load (the chirping mechanism).
	7. The class analyzes its inquiry strategy and then applies its knowledge by exploring electrical circuits with batteries, foil, and lightbulbs.
	   • She pushes her advanced learners (including GATE students and ones who excelled earlier in this lesson) to build parallel circuits after demonstrating series circuits.

*Britni at interactive
whiteboard, seed game*

Britni Hong

| Figure 7.6 | *Stages of the concept attainment model.* |

	Before the lesson, select a concept or rule and collect a wide variety of examples and nonexamples of your concept.
Open	1. To build interest, briefly display some of the items. (Items can vary. Examples include words, objects, pictures, and places on a map.) 2. Introduce the students' task: to discover your rule for grouping.
Body	3. One at a time, present the items that serve as examples or counterexamples of your grouping. State whether each item belongs or does not belong to your group, perhaps by calling each a *yes* or a *no*. 4. Continue presenting examples and counterexamples, providing opportunities for students to share their hypothesized rules and discuss them with their peers. Guide students' discussion to be certain that their proposed rules conform with all the data you have presented. Provide examples that challenge students' erroneous rules.
Close	5. When most students have induced the rule, furnish a final chance for consensus. Allow the rule to be stated aloud for the class. 6. Invite students to explore further examples or to group the data according to a criterion they select. 7. Process the activity by making observations about the process and content as appropriate.

and, finally, the rule (or concept) for grouping is induced. In the photo, Britni is leading The Seed Game. Using the interactive whiteboard, Britni leads her audience to sort examples of seeds, placing the photos onto the left black rectangle or on to the right. Eventually her students correctly conclude that Britni's rule is how seeds travel: seeds in one group travel by wind; seeds in the other group travel by animal. The students attained the concept of modes of seed dispersal.

Stages of the Concept Attainment Model   Figure 7.6 delineates the stages of the concept attainment model. Notice that the teacher presents one item at a time. It may be necessary to change the order of presentation or to gather new items to challenge the students' emerging hypotheses. Occasionally students discover a rule that is accurate given the data they observe but is not the rule or concept you meant to illustrate. Be certain to provide many different-looking or different-sounding examples of your concept so that students can focus on the critical attributes of the rule. If students induce a rule other than the one you planned, you may need to provide additional examples that contradict their rules.

A Sample Concept Attainment Lesson Figure 7.7 presents a sample lesson using the concept attainment format.

Learning Cycle

The learning cycle approach is inductive in that it moves from firsthand experiences to well-formulated understanding of the content and real-world application. It is based on constructivist learning theory that defines learning as both the process and the result of questioning and interpreting, the application of thought processes and information to build and improve our understandings, and the integration of current experiences with past experiences (Marlowe & Page, 1998). The learning cycle model differs from other inductive approaches in that the first and last stages of the lesson must be based in real-world or realistic experiences. The learning cycle approach can level the playing field by ensuring that all students have firsthand experiences to build background knowledge and deepen content knowledge. This is especially important for English learners and for students whose background experiences may be limited (Guillaume, Yopp, & Yopp, 1996). It also can foster the development of content vocabulary (Spencer & Guillaume, 2006).

Description of the Learning Cycle Model A learning cycle begins with a real-world problem or event that piques students' interests and fuels one or more questions for exploration. A personal story, discrepant event, current event, toy, poem, or thoughtful question from a student or the teacher can all serve to engage the students. Next, students interact with data sources and concrete materials to explore the problem or question(s). Exploration builds background knowledge, from which more abstract understandings arise. After students have firsthand experiences the teacher begins to formally help students to systematize their knowledge, label concepts, and generate explanations. Finally, students apply their newly formulated knowledge to a similar real-world problem or event.

Stages of the Learning Cycle Model Different versions of the learning cycle approach to planning and instruction vary only slightly in the number of stages they propose, typically between three and five. Figure 7.8 depicts the phases of the learning cycle using one popular version of the model. This version of the learning cycle embeds assessment in each phase of the lesson. Another useful version of the learning cycle model is the five E approach: engage, explore, explain, extend, and evaluate.

A Sample Learning Cycle Lesson The lesson in Figure 7.9 is a visual arts lesson for high school students that follows the learning cycle model. Notice that a single lesson can last more than one day and that it can make use of many kinds of resources. In following the learning cycle model, the lesson begins with a real-world phenomenon to engage the students (discussion of a painting), explores ideas related to that phenomenon (examination of the use of color in many other works), develops concepts surfaced through the exploration phase (color concepts), and ends with a connection back to the real world (creation of students' own works that make use of what they learned through the lesson, principles of color use).

Concept Formation

Hilda Taba's (1967) strategy allows learners to build new ideas by categorizing specific pieces of data and forging new connections among those data.

Figure 7.7   *A sample concept attainment lesson.*

Objectives:	Kindergarten students will distinguish between examples and nonexamples of a triangle. Students will group items based on relevant attributes.
	Preparation: The concept attainment strategy is new to the teacher, so he conducts Internet research to read up on it. He finds a particularly helpful set of materials at the Georgia Department of Education Web site (http://www.glc.k12.ga.us/pandp/critthink/ conceptattainment.htm).
Open	1. "Come sit with me here on the rug and have a look at some of the things I brought today." • Teacher draws two students near him. His student with a visual impairment sits on his left. His student who is physically very active sits on his right. • Teacher takes turn allowing first the student on his right and then the one on his left to pull items from a bag. • All students are allowed to handle and comment on a few of the items.
	2. "Some of these items are members of my club, and some are not. Your job today is to discover the name of my club. Then we will know which items can join and which cannot." 3. "I will place the members of my club in this hoop of yarn. Items that are not members will go outside the hoop. Ready?" He guides the hand of his student with the visual impairment over the yarn hoops. He speaks soothingly to refocus the student on his right who is beginning to bounce.
Body	4. Teacher shows one item at a time, placing it in the hoop if it is a triangle and outside if it is not. He provides plenty of examples and nonexamples that vary not only in the number of sides and angles but also in color, size, and texture. 5. After presenting five or six items, teacher encourages the children to guess where he will place subsequent items and guides them to explicitly state their hypotheses: "Whisper to your neighbor what you think is the name of my club." Teacher helps students test their hypotheses by examining the present examples and by adding others.
Close	6. When most students have demonstrated knowledge of the "triangle club" rule, teacher invites students to state it aloud: "Okay, club experts, what is the name of my club? Everyone, say it aloud on three. One . . . two . . . three!" "Triangles" students shout. 7. "Who can look around the room to find a member of my club? Who can find a nonmember?" As most students look around, teacher provides three more samples for the students at his side and for two others who especially like to work with the teacher. 8. Students share examples and nonexamples they have found. 9. "Let me see if I understand the rules about triangles, then. Does size matter? Does color? Texture?" (All: "No!") "What matters about a triangle is that it has exactly three sides and exactly three angles." 10. "After recess, I will place these objects in a center so that you can think of your own club using the objects." Teacher includes different types of triangles such as right, isosceles, and equilateral triangles, knowing that some students will be ready to informally examine the size of their angles. 11. Extension: Students are so excited by the "game" of sorting objects into clubs that the teacher creates a few drag-and-drop concept attainment Web pages for other concepts the students are studying. • They try the activities during center time in class, and they log on at night and play the games with their families too. • Some parents report playing the "club game" while they are waiting at the doctor's office or for the bus.

Figure 7.8   *Stages of the learning cycle.*

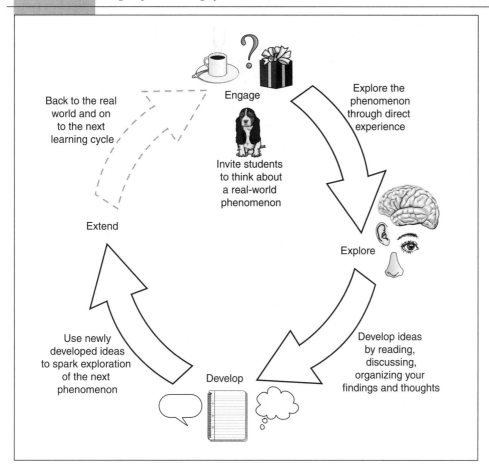

Open	1. Engage: Provide a brief real-world phenomenon, an object, or an issue that engages students' interest in the topic and fuels one or more questions for investigation.
	• Listen carefully to determine students' prior knowledge related to the topic and to expose their questions.
	• Do not provide explanations of phenomena yet.
	• Make a list of students' questions.
Body	2. Explore: Provide materials so that students engage in firsthand experience with the issue under study.
	• Students begin to address their questions from the prior phase.
	• They begin to generate new concepts and questions. Observe students carefully to determine emerging concepts and vocabulary.
	3. Develop: Systematically develop the concepts that arise during the exploration phase.
	• Supply vocabulary terms appropriate given students' experiences.
	• Provide direct presentations of the information and reading experiences as necessary so that students refine their understanding.
Close	4. Apply: Present a new problem or situation that can be addressed given students' newly formed understandings.
	• Connect to the real world.
	• Use the real-world connection as the starting point for the next learning cycle.

A sample learning cycle lesson.

Objectives:	Tenth-grade students will analyze works of art to determine principles of color use. Students will create their own work of art that uses color to convey a message.

Engage
(Open)
	1. With zydeco, Cajun, or jazz music playing in the background, the teacher shares a brightly rendered watercolor painting from New Orleans.
	2. "Years ago I took my favorite vacation and bought this painting. Looking at this painting, where do you think I went?"
	  • She supports the students' guesses by asking for their evidence. "What about the picture makes you say, 'Europe'?"
	  • They discuss, among other student-generated topics, the architecture portrayed in the painting.
	3. Once the students conclude that the painting depicts a courtyard in New Orleans, teacher asks students to examine how the artist used color to capture the sense of energy, cultural fusion, and joy that many people associate with the city.
	4. To set the stage for exploration, teacher states that artists throughout time and all over the world use color to convey or enhance the message or mood of their works.

Explore
(Body)
	5. Teacher sets the task: "I reserved the laptops for tomorrow. Your job will be to go on a virtual tour of museums around the world and download examples of visual art that use color in a variety of ways. You will share your examples with the class."
	6. The next day, the students boot up the laptops and connect to the Internet for their tour. It launches with a visit to the National Gallery of Art (http://www.nga.gov).
	  • The teacher supplies URLs of other museum sites, and in pairs, students find examples of art that vary in their use of color to convey mood and message.
	  • When permitted, students print out copies of the art and create a class gallery of the varied works. Or they leave the image displayed on their screens. Another option is to load images into a google.docs presentation for a virtual gallery.
	  • Teacher and students add reproductions such as posters of famous works and their own works to the gallery as well.
	  • A few students have created and shown their own works at festivals. These are added to the gallery.

Develop
(Body)
	7. The following day, teacher commends the students on their diligent searching: "We have created quite the collection of works in our class gallery. Very impressive! Your next task is to study all the works to determine themes in how color is used."
	8. Students tour the class gallery, grouping works that create similar moods or convey similar messages. They test the hypotheses they formed in viewing works they found with their partner on the virtual tour by studying the larger set of works found by their classmates.
	9. The day ends with the students writing and submitting journal entries on their tentative conclusions about the use of color.
	  • One student writes, for example, "When artists use a subdued palette, it expresses a calmer message. Mixing black with the colors adds an air of sadness to the work."
	  • Two students, including one with a developmental delay, dictate their entries into the computer near the door that has speech recognition capacities. They print out their work and take it home to practice reading it.
	10. That night, the teacher studies the students' entries and reproduces some of their most telling findings using presentation software instead.
	11. The next day, the teacher lectures on the use of color, drawing from the concepts and tentative generalizations about color students recorded in their journals.
	  • She introduces terms such as "hue," "value," and "saturation" to formalize what the students stated informally in their entries.
	  • For homework, students read from their text a chapter on the use of color.
	  • Two or three who experience reading difficulties read a compact disc version, in which the teacher has highlighted key ideas and terms.

Apply (Close)	12. Students select a life event that evoked strong emotions from them.
	• They create a work using a medium of their choice and use color to convey their intended emotions.
	• Students plan a gallery showing, including background music related to their works. Families (and other supporters) attend the lively showing.
	• Students begin to notice, now, differences in artists' use of *line* in addition to color. Teacher begins to think about line as the next element for study.

Description of the Concept Formation Model   Often deemed "list–group–label," concept formation should increase students' ability to process information. Students begin by developing extensive lists of data related to a topic or question. Next, they group the data based on criteria they select, and they develop labels for their groups. The labels of the groups convey a concept or generalization. Oftentimes students are asked to re-sort data in different ways. Lessons often conclude with students using the information in a new way, such as by composing an explanatory paragraph.

Concept formation can be used to induce one particular concept or can be used in a divergent manner so that a number of accurate concepts or generalizations result. It has a wide range of applications. One is to consolidate concepts at the end of a lesson, as in the Teaching Tip.

Figure 7.10   *Stages of the concept formation lesson.*

Open	1. Challenge the students with a question about the topic that will encourage them to generate an extensive list.
Body	2. *List:* In full view, record students' contributions in the form of a list. Some teachers use sentence strips, large cards, or the interactive whiteboard.
	3. *Group:* Invite the students to place similar objects together. Questions such as "What goes together?" can elicit grouping.
	4. *Label:* Ask students to label their new groups: "What can we call this group?"
Close	5. Call students' attention to new concepts that arise from their groupings.
	6. Categorize new pieces of information according to the students' system and invite them to regroup and label the information.
	7. You may require students to use the information in some way, such as through a writing or retelling assignment.

Stages of the Concept Formation Model   Figure 7.10 lists the stages employed in the concept formation lesson. The Teaching Tip gives some ideas for a concept formation quick start.

A Sample Concept Formation Lesson   Figure 7.11 gives a concept formation lesson I used with second-graders. In this lesson, students generated many words related to the topic *water*. They sorted the words into groups that shared certain characteristics. I was surprised that students initially grouped the words according to **linguistic** clues rather than by **semantic** clues. With prompting, students regrouped words in a few different ways to discover that water can be both helpful and harmful to humans. Finally, they wrote books about how we interact with water.

Teaching Tip

CONCEPT FORMATION QUICK START

Use a mini-concept-formation activity to close your lesson or as a review. Here's how.

1. Choose some content terms, perhaps between 5 and 10. Remember your vocab cards from the Teaching Tip (p. 77)? Use those. Or have the students pick the words. Be quick.
2. Put the words on cards or large sticky notes and display them. Use magnets to hold them to the board if you wrote cards. Or display them on the interactive whiteboard.
3. Have students group them. Which words go together? Regroup them in a different way.
4. Ask students to name the groups, then use the group labels in a sentence.
5. Alternatives: Students can sort cards with small groups at their seats. Or you can hand each student a card and have the students move around the room to form groups.

Figure 7.11   *A Sample Concept Formation Lesson*

Objectives:	Second-grade students will form two accurate statements about the interrelationship of humans and water.
	Students will group data in rule-governed ways.
Open	1. "Class, come sit with me and listen to my rain stick." Students join teacher and listen intently as she turns the column once, then twice.
	• They chat briefly about their experiences with similar instruments.
	• One student visited family in Chile, birthplace of the rain stick.
	• "I brought my rain stick in today because we are beginning to study weather."
	2. "Let's begin today by writing down as many water words as we know. I will write the words here on index cards."
Body	3. *List:* The class creates an extensive list of water words. Examples include *evaporation, puddle,* and *mudslide.* When the students' listing slows down, the teacher prods their thinking: How about frozen water?
	4. *Group:* Teacher calls the class of 20 to the carpet, and in their circle they lay out all the index cards that list their words. "That's quite a list, my friends! Now let's think about putting some of the cards together in groups. Who sees some cards that go together?"
	Teacher jokes with students, suggesting that they sit on their hands, because each is so eager to group the cards. She makes a note to herself that making individual or partner cards may work even better than class cards for grouping. Students group words into those that include *-ation* within them and those that do not.
	Teacher praises the ingenuity of their grouping and then asks students to regroup them another way. Students continue grouping until each card is with others. Teacher encourages students to collapse groups and to consider cross-groupings.
	5. *Label:* Students dictate the names of the groups they have generated, and the teacher writes group names on new cards, which she places near the three groups: *Ways water helps us, Ways water can be dangerous,* and *Other water words.*
Close	6. Teacher leads students to draw conclusions about the groups they have generated. Students conclude that humans interact with water in many ways, both helpful and harmful.
	7. Teacher provides materials and instructions for students to make water pop-up books that contain two accurate sentences of ways that humans interact with water. Later, students read their books aloud to their sixth-grade buddies.
Extension:	Because the students were so eager to sort the cards, teacher knows students need more opportunities to work with the words. She transfers the words to a computer file and each day for the next week students begin the day by coming up to the interactive whiteboard and dragging and dropping terms into new groups.

Unguided Inquiry

Through unguided inquiry, students address a problem or issue through firsthand experience with plentiful materials and information sources. The teacher serves as a facilitator instead of as a presenter. Many possible answers or solutions may be generated. Glasgow (1997) touts the contemporary relevance of unguided inquiry, which he calls **problem-based learning**:

> In most professions, knowledge is dynamic and requires current understanding for optimal success with contemporary problem solving. Information, concepts, and skills learned by the students are put into memory associated with the problem. This improves recall and retention when the students face another problem . . . Problems actively integrate information into a cognitive framework or system that can be applied to new problems. (p. 42)

Problem-based learning involves small groups of students locating and using rich resources (often with technological ones playing a prominent role) to solve a real or realistic problem. For example, first-graders may need to determine the best pet for their class (Lambros, 2002). Secondary students may need to address a moral dilemma problem, such as suggesting a course of action for a doctor who was just called by a parent confessing that the parent broke into the pharmacist's shop for drugs a child needed to survive (Slavin-Baden & Major, 2004). Problem-based learning and other forms of unguided inquiry can be implemented at all grade levels, in both general and special education settings, and across the curriculum (Audet & Jordan, 2005).

Description of the Unguided Inquiry Model   Unguided inquiry can be used in any subject matter through which students can personally experience a problem and then work firsthand with data to address (and perhaps solve) that problem. In social studies, for example, students may frame the problem of homelessness in the local community either by experiencing homelessness themselves or by observing others who are homeless. They work to define the problem by formulating a question, to investigate the issue through reading and interviewing, and then to generate possible solutions. Their efforts may lead them to fund-raising or other social action opportunities. In mathematics, students may design survey studies that allow them to collect, analyze, and present data and then act on their findings.

Although unguided inquiry leads students to gain understanding of disciplinary content, the teacher may not be able to determine in advance which understandings will be developed. Rather than presenting information directly, the teacher provides for a rich environment and gently guides students' efforts to discover relevant information and address the problem productively.

Stages of the Unguided Inquiry Model   Figure 7.12 gives stages of the unguided inquiry model.

Figure 7.12   *Stages of the unguided inquiry model.*

Open	1. Present or capitalize on a problem that has multiple solutions and that captures the interests of students.
Body	2. Guide students in clearly stating the problem, perhaps by formulating a question.
	3. Lead a discussion of methods that may allow students to address the problem. Set the guidelines for study. Provide access to a variety of appropriate resources, including concrete materials and information sources.
	4. Monitor students as they employ their methods, helping students to revise and refine their methods as appropriate.
	5. Encourage students to take action based on findings, when appropriate.
Close	6. Direct students to draw conclusions regarding (a) the problem and (b) the processes of investigation.

A Sample Unguided Inquiry Lesson Figure 7.13 recounts an unguided inquiry lesson, inspired by Project WILD's (2001) lesson, "No Water Off a Duck's Back." Students of all ages participate thoughtfully in the lesson, creating and cleaning up the *simulation* of oil spills.

Strengths and Criticisms of Inductive Strategies

Each of us probably has a story that illustrates the old saying "Experience is the best teacher." Experience allows us to form rules that can be useful in guiding our behavior and solving related problems in the future. Most of us report that when we generate the rules by distilling experience rather than simply by reciting the rules we have heard stated for us,

Figure 7.13 *A sample unguided inquiry lesson.*

Objectives:	Seventh-grade students will describe useful techniques for cleaning oil spills and state at least one possible drawback of each technique. Through a closing discussion or product of their choice, students will demonstrate the ability to clearly define a problem, to employ an appropriate method, and to analyze their results.
Open	1. Teacher projects an Internet image from a news magazine of an oil-soaked bird and leads students to conclude that an oil spill at sea was responsible for the bird's condition. 2. Using Inspiration (http://www.inspiration.com), the class together begins to create a semantic map on oil spills. Students move into small heterogeneous groups and continue adding to a small-group version of the map. 3. Teacher focuses students' attention on the portion of the map that lists a few cleanup methods: "Let's think about this part of the map. You already know some ways that specialists attempt to clean up spills at sea." 4. Teacher shows a clear container with water and vegetable oil meant to simulate an oil spill. "Here I have my own spill."
Body	5. Teacher directs pairs of students to phrase the problem for investigation as a question. Students share their questions aloud and revise based on peers' ideas. 6. Students spend one period reviewing books, encyclopedias, newspapers, and Internet materials to study cleanup methods. The teacher quietly assigns each student to a particular source given information on students' reading level, but she allows them to read their choice of additional materials as well. Materials include sources in Russian and Korean to provide primary language support for her English learners. 7. The next day, students bring in some cleanup materials and place them with those gathered by the teacher. Materials include coffee filters, detergents, soaps, sponges, eyedroppers, and paper towels. 8. In pairs, students devise and record a plan for cleaning up the vegetable oil spill. Partner groups exchange plans and ask each other a few questions to troubleshoot before spill cleanup begins. 9. Before distributing materials, the teacher quietly pulls two students with marked behavior difficulties to her. She makes each of them manager for particular materials and reinforces the rules for handling other materials appropriately. 10. With plans in hand, each pair creates its own oil spill using one tablespoon of vegetable oil in a pan of water. Students implement their plan to clean up the slick. Teacher monitors, prompting students to work carefully and to record their efforts in specific detail. She attempts to enrich their thinking through strategies such as visits to other student groups for observation.
Close	11. As testing concludes, teacher guides students in constructing a class chart of cleanup methods and their potential usefulness. The class also discusses drawbacks of its methods and reflects on how its future tests may be improved by the strategies students attempted in this inquiry. 12. Students choose a format to share what they learned and to evaluate their success as problem solvers. Teacher encourages intensely curious students to conduct future investigations on cleanup methods for oil spills on land.

learning is more potent and tends to be longer lasting. Inductive strategies capitalize on the tremendous power of discovery learning.

Additionally, one widely professed purpose of education is to foster students' ability to think independently, to find order and patterns in the huge amount of information that confronts us daily. Inductive approaches are useful for that purpose because they provide students with opportunities to frame problems, to select appropriate methodologies, and to analyze their reasoning. To expand students' ability to face problems and complicated issues, inductive strategies focus on the processes of questioning, gathering information, and learning, in addition to content mastery. Recall that the skills and dispositions necessary for the generation of new knowledge are considered essential for the 21st century.

Finally, inductive strategies make use of many principles from Chapter 6: They connect easily with the lives of the learners by using student interest and frequently allowing for some student choice in the methods of study and the pacing of the lesson. Inductive approaches address human nature and needs by sparking and sustaining curiosity and by encouraging students to be puzzlers and problem solvers. Further, inductive strategies often make use of a wide range of information sources and real-world materials, which results in an enriched learning environment. When students engage in unguided inquiry into problems they themselves experience, they have the important opportunity to question existing conditions and to work on improving one piece of the world.

Inductive strategies can be criticized for a number of reasons. First, because student input can so dramatically shape the direction of the lesson—not only its pacing but in many cases its content as well—it can be difficult for the teacher to predict a lesson's content outcomes. Releasing partial control to students can be unsettling to teachers because they must approach content and time decisions with greater flexibility, especially in divergent lessons. Whereas the outcomes in a directed lesson are clear at the outset, divergent inductive lessons such as unguided inquiry result in multiple generalizations. Some teachers feel that this divergence places heavy demands on their own stores of knowledge.

The divergent, somewhat unpredictable nature of certain inductive methods also worries some teachers because of the pressure they feel to systematically treat a large body of content information in short periods of time. Focusing study on relevant, real-life problems may not allow for orderly treatment of some of the more mundane topics teachers are expected to address.

Finally, inductive lessons require resources and time. Whereas it takes very little time for a teacher to directly *state* a generalization, *inducing* a generalization requires repeated and varied experiences. Although they can produce lasting and memorable learning, inductive strategies can be less time efficient than direct instruction.

When will you use inductive methods? Check your stance toward education to gain a sense of what you want students to be able to do as adults. If you include outcomes such as the ability to analyze information sources, to think critically and creatively, or to solve complex problems, you need to master and employ inductive strategies. Because of their potential to address both content and thought-process goals, I hope you will use inductive strategies frequently. As a general rule, when you plan your lessons, ask yourself: "Could the students effectively discover these points for themselves if I arranged conditions appropriately?" If your answer is yes, use an inductive strategy. My own stance toward education reminds me not to tell students that which they could discover on their own. The last strategy addressed in this chapter, cooperative learning, can include both inductive and deductive approaches.

Cooperative Learning

Popularized in the 1970s and 1980s, cooperative learning was formulated as an attempt to move classroom practices away from the highly individualistic and often competitive emphases of the typical American classroom. Cooperative learning includes a family of methods and structures designed to capitalize on every classroom's diversity and to enrich students' cognitive learning and social behaviors (Jacob, 1999; Johnson & Johnson, 1999). Related terms include *peer-mediated instruction* and *collaborative learning*. Often these terms are used interchangeably, although precise distinctions do exist. For instance, some say that cooperative learning requires a shared product of learning; collaborative learning does not.

Through cooperative learning, students work together to meet goals and build social skills.

Source: Scott Cunningham/Merrill.

Research on peer-mediated instruction (including cooperative learning) is extensive, with studies spanning a century and many countries, grade levels, subject areas, and populations (including general and special education) represented. Results are positive (Hall & Stegila, 2003). Cooperative learning is effective for encouraging content learning, social interaction, and students' attitudes toward learning and the subject matter. Examples of its effectiveness include a meta-analysis of the research by Marzano et al. (2001) and studies by Maheady, Michielli-Pendl, Mallette, and Harper (2002) and Baker, Gersten, and Lee (2002). Even very young children can use cooperative learning in its simple forms.

Description of the Cooperative Learning Model   In cooperative learning lessons, students are expected to help each other learn as they work together in small groups. Groups can be temporary or yearlong. Frequently, cooperative groups include four members, but other configurations also exist. Cooperative learning is more than simply assigning students to work together and then issuing group grades. According to proponents (Kagan, 1994; Slavin, 1995) cooperative learning needs to accomplish three basic principles:

1. *Positive interdependence.* Conditions must be arranged so that students are dependent on each other for success. This interdependence can be facilitated by providing group awards or by structuring tasks so that individual students cannot complete them alone.
2. *Individual accountability.* Each student must remain accountable for exhibiting mastery of the content.
3. *Simultaneous interaction.* Lessons should keep a maximum number of students overtly active at once. This is in contrast to traditional lessons in which only one student in the entire class speaks at a time.

A fourth principle is *equal participation* (Kagan 1994). Students need to make balanced contributions to the group's work. Kagan argues that to accomplish these principles, teachers must:

*   Structure teams so that they are heterogeneous. Ability, language, gender, and ethnicity may be criteria teachers use to sort students into teams where members differ.
*   Use team-building and class-building activities to create the will to cooperate.
*   Use management techniques specifically suited for group work. Examples include a quiet signal to regain students' attention and the use of assigned roles within teams.
*   Explicitly teach social skills such as listening and conflict resolution techniques.

In sum, cooperative learning lessons structure resources and activities so that students remain responsible for their own learning and become responsible for assisting their teammates in learning.

Stages of the Cooperative Learning Model   Although for many teachers cooperative learning has come to mean simply allowing students to help each other, there are scores of formal cooperative learning structures that breathe life into the principles of cooperative learning. The stages listed in Figure 7.14 do not represent a single lesson. Instead, they suggest a sequence of events that take place over an extended period of time as a teacher works to establish a cooperative learning classroom.

Individual cooperative learning lessons that make use of a variety of structures can be embedded within this sequence. There are plentiful structures and resources on the Web. For example, try the links at CAST's site: http://aim.cast.org/learn/historyarchive/backgroundpapers/peer-mediated_instruction. In the meantime, here are four to get you started.

1. *Jigsaw II* (Slavin, 1995): Students in heterogeneous teams read the same chapter of material, with each member focusing on particular "expert" topics in the chapter.

Figure 7.14   *Stages of the cooperative learning model.*

Form teams and set the stage	1. Select the dimensions along which students will be heterogeneously grouped.
	2. Use assessment results and demographic information to place students into groups of four that include members who differ according to the selected dimensions. For example, each group may have two high achievers, two lower achievers, and be balanced in terms of girls and boys and English and Spanish speakers. Random teams, interest teams, or skill teams may also be used.
	3. Teach a defined and explicit set of social behaviors. Examples include active listening and responding in positive ways to peers' contributions.
Implement cooperative management system	4. Select and teach a quiet signal. Examples include a raised hand, a flick of the lights, a noise maker, and patterned hand claps.
	5. Teach students to distribute and collect materials within their teams.
Build teams	6. Encourage students to rely on each other by using team-building activities. Examples include team interviews and developing team names or hats.
Teach social skills	7. Directly teach students to interact in positive ways.
	• Post a list of the behaviors you expect to see and model those behaviors for the students.
	• Consider assigning roles such as encourager and task master to help students learn skills.
	8. Monitor social skills. Reinforce appropriate social behaviors. Allow students to evaluate their own use of social skills regularly.
Use cooperative learning strategies throughout instruction	9. Select from a variety of structures to embed cooperative learning within your regular instruction.
Analyze and revise	10. Monitor students' growth in social skills and encourage them to self-monitor through self-assessments.
	• Reorganize teams as appropriate.
	• Set new goals for yourself and your students based on their current work.

Students meet in groups with other experts to discuss the material and decide how to present it to group members. Back in their home teams, members teach each other their expert topics, ensuring that each member has mastered all topics. Students are assessed on the material, and the teacher records both individual scores and team scores that are based on the improvement gains of each individual student. (Focus on Content mastery)

2. *Inside–outside circle* (Kagan, 1994): Two concentric circles form, and students face each other. Partnered with the outside circle person directly across from him or her, each inside circle student shares and then listens as the outside circle person shares. The outside circle rotates so new partners can converse. (Focus on Information sharing)

3. *Student-teams achievement divisions* (STAD; Slavin, 1995): Based on the lesson objective, the teacher presents new information in a manner that closely relates to quizzes students will take later. Then team members practice the information together, using worksheets or other materials. Team members' responsibility is to ensure that all members have mastered the content. Next, every student takes a quiz on the material. Individuals receive scores based on their improvement over time. Team scores are determined by combining individual improvement scores. Recognition is given to teams based on their team scores. (Focus on Content mastery)

4. *Team statements* (Kagan, 1994): Each person writes an individual statement about a topic. Students share their statements and then develop a team statement that synthesizes each of the individual statements. (Focus on Thinking skills)

A Sample Cooperative Learning Lesson   Figure 7.15 shares a sample lesson for second graders that uses three of Kagan's cooperative learning structures.

Figure 7.15	*A sample cooperative learning lesson.*

Objectives:	Second-grade students will synthesize information from their aquarium field trip as evidenced by their descriptions of the murals they create.
	Students will exhibit two social skills: listening to each other and asking the teacher a question only when no group member can answer it.

Open	1. The class gets ready to learn.
	   • Class is seated on the floor in a misshapen circle.
	   • A fully included student using a wheelchair is sitting next to several friends who like to help out.
	   • The teacher directs students to choose a partner by making eye contact with a person nearby and linking up.
	   • She watches to ensure that all students are matched in a respectful way, and then she has them number off (1 and 2).
	2. Teacher states, "Here are some plastic animals like the animals we saw on our aquarium field trip. I have plenty. Partner 2, come here, choose one, talk to your partner about what you remember about the animal on the trip, and then return it to the center so that Partner 1 can choose another animal."
	3. Teacher watches the partner group with her fully included student to ensure that the student's partner doesn't do too much for him. She monitors others as well.
	4. Teacher compliments the students: "Do you know what I noticed as you were talking? When your partner spoke, you really listened. I could tell because you were looking at your partner, nodding and sometimes smiling. You didn't interrupt either. Careful listening is the social skill we'll practice today and tomorrow. What does it *look like* to listen carefully? What does it *sound like*?" A brief discussion ensues and the teacher charts their responses.
	5. "I can tell from your conversations that you learned many things from our field trip. Today you will have a chance to share what you learned by creating a team mural. Tomorrow we will describe our murals to each other."

Body	6. Each partner group joins up with another to form teams of four and they renumber, 1–4.
	7. At their team tables, students fact-storm on their trip.
	• Using a strategy called roundtable, one student writes a memory from the aquarium trip on a large sheet of paper, then passes the paper to the next member. The partner of the fully included student takes his dictation.
	• Students continue writing for about 10 minutes, until the paper is full.
	• "Now that you have so many animals and plants recorded, see if your team can group them in some logical way. Write on the chart."
	8. "Use your groupings to create a mural. Look toward the back of our room and you will see many materials you may use."
	• Students: "Dude! Glitter!"
	• Teacher continues: "Here's the rule for making your mural. I have made a sign that describes your job. See? Member 1, you are in control of the scissors. Only you may cut. Member 2, you are the magazine monitor. Any pictures selected from the magazine are your responsibility. You see that you may need 1 to cut for you, right? Member 3, your job is Fancy Material Captain. Glitter and crepe paper belong only to you. Member 4, markers are your job."
	• She checks for understanding on directions. Satisfied, teacher states, "Use your charts and get to work."
	9. Children work until lunch on their murals.
	• Teacher monitors to be certain that members are making their unique contributions based on their roles.
	• When individuals ask her questions, she asks, "Have you asked each person in your group that question yet?"
	• She applies some time pressures to keep groups productive, and she reinforces the listening skills students demonstrate.
Close	10. The next day: To share their murals and allow the teacher to assess the first objective, students use the "one stay, three stray" structure.
	• All Number 1's stand by their group mural and describe it to three visitors.
	• Next, Number 2's stay and describe while the others stray to see the murals of other groups.
	• Teacher takes anecdotal notes on students' presentations.
	• Back in their home groups, groups write one statement about what they saw and heard about other groups' murals.
	• Statements are posted near the murals.
	11. Students talk briefly in their groups to evaluate their social skills.
	• They focus on the chosen skill, careful listening.
	• They discuss the questions "What did we do well as a group today?" and "What will we work on for next time?"

Strengths and Criticisms of the Cooperative Learning Model   Cooperative learning offers refreshing changes to traditional classroom practice. First, it breaks the typical discourse pattern where teachers do most of the talking. It can enliven a classroom because it allows a far greater number of people to talk—to develop oral communication skills—at once. Second, cooperative learning changes the typical expectation that students need to succeed only as individuals and instead builds as norms social interaction and interdependence. Third, whereas student differences are sometimes seen as problematic, cooperative learning suggests that the more diverse the group, the richer the potential outcomes. Fourth, cooperative learning meets many of the principles addressed in Chapter 6. It is highly interactive, it capitalizes on human nature by allowing students to be actively involved throughout the lesson, and it allows students to form connections to the subject matter and with other students.

Teaching Tip

COOPERATIVE LEARNING QUICK STARTS

Use quick collaborative activities to increase interaction, language, and learning. Here are three to get you going.

1. *Peer teach:* Pause a few times during a lesson. Have one partner reteach the content to the other. They switch roles next time.
2. *Traveling partners:* Before the lesson begins, have students sign up for traveling partners. Each records the other's name. Or you designate the partners. They should not sit near each other. When it is time during the lesson, signal students to travel to their partners. Partners might work a problem, discuss an issue, or check over their notes. Signal when it's time to head back to their seats.
3. *Four-two-one:* At the end of a lesson, have students individually write down what they think are the four most important words from the lesson. In partners or small groups, have students share their words and then devise a list of just two important words. Everyone must agree. Finally, in partners or small groups, they pick the one word that captures the lesson best (Rogers, Ludington, & Graham, 1999).

Still, cooperative learning brings some difficulties. Cooperative learning lessons can take more time than traditional presentations because students are simultaneously learning social skills. Cooperative classrooms require diligence from the teacher in terms of classroom management. It takes skill to harness students' energy and ensure that students are working productively. It can also be a challenge to guide students in solving their social difficulties when a teacher's temptation is to quickly solve the problem and move on. Finally, it is the teacher's responsibility to structure lessons that require every student to contribute to the group's work. One of the greatest challenges of cooperative learning is to bar the possibility that students can freeload.

When will you use cooperative learning? Informal techniques such as partner sharing are easily integrated into traditional instruction. Try the three cooperative techniques given in the Teaching Tip. Individual lessons that employ cooperative structures are also possible. Structuring your entire classroom around the principles of cooperative learning will probably require you to receive additional training or to study some of the excellent resources that describe cooperative learning methods. As you consider cooperative learning, remember the power of your role as instructional leader. You must arrange events so that you can manage students' behavior, monitor their social skills, and ensure that they truly are helping each other succeed. Think through your activities, anticipate trouble spots, and plan some alternative responses to keep your cooperative lessons productive. Also consider whether and how technology might enhance your selection of instructional strategies.

Parting Words

Classroom teaching is so demanding that it is easy to retreat to instructional methods that do not require us to consider best practices, to enact our stances toward education, to stretch as professionals, or to stray from the ways we were taught as children. However, teaching is more than telling. Skilled teachers can use a number of instructional strategies to suit their purposes and encourage different kinds of growth for their learners. Make learning and using a number of instructional strategies a priority, perhaps selecting one or two based on your work from the Before You Begin Reading exercise in this chapter. When you try any new strategy, think very carefully about what you will say at each point, what you will expect from the students, and what you will do if things do not go as planned. Expect that you will need repeated opportunities to practice new strategies; in fact, research on staff development suggests that a strategy may not feel natural until you try it about a dozen times. A dozen times! Further, be vigilant in thinking about how using a variety of instructional strategies can help you differentiate your instruction so that it pushes all of your students to their learning potential. The harder you work to build your instructional repertoire, the better able you will be to help your students grow and develop.

Opportunities to Practice

1. Record yourself teaching or ask for permission to observe another teacher. Tally the number of questions the teacher asks and how many the students ask. Analyze your data of question–answer patterns according to some of the topics given early (pp. 144–145) in this chapter. What is your evaluation of the questioning you observed?

2. Observe another teacher lead a lesson. Afterward, discuss with the teacher the choices he made about instructional strategies. Ask him how many of the strategies from this chapter he knows and which he prefers. If an observation is not possible, try analyzing the teacher's editions from a published curriculum series. How many of the strategies are suggested? What is your evaluation of the use of instructional strategies? What changes might you suggest?

3. Make a prioritized list for yourself of the strategies you will work to master. Busy? I suggest you choose, for a start, direct instruction and one other strategy. Study the stages of the models as if you are studying for an exam. Commit them to memory and then bring them to life through intense effort to model them each a couple times. Work with a colleague and discuss your experience.

4. Write two contrasting lessons using strategies from this chapter. Use an objective from your classroom or the following one: "Students will retell three major events from a story [name one] in the correct sequence." Blank lesson plan forms are included in Figure 7.16.

5. Figure 7.16 includes lesson plan formats for each of the instructional models and strategies in this chapter. Use them as you plan lessons that incorporate different strategies. Remember to include cognitive, affective, and psychomotor objectives as appropriate. Also, include assessment to match each of your objectives.

Web Sites

Use the names of strategies given in this chapter to conduct your Internet search for teaching techniques. Examples include the following:

http://www.imsa.edu/team/cpbl/cpbl.html
Center for Problem-Based Learning by Illinois Mathematics and Science Academy. Start with the tutorial, then move to Sample Problems.

http://www.thirteen.org/edonline/concept2class/
Concept to Classroom. This site offers free online workshops in topics such as cooperative learning, inquiry-based learning, and Webquests. Solid information is supplemented with video.

http://www.inquiry.uiuc.edu/
The Inquiry Page. Includes a helpful inquiry cycle and examples of inquiry in practice. Browse the inquiry units, but be sure to evaluate the submissions using your knowledge of the critical attributes of inquiry.

http://olc.spsd.sk.ca/DE/PD/instr/index.html
Instructional Strategies Online. This site groups dozens of methods within a handful of strategies. A valuable resource, it provides background, step-by-step directions, and plentiful resources to help you master a variety
of techniques. One example from this chapter is concept attainment.

The instructional strategies presented in this chapter are just a subset of the myriad strategies you can try. Others, such as virtual field trips and simulations, are also readily available. To get started, try these sites:

http://www.awesomelibrary.org/
Awesome Library. Look around, or search for the word "simulation" within the site and locate many activities that allow students to experience content through memorable, role-play-type activities.

http://www.uen.org/utahlink/tours/
Virtual Field Trips by Utah Education Network. This site provides great links and prepares students for their virtual travels.

http://webquest.org/
WebQuest News. This site presents WebQuests by their founder, Bernie Dodge at San Diego State University. Membership in the QuestGarden community has a fee, but teachers can search WebQuests by grade level and content area for free.

Figure 7.16 *Lesson plan formats.*

Direct Instruction Lesson

Objective(s):   Materials:

Expectations for behavior:

Open	1. Anticipatory set: • Focus: • Objective: • Purpose:
Body	2. Input: • Provide input: • Check for understanding: 3. Guided practice:
Close	4. Closure: 5. Independent practice:

Inquiry Training Lesson		
Objective(s):		Materials:

Open	1. Discrepant event: 2. State students' task:
Body	3. Elicit questions that verify conditions and events of the discrepant event: • Sample acceptable questions: • Sample prompts to encourage appropriate questions: 4. Elicit questions that test hypotheses: • Sample acceptable questions: • Sample prompts to encourage appropriate questions:
Close	5. Guide students to formally state their explanations:

(continued)

Figure 7.16 *Lesson plan formats (Continued)*

Concept Attainment Lesson

Concept or rule to be discovered:

Objective(s):

Materials (list examples and counterexamples of your concept):

Open	1. Briefly display objects: 2. State students' task:
Body	3. Present examples and counterexamples of the concept or rule (list the order in which examples will be presented): 4. Allow students to test their hypothesized rules by (a) citing their own examples and nonexamples and/or (b) talking with peers. Prompts:
Close	5. Allow the rule to be stated for the class: 6. Allow for observations of the content and process of the lesson: 7. Invite further exploration (e.g., allow students to create their own groups):

Learning Cycle Lesson

Concept or rule to be discovered:

Objective(s):

Materials:

Open	1. Engage (use a real-world phenomenon to hook the students; elicit questions; determine background knowledge):
Body	2. Explore (work with concrete materials; determine emerging concepts and terms):
	3. Develop (formally develop concepts and terms from the explore phase; use readings, direct presentations, and other methods to ensure mastery of the objective):
Close	4. Apply (provide a novel problem to which new knowledge can be applied or make some other real-world connection):

(continued)

Figure 7.16 *Lesson plan formats (Continued)*

Concept Formation Lesson

If specified, concepts or generalizations to be discovered:

Objective(s):

Materials:

Open	1. Introduce the topic and ask a question that will generate a list of terms:
Body	2. List (prompt students to generate an extensive list related to the topic):
	3. Group (prompt students to group items from the list):
	4. Label (prompt students to name the groups):
	5. Optional: Regroup (prompt students to find other ways items can be grouped):
Close	6. Call students' attention to the concepts or generalizations that arise from their groupings. Prompt:
	7. Extend learning through an additional assignment, such as a drawing, writing, or speaking opportunity:

Unguided Inquiry Lesson

If specified, concepts or generalizations to be discovered:

Objective(s) (consider both content and research skill or process objectives):

Materials (list concrete materials and information sources):

Open	1. Present stimulus material that suggests a problem or issue for study:
	2. Guide students to state the problem in clear terms. Prompts:
	3. Decide on appropriate methods to address the problem. Prompts:
	4. Set the guidelines for study. Prompts:
Body	5. Monitor students as they employ their methods. Prompts to encourage careful study:
Close	6. Encourage students to draw conclusions regarding (a) the problem and (b) the processes of investigation. Prompts:

(continued)

Figure 7.16 *Lesson plan formats (Continued)*

Cooperative Learning Lesson

Content objective(s):

Social skill objective(s):

Materials:

Prelesson questions	a. How are teams formed? b. What quiet signal will you use? c. What team-building and class-building efforts have you taken or will you take?
Open	1. Focus students' attention and allude to the lesson's content and activities: 2. State expectations for cooperative work and teach social skills:

Body	3. Use a cooperative learning structure to present information or encourage discovery learning. Samples from Chapters 5 and 6 include the following:
	
	   blackboard blitz inside–outside circle round table
	
	   brainstorming jigsaw roving review
	
	   four corners numbered heads together stand to share
	
	   gallery walk one stay, three stray values lineups
	
	   group problems peer interviews
	
	4. Monitor students' use of social skills. Sample prompts:

Close	5. Summarize the learning. Prompts or cooperative strategy: 6. Process students' use of social skills:

Student Assessment

8

Before You Begin Reading

Warm-Up Exercise for Assessment

Think back to your years as a student. How did your teachers know whether and what you learned? What kinds of feedback did you receive? Take three minutes to jot down as many different assessment strategies as you can recall experiencing.

Now mark each of these statements with agree or disagree:

1. Teachers knew me as a multifaceted person with varied strengths and skills.
2. Teachers were interested in my own assessments of my work.
3. Teachers encouraged me to set my own learning goals.
4. The feedback I received from tests and other assessments helped me learn.
5. Teachers changed what they did in the classroom based on student assessment data.

Finally, evaluate your answers for statements 1 through 5. Were your experiences with assessment as a student positive? Would it have been better if teachers had assessed your learning differently?

Here is a chance for you to use effective practices from both the past and present to make a difference for today's students. Use your conclusions to help make sense of the following chapter and to build your own system for assessing student progress.

"The greatest magnifying glasses in the world are a man's own eyes when they look upon his own person."

—Alexander Pope

Assessment is the magnifying glass we use to look upon our efforts in education. Through assessment, we gather, analyze, and use information about schools' work and students' progress. We use the assessment magnifying glass for many purposes such as checking the health of our schools, communicating our efforts to the public, and comparing ourselves to other nations. Our primary purpose of assessment, though, is student growth. This chapter addresses student assessment in the following sections:

- Principles of Assessment
- Assessment Basics
- The Assessment Landscape
- Classroom Assessment Step by Step
- A Note on Grading
- A Sampler of Assessments

Principles of Assessment

Assessment of student learning is multifaceted and complex, and to do a good job at it, we must use a number of principles to guide our actions, no matter the level or type of assessment. In our assessments, we need to:

1. Measure what we value.
2. Include students.
3. Be fair.
4. Use what we learn.
5. Add to the bigger picture.

These five principles are introduced briefly here and reoccur as themes throughout the chapter.

1. *Measuring what we value.* At every level (globally, nationally, professionally, and individually) we give serious deliberation to what we should accomplish through education, and we embody those wishes as goals in a variety of forms such as philosophies and mission statements. Assessment is the vehicle we use to ascertain our progress toward our goals and to adjust our course of action. Assessing what we value entails ensuring that our assessments address all of our goals—not just a narrow range of them—and both short- and long-term targets.

(Assessment principle: Measure what we value.)

2. *Including students.* Although assessment often appears to be done *to students* rather than *with students*, the ultimate goal in assessment is self-assessment (Costa & Kallick, 2000). Only when they are effective self-evaluators will students be autonomous individuals who can motivate their own learning and action. Thus, our efforts must include assessment *of learning* (to check progress), *for learning* (to guide next steps), and *as learning* (to help students grow as self-evaluators).

3. *Being fair.* To provide a true picture of what students know and can do assessments must be systematic. They must provide **valid** and **reliable** information for all of our students. A *valid* assessment measures what it was intended to measure and allows us to draw accurate inferences. Confounds to validity include, often, English language proficiency and reading skill.

Either of these variables might affect a student's score on the fourth-grade science item found in Figure 8.1. A *reliable* measure gives consistent results under different conditions and with different raters. To be fair, assessments also need to be unbiased and equitable. Using **multiple measures** increases the odds that we build fair, accurate, and rich portraits of student progress.

4. *Using what we learn.* Assessment results must be useful. By providing information about students' progress toward goals, assessment data should inform our instruction and other next steps

| **Figure 8.1** | *Sample science assessment item.* |

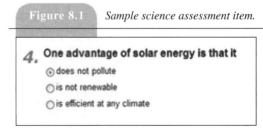

Source: National Center for Education Statistics' Kid Zone (http://nces.ed.gov/nceskids/eyk/) Permission pending.

such as schoolwide program revision. Assessment should also guide the selection of future learning goals.

5. *Adding to the bigger picture.* Information about student progress is collected over time and from many sources. Assessment efforts need to add to the bigger picture of what we know about each of our individual students. Each assessor fits into a variety of assessment systems and must contribute to the bigger picture(s) of what we know about our students. Each assessor must also develop and implement effective assessment systems at her own level of influence.

Assessment Basics

As you consider your important role as an assessor and pursue effective assessment, several basic concepts may be of service.

Different Assessments for Different Purposes

Although schools focus on the cognitive domain, our student learning goals do fall into several domains (cognitive, psychomotor, and affective). For example, the National Science Education Standards require students to master the *abilities* necessary to do scientific inquiry, which include, for instance, *employing equipment and tools* to gather data (National Research Council, 1996). Those abilities include psychomotor skills like handling equipment precisely and safely. The standards also emphasize *appreciation* for science as a way of knowing the world and the *dispositions* and *attitudes* associated with science. Because domains vary, so must our assessments to measure students' progress. Students' use of tools of science might be assessed through a performance task, and their attitudes might be assessed through observation. Stiggins (2001) suggests that teachers use assessments to measure a variety of targets, including:

- Knowledge and understanding
- Reasoning
- Performance skills
- Proficiency in creating products
- Dispositions

In addition to classroom assessments, students face a variety of other assessments. Achievement tests are common, as are aptitude tests (which measure aspects of ability), interest inventories, and diagnostic measures that might screen for health or learning conditions. Each of our many assessments needs to match our purposes.

Norm- and Criterion-Referenced Assessments

Measures can compare individuals' results to a group or to an external standard. **Norm-referenced** measures compare an individual's performance with that of a norming group. How well an individual does depends on the achievement of others. Think of grading on a curve: A score of 75 percent might bring you any grade from A to F depending on how your classmates do. A common norm-referenced score is a **percentile,** the score below which that percentage of the scores falls. A score at the 90th percentile means that 90 percent of the people who took the test scored below that score. Another example is a **grade equivalent score** (GE), which tells the grade and month (1-9) of the average person who achieved a given score.

Criterion-referenced assessments instead compare each individual's score to a standard. One's progress on a criterion-referenced measure is not influenced by others' scores. Your score of 75 percent would earn a C (by common convention), regardless of your peers' scores. A common criterion-referenced practice is pass/fail grading using a predetermined cut score. A driver's license test is an example. Another is the determination of students' grade level proficiency, where scores fall into performance levels such as "advanced," "proficient," and "basic" depending on predetermined criteria.

Both norm-referenced and criterion-referenced scores provide useful information; using both gives us a more precise picture of student progress. For instance, at the doctor's office, it's helpful to know both a child's weight measurement and its percentile. The former (say, 72 pounds) gives an exact, criterion-referenced measure, and the latter (say, 68th percentile) allows us to compare the child's weight to that of his age mates. Knowing both pieces of information is helpful to the child, the parents, and the doctor for making future decisions about things like nutrition.

Standardized and Local Assessments

Standardized tests are developed, administered, and scored under systematic conditions. They are meant to provide results that can be compared across large numbers of students. Examples include the Iowa Test of Basic Skills (ITBS) and the Comprehensive Test of Basic Skills (CTBS). Local assessments, on the other hand, are developed, implemented, and analyzed with the local context in mind. District writing exams are an example of a local assessment. Both types of assessment—large-scale and local—can contribute unique information to our understanding of students' progress. The trick is to be smart in considering the kind of information that each can provide.

Formative and Summative Assessments

Assessments whose primary purpose is to inform us of students' postinstructional performance are **summative.** Statewide achievement tests are an example. Even though we do use the results to shape future planning, the achievement tests' immediate and primary focus is to report students' performance for the year. Summative assessment is assessment *of learning.*

Formative assessment is assessment *for learning.* The primary purpose of formative assessments is to give current information about students' progress that helps us shape (or "form") our actions to better meet students' needs. Research indicates that formative assessment has a strong positive effect on student learning (Black & Wiliam, 1998; Herman, Osmundson, Ayala, Schneider, & Timms, 2006; Popham, 2008). Indeed, much interest in today is centered on the power of formative assessment to improve teaching and learning. Formative assessment can occur *before instruction,* providing diagnostic information, and *during instruction,* providing **progress monitoring** and opportunities to modify the pace, content, and approach of our lessons in response to students' unfolding needs. Students should be active in formative assessment: "Formative assessment is a planned process in which teachers *or students* use assessment-based evidence to adjust what they're currently doing" (Popham, 2008, p. 6; emphasis added).

Assessment *for learning* involves students in determining their current performance, setting goals, and ascertaining progress toward those goals. "When students and teachers become partners in the classroom assessment process, both working in the service of student success, research from around the world reveals that the result is profound achievement gains for all students" (Stiggins, 2009, p. 420).

Balanced assessment systems include both formative and summative assessments. Formative assessment provides guidance along the road, and summative assessment tells us when, whether, and where we've arrived. Both are necessary for guiding student growth (Kennedy, Chan, Fok, & Yu, 2008).

The Assessment Landscape

Your work as an assessor puts you and your students on the map. Let's examine the landscape of assessment from afar and up close.

International Assessment Landscape

At the global level, student assessment allows us to compare our students' attainments to those of students around the world. Analyzing international results can provide insights into our practices and policies and suggest avenues for improvement. Dozens of countries participate in each of two major international assessment programs: the Trends in International Mathematics and Science Study (TIMSS) and the Programme for International Assessment (PISA).

PISA is a triennial assessment of 15-year-olds' capacity to analyze, reason, and communicate effectively in the areas of mathematics, science, and reading. PISA's literacy emphasis is on applying knowledge as students pose, solve, and interpret problems in a variety of settings (OECD, 2010). The test also asks students to assess their attitudes, motivation to learn, and learning strategies. Future versions will measure ICT competencies and consider use of computer-based assessment tools such as **adaptive testing.** Adaptive testing matches the level of the test to students' performance so that they need not complete all items including ones that are too easy or too difficult for them. U.S. students' performance on PISA was significantly below the international averages in science and mathematics (OECD, 2007). As a side note, the gender differences explored in Chapter 4 are alive across the globe in PISA results; females dramatically outscored males in reading. Males in many countries marginally outperformed females in mathematics, and no gender differences in science arose.

Administered every four years, the Trends in International Mathematics and Science Study examines the mathematics and science knowledge that fourth- and eighth-graders are likely to have learned in school (NCES, 2010h). U.S. students recently scored above international averages in science and mathematics at both grade levels (IEA, 2007a, 2007b). Figure 8.2 gives international comparisons related to the fourth-grade science question—A TIMSS question—given in Figure 8.1. Go to the NCES Kids Zone site and try some questions yourself. Comparisons of these TIMSS and PISA results suggest that U.S. students did better at displaying factual knowledge than they did at reasoning in complex tasks.

Figure 8.2   *International comparisons on science assessment item.*

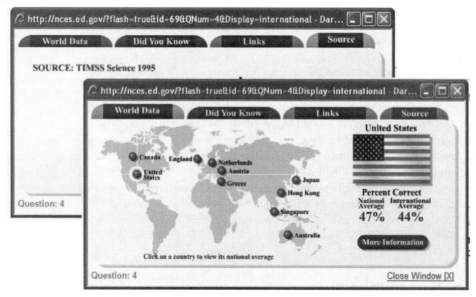

percent correct responses to the fourth-grade science item, "one advantage of solar energy is . . ."

Source: National Center for Education Statistics' Kid Zone (http://nces.ed.gov/nceskids/eyk/) Permission pending.

National- and State-Level Assessment Landscape

The National Assessment of Education Progress (NAEP), deemed the nation's report card, is the longest running, largest standardized assessment employed across the United States. Participation is now mandated by the Elementary and Secondary Education Act (No Child Left Behind). Every four years, a sample of fourth-, eighth-, and twelfth-grade students in every state completes the NAEP in several subject areas. Questions include both **constructed response** and **selection-type** items. Visit http://nces.ed.gov/nationsreportcard/ to view a wealth of information such as long-term trend data, your state's profile (including expenditures per pupil, percent of students with individual education programs, and percentage participation in English proficiency programs), and released test items (click on "sample questions").

Although mandated, the NAEP is not considered by most as a high-stakes test because its results have no tangible consequences. Instead, NCLB's accountability requirements are tied to mandated statewide achievement tests. Beginning in grade three, students are assessed annually using standardized tests that measure progress toward state content standards. Students' achievement falls into performance levels such as "advanced," "proficient," "basic," and "below basic." Each school—and each subgroup of the school's population—must make **adequate yearly progress** (AYP) toward NCLB's goal of 100 percent of students attaining grade level proficiency by 2014. Schools that do not make AYP are subject to sanctions and possible takeover. Revisions under consideration for the reauthorization of NCLB focus more on growth-based models and less on punishments or sanctions.

We can draw a number of conclusions about the standardized testing landscape in the United States. First, tests are developed, administered, and analyzed by people external to the local schooling context; this is not the case everywhere (Darling-Hammond & McCloskey, 2008). Second, our tests focus more on recall of factual information through selection-type items than do the tests of countries that score well on PISA. In such countries, tests focus more on open-ended items that require extensive writing and analysis and application of knowledge (Darling-Hammond & McCloskey, 2008). Third, our tests affect the curriculum by changing its scope (typically narrowing it), the forms of knowledge it embodies (typically isolating information into discrete bits), and our instructional approaches (typically moving them to teacher-centered techniques) (Au, 2007; Laitsch, 2006).

Perhaps for these reasons many oppose standardized testing in the United States. Vocal critics (e.g., Kohn, 2001; Valli, Corninger, Cambliss, Graeber, & Buese, 2008) condemn standardized tests as incapable of measuring important outcomes, of limiting our vision of what is important, of weakening student-teacher relationships, and of being biased against groups such as English learners (Menken, 2008), students from ethnic and racial minority groups, and students from low-income homes (Johnson, Johnson, Farenga, & Ness, 2008). Some seriously doubt the ability of standardized tests to measure the types of learning and intelligence that relate to success in the real world. Sternberg (1997a, 1997b), for instance, argues that successful intelligence—the ability to adapt to one's environment to accomplish goals—is not measured by standardized tests. Sternberg also asserts that standardized tests emphasize conformity in thought instead of valuing diverse approaches to learning.

Those who offer support of standardized testing (e.g., Phelps, 2005) advance a number of arguments in favor of testing. They state that public support for high-stakes testing is consistently positive; as education is a public endeavor, our profession must remain accountable to its constituents. Proponents also point to benefits such as the power of standardized tests as diagnostic and motivational tools. Some proponents recognize the limitations of standardized tests and suggest that we focus efforts on improving our testing practices. Darling-Hammond and McCloskey agree:

> While U.S. accountability efforts have focused on achieving higher test scores, they have not yet developed the kind of teaching and learning systems that could develop widespread capacity for significantly greater learning . . . for today's knowledge based economy: the abilities to find, analyze, and use information to solve real problems; to write and speak clearly and persuasively; to defend ideas; and to design and manage projects (2008, p. 271).

The School-Level Assessment Landscape

Stories of schools across the nation that are in fact working diligently to increase success for all students—and succeeding admirably—abound. Examples include case studies from individual schools and consortia that include the entire range of student population variables (e.g., Allen, Ort, & Schmidt; 2009; Baker, Gersten, & Lee, 2002; Brookhart, Moss, & Long; 2008; Frey & Fisher, 2009; Mokhtari, Thoma, & Edwards, 2009; Reeves, 2003). A number of common threads run across these success stories. Promising assessment practices include:

- Teachers and other participants (students, families, and administrators) work together at the local level, as school teams, for student progress.
- Team members maintain a very sharp focus on student learning goals and on continuous improvement.
- Teacher teams together develop and administer frequent formative assessments. One benefit is that this deepens teachers' knowledge of their content and of assessment.
- Teams regularly discuss student assessment data and then modify instruction to improve learning.
- Teachers include students in assessment *for* and *as* learning. Students set their own goals and monitor their growth toward those goals.
- Teachers move toward writing intensive, performance-based assessments.

When asked during your job interview, "Do you have any questions for us?" ask about the school's approach to student assessment. If you have a choice, join a staff that is deeply engaged in the shared pursuit of student growth through a schoolwide effort to learn and to improve decision making through assessment.

Classroom Assessment Step by Step

We've zoomed in from the international perspective on assessment to the school level, locating you precisely on the assessment map. Now let's delve into the student assessment role over which you have the most control: classroom assessment. This step-by-step process describes the classroom assessment process whether you are part of an effective staff team or working independently. You'll see that the process embodies our principles of assessment. As a refresher, the principles state that we need to:

1. Measure what we value.
2. Include students.
3. Be fair.
4. Use what we learn.
5. Add to the bigger picture.

The five steps described here take you from goal setting through assessment and instruction—and back again. The graphic in Figure 8.3 expands the goals → teach → assess cycle presented earlier.

1. Choose Your Assessment Targets

As Figure 8.3 shows, classroom assessment starts in the planning phase (Gronlund, 2004). Begin the assessment process by selecting learning targets. Because we need to measure

Figure 8.3   *Classroom assessment cycle.*

Determine assessment targets (learning goals).

Preassess; analyze results.

Adjust learning targets.

Plan for inclusive, responsive instruction.

Teach.

Monitor, reflect, adjust.

Teach.

Postassess; analyze results.

Source: Inspired by Ainsworth and Viegut (2006).

Teaching Tip

ASSESSMENT VERSUS EVALUATION

Assessment is the act of gathering information about student progress. Evaluation assigns a judgment, or value, to that information. Grading is thus an evaluative activity. Assigning accurate and meaningful grades is a difficult endeavor, fraught with many logistical and ethical issues (Deddeh, Main, & Fulkerson, 2010; Pope, Green, Johnson, & Mitchell, 2009). Grades should be well supported by assessment results, so think about whether and how you'll assign grades as you consider any assessment issue.

what we value, start with the broad view for yearlong targets. Check sources like your stance toward education, the school's mission statement, and 21st-century skills. If you want your students to "Demonstrate originality and inventiveness" (Partnership for 21st Century Skills, 2009, p. 3), this goal becomes an assessment target. View the school's report card for potential targets, as you will be responsible for assessing students in its required domains. Also review mandated assessments such as your statewide assessment. Both the **blueprints** that lay out content and format for these exams and released items are widely available online.

In surveying, a benchmark is a point of reference for measurement. Schools set benchmarks too. Benchmarks are intermediate goals that are measured throughout the year using the district's choice of measurement tools. They serve as a reference point for students' rate of progress as they prepare for year-end testing. Herman, Osmundson, and Dietel (2010) argue that benchmark assessment stands between the classroom's formative and the state's year-end summative assessment because benchmark assessments give both summative information on students' progress to date and formative information for planning instruction. Check your district's **benchmarks** in order to help you set your goals and begin planning for assessment. This broad view of learning targets can help you ensure a coherent approach to teaching, learning, and assessment.

Then get more specific by setting targets based on content standards. Ainsworth and Viegut (2006), like others, suggest that we first examine our standards to prioritize them. Many states or schools offer or devise lists of "power standards" that receive the instructional emphasis. Next, study your standards in detail to analyze their demands. Ainsworth and Viegut offer a helpful, four-step process for analyzing the demands of content standards.

1. "Unwrap" a standard by underlining important concepts and ideas (what students need to know—the nouns) and circling the verbs (what students need to be able *to do* with the information).
2. Create a graphic organizer such as a diagram or bulleted list to represent the unwrapped standards. Include a little information about the instructional context in which ideas will be presented.
3. Determine the big ideas from the unwrapped standards. Big ideas are generalizations that transfer across time and culture (recall the Big Idea unit planning strategy from Chapter 5).
4. Write essential questions that will be answered through instruction. Look at your big ideas and infer the questions that they answer.

Figure 8.4's four panels give a highly abbreviated example of these four processes for a single fourth-grade draft geometry standard from the Common Core Standards (Common Core State Standards Initiative, 2010).

Instructional time is short and integrated learning can be powerful learning, so also consider standards from other areas that can be addressed in tandem. Examples include English language development standards, Information and Communication Technology standards (like ISTE's student standards), social skills, and writing standards.

The unwrapping approach is useful for determining targets for many timeframes—for an entire year, a unit, or a single lesson. Whether you use the unwrapping method or a

Figure 8.4   *Unwrapping a fourth-grade mathematics standard.*

1. Unwrap the standards.
 	
(CLASSIFY) <u>two-dimensional (2D) figures</u> based on the presence or absence of <u>parallel or perpendicular lines,</u> or the presence or absence of <u>angles</u> of a specified size. (RECOGNIZE) <u>right triangles</u> as a category, and (IDENTIFY) <u>right triangles.</u>
	2. Create a graphic organizer.
	
	Concepts: Attributes of 2D figures
	    • Lines: Parallel, perpendicular
	    • Angles: Right, other sizes
	Concept: Classes of 2D figures
	    • Triangles
	      —Right triangles
	Skills: Be able to do
	    • Recognize
	    • Identify
	    • Classify
	Context: Geometry unit with architecture focus

3. Determine the big ideas. 1. Two-dimensional figures are comprised of lines and angles arranged in characteristic ways. 2. Two-dimensional figures can be identified and classified by their attributes such as lines and angles.	*4. Write essential questions.* 1. How do the lines and angles in 2D figures vary? 2. How is it useful to identify the lines and angles in 2D figures?

different one to analyze the standards, the point is to dig deeply into exactly what students need to know and be able to do when they master the standards. Without careful study, it may be tempting to give the standards a cursory glance and treat them as items on a check sheet to quickly check off and move on rather than teaching and assessing them deeply.

2. Choose Your Assessment Strategies

Whether you are assessing learning for an entire unit or a single lesson, you next determine how you will assess students' mastery of each target. As you select your assessment strategies, remember that there are many options available to you; the sampler in the next section of this chapter lists a dozen or so.

Select strategies that match the intent of the standard for what students should be able to do with information. Be sure to select assessments that match your objectives. As a general rule, *go deep and go varied*. Work toward requiring students to apply information in real-world contexts and represent their knowledge and abilities in a number of ways.

In developing or selecting your assessments, consider the role that ICT can and should play. Computer-based technologies expand our options for assessment dramatically. They allow for richer products such as digital videos, presentations, and wikis (Salend, 2009). Inventive computer-based assessments contextualize context within realistic problems in virtual worlds and mirror conditions of life and learning in the 21st century (Svihla, Vye, Brown, Phillips, Gawel, & Bransford, 2009). Digital technology also can help us provide universal access for students during our assessments by allowing for differentiated input (e.g., larger text, speech readers, languages other than English) and output (e.g., speech-to-text programs and modified keyboards). Computer-based approaches to assessment can also simplify your assessment life through item banks that allow the creation of multiple forms of a test, and computer-based tests can provide immediate feedback for students.

21st Century Teaching and Learning Tip

CREATE FREE ONLINE QUIZZES

You and your students can create quick quizzes online for free and embed them into your Web sites or blogs. Search the term "create free online quizzes" and you'll find sites such as Google Docs, MyQuizCreator, Quizilla, MyStudiyo, ProProfs, Classmaker, QuizCenter, QuizBox, and EasyTestMaker.

Three questions to consider as you develop or select your assessments are:

- What is my range of options, from traditional to alternative?
- How can I be fair with my choice of assessments?
- How can I assess before, during, and after assessment?

Both traditional and alternative assessments can provide useful information. Traditional measures include paper/pencils tests with their selection-type or constructed-response items. Alternative (or authentic) assessment measures offer a rich complement to traditional assessments by providing context-embedded, multifaceted portrayals of what students know and can do. Examples include performance assessments and portfolios. Because they provide rich contexts and require multifaceted responses, alternative assessments are inclusive of a range of student needs, including those of English learners (Medina-Jerez, Clark, & Medina, 2007) and of students with special needs (Layton & Lock, 2007; Vacca, 2007).

To be fair, consider assessment strategies that allow all of your students to demonstrate what they know and can do. Consider the validity of your measures given your purposes and each of your students. Also select assessments that you can score reliably. A top concern of teachers in one study was "score pollution," where teachers' perceptions of students' behaviors or characters influence the grades teachers give (Pope, Green, Johnson, & Mitchell, 2009). Being fair may require you to use more than one measure and differentiate your assessments.

Chapter 4 introduced approaches to provide responsive and inclusive instruction; those approaches also provide guidance for us as inclusive assessors. For instance, you may need to include additional visual supports or examples, read directions aloud, or provide extra work time. Here are other examples of inclusive assessment practices:

- English learners may need to express their learning in the primary language, may require the use of a dictionary, or may respond to closed-ended prompts rather than constructed-response ones.
- Struggling readers may listen to the computer read the test to them as they wear headphones.
- Gifted students may be expected to respond to an assessment prompt with greater complexity or in greater depth.

We should consider adjustable classroom assessments that allow all students to reveal what they know (Gregory & Kuzmich, 2004). The Inclusive and Responsive Teaching Tip

Inclusive and Responsive Teaching Tip

TIERED ASSESSMENTS

1. Determine what full proficiency of the content standard would look like. What evidence would you accept as mastery?
2. Use that level as the minimum acceptable level; all students must demonstrate mastery at that level.
3. Adjust the complexity or challenge of the assessment for students who are working at higher levels of readiness. For example, students at lower levels of readiness might demonstrate proficiency by graphing linear equations where variables are whole numbers and they are given the graph. Students at higher levels might graph variables that are fractions or absolute values, and they might generate the graph themselves.
4. Learning menus and learning contracts, where students choose their assessments on occasion, are also adjustable assessments (Wormeli, 2006).

provides one example of adjustable assessments: tiered assessments (Tomlinson, 2001; Wormeli, 2006).

Finally, choose assessments that allow you to check student progress at each phase of instruction. Check to determine whether there are mandated assessments such as benchmark tests or publisher tests for the content standards at hand. Many mandated assessments serve summative purposes. That won't be enough. You need both formative and summative assessments, ones that give you information about students' thinking before, during, and after instruction.

Formative Assessment—Preassessments   On the day before her lesson on the Eighth Amendment, a social studies teacher hands each small group an envelope of ten statements she selected from the supplemental workbook and cut into strips, five with true statements about the Eighth Amendment, and five with false. Strip number 3 reads, for instance, "The Eighth Amendment prohibits the federal government from punishing citizens for their crimes." The students work in their groups to sort the statements into two stacks: true or false. Statement 3 goes in the false stack. The teacher circulates and notes that most students already know about the protection against cruel and unusual punishment, but few know about the protection the Eighth Amendment provides against excessive fines. She focuses tomorrow's lesson more clearly on that provision. This teacher's engaging 10-minute activity (a true/false sort from Guillaume, Yopp, & Yopp, 2007) is an example of formative assessment that can be used prior to instruction. Other ideas for rapid preassessments are homework, group problems, and brainstormed lists. Student interviews (see Teacher Talk), traditional pretests, and journal entries are other examples of preassessments. Consider whether it is appropriate to use the same assessment as a preinstructional and postinstructional measure. Be careful, though, that your preassessments do not discourage students by presenting pages of items of content they don't know.

By assessing students' prior knowledge, teachers' lessons have a greater chance of connecting to what students know. Results on preinstructional assessments may tell you, for instance, that students do not have the background knowledge necessary for success in the unit you were planning or that they have already mastered the standards you intended to teach. In either case, had you not preassessed students, you would have wasted valuable instructional time and effort. Preassessments are also important in helping you to determine special interests and needs students may have so that you can differentiate your instruction to provide all students with powerful learning. Adjust your learning targets based on the results of your preassessments.

TEACHER TALK

Three practicing teachers reflect on the power of prior-knowledge interviews, where they talked with individual students to discover what the students knew about specific science content:

1. "My [middle school] student felt privileged to share her knowledge with me one-on-one. I don't often take the time to sit with one student and listen carefully to her view of the world."

2. "I taught my same students last year, so I know what they were exposed to in science. I couldn't believe that my prior knowledge interview student didn't have the concepts I thought I taught so well last year. He could repeat definitions that we memorized, but he hadn't glued those definitions to real ideas or explanations of the world. It was a humbling experience."

3. "I interviewed a small group of kindergartners to discover what they knew about sinking and floating. I know people learn things at home, but I was amazed at all the connections these five-year-olds made with their outside lives. They talked about going fishing, about throwing pennies into a fountain, and about playing with bathtub toys. I learned vividly that even my very young students are working hard to make sense of things."

Teaching Tip

WIPE BOARDS

Recall, from Chapter 6, that there is research support for the use of response cards as an active participation strategy. For an inexpensive class set of wipe boards, place card stock into a plastic page protector and hand it, and a dry erase marker, and a tissue to each student. I have found, to date, 84 uses for these boards. Here are a few:

- Every student can now "do the problem on the board" and hold up work for you to quickly assess.
- Everyone can spell out the words at a spelling bee now; this way the students who need the most opportunities to practice spelling get to keep spelling long after they'd typically be "out."
- Place colored card stock *and* white paper in the page protector. Students can flash the colored side for "true" and the white side for "false" when asked a question.
- Slip a hundreds chart, worksheet, map, or periodic chart into the page protector. Students can follow your directions, practice naming countries or tracing routes, circle nonmetals . . . in short, all students can stay actively involved while leaving a record of learning that you can quickly check before they erase.

Formative Assessment as Progress Monitoring—Assessing During Instruction   Select a variety of strategies to find out what students are learning as you teach. Any assignment or activity that you provide for practice can serve as a formative assessment. Class discussions (with you taking notes), homework pages, worksheets, daily quizzes—on paper or using student responses systems, in-class writings, and blog entries are few ways that you can gather data to monitor students' progress.

To provide informal progress-monitoring information and make mid-lesson adjustments, you should also employ active participation strategies where every student responds. One quick and engaging tool is the use of wipe boards, which are a form of response cards, as described in the Teaching Tip. Response cards, including wipe boards, support engagement, behavior, and achievement. They provide a greater range of students with immediate access to teacher feedback. Students can flash colored cards or complete drawings instead.

Partner talk is another active participation strategy that provides informal assessment information. You might pause during a lesson and ask students to talk with a partner: "Tell your partner one thing you know from the lesson and one thing that makes absolutely no sense. You have two minutes, and then be ready to report." This progress-monitoring strategy can allow each person to safely express his fragile, newly forming knowledge and provide you with new directions for attacking difficult concepts. It also provides a context for language use and development. Active participation strategies can be used during every instructional phase to prove assessment information, as shown in Figure 8.5.

Formative and Summative Assessment—Assessing After Instruction   Ensure that you select postlesson assessments that will allow you to determine the level at which students master your objective. Some checks on objectives will be brief and informal, and some will be much more complex and formal. One "quick check" strategy is to collect and analyze short student work samples. For example, to close a lesson, you have your chemistry students write brief responses to the prompt, "What is the difference between endothermic and exothermic reactions?" You collect their responses and sort them into two stacks: Those who recorded a correct difference, and those who did not. You count how many are in each stack and determine whether to **reteach** or move on. This use of a postinstruction assessment is *formative* because the results are used to shape instruction for the following day.

Postinstruction assessment that is used in a *summative* way instead provides a (relatively) final picture of what students know and can do related to the learning targets standards at

Figure 8.5 *Using active participation strategies to assess student learning throughout all phases of instruction. Refer to figure 6.6, p. 131 (currently).*

Preinstruction Assessments	4. Share a story
	12. Quick writes
	20. Values lineup
	28. Brainstorming and fact-storming
	• Drawings: Students draw a picture of the content and use drawings to describe their knowledge.
	• Four corners: Students respond to prompts that have four possible answers and then go stand in a corner of the room that matches their response. They discuss with corner mates or others.
	• Peer interviews: Students interview each other on prior experiences with the topic.
	• Prior knowledge interviews: Teacher observes students completing a task and asks a few gentle questions.
During-Instruction Assessments	1. Choral response
	2. Whip
	7. Flash cards
	8. Finger signals
	9. Wipe boards
	10. Letter and number tiles
	14. Peer coach
	15. Student-led recitation
	16. Numbered heads together
	17. Toss the ball
	18. Talk to your partner
	27. Sorts
	29. Partner journals
Post-Instruction Assessments	11. Comprehension check
	13. Fuzzy points
	22. Charts and diagrams (individual, group, or whole class)
	25. Student quiz
	30. Blackboard blitz
	31. Gallery tour
	• Graphic organizers: Alone or with assistance, students create visual displays of content information to illustrate their understanding of key concepts and relationships.

hand. In choosing your summative assessments, consider traditional tests created by publishers or by you and your team, and consider performance-based alternatives such as multimedia projects or in-class demonstrations. Most teachers grade students on a mix of formative and summative assessments. Others (e.g., Deddeh, Main, & Fulkerson, 2010) argue that in truly standards-based systems, formative activities—though very important—are for practice only and that term grades should be based entirely on summative assessments. Many such teachers allow students more than one attempt on a summative assessment. For example, algebra teachers I know allow students to retake an exam (actually an alternate form of an exam), no matter the initial grade, as long as students complete a self-analysis of their performance and prepare for the retake. Teachers who employ this practice argue that students master content at different rates and that it increases students' motivation to learn and achieve.

3. Include Your Students

Figure 8.6 is a self-portrait my son Alex drew near the beginning of his kindergarten year. "Good detail," said his mother. "Lots of realistic subtleties! Smart kid!" In the right-hand portion is the self-portrait Alex completed near that year's close. "Yikes!" said his mother. "Less detail. No pupils, no digits, no feet, no hair! No growth in fine motor abilities!" I struggled with my interpretation of those portraits until a wise teacher suggested that I ask *Alex* to analyze the portraits.

Alex easily explained to me the significance of the second portrait. There was less detail, yes, but, he held up both arms, made fists, and flexed his biceps, "Mom, look how *strong* I am!" Alex's most treasured change of his kindergarten year was that he had become physically more capable, much stronger: Superman strong! Had I not asked Alex to attach meaning to his work, to self-evaluate, I would have been left with an unnecessarily limited conclusion about his progress.

Students as Assessment Partners   Alex's self-portrait experience reminded me of a critical principle of assessment: We need to involve students as full partners in the assessment process. Our responsibility is to help students gain the dispositions and skills that will allow them to set goals and monitor their progress in working toward those goals. In doing so, we need to help even the youngest students move from making decisions on assessments without conscious thought to the *strategic* and *reflective level*s of metacognitive practice where they thoughtfully employ a set of strategies to monitor their own thinking and plan for self-improvement (Bingham, Holbrook, & Meyers, 2010).

Figure 8.6   *Alexander's self-portraits.*

| Alex's Early Kindergarten Self-Portrait | Alex's Late Kindergarten Self-Portrait |

Figure 8.7   *The classroom assessment cycle with students as assessment partners.*

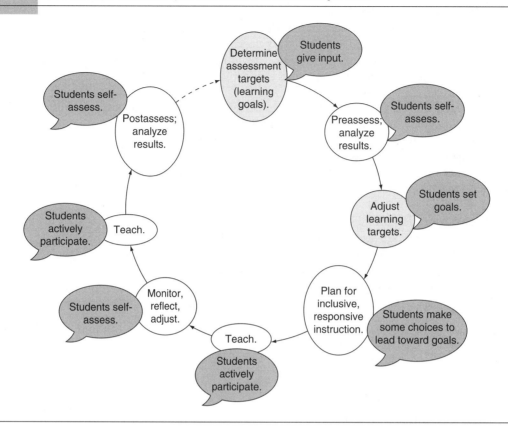

Figure 8.7 gives the assessment cycle again, this time with student input at each step of the way. As you plan to include your students as assessment partners ask about each phase of the cycle:

- How might they have some choices in what they learn and how it will be assessed?
- How can students set their own goals related to the specific content?
- How can they track their progress throughout the learning?
- How can I help them reflect on their learning and set new goals?

Figure 8.8 provides numerous examples of how you can include your students' voices and choices in your assessment by helping students set goals, make assessment choices, self-reflect, and evaluate instruction.

Peers as Assessment Partners   In our efforts to enhance students' skills as evaluators, we can help them to evaluate products from their peers as well. Through peer assessment, students learn to assess the quality of a product or performance without reliance on the teacher. Peer assessment can be informal, such as when students edit each other's work or review homework problems together. It can also be more formal, as when students rate the social skills of group members at the close of a cooperative learning experience.

Families as Assessment Partners   Assessment must include not only students and their peers but families as well. Professional guidelines for teachers (such as the National Board for Professional Teaching Standards, 2002) make it clear that teachers and schools need to take the lead in including families in the process of schooling, including the assessment phase. Families' role is far greater than simply ensuring that students get to bed on time and eat a hearty breakfast before the big tests. Your communication with family members about assessment should be goal-driven, multifaceted, and inclusive of their

Figure 8.8   *Involving students in assessment.*

Goal Setting	• Students discuss previous years and create a chart at the beginning of the year of topics they would like to study. • Students provide input into the course content, choosing units and lessons based on assessment results and their interests. • Students examine their records (portfolios, work samples, and report cards) to set class and personal goals. • Students keep individual records of their progress. They discuss progress and revise goals with their teacher. • Students end an examination by answering the question, "What would you like to learn next?" • Students write a note to their teacher explaining what she should focus on as she assesses a piece of writing or a performance. • The teacher invites students to write long-term goals and seal them in envelopes. The teacher may mail these letters back to students when they reach a certain age.
Student Choice	• Students select some forms of assessment. Teachers who implement multiple intelligence theory often allow students to choose from among seven or eight assessment formats. • Students work in groups to list what they consider the key content to be assessed. • Students develop some questions or prompts for the assessment. • Students select writing prompts or test items from a larger bank. • Students respond to prompts that allow for a broad range of appropriate responses (for example, "Devise a method of sharing equally"). • Students have some say over the assessment conditions (for instance, students are allowed to move to the library if they need isolated conditions or are allowed to have a prompt read aloud to them).
Self-Reflection and Self-Evaluation	• In small groups or in their journals, students discuss their thinking or analyze a problem. • Before submitting work, students analyze their growth, in writing or in a conference. • Before submitting work, students turn the paper over and write to their teacher: "What would you like me to know as I read this paper?" • Students study good and poor examples of the product to be created and assessed. They develop rubrics for use in scoring their products. • Students use rubrics or a checklist from the teacher to assess their own work before submitting it. • Students grade their own papers and hold onto the grade. They compare their analysis with the teacher's analysis and discuss. • Students reflect on their progress over time by comparing work samples from different time periods.
Evaluation of Teaching and Assessment	• Students rate problems and exercises for appropriate level of difficulty (too easy, just right, or too difficult) and for appropriateness of content. • In their journals or on anonymous slips of paper, students tell the teacher what worked well in facilitating their learning and what may have worked even better during particular lessons or units. • Students periodically rate the teacher's instruction, giving specific praise and criticism. Using a specific format can help structure feedback into a format most useful for the teacher, but open-ended questions are important as well. • The teacher regularly provides students with choices for future activities based on the class's assessment of current activities. • The teacher shares his instructional goals with students and revises the goals based on ongoing assessment.

Inclusive and Responsive Teaching Tip

INCLUDING FAMILIES AS ASSESSMENT PARTNERS

- Solicit family input on learning goals.
- Frequently provide newsletters about student learning. Include samples of students' learning products on your web page. Maintain e-mail contact regarding assessment information.
- Try a dialogue journal where you, a family member, and the student communicate about student progress.

- Include family members in regular assignments. One idea is to weekly have students describe to a family member three things they learned. The family member records three things they learned. The family member records those things (in English, the home language, or in another format), perhaps adds a comment, and signs a form.
- Invite family members, baby-sitters, or friends into your class to listen to oral reading, translate, or work with students who need extra support during assessments.

perspectives. The Inclusive and Responsive Teaching Tip gives a few ideas for including families as members of the assessment community.

Another example is **student-led conferences** (Bailey & Guskey, 2001; Benson & Barnett, 2005), where students facilitate a discussion of their progress among family members, teachers, and themselves. This approach to conferencing seems especially popular at the middle school level, but all students can succeed with these conferences. Search "student-led conferences" on the Web for a host of resources, including guidebooks and videos, regarding student-led conferences.

Technological tools also keep us in touch with families regarding assessment. Many teachers use blogs, Web sites, and school-based email to keep in touch with families regarding student progress. Some schools have autodialing systems that notify families about upcoming events—including tests and major assignments. Also, in virtually every state, schools have **Student Information Systems,** or centralized data tracking systems that allow personnel to monitor students' progress over time and to provide more efficient communication and decision making based on student data. Students and families typically have access to these systems through password-protected sites.

Upon log in, families can see everything from daily attendance, to immunization records, to missing assignments and current grades, to transcripts. Students and family members can also communicate directly with teachers and schools via email through such systems. Providing real-time access to students' activities and performance gives parents the information they need to be well-informed partners in schooling.

4. Employ Your Assessments and Analyze the Data

Once you've developed or selected your assessment tools and strategies, employ them throughout the cycle: before, during, and after instruction. Adjust the assessments you use based on your progress monitoring, and adjust your instruction based on your assessments. Keep students actively engaged in instruction and monitoring their own progress.

As you plan to analyze your data, keep your eye on the learning targets that the assessments are to measure, and remember the purpose of each assessment.

Informal Data Analysis: Quick Scans When the stakes are low, as for many preassessments and for progress monitoring through active participation strategies, a quick analysis of whether students are on track is probably sufficient; you and the students simply need to know whether the class is making adequate progress and gain a rough idea of the concepts or skills that might be impairing progress. Students can complete a quick scan to self-monitor. For instance, at the end of a period where your students were tackling a tough problem in small groups, you might ask students to rate their own use of learning skills on a couple questions ("I helped make decisions and solve problems" and "I took risks by exploring something new to me") and then set goals for tomorrow based on their answers.

As another quick scan, a brief glance at the report generated from a clicker pre-quiz (using a student response system) for a sixth-grade geology unit is enough to reveal that two-thirds of the class needs more information about processes that shape the earth's surface (Figure 8.9; The answer is false. Water is the dominant process that shapes the earth's surface.).

For yet another quick scan, you can sort student papers into two stacks: "Getting It!" and "Not Yet!" (as in our earlier chemistry example). If you needed more detailed information from the chemistry students' quick writes, you could further sort the "Not Yet!" examples into stacks based on students' apparent misconceptions. For example, one group may have understood something about energy entering and leaving reactions, whereas one group did not even mention energy. Then you could plan to follow through based on those types of errors.

Formal Data Analysis   Quick data scans are appropriate when you need a rough idea of students' current progress and needs. At many times more formal analytical approaches are appropriate. Formal approaches allow you to be systematic (fair) and to pinpoint more finely students' needs and growth.

One of the most prevalent and useful scoring tools is a rubric. A rubric is a scoring guide that specifies the criteria against which an item will be assessed. Rubrics can be used for scoring many kinds of complex works. Writings, performances, portfolio entries, constructions, and digital projects can all be assessed through rubrics. A **holistic rubric** (one that addresses the overall characteristics of the entry and yields a single score) is found in Figure 8.10.

An **analytical trait rubric** assesses individual traits, or components, of the performance separately (Arter & McTighe, 2001). An analytical trait rubric contains two kinds

Figure 8.9   *Quick scan analysis through audience response data.*

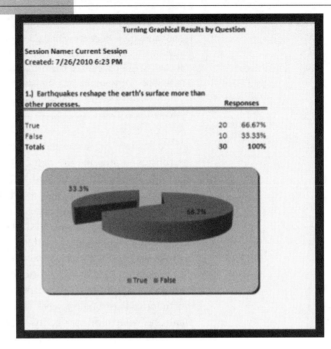

Figure 8.10   *A sample holistic rubric for scoring portfolio entries.*

Score 3	Score 2	Score 1
Entry briefly describes the item that follows but devotes more attention to careful analysis.	Entry describes the item that follows and reflects on it in brief ways.	Entry is solely a simple description of the item that follows. Description may be quite long.
Entry reflects on the author's thinking in meaningful ways.	Entry includes superficial or limited information about the author's thinking.	Entry does not include information about the author's thinking.
Entry addresses content-area concepts accurately and in ways that enrich the reader's understanding of the item that follows the analysis.	Entry addresses content-area concepts in limited, accurate ways.	Entry does not reveal content-area knowledge or content information is inaccurate.

Teaching Tip

NO GUESSING ALLOWED: POST SAMPLE WORKS

The more time students spend guessing what you want, the less time they spend learning. Also, guessing makes people feel dependent rather than powerful. Obtain samples of student work at each of your specified performance levels (e.g., "Not Yet," "Getting There," and "Got It!" or maybe "Developing," "Competent," and "Exemplary"). Post these works on the wall—or online—with a copy of the rubric.

of information: the scale and the dimensions. The scale—usually posted along the top of the rubric—represents the range of performance levels, such as 1, 2, and 3, or "standard not met," "standard met," and "standard exceeded." The dimensions are the individual categories upon which the work will be assessed. They are usually placed along the side. One example is: content, organization, and convention. Another example is creativity, accuracy, and presentation. Visit the Discovery School Web and the Rubistar sites at the close of the chapter to view many examples of analytical rubrics. You may find one to borrow, and you will find many sites that allow you to create your own rubrics.

If you use an existing rubric to score students' work, be sure to share it with them in advance, teaching them its properties and studying examples so that they understand the characteristics of quality work (see Teaching Tip). Students are far more likely to understand and value a rubric deeply if they have helped create it, so at least occasionally it can be productive to help students create the rubrics by which their work will be assessed.

Another formal approach to data analysis is **error pattern analysis.** For skill areas where accuracy is important—such as spelling, beginning reading, writing, mathematics computation, and speech production—error pattern analysis helps you and the student examine the student's work for patterns of inaccurate or missing concepts and skills. It is based on the notion that most of the errors students make are not random; they reflect some incorrect hypothesis or mental rule (McMahon-Klosterman & Ganschow, 1979). By analyzing patterns in incorrect responses, you and the student can find the source of the misunderstanding and build accurate concepts and skills to improve performance. For instance, in mathematics, you might analyze a second-grader's work in subtraction with regrouping to discover that he doesn't regroup tens into ones; he just subtracts the smaller number from the greater number. Here are some general steps for error pattern analysis no matter the subject or grade level.

1. Gather student work samples and, if possible, copy them for markup purposes. In the case of reading, speech, and language, you may use recordings (audio or notes) of the students' production.
2. Mark items as correct or incorrect. (Mark the errors.)
3. Glance at the correct items to be sure they are correct for the right reasons (not just lucky guesses or application of an incorrect rule that happens to work).
4. For incorrect items, cluster the errors students make. In writing, you may note subject/verb disagreement, for instance. In spelling, you may note that the student is not doubling the final consonant before adding a suffix when necessary.
5. Prioritize the error patterns. Determine which should be addressed first.

Error pattern analysis is a very powerful strategy for diagnosing and correcting the kinds of mistakes students make because it is efficient; through it we correct not individual errors but the misunderstandings that lie beneath them. This is a useful process to teach students as well.

Electronic gradebooks and spreadsheets are also helpful tools for understanding classroom assessment data. If students' names are entered in rows and data (such as individual quiz items) are entered as columns, you can sort the data to identify different patterns. For instance, you can see which students are scoring near the top and bottom of the class to be sure to plan appropriate follow-up for those groups, and you can analyze patterns within the data, such as the item people tended to miss most often. In Figure 8.11, it's clear that

Figure 8.11 *Sample spreadsheet with sorted data.*

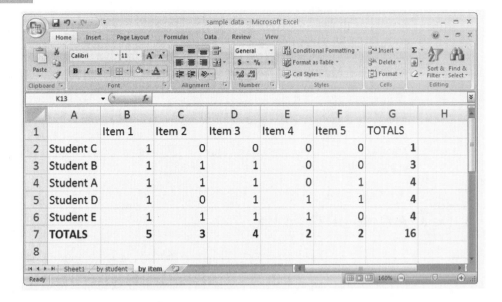

	Item 1	Item 2	Item 3	Item 4	Item 5	TOTALS
Student C	1	0	0	0	0	1
Student B	1	1	1	0	0	3
Student A	1	1	1	0	1	4
Student D	1	0	1	1	1	4
Student E	1	1	1	1	0	4
TOTALS	5	3	4	2	2	16

Student C needs particular support and that the concepts from Item 5 need more attention for the entire class. These applications also calculate statistics that can be useful in analyzing students' performance.

Error pattern analysis of another sort also occurs as teams of teachers examine performance patterns in their standardized test data. Reports give performance by grade level in each assessed area, both in terms of criterion-referenced information (such as raw scores and performance levels) and norm-referenced information (such as percentiles). Results are provided in clusters of state standards so that teams can determine patterns of strength and new areas of instructional emphasis for the coming year. By contributing to these discussions and by working with grade-level or department teams to analyze student work, and by using Student Information Systems, you contribute to the larger picture of student progress as measured through assessment.

5. Use What You Learn

Use your assessment results to guide what happens next in your classroom. For example, despite the fact that teachers in two studies could accurately discern error patterns in students' work, they did not base their plans for instructional intervention upon those error

Teaching Tip

TEST AND THEN RETEACH

- Analyze the results of a paper-and-pencil test and look for the four to seven major error patterns or gaps in students' thinking.
- Form flexible groups that are composed of students with similar gaps.
- Spend a bit of time working with each group, providing instruction tailored directly for the need they displayed on the test.

For instance, on day 1, your students take the district's multiple-choice benchmark test in mathematics. The test is computer scored and returned to you on day 3. On day 4, you spend 20 minutes in small-group time, discussing only item 1 of the test. Your groups are a, b, c, d, or e, depending on their selected answer to item 1. On the next day, you meet again for item 2, and so on for the four problems students missed most.

patterns (Cooper, 2009; Riccomini, 2005). Be sure to use what you learn. The Teaching Tip gives one idea for reteaching after a multiple-choice test.

If students demonstrate deep mastery of the content, you may need to increase your pace or skip ahead. If many do not, you have some choices to make: Should you stick with the pacing guide or stop and reteach? This is a common dilemma. It can be helpful to understand the structure of your curriculum. For instance, some curricula "spiral" or revisit content at deeper levels in subsequent units, so students will be given further opportunities to master information. You can also pull small groups of students during a few minutes of reteaching time, use family volunteers to work with individuals throughout the day, work with them outside the class period, or provide other opportunities for independent content learning outside the school day, such as Web-based instruction. You can differentiate homework, too, to ensure mastery. Finally, use what you learn to help you start the cycle anew: to plan the next set of learning targets.

A Note on Grading

To manage the dilemmas associated with assigning grades to students' performance, you need to reason your way through each issue with a good deal of thought. The grades you record need to follow the same guidelines as your assessments. In general, you need to assign and then grade the things that matter; you need to capture a rich portrait of what students know and can do; you need to be fair and systematic, including the students; and you need to be efficient. Here is some advice for grading.

1. Find a copy of the grade report used for your level before you begin teaching and entering grades. Check the alignment of the report card with your content standards. Determine whether each item is assessed every term. Use that information to guide your long-term planning. Use the report form to structure your grading, but also collect other information that is important to you and may not show up on the grade report.

2. Inform students of criteria for grades in advance. Students who receive challenging assignments and have clear grading criteria perform better than those who don't (Matsumura & Pascal, 2003). In every case possible, allow student input into grading criteria, perhaps using strategies such as backwards planning.

3. Think about the role of daily homework in students' overall grades. If a student aces every test but refuses to do homework, should the final grade be an F? If so, you will be awarding a grade for something other than content mastery, which was demonstrated through exam performance. Is that other criterion reasonable and clearly specified?

4. Similarly, check grading policies for students with significant academic disabilities. How will you denote that a student may be performing consistent with capability, but still be earning a failing grade? Many teachers worry about the demoralizing effects on students who consistently earn failing grades despite their best efforts, yet these teachers appreciate the importance of consistent standards.

5. Be careful of how much weight you place on assignments that are completed outside of class. Unless you specify that family members should be involved in completing a major project, you probably need to be guarded in the importance you award it. For instance, some middle school teachers are tempted to weight a science fair project heavily despite the fact that it is completed almost entirely at home. Under these conditions, the teachers cannot be sure whose work they are grading. Additionally, not all homes have the resources to support students in projects such as these. Be sure to provide in-class instructional support for any major project and have checkpoints along the way.

6. Be careful of how you award extra credit; use it to reward appropriate performance. As a counterexample, I have witnessed teachers award extra credit points when their students donate the novels they purchased to the class library. In a sense, students buy a portion of their grade if they can afford the price of a novel. Similarly, some teachers award extra credit points at the end of a term if students did not use their

allotment of bathroom passes. In both of these cases, nonacademic performance (financial donations and bladder control) is rewarded with academic grades. Additionally, if you award extra credit, ensure that its weight as a portion of the grade reflects your priorities.

7. Don't write a grade on every piece of paper. Some assignments are just for practice. In fact, many teachers judge homework assignments as complete or not and reteach to address errors. Or they collect and grade a sample of homework. Also, feedback needs to be timely for it to be useful to the learner. Don't collect stacks of papers if you cannot return them for weeks.

8. When you grade papers, be specific in your feedback. "Great job" feels good, but it doesn't give advice on how to repeat the performance for next time. If you write praise, make sure it is based on the quality of the performance and not on your opinion as an authority. "Your use of color creates a sense of excitement" is more relevant and helpful than "I love your use of color."

9. Instead of entering percentages in your grade book (paper or electronic), translate grades into smaller numbers. Some teachers use a 1- to 12-point system, others use a 1- to 5-point system. If you keep a paper gradebook, consider adding the points as you record them so that your work is done at the end of the term. Using smaller numbers not only makes figuring totals easier, it avoids penalizing students for low scores the way entering tiny percentages can. (Mathematically, it is difficult to overcome even a single 23%.)

10. After you figure grades, check again that marks accurately reflect your global assessment of each student's growth. Be prepared to defend every grade you report to families. Be open to the possibility that you may have misgraded. Be ready to say what students will need to do differently for different marks.

11. Be careful in the words you write in the comment section of a grade report. Remember that those words will be the ones that follow students for years after they leave you. Include only relevant comments. Be constructive. Point out every student's growth.

12. Work with grade-level and department teams to develop common, consistent, and fair approaches to grading student work.

A Sampler of Assessments

You may choose from hundreds of available assessment techniques and tools. This sampler describes in a nutshell 10 classroom assessment techniques.

Traditional Tests

Traditional paper-and-pencil measures can be furnished through adopted textbook series or written by teachers (most typically alone or in teams with other teachers, but students can also contribute items). Some common types of questions on traditional tests include selection-type and constructed response items. Objective items tend to be time-consuming to write but quick to grade and are subject to little interpretation from the grader. Open-ended questions include short-answer items, essay questions, and less traditional variations such as graphic organizers and pictorial representations of students' knowledge. Teachers' time investment with open-ended items tends to be not in the writing phase but in the assessment phase. Open-ended items require more judgment from the grader than do objective items. If you write your own tests, consider the following:

- Include a mix of selection-type and constructed-response items so you have a richer picture of student knowledge.
- Make the response format efficient for students so that it is less tiring and so that there is no question about what they wrote. (For example, have them circle T or F rather than writing the word.)

- Make the prompts clear and specific so that students understand the parameters.
- Keep your tests short. Any test is just a snapshot.
- Include common errors among the choices. This can increase the validity of your measure. (Wormeli, 2006)

Attitude Surveys

Usually developed by teachers, attitude surveys are paper-and-pencil scales that assess students' preferences and feelings toward a topic or skill. Some prompts are closed-ended. For instance, students can rank order lists of subjects in terms of their preferences or agree/disagree with a set of items. In Kagan's (2001) Spend a Buck, students "spend" their hypothetical dollar as they wish to vote for certain items on a scale. For young students, a survey item can be read aloud while the students circle one of a continuum of faces, very happy to very sad. Open-ended items allow for a broad range of student responses. An example is "What I would like you to know about me as an artist is _____." Many teachers use attitude surveys near the beginning of the year to become acquainted with their students.

Products

Students submit items to demonstrate their understanding or skill. Examples include student-composed newspapers, digital stories, brochures, dioramas, posters, works of art, multimedia presentations, and scientific or practical inventions. Many performance-based assessments result in products.

Portfolios

Portfolios are collections of work samples over time and from a variety of contexts, together with students reflections on those work samples (Hebert, 2001; Stefanakis, 2002). Some items are typically chosen by the teacher, and some are student selected. Students write reflections about the entries in order to discuss their learning. Portfolios can be hard copy or they can be electronic. Two benefits of the electronic portfolio are its portability and multimedia format. Conduct a Web search using the terms "student portfolios" and "electronic portfolios" for plentiful examples.

Journals

Used primarily for informal assessment, journals can be completed by children as young as kindergartners. Students can respond to prompts from the teacher in pictures, symbols, or written words. They may also write with no prompt from the teacher. One of the primary benefits of journals is that they have a broad range of applications. Students can use them to describe their thinking, to document their experiences, to ask questions, to converse with a peer or the teacher, and to analyze their growth. Sample journal prompts include "What is mathematics?" and "How do you use mathematics in your daily life?" (Newmann, 1994).

Performance-Based Assessments

Students demonstrate competence by applying knowledge in a real-world setting, through a performance. Discrete skills such as cutting, counting, shooting a basket, or focusing a microscope can be assessed through student performances, as can more complex behaviors such as reading and social problem solving. Performance-based assessment is a major trend in assessment for the 21st century (Darling-Hammond & McCloskey, 2008).

Teacher Observations

Teachers observe students working and interacting under typical classroom conditions. Examples include students' use of science process skills, their play behavior, and their ability to work as part of a team. To be systematic in their observations, teachers keep anecdotal records that describe their students' behaviors. Some teachers take notes on individual students, date the observations, and then collect them in file folders. This system allows teachers to analyze individual students' performances over time.

Interviews

In clinical interviews, teachers work with one student, or just a few students, at a time. Students typically complete a task that allows the teacher to probe their reasoning. For instance, in an interview to assess a student's prior concepts in science, a teacher might sit with the student and display a house plant. The teacher may ask her pupil to describe the plant and to hypothesize about the functions of the plant's parts. In a reading interview, a teacher might ask her student to point out and discuss features of the text that help convey the text's message.

Drawings and Diagrams

Drawings and diagrams allow you to tap into students' knowledge through visual means. Drawings used over time are often highly effective at demonstrating change in students' thinking and abilities. Students can draw their understandings of specific terms, emotions, experiences, and objects throughout history. One example is provided in Figure 8.12. The left side shows Zachary's portrayal of a squid when he was 4 years old. The right column was completed 5 years later. Both pictures demonstrate that he had some understanding of the external structure of a squid, and we see significant growth over time. Further, we see that he has some ideas still developing, even in his later drawing. For instance, the chromatophores (spots) are actually grouped, not randomly spread over the squid's body.

Figure 8.12   *Compare the two drawings and view Zachary's knowledge as emergent: What does he know about squid structure? How has it changed over time? What does he need to understand next?*

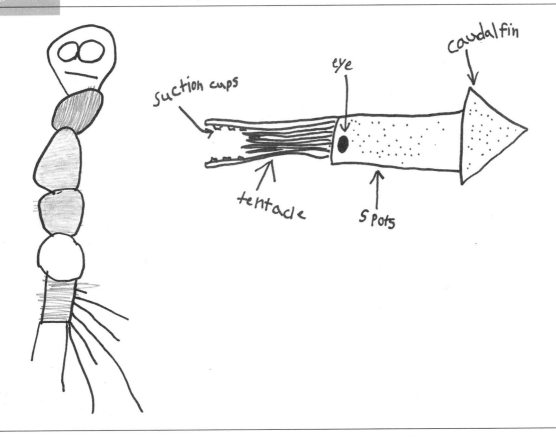

Graphic Organizers

In addition to drawings, students can also complete a variety of graphic organizers (introduced as an instructional tool in Chapter 6). One widely used organizer is the concept map (Novak, 1990, 1991, 1998). Research on concept mapping indicates that it support students' achievement and helps them organize and represent their knowledge (Edwards & Fraser, 1983; Novak & Gowin, 1984). As the sample concept map in Figure 6.9 shows, a major concept or term is given at the top of the map. Beneath it, subconcepts are presented hierarchically. Each concept is related to one above it with a line or an arrow and a verb phrase that specifies the nature of the relationship between the two concepts. Often concepts are connected to more than one other concept. In general, the more concepts listed on a map, and the more accurately and richly connected they are, the better developed the author's thinking about that topic.

Parting Words

Assessment of student progress is a messy business. Something as simple as writing a letter grade on a student paper requires us to ask ourselves difficult questions such as, "What does this letter represent? Is it growth over time, or does it show that this is one of the best papers in the stack? Does it deserve this letter when the writing is so flawed, despite that it shows understanding of the content?" Teaching is a complex moral endeavor, and the weight of an evaluator's role should be great. However, there is also incredible power that comes through assessment. When you conduct valid assessments, you peer through a window into students' thinking and gain entrée to avenues that can propel your students' growth and development. When you help them improve as self-assessors, you teach them dispositions and skills that will useful to them daily as autonomous beings.

Opportunities to Practice

1. Pull out your stance on education from Chapter 2 and the two or three overarching goals you developed in Chapter 5 as a result of your stance. Reread your stance and goals with an eye toward assessment.

   a. As you develop your assessment system, think about what kinds of information you will need to gather as a result of your view of what is important. How can you gather that information in ways that remain true to your convictions?

   b. In evaluating your assessment system, consider the following: How does this system reflect your view of the good society? Of the purpose of education? Of teaching? Of learning? If you find little concrete evidence to link your stance toward education with your system for assessing student learning, you probably need to spend a bit more time revising the system—or the stance—to more accurately reflect your professional views.

2. Use the Assessment Analysis in Figure 8.13 to evaluate the potential of one of the instruments in use in a classroom, and try it with any newly discovered assessment strategy.

3. If you are currently teaching, try one of the assessment strategies from earlier in this chapter. Reflect on the experience. If it provided useful information, what would you need to do to arrange your classroom to include this strategy in your assessment system?

4. Survey your students on their opinions about assessment. Use the survey to determine how they prefer to demonstrate their learning. Ask about how teachers help them learn to assess their own work. Share your results.

5. Try one of the Teacher Tips from this chapter. Examples include using an audience response system or wipe boards for formative assessment and writing an online quiz.

6. You saw Alex's kindergarten self-portraits in Figure 8.6. Now look at Figure 8.14 for the final version, completed at the end of his K–12 years. Make a list of all the ways his portraits have changed from kindergarten to grade 12. Have they retained any commonalties? (By the way, when I showed Alex the kindergarten portraits, he said, "Now I don't feel so bad about how this one looks." He appreciated his growth over time!) Where would you guide him next as an artist?

Figure 8.13 *Assessment analysis.*

Instrument: Intended Purpose: Check Use(s): _____ Before Instruction _____During Instruction _____After Instruction		

Criterion	Evidence or Notes	Usefulness for Intended Purpose

1. Instrument measures valued outcome(s). Domain(s):
  a. Cognitive
  b. Affective
  c. Psychomotor
	Valued outcomes:	1. low medium high
		
		a. low medium high
		b. low medium high
		c. low medium high

2. Instument's use can include students as assessment partners
  a. Goal setting
  b. Student choice
  c. Progress tracking
  d. Reflection on learning
  e. Families as partners
		a. low medium high
		b. low medium high
		c. low medium high
		d. low medium high
		e. low medium high

3. Instrument contributes to fair assessment
  a. Every student
  b. Valid
  c. Reliable
		a. low medium high
		b. low medium high
		c. low medium high

4. Results from the instrument have a high potential of being useful.		4. low medium high
5. Instrument is likely to provide information that contributes to the bigger picture of student progress.		5. low medium high
Overall evaluation of the instrument for intended use:		

Figure 8.14   *Alex's drawing.*

 Web Sites

http://act.org
> *ACT. The ACT is a widely accepted college admissions test. Read about the test your students may take. Check resources for educators and parents (including a student blog).*

http://www.cse.ucla.edu/
> *CRESST: National Center for Research on Evaluation, Standards, and Student Testing. Contains resources that are both scholarly (see the Reports and Policy Briefs) and practical (see the pages for Teachers and Parents).*

http://school.discovery.com/schrockguide/assess.html
> *Discovery School's Kathy Schrock's Guide for Educators: Teacher Helpers Assessment and Rubric Information. This guide contains many Web-based resources for classroom assessment and grading, including alternative assessments and report card comments.*

http://www.ets.org/
> *Educational Testing Service. Go to "Tests" to read about many of the tests you and your students may take.*

http://www.fairtest.org/
> *FairTest. The Web site of the National Center for Fair and Open Testing, which promotes "fair, open, valid and educationally beneficial evaluations" and "works to end the misuses and flaws of testing practices." Check the "What's New" page for the Center's work directed toward NCLB, and see the K–12 testing page.*

http://www.inspiration.com
> *Inspiration is a commercial software product that allows you and your students to develop concept maps and other graphic organizers. You can download a free trial version of the software at this site.*

http://www.lasw.org/
> *Looking at Student Work. Gives strategies for teachers to work together and with families to examine student work for a number of purposes. The site includes protocols and strategies for analyzing student work.*

http://nces.ed.gov/nationsreportcard/
> *The Nation's Report Card: The National Assessment of Education Progress program. Read the findings by state or subject matter. Click on "Sample Questions" to try released items in a variety of subject areas and grade levels.*

http://www.nclb.gov/
> *The No Child Left Behind Web site.*

http://www.pisa.oecd.org
Organization for Economic Co-operation and Development: Programme for International Student Assessment. Read about what this international assessment measures, which 65 countries participated in 2009, and how students fared.

http://rubistar.4teachers.org/index.php
Rubistar. Create your own rubrics at this site. Continue to explore rubrics at http://www.internet4teacher.com.

http://www.internet4classrooms.com/links_grades_
kindergarten_12/assessment_tools_teacher_tools.htm
Internet4Classroom's Assessment Tool's page. Many links to rubric builders, test makers, and alternative assessment formats.

Also try searching with search terms for specific issues and strategies in assessment. Examples include:

Authentic assessment
Classroom assessment (sites give assessment techniques)
Formative assessment
Gradebook programs (many sites have free downloads)
Performance assessment
Portfolio assessment
Standardized testing
Statewide achievement testing

Managing the Learning Environment

9

Before You Begin Reading

Warm-Up Exercise for Managing the Learning Environment

Think of a store or other business that you hold in high regard: a place of business where you actually do not mind spending your time. Got it? Jot down some brief notes in response to each of the prompts.

1. Describe the physical space. What aspects of it appeal to you? Do any make your life more difficult? Which?

2. Describe how time is used within this store or business. What aspects please you? Which irritate you?

3. Describe typical interactions in this business. What do you expect? What happens when interactions are not up to your expectations?

4. You wrote the responses from the perspective of a customer. How (if at all) would your responses have changed if you wrote from the boss's perspective? From an employee's? Analyze whether your responses can teach you anything about the way you would like to manage your classroom.

"Never before have we had so little time in which to do so much."

—Franklin Delano Roosevelt

You have so much to accomplish with your students! As you teach them content, you must manage them as groups within a tight space, with limited materials, and with never enough time. The work you've begun as an inclusive and responsive teacher continues right through your classroom management. That is, you continue to focus on improving your understanding of yourself and your students; build relationships of acceptance, trust, support, and communicate high expectations; and use inclusive and responsive management approaches that value students as individuals while pushing them toward success. The research on classroom management provides three very clear directions for effective classroom management.

1. Effective managers conduct all classroom management within the context of trusting, caring relationships and toward the goal of helping students manage themselves, individually and as a community (Bondy, Ross, Gallingane, & Hambacher, 2007; Brophy, 2010; Freiberg, 1996; Weinstein, Tomlinson-Clarke, & Curran, 2004).
2. Effective managers maintain a structured, predictable, and task-oriented learning environment (Brown, 2004; Simonsen, Fairbanks, Briesch, Myers, & Sugai, 2008).
3. Effective managers maximize learning time by engaging students and minimizing disruptions (Jones, 1987; Palumbo & Sanacore, 2007).

Effective classroom management not only makes life more pleasant for everyone, it teaches important social skills and translates into student achievement (Bohn, Roehrig, & Pressley, 2004; Emmer, Evertson, & Anderson, 1980; Evertson & Emmer, 1982; Freiberg, Connell, & Lorentz, 2001; Freiberg, Huzinec, & Templeton, 2009).

This chapter encourages you to develop a classroom management plan that shapes a productive and humane learning environment. Research indicates that classroom management systems must be coherent, consistent, positive, and proactive (Miller & Hall, 2009). In order to help you build such a system, the chapter addresses four components of classroom management:

- Creating community: Managing classroom ambience
- Managing physical space
- Managing resources: The stuff of teaching
- Managing time

> **REMEMBER THE LAW**
>
> Protect physical safety.
>   Provide adequate supervision.
> *Refresher from Figure 1.2.*

Creating Community: Managing Classroom Ambience

An inclusive and responsive teacher provides an environment where students behave appropriately from a sense of responsibility for themselves and for each other rather than from fear of punishment or desire for a reward (Metropolitan Center for Urban Education, 2008). Your central task is to meld a group of individuals without common ground or goals into a classroom community. Kohn (1996, p. 101) defines the classroom community as

> a place in which students feel cared about and are encouraged to care about each other. They experience a sense of being valued and respected; the children matter to one another and to the teacher. They have come to think in the plural: they feel connected to each other; they are part of an "us."

Such a community recognizes each person's experiences and perspectives.

Know Thyself

The task of understanding others begins with us recognizing the limits of our own understandings. In a testament to the importance of self-awareness, an ancient Greek inscribed

21st Century Teaching and Learning Tip

BUILDING CULTURAL PROFICIENCY

Skilled citizens of the 21st century communicate and work effectively with diverse teams by responding open-mindedly to others' values, respecting differences, and using social and cultural differences to increase innovation (Partnership for 21st Century Skills, 2009). To increase your cultural proficency, visit the Web and search "cultural proficiency" and "cultural competence." Try some of the assessments (such as the Cultural Proficiency Receptivity Scale) and activities, and check out the many podcasts that provide information on cultural profiency as well. Great resources to get you started are at Cecil County Public Schools site (http://staffdevelopment.ccps.org/ETMA/CulturalProficiency.html).

the advice "Know thyself" (γν ῶθι σεαυτόν) on the Temple of Apollo at Delphi. Just as is the case with our instructional decisions, facets of our identity such as our own upbringings and personality quirks influence our classroom preferences. Factors such as our generation, gender, ethnicity, and social class affect our management decisions, often in subtle or unconscious ways (Weinstein, Tomlinson-Clarke, & Curran, 2004). As an example, teachers commonly use nondirective strategies like hints ("Everyone should be working right now") despite the mismatch this may create for the many students whose families (such as many African-American families) use more directive approaches to discipline (Brown, 2004; Ware, 2006). Building cultural proficiency, including self-awarenss is an important goal (see the 21st Century Teaching and Learning Tip). Exploring our own identities can help us to make informed management decisions. To create community, ensure that the classroom reflects your students as individuals and, over time, the group you become together (e pluribus unum: Out of many, one).

E Pluribus . . .

Use a variety of strategies to ensure that your room recognizes every member. You can help members get to know each other through strategies such as oral history interviews, artifact interviews, and ice breakers such as "Find someone who. . ." mixers. You can use bulletin boards where each student has a place to pin treasures like sports awards, community service recognitions, pictures of pets, and personal mementoes. You can invite students to share their school-appropriate music choices for playing during transitions or work periods. You might hang a world map under the title Everyone Is from Somewhere and ask students to add push pins for their families' roots. When teacher Jennifer Cunningham learned that her class would include a student just arrived from Russia, she researched words for common classroom objects and hung the Russian (and English) terms around her room.

. . . Unum

It's also important to use activities to forge a sense of the group. Many strategies are worth a try. Make a list of a dozen or more quick jobs that students can accomplish as managers; contributing from day 1 to the functioning of the classroom increases students' sense of ownership and can save you hours of instructional time. You might together brainstorm a list of community characteristics that members appreciate. Students might create a class Magna Carta (Freiberg, 1996). You can hold regular community circles, or **classroom meetings,** where students recognize each other's efforts and address an agenda of issues they select. Meetings are productive for all and have been shown effective for increasing the social inclusion of students with special needs (Frederickson, Warren, & Turner, 2005). You can invite students to plan and create a whole-class bulletin board, maybe to accompany the current unit or season. Students might enjoy making a class scrapbook, time line, or Web site to capture its unfolding history. One classroom job can be photographer; have this manager collect photos of students that can be shared in celebratory slide shows. Eating together nearly always builds community and provides an opportunity to talk about food rituals from students' worlds. You can also capitalize on those moments in history that

Inclusive and Responsive Teaching Tip

ROBIN'S TIPS FOR BUILDING COMMUNITY

Robin Mackie thoroughly enjoys her job teaching middle school students' English Language Development (ELD). Robin focuses on rigor and student engagement within a context of community. Here are 18 of Robin's strategies for creating community.

1. I tell them I care for them like a mother hen cares for her chicks.
2. I teach and enforce manners. I do not banter with students.
3. I have a sense of humor and tell stories to the students about my childhood and random silly things to be human to them.
4. I share my feelings and let them know they have power to hurt or heal with their words—other students and me.
5. I ask forgiveness for my mistakes individually or to the whole class.
6. I use positive touch—hand on shoulder, knuckles, hand-shake; I give hugs to girls and side squeezes to boys.
7. I have a teacher Facebook account.
8. I attend community events when possible.
9. I call home during class sometimes to say hello to sick students.
10. I decorate the classroom with their help.
11. I make a banner with all my advisement students' pictures on it.
12. I bring treats on special days.
13. I give birthday goodie bags and certificates. I post birthdays in my window.
14. I use Participation Cards to ensure equal participation.
15. We discuss sports and other topics in class.
16. We watched YouTube videos in Gujarati of a hip-hop song my student Adya liked, and she taught us how to sing it.
17. We use real adolescent issues to discuss grammar and writing.
18. I read aloud great books, especially ones with fun "voice." The room is always silent and they beg me to read longer.

Robin Mackie

bring you together. For example, when it snowed one day (very unusual!), my sixth-graders and I spent a cold 20 minutes outside enjoying it rather than attending to the lesson in my plan book. The Inclusive and Responsive Teaching Tip shares other strategies for forging a sense of community.

Creating Community Using a Range of Strategies

As Robin's tip indicates, you'll need to actively employ a broad range of strategies to build classroom community. The range includes your modeling of genuine respect and regard, the choices you make for the physical environment, your procedures and routines for conducting business, and the ways you communicate with the students and require them to communicate with each other.

Classroom community begins to develop through the tone, or ambience, you create from the first day of school. *Ambience* refers to the mood or atmosphere of your classroom environment. Some classrooms are subdued and businesslike, some are homey, and others are full of noise and excitement. Classroom ambience can vary widely and still encourage student success. Although what works best for each of us varies, you probably want to establish an ambience that

- *Encourages students to take risks* by providing for emotional safety and a sense of belonging.
- *Provides for intellectual stimulation* by including appealing displays, plenty of resources, and interesting objects.

- *Fosters social interaction* by providing space and opportunities for students to work together.
- *Conveys a sense that school is a pleasant experience.*
- *Communicates your stance toward education* without you saying a word.

Metaphors and other analogies can provide a starting point for helping us think about ambience. You may recall, for instance, the metaphors for teaching suggested in Chapter 1's Opportunities to Practice, Exercise 2. Refer back to your stance on education as a guide for the kind of atmosphere you would like to establish. Skim your stance and compose a single-sentence simile: "I want my classroom to feel like a _____." Sample responses that may fill in the blank include the following:

- *Board room* (where powerful people meet to accomplish important things)
- *Garden* (where beautiful, dissimilar plants are given everything they need to flourish and bloom)
- *United Nations* (where people from around the world work toward international cooperation)
- *Home* (where people who care about each other live together in comfortable surroundings)
- *Hospital* (a clean, safe environment where people leave healthier than when they entered)
- *Sports camp* (where individuals hone their skills in preparation for the big game)

Analogies provide very different directions for the kinds of physical arrangements, displays, furnishings, routines, and activities that teachers select in managing their classrooms. Imagine, for example, how differently a home and a hospital classroom would appear at first glance.

Home
- Overall atmosphere is cozy and warm
- Displays are personalized and cluttered
- Desks are arranged in groups for interaction
- Each group has materials at the center
- Several ongoing projects are out in view
- Lots of personal touches: fabric curtains, lamps, colorful rug, radio, potted plants, and rocking chair

Hospital
- Overall atmosphere is neat and calm
- Wall displays have coordinated backgrounds
- Desks are arranged in rows for efficiency
- Materials are placed out of sight
- All surfaces are clean and shiny
- Colors are limited but carefully used

Select a physical arrangement, time schedule, routines, and instructional activities that build community and convey your convictions about what education should accomplish. Students can contribute. You might ask students as homework to create a map of the perfect classroom, given the furniture and resources available to you (Thorson, 2003). Students could present maps and then decide on a single map or a combination of maps to try out in

Teaching Tip

THINK TWICE ABOUT WINNERS AND LOSERS

Inclusive and responsive teachers base decisions on solid knowledge of their specific students. Mild competition can enhance engagement (Marzano, 2007), but not everyone enjoys it. Survey your students to determine how many of them enjoy friendly classroom competition. In my experience, about one-half the students in a class enjoy competition. Work their preferences into the classroom in ways that help them feel welcome and yet do not detract from the sense of community. You might undo the sense of community you try so hard to maintain by using a game if students focus more on winning and losing than on the learning. Try some alternatives: "Let's see if we can beat our best class time (or scores)." "To win this game, each team needs five examples." "Each presentation will receive an award. Be listening to see what each one does best."

your room. It is ultimately the *people*—the way they treat each other and the way they care for their space—who define the ambience. Additionally, you can help students feel like they belong by making careful choices about the games you play; see the Teaching Tip.

Turn to Figures 9.7 and 9.8 now to begin planning for your own management system, including ambience. Community develops, in part, through your decisions about managing the classroom's physical space.

Managing the Physical Space

Consider the range of learning goals for your student and use your physical space to match those goals. Visualizing the classroom as "learning space" (Faltis, 2001) and breaking away from the traditional "teacher up front, students facing forward" pattern may allow you to identify many areas in the classroom where teaching and learning can occur. Think about the different kinds of space you and your students will need. At the elementary level, these spaces typically include an area for desks or tables for seatwork, at least one area from which you can teach the whole class, small-group work spaces, and an area for messy tasks. Secondary classrooms typically make fewer provisions for student movement or a variety of activities in part because classrooms tend to serve more specialized purposes, such as cooking rooms and science laboratories.

Although your physical space should be carefully structured, it should also allow for flexibility (Simonsen, Fairbanks, Briesch, Myers, & Sugai, 2008). Teachers at all levels should remember to use student seats flexibly, rearranging the room as dictated by instructional activities. Because a variety of grouping patterns can be effective for supporting student engagement (Bohn, Roehrig, & Pressley, 2004; Vaughn, Hughes, Moody, & Elbaum, 2001), you will no doubt want to be able to rearrange student seats so that they can work total group, alone, in partners, and in small groups (that's TAPS from Chapter 4).

Also consider using your wall space, windows, and ceiling (if allowed) to their fullest advantage. Enrich the environment with special-interest areas such as a puzzle center (you too, high school teachers), a class library, or a music center. Ensure that you minimize distractions and overcrowding and that activities and traffic can flow easily (Simonsen, Fairbanks, Briesch, Myers, & Sugai, 2008).

Rich resources are more fully utilized when they are organized efficiently.

Source: Anthony Magnacca/Merril

As you arrange for the different areas in your classroom, be certain that you can **monitor** students at all times and that they are free from the threat of physical danger. For instance, do not allow them to stand on a chair stacked on a desk so that they can reach a top shelf. In addition to safety, your choices for arranging the physical space can be used to enhance the spirit of cooperation. Glance around the room and see what the arrangement says about the balance of power, about student choice, about meaningful study, and about a sense of the group. Finally, when considering each option for the layout of space and resources, ask yourself two questions:

- Is it productive?
- Is it efficient?

Is It Productive?

Productivity requires that:

1. *The space allows for a balanced variety of activities.* You address students' physical, social, and emotional needs when you provide for shifts in movement. For young students especially, plan to balance seat time with floor time, whole-group instruction with individual or small-group work, and quiet activities with more boisterous ones. School tends to be a highly public place. Design an area that allows for privacy within safety constraints and crowded conditions.

2. *People can see and hear each other.* Charney (2002) contends that for students to feel safe they must feel seen. She arranges her classroom with few visual barriers so that when positioned at her work space, she can see the entire class. You need to be able to see students, and they need to be able to see you—and each other. Research indicates that face-to-face seating arrangements facilitate student interaction, and that students ask more questions in such arrangements (Marx, Fuhrer, & Hartig, 1999). You'll recall from Chapter 7 that student-generated questions facilitate learning.

When it's time for students to look at you for whole-class instruction, some may need to turn their desks toward you. Teach them to quickly rearrange their seats so that they can participate in the lesson. So that students can hear other members of their group during cooperative lessons, you can teach them to use "six-inch voices," which are voices that can only be heard from a distance of six inches.

3. *The students are able to focus their attention on the task at hand.* Sit in the students' desks and look up to check visibility of the screens and other instructor stations. Try anticipating potential problem areas from these new vantage points. Is your directed lesson competing with a colorful bulletin board or the aquarium behind you? Are some students looking into the light because they face windows? Is the noisy science center positioned far enough away from your math group to allow students to focus on their work? Will the students working on the computers distract the others?

Is It Efficient?

Efficiency in the physical layout allows you and the students to complete tasks without delays. Efficiency requires that

1. *You can get to each of the students quickly.* Physical proximity is important for encouraging appropriate behavior, providing assistance, and ensuring safety. Fred Jones (2000) emphasizes that the greater the physical distance between students and teacher, the less likely students are to remain **on task.** Arrange your room so that you can quickly get to each of the students by positioning furniture to create wide walkways. Jones suggests that tables and desks be arranged so that the traffic pattern forms a loop, or circuit. Figure 9.1 gives a sample floor plan with the loop marked.

2. *The students can get to each other.* Student access to peers is helpful in efficient distribution of materials and in small-group and partner work.

3. *You and the students can get to the materials.* Much time can be wasted as students wait for paper or other supplies. Position materials for easy access. For instance, store

Figure 9.1   *Sample floor plan with teacher's loop marked.*

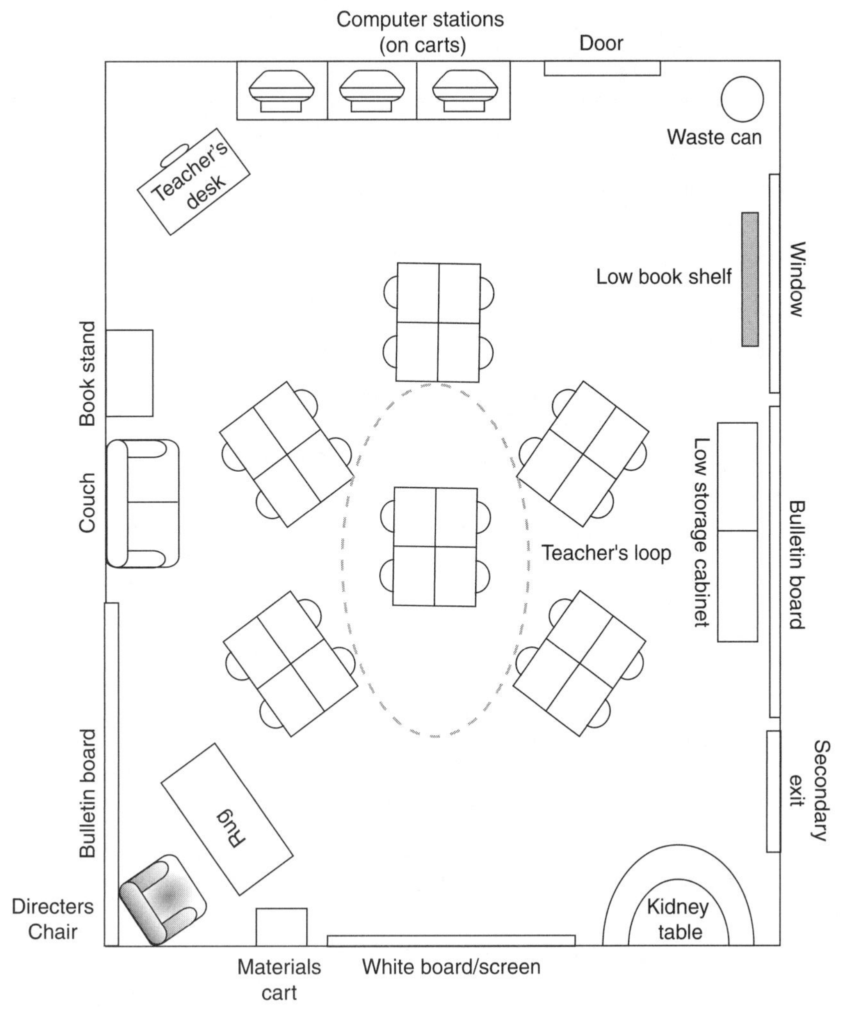

Computer stations
(on carts)

Door

Waste can

Teacher's desk

Low book shelf

Window

Book stand

Teacher's loop

Low storage cabinet

Bulletin board

Couch

Bulletin board

Rug

Directers
Chair

Secondary
exit

Kidney
table

Materials
cart

White board/screen

materials as close as possible to the area where they will be used. Then train students how and when to distribute and use the materials. Some teachers assign two or three students to be paper passers, so that the teacher gives a word and three assistants snap to work. In cooperative learning classrooms, each group typically has a supply sergeant who is responsible for gathering and collecting materials. If students fill the supply role in your classroom—and you have trained them well—let them know that if they cannot perform, they lose the job. Doing so prevents students from dawdling and allows them to take pride in a job that must be done well.

4. *You and the students can get other places easily.* Arrange furniture and work areas to avoid traffic jams. Think about areas that tend to draw crowds (the pencil sharpener and the drinking fountain, for instance) and provide wide margins for each. Position student seats so that these high-draw areas do not interfere with their work. Be certain that all students can reach the exits quickly in times of emergency. Figure 9.2 reviews sections of the classroom's physical space and provides guidelines to consider for each area. After you've arranged your room, sit in some of the students' desks around the room.

Figure 9.2 *Checkpoints for a classroom's physical space.*

Work Areas	Checkpoints
Desks or tables for seatwork	• Match seating arrangements with your stance and the instruction you hope to provide. • Rows can be effective—especially for new teachers—if the instruction is good and desks are used flexibly. Rows may be useful, at least for the first days of school, until students have learned your expectations about talking and work times. But don't let rows interfere with the development of a sense of community. • In row configurations, short and shallow (many columns with few desks) is typically better than narrow and deep (few columns with many desks). • Row clusters, in which two or three desks are pushed together and yet still point forward, save space and encourage interaction. Two large, nested horseshoes serve a similar purpose and create a sense of group belonging. • Small clusters of desks (usually four) that face each other promote social interaction. Slant the groups for better views of the front board. • Try a single large circle for classroom meetings. • If possible, avoid using all the floor space for desks. • Be certain that students fit their desks. Make a switch or call the janitor if they do not.
Whole-class instruction station	• Position your media equipment so that all students can see when seated at their desks. • Use a small table or cart to keep instructional supplies available. • At the elementary level, save enough floor space so that you can pull the entire class "up to the rug" or "over to the rocking chair" to work with all students in a more intimate setting. Reading aloud and class discussions are often more effective when students are seated in close proximity. A change of pace can be good for behavior and materials management, too. Consider alternatives if students object to sitting on the floor.
Areas for small-group instruction	• If space allows, use a round or horseshoe table for small-group instruction. • If space is tight, consider using space outside the classroom door or borrow from another area such as your library. Make the area off-limits if you are instructing there. • Position yourself so that you can see all students. Keep your back to the wall.
Special-interest areas	• Include learning centers such as a class library, an author's corner, a science center, a technology area, a pet area, or an art area. Even a small counter space works. Try a claw-footed bathtub filled with pillows for reading or a tropical rain forest for independent work. • Students and their families sometimes like to contribute materials for these areas, but you will need to teach students to handle materials carefully. • Include a private area for quiet reading. This space or another may be used for students who need to be temporarily removed from the group. • Special-interest areas can be permanent or can evolve with the interests and needs of your class.
Work spaces for messy tasks	• Place the painting or art center near the sink for easy cleanup. Teach your students to place newspaper under their work and to properly care for materials. • Space outside the classroom door can be used if you can monitor all students. • Position materials for active lessons away from your whole-group instruction station so that you can monitor from afar as individuals go up to gather materials. • Place the materials distribution center away from students' work desks, to the extent possible. • Obtain a large sheet of heavy plastic or an easy-clean rug if you need to protect carpet.

While the ideas are rolling, you may want to turn ahead to Figure 9.9 and design the physical layout of your classroom.

Managing Resources: The Stuff of Teaching

Managing a classroom means managing many resources. Three considerations for resource management include paper flow, digital equipment, and communications.

Paper Flow

One prominent management issue is managing the paper flow. Many new teachers—even those who felt otherwise well prepared—struggle to stay afloat of their paperwork. An important early lesson is to devise *systems* for managing the paper flow. They develop, for example, homework folders that go home and get reviewed periodically by families, they work with volunteers to organize upcoming materials and check in papers that come from home, they devise planners in which students record their assignments, and they identify spaces where students submit their work. In classrooms where students share the leadership, students can apply for some fifty manager tasks—which they complete in 60 to 90 seconds—that would otherwise need to be handled by the teacher (Freiberg, Huzinec, & Templeton, 2009). Implementing systems for managing resources allows teachers to streamline their efforts and spend more time on instruction than on checking homework.

Morris (2000) provides an example of a system that can be useful for many such necessary management tasks: student numbers. He assigns each student a number, and this number is used for several purposes. For instance, students collect and mark homework as completed using their numbers rather than names. Their papers can be quickly collected and placed in numerical order for easy entry into the paper or electronic grade book. Materials, even individual crayons or pencils, can be marked with students' numbers for quick identification. Students can "sound off" by number at a fire drill to ensure that all are present. Numbers can be recorded on cards, craft sticks, or in smart phone applications ensure that students are called on equitably.

Digital Equipment

ICT equipment plays an increasingly large role in U.S. classrooms. Many rooms are equipped with projection systems, document cameras, and interactive whiteboards. If these are permanent, consider their location as you choose your instructional stations. Remember a basic rule of classroom management and discipline: Face your students. Keep your back to the wall. Arrange the equipment so that you can see the students' faces as you use it. For instance, place the document camera near the front of the room, with the screen behind you and the students in front of you (recall Paola using the document camera on page 127). If the equipment is movable, ensure that it is secured safely on carts and that you have a routine for where to store it when it is not in use. One classroom manager job can be projection specialist. At a signal, the specialist can quickly move the equipment into place and return it afterward.

Another resource management question is how to integrate the classroom's single classroom computer meaningfully into instruction. Three-quarters of all American classrooms have between one and five computers in them. Teachers often struggle to use these single or few computers to their full instructional advantage.

The single computer can be used both as a teacher tool and as a student tool. The teacher uses it as a tool for preparing instructional materials, communicating with families, and keeping track of student progress. If the computer can be connected to a projection system so that all can see the screen, it becomes the teacher's whole-class instructional tool. He can use the computer to model the writing process or to do shared writing, to draw concept maps, to present still photos or short video clips that enrich the lesson. If no projection system is available, students can view images before instruction in small groups.

A single computer can also be used as a student learning tool. Individual students can provide input to larger products such as brainstorming lists. They can work in small groups to create documents, drawings, or maps. Individual students can use the computer to reinforce their lessons, for instance through drill programs that practice previously presented objectives, or by hearing content presented in their home language. Computers can be used as assessment tools, and they can be used by individuals or small groups during work time. To ensure that all students work on the computer, their teacher creates a schedule and posts it so that small groups or partners can check and monitor their own visit. The teacher also may hang a check sheet near the computer so students check off their names as they complete their computer activities.

If your classroom has several computers, think about where to place them. Some teachers place them all in a row along a wall of the classroom in order to create a work zone. Other teachers spread the computers throughout the class. Some teachers find it important to arrange the computers so that they can see the screens as students work. Watch the cords are safely concealed or secured. Number the computers so that you can direct students to them easily. Keep log in and other directions posted near the computers, and consider placing a kitchen timer near each so that students can monitor their usage. Train ICT student experts as one of your rotating classroom jobs so you don't spend your time unjamming a printer when you should be supporting student learning.

Think security when you consider storing other expensive equipment such as calculators, cameras, wireless devices, handheld microscopes, and response systems. Such equipment is best kept locked. At minimum, store it behind closed cupboard doors near the teacher's station where students are unlikely to wander, particularly if a substitute teacher is in charge. Each piece should have a protective case and be labeled so that it can be matched with its peripheral equipment and stored efficiently.

For equipment that you share with other teachers, such as laptops on a cart, be sure to learn about the checkout procedure. Request the equipment far in advance so that it will be ready when you need it. Check all equipment upon receipt so that you are not held responsible for equipment that you received damaged or incomplete. Test it all the day before you use it. Charge all batteries, ensure that the appropriate software is loaded and that Web sites are bookmarked. Match cables and cords to their respective machines. Enlist equipment managers to help with this process and to check the equipment all back in, piece by piece, when it's time to return it.

Communications

Families are one of your greatest resources. Plan carefully to implement your plans for family partnerships (from Chapter 3). Develop a plan for family and friends who can volunteer. Keep an instructional activity (such as flashcards) ready for volunteers to work with individual students. Have materials in need of preparation ready, too, in case your volunteer prefers that sort of contribution.

Also make a plan to maintain records of your communications with family members to ensure that you are regularly and equitably engaging families as educational partners. Student Information Systems (Chapter 8) make efficient use of time, aid in analysis, and foster timely communications with students and families. Also keep a contact log for family phone calls and other communications. Word-processed tables and spreadsheets can both be used for this purpose, although spreadsheets make it easier to manipulate your data for different purposes. List the date, time, student, family member, description of the issue, and plans for resolution if appropriate. Post assignments and major events for students and families via e-mail or through your own Web site.

Experienced classroom managers sometimes use their resource management systems so effortlessly that it can be hard to appreciate them. Watch your mentors carefully and jot down some notes about how the teacher manages the scarce resources and plentiful paper we find in most classrooms.

Managing Time

Alarming studies (e.g., Jones, 1987) indicate that teachers lose up to half of their instructional time through inefficient management. Imagine wasting *half* of the precious time you have with your students. Use your classroom time as gold; wasting a single minute costs everyone in the class, and those costs can never be recouped.

Maximizing Academic Learning Time

Using your time as gold means that you need to *maximize* the time your students spend engaged in learning and *minimize* the time they spend in other ways in your classroom. The total amount of classroom time can be divided into three nested subsets: allocated time, engaged time, and academic learning time. These aspects of time are presented in Figure 9.3, which makes it clear that your job as a time manager is more sophisticated than just ensuring that students are busy at *something*. You want the bull's-eye in Figure 9.3—academic learning time—to expand so that it crowds the other two circles. Your job as a time manager is to ensure that students are experiencing success in work related to lesson objectives. Students are not using their time well if they are staring at the right page in the text but have no idea what it means.

Figure 9.3   *The target for classroom instruction.*

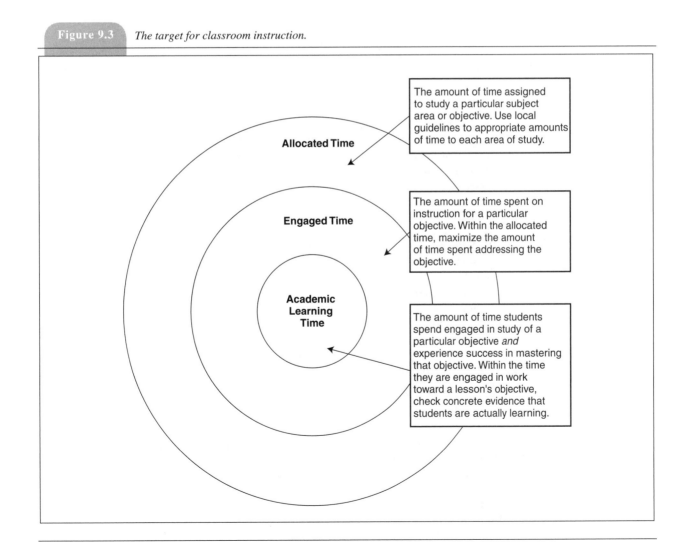

Allocated Time

Engaged Time

Academic Learning Time

The amount of time assigned to study a particular subject area or objective. Use local guidelines to appropriate amounts of time to each area of study.

The amount of time spent on instruction for a particular objective. Within the allocated time, maximize the amount of time spent addressing the objective.

The amount of time students spend engaged in study of a particular objective *and* experience success in mastering that objective. Within the time they are engaged in work toward a lesson's objective, check concrete evidence that students are actually learning.

An effectively managed classroom results in greater academic learning time.

Source: Karen Mancinelli/Pearson Learning Photo Studio

Maximize learning time by using everything you know about providing engaging, responsive instruction. Think carefully, for example, of your use of video in the classroom, as it is sometimes poorly used (Hobbs, 2006). Hobbs recommends that, in order to use media well, teachers should:

- Set clear instructional purposes.
- Make use of functions such as pause and review to enhance learning.
- Stay mentally engaged throughout the showing (do not do other things).
- Avoid noninstructional uses such as video as a reward, time filler, or a way to control student behavior.

Maximizing learning time also includes helping students learn to manage their work time. The Teaching Tip gives one suggestion for doing so.

You also maximize learning by minimizing the amount of time spent on business items. One guaranteed way to minimize wasted time is by using **routines** for recurring events (Marzano, 2007). Routines offer the added benefit of providing predictability, confidence, and security, especially for students who are accustomed to strict family structure, are lacking in structure at home, or have physiological needs for clear and calm behavioral support (Gootman, 2001). You will need both noninstructional and instructional routines.

Teaching Tip

KEEPING TRACK OF TIME

It's easy for teachers and students to lose track of time during small-group or independent work time. Help students learn to gauge time by calling their attention to time requirements. Displaying a timer seems to be far more potent then telling them to watch the clock, and it removes you from the burden of timekeeper, where your announcement "time's up!" is likely to be met with a chorus of "No!" Some teachers use a kitchen timer or their smart phone timers. Interactive whiteboards have a timer function, too. If you have a projection system for your computer, try this free timer and stopwatch: *http://www.timeme.com/*. Time manager can be another classroom job.

Noninstructional Routines

An initial investment in teaching your students to run the business of your classroom will save vast amounts of time over the course of the year. It will save you from 2,043 questions about where homework belongs or whether it is okay to sharpen a pencil. Research indicates that effective managers devote considerable time in the first days of the year teaching their procedures and routines (Bohn et al., 2004; Emmer et al., 1980; Evertson, & Emmer, 1982; Marzano, 2007). The Teaching Tip gives advice based on this research to get you off to the right start.

Figure 9.4 lists some of the recurring "business" events that occur in classrooms for which you may wish to establish and teach set procedures. Teach the most immediate

Teaching Tip

OFF TO THE RIGHT START

During the early days of the term, be sure to:

✔ Set high expectations for what all students can learn.
✔ Offer engaging learning activities.
✔ Establish your routines and procedures.
✔ Praise specific student success and behavior.
✔ Encourage student self-regulation.

Figure 9.4 *Recurring events that might benefit from a routine.*

- What to do when class begins
- What to do when class ends
- How to enter and exit the classroom
- Taking attendance
- Opening exercises
- Getting lunch count
- The rules for having water at desks or getting a drink of water
- When to use the restroom
- How to behave in each area of the classroom
- When and how loud to talk
- When to sharpen a pencil
- Where and when to get paper and other supplies
- How to head a paper
- What to do if a computer stops working
- Where and when to submit completed work
- How to gather work for absent students
- How to complete homework when returning from an absence
- What to do if the teacher steps out of the classroom
- What to do when a visitor comes
- Who will and how to help a substitute teacher
- Who will and how to run errands for the teacher
- What to do in case of emergency

routines (what students should do when they enter the classroom in the morning, how you will take roll, what is expected in each area of the classroom, what happens at the end of the period) early on. Over time students can master each of the routines that will help them run the classroom, even in your absence. The beauty of good routines is that they set the expectation that students are responsible and capable of running the show, they help students feel secure in the predictability of their environment, they reinforce your expectation that student learning is your highest priority, and they save you from countless mundane decisions.

When you teach a routine, do it purposefully with a carefully chosen instructional strategy. I have seen some teachers gracefully coax their students into routines solely through subtle modeling. More often, direct instruction (recall Figure 7.2) is employed to efficiently ensure that each student understands and can use the routine. The younger the student, the more direct instruction may be necessary. Through direct instruction, you

- Present critical information on the routine.
- Check for student understanding.
- Practice the routine with the students.
- Observe students as they practice the routine independently.

Reteaching repairs misunderstanding at any point (Wong, 1998). For example, Ms. Garcia wants to teach her third-graders to get to work immediately when they enter the classroom each morning. She clarifies her own expectations and writes them on a chart. Then she teaches her students: "There are three things to be done each morning when you step into the classroom." Pointing to her chart and using appropriate hand gestures to support her message, Ms. Garcia states: "First, put your things away. Second, move your photo to the 'buying' or 'bringing' lunch string. Third, take out your journal and begin writing." After checking for understanding, Ms. Garcia provides guided practice: "Let's pretend it is morning now. Pick up your backpack and meet me in line. My bet is that all of you will be able to do each of our three morning tasks without a single reminder!" Students giggle as they indulge Ms. Garcia in her charade. She laughs along and provides plenty of praise for students as they get started on their own. If students fail to carry out one or more of the steps, she stops them, reteaches the step(s) they missed, and they try again. She leaves her chart posted for two weeks, until students have internalized the routine.

You will select noninstructional routines based on your own preferences and the ages of your students. Let's explore alternatives for one of the most common noninstructional routines: taking attendance.

Some teachers choose to call out students' names for daily roll so they have the opportunity to greet students as individuals: "Good morning, Tran. Good morning, Chelsea." Calling students' names in this way establishes daily positive contact with all students. However, calling each student's name aloud daily only to listen for a rote response ("Here!") is a waste of instructional time, especially for secondary teachers who have limited time with each set of students and must take attendance five or more times per day. If name-calling during roll is not used as an instructional or interactional tool, consider an alternative that takes far less time:

- As students work in their journals or complete some other task right after the bell, you can glance over your seating chart and the classroom to silently check and record absences.
- If students are in groups, one member can report absences for each group.
- An attendance manager can take roll and enter it in the computer or run it to the office.
- Students enter the room and move personal markers—such as clothespins, cards, or magnets with their names on them—to a new area to indicate that they are present. One first-grade teacher I know photographs her students during the first week, cuts out the figures, and glues magnets to the back. Students move their photos each morning. She simply glances at the few remaining names or photos to determine absences. These photos can also be used for graphing experiences in mathematics. See Figure 9.5 for an example of how this strategy can be used to instructional advantage.

Instructional Management and Routines

In his influential research, Kounin (1983) studied how teachers organize and manage their lessons and found that three aspects of lesson movement correlated well with management success:

- *Smoothness.* Does the lesson flow from start to finish, adhering to a set focus? Is it free from abrupt changes in what students are asked to do?
- *Momentum.* Does the lesson move along without lags created by the teacher over-explaining (the yack factor) or overdwelling (the nag factor)?
- *Group focus.* Is the teacher able to concentrate on the entire group of students as a unit?

In the same way that routines can help with noninstructional issues, routines can also help smooth instructional movement wrinkles. Typical creases that can be ironed out through careful attention to instruction include the following:

- Pacing
- Transitions
- Providing assistance
- Making every minute count

Figure 9.5   *Take roll and teach . . . at the same time.*

As students enter the room, they move their marker in response to a question. Their answers build a class graph, which is discussed during opening exercises or a relevant lesson.

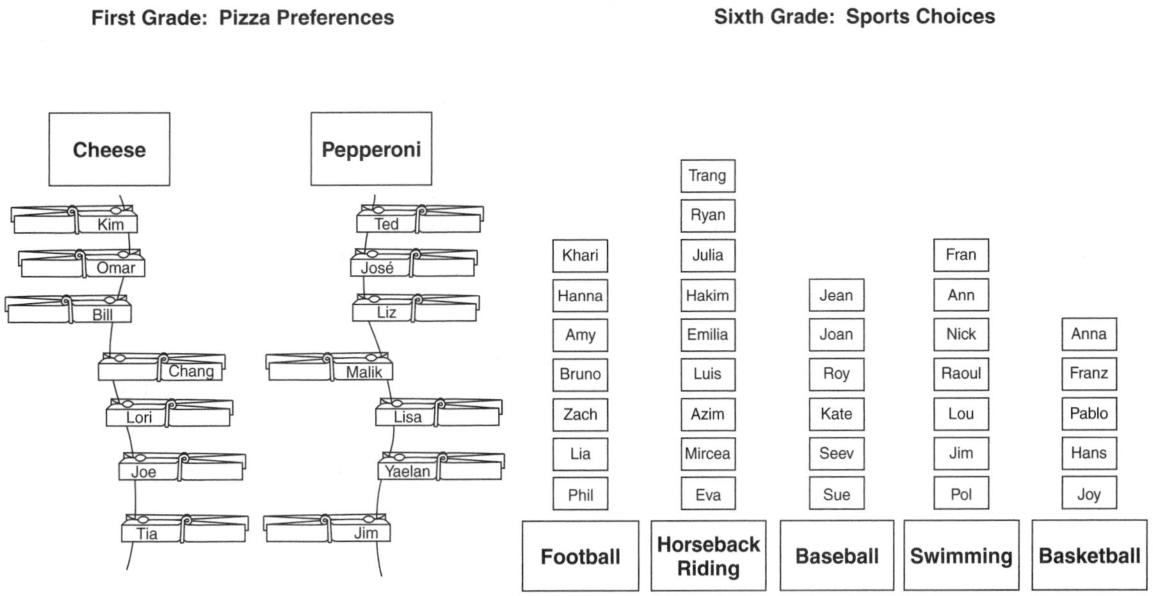

First Grade: Pizza Preferences

Cheese

Kim
Omar
Bill
Chang
Lori
Joe
Tia

Pepperoni

Ted
José
Liz
Malik
Lisa
Yaelan
Jim

(Markers are clothespins with students' names. Graph is two pieces of string taped to board.)

Sixth Grade: Sports Choices

Football	Horseback Riding	Baseball	Swimming	Basketball
Khari	Trang		Fran	
Hanna	Ryan	Jean	Ann	
Amy	Julia	Joan	Nick	Anna
Bruno	Hakim	Roy	Raoul	Franz
Zach	Emilia	Kate	Lou	Pablo
Lia	Luis	Seev	Jim	Hans
Phil	Azim	Sue	Pol	Joy
	Mircea			
	Eva			

(Markers are tiles attached to magnets. Graph is cookie sheet or magnetic white board.)

Pacing   Pacing refers to the speed at which instruction is delivered. Pacing often presents difficulties for new teachers because it demands an understanding of student development, and in-depth knowledge of students grows primarily through experience. A well-paced lesson devotes just enough time to developing concepts and ideas (Sangster, 2007). Lessons must progress slowly enough to ensure student understanding but quickly enough to

1. Maintain student interest and attention.
2. Minimize opportunities for misbehavior.
3. Make efficient use of a time within a crowded classroom schedule.

To gauge the pace of your lessons, start by watching for cues from the students. You may select a couple focus students with disparate needs—for example, a student with an identified learning disability and one who learns quickly. Do they appear anxious? You may be moving too quickly. Are they snoozy? You may need to pep things up. Is one antsy? You may need to switch activities. Overwhelmed? You may need to let them process information for a bit before moving on. Do not rely solely on students' body language, though, because it can be limited and misleading. Use progress monitoring strategies such as unison response. Figure 8.5 provides information about student learning to adjust your pacing.

As you observe a variety of experienced teachers, you will note that they pace their lessons differently, depending on both their students and their own preferences. I prefer an air of productive hurrying. I like students to glance at the clock, surprised that our time is up, when I close the lesson and say good-bye. To ensure that lessons do not drag, tell students how much time they have for each task and stick fairly closely to your stated limits. Especially during group work, students of all ages seem to take as much time as they are given to complete their work. You may bend your rule a bit if they groan at your one-minute warning ("Okay, but in two minutes you will be ready to report. Hurry!"), but if you double your initial time allotment, you will teach students that they need not focus and work productively or that you can be swayed easily to relax your requirements. Send the message that time is golden. In doing so, be certain to use each spare moment to instructional advantage. Have a plan if your lesson runs short, as in the Teaching Tip.

Transitions   Transitions are the periods between one activity and the next. Teachers at all levels need to switch activities efficiently *within* lessons. Teachers with multiple subjects also must manage transitions *between* lessons. Murphy must have a law to account for the fact that students—no matter the age—can remain attentive during an entire lesson and then hang from the ceiling in the two minutes between one activity and the next. In fact, transitions are one of the top three management trouble spots (transitions are are joined by the first and last 5 minutes of the period or day; Freiberg, Huzinec, & Templeton, 2009). To encourage smooth transitions:

1. Anticipate transitions as trouble spots. Have your own materials ready. Be watchful and businesslike.
2. Plan for transitions as a mini-lesson: What exactly do you need students to do in switching activities? Tell them. Monitor their behavior and redirect as necessary ("Stop. You forgot the part about silence. Let's try again.").
3. Practice completing transitions in limited time. Challenge students to prepare for the next lesson in less than 60 seconds. Invite them to beat their previous times. Make it a wager if you are the betting type. Some teachers time their students during transitions and other routine events. Seconds not wasted can be spent during preferred activities later (F. Jones, 2000).
4. Use a change in space to ease transitions: "Finish up your comprehension questions and meet me on the rug by the time I count down from 20."
5. Make transitions serve double duty. For example, some teachers have primary-grade students sing as they move from one activity to the next. This keeps the students

Teaching Tip

WHAT TO DO WHEN—YIKES!— THE LESSON RUNS SHORT

As new teachers learn to gauge pacing, lessons occasionally take less time than expected. For *every* lesson you plan, have a brief, stand-alone activity ready in case the lesson runs short. Practice pages and extension activities are examples. Be certain that the extra activity is meaningful.

If you really get stuck, try some of the sponges in Figure 9.6 on page 227 or the independent activities listed in the upcoming subsection "Making Every Minute Count."

instructionally focused and limits the transition period to the length of the song. A secondary teacher may play one song on the computer to signal the start and finish of the transition. Other options include reciting math facts and picking up trash as students move from one activity to the next.

Providing Assistance   Students often lose learning time during independent work periods because they sit and wait for the teacher's help. Make a plan so that you can provide assistance to all students who ask—before their hands fall asleep in the air. The first way to ensure that you provide timely individual assistance is to monitor the kinds of assistance that students request. Imagine that you just gave instructions for a social studies assignment and eight students surround you, papers rustling, questions poised. Their presence is a sign that you need to reteach: You discover that they do not understand how to read the scale on the map. Stop answering individual questions and reteach the entire group. (See the Teaching Tip.) Or poll the class and pull aside a small group for further explanation of the map's scale. If you have developed a safe environment, students generally will not mind taking you up on your offer to join them in the back for an encore.

After ensuring that students as a group understand concepts and your directions, think about how you can make sure that students get the help they need with as little time away from learning as possible. Following are four strategies teachers find useful:

1. Use praise–prompt–leave (from Figure 7.2). When you address a student's question, give a specific compliment for what he has done right, prompt him quickly on what he needs to do next, and leave. Providing efficient help allows you to interact with more students. Fred Jones (2000) admonishes us to spend no more than 20 seconds as we provide assistance to individuals.

2. If students are seated in groups, teach the students that there can be no *individual* question for the teacher, only a *group* question. That way, students are expected to ask two or three peers before they ask you. You not only save time but also display the expectation that students can and should help each other.

3. Check the work of one person in each row (or group) who is likely to succeed quickly. Put her in charge of answering the questions in her row.

4. Use a signal other than the raised hand. Students can stand a red card or plastic cup on their desks, for example, if they need your assistance. Teach them to work on another section of the task until you arrive.

Making Every Minute Count   You want students engaged in learning even when you are not providing formal instruction. Make every minute count by

- Having a plan for what students should do if they finish early.
- Using "sponges" to soak up spare minutes.

Students work at different rates, and, at least at the elementary level, at some point each will approach you and say, "Teacher, I finished. What should I do now?" Develop some instructionally sound responses and teach students—even kindergartners— to select and complete learning activities without your assistance. Write (or draw)

Teaching Tip

RULE OF THUMB FOR RETEACHING

Choose a number, five or fewer, as your limit. Let's say four. If four of your students ask you for the same kind of help, do not answer individual questions; reteach the group: "I did not make this as clear as I had hoped. Many people are asking about _____. Let me explain in another way." Stick with your limit.

acceptable choices on a chart, post the chart, and teach students to follow the chart. Then if they ask, "What should I do now?" you just point to the chart. Add new choices occasionally. Depending on students' age, some widely applicable choices include the following:

- Complete product option contracts (one strategy for differentiating instruction, p. 64).
- Add to the class's *Great Quotes Graffiti Board.*
- Play a thinking skills game (e.g., chess, checkers, or a board game). Have an interactive whiteboard? Try Set (www.setgame.com) or the *New York Times* daily news quiz (http://learning.blogs.nytimes.com/).
- Read a good book.
- Write a letter to a friend in the class. "Send" it through the class post office.
- Study the globe.
- Practice skills (e.g., printing, spelling words, math facts, and vocabulary cards).
- Work at a station (e.g., for science, art, building, puzzles, or technology).

Just as you can count on students finishing at different rates, you can bet there will be downtime, or brief periods when your class is waiting for an assembly, class pictures, or a guest speaker. Soak up those spare minutes with sponges, which are activities that encourage learning but do not require much preparation. For example, when the first assembly runs late and your class is waiting to join the second one, you might ask students of any age, "Have you lived a million seconds?" Students can also estimate their age in minutes, days, weeks, or months. Then you can quickly check their predications by visiting http://www.mathcats.com/explore/agecalculator.html. Calculations are completed so quickly that the site is sure to spark some interesting questions for exploration. The first assembly is *still* not out? Discover what happened on this day in history by checking the headlines: http://dmarie.com/timecap/. Secondary students will be enthralled by http://peteranswers.com But first search "How does Peter answers work?" Some additional sample sponges are given in Figure 9.6. Write sponges in a computer file, on index cards, or in a small notebook in advance so that you can choose one and get right to work. Students can even be taught to select and lead sponge activities. While you are thinking about time management, you may choose to use Figure 9.10 to make a tentative plan for using classroom time well.

Your Own Management Plan

You have an empty room, a class list, and sets of texts. Where do you go from here? How will you establish a cohesive community? Figures 9.7 through 9.10 can help you establish an initial classroom management plan that is consistent with the major points of this book and that can set you on your way to establishing a productive and humane learning environment. Because some teachers, particularly secondary teachers, "float" from room to room rather than being assigned a single room, Figure 9.11 may be helpful in helping you think about some key management issues within a single period (inspired by Emmer, Evertson, & Worsham, 2002). You will revise your plan in response to your students and your growing expertise, so use this draft to brainstorm. You may wish to first try the exercise employing Figure 9.12 at the end of this chapter if you have not yet had many opportunities to observe classrooms.

| Figure 9.6 | *Sponges for spare moments.* |

1. Read student requests from a book of poetry (anything by Shel Silverstein is a sure bet).

2. Practice logical questioning with a game of 20 Questions.

3. For young students, play Simon Says to hone listening skills. Or, play it in a different language.

4. Count as high as you can as a class by ones, twos, fives, tens, threes, or sevens. A variation is to count by ones and say *buzz* to replace multiples of a given number: "8, 9, buzz, 11," for example, for multiples of five.

5. Individually, in pairs, or as a class, list as many compound words, state capitals, homonyms, mammals, cabinet members, African countries, prime numbers, chemical symbols, or anything else as you can.

6. Sharpen estimation skills by estimating and checking an unknown quantity, amount, or duration of an event. For example, "How many seconds can you stand on one foot? With your eyes closed?" "How many beans fit into my hand?" "What is the total value of the seven coins in my pocket?" "How many insects are on earth?" Use the World Almanac or a book of world records for information.

7. Write brief group stories. One person writes the opening, folds back all but the last line, and passes it to the next author.

8. Practice classification skills with "Who's in My Group?" Call students who meet an unstated criterion of your choosing (such as black hair or earrings or laced shoes) to the front of the room to be members of your group. The rest of the class guesses the rule. Be tricky and use more than one criterion. Or, allow students to make the rule and call up the groups. For older students, draw the dichotomous key to demonstrate your grouping.

9. Pull out a set of simple objects and list scientific observations about them. See how long of a list you can create. Then see if students locate a particular object in the pile purely by reading or listening to peers' observations. Work on improving the quality of their observations over time.

10. Pull down a map and play "I'm Thinking of a State (or Region or Island)" by allowing students to ask questions to discover your state. Allow a student to lead the next round. Or, in a less structured activity, find out how many countries are represented in the travels (or ancestries) of your students. Where is the farthest north anyone has traveled? East?

11. Tell students a story. Invite one of them to tell a story or do a trick.

12. Do some genetics research: See how many can curl their tongues, for instance. Who has a hitchhiker's thumb? Attached earlobes?

13. Try some at-your-seat gymnastics. Can students clasp their hands behind their backs if one arm reaches from next to the head and the other comes from below? Can they rub their stomachs and pat their heads at the same time? Drum their fingers starting with the pinkie, then starting with the thumb?

14. Talk about the world. What have students read on the Web today? In the paper? Seen on the news?

Figure 9.7   *The big view: Guiding forces in my management plan.*

1. The law:
   ☐ Reread Figure 1.2 on teachers' legal responsibilities. Notes:

   ☐ Check with administrator or mentor for expectations and sources for local laws.

   ☐ Things to keep in mind:

2. The setting:
   ☐ Check your work in Figure 1.1 to refresh your thinking about the specific locale and the expectations it provides.

   ☐ Things to keep in mind:

3. My stance toward education:
   ☐ Glance at your work in Chapter 2 to refresh your memory of your big view of teaching.

   ☐ Complete the following stems:
   A good society

   A community

   The purpose of education

   People learn by

   Good teachers

Figure 9.8   *My plan for creating positive classroom ambience.*

☐ I want my classroom to feel like a _____.
☐ I will foster a sense of community by:

☐ Physical arrangements to create that tone
    Work space (tables and desks):

    My instruction station:

    Small-group instruction area:

    Special-interest areas:

    Wall and ceiling space:

    My work space and storage areas:

☐ Other furnishings and strategies I will use to create that ambience:

Checkpoints
Does the room provide for

☐ Emotional safety and a sense of belonging?
☐ Intellectual stimulation?
☐ Social interaction?
☐ Pleasant experience?
☐ Student responsibility?

Figure 9.9   *My plan for arranging classroom space.*

The Perfect Classroom: A Map

Checkpoints

☐ Is it safe? Can I monitor?

☐ Does it encourage community?

☐ Is it productive?

☐ Is it efficient?

☐ Does it make full use of available resources?

Figure 9.10	*My plan for using classroom time well.*

☐ Check with administrator or mentor for requirements or guidelines on allocated time.

Sample Classroom Schedule

Routines

☐ **Some of my noninstructional routines:**

    Taking attendance:

    Opening exercises:

    Expected behaviors for each area:

    Two more routines to use (review Figure 8.4):

☐ **Instructional routines:**

    Providing assistance:

    Sponges:

    Independent work activities:

Involving Families

☐ Routines for involving family and other volunteers:

☐ Routines for communicating regularly with families:

Figure 9.11   *Management plan for a single period of the day.*

1. Opening Procedures	2. Rules and Procedures	3. Dismissal Routines
Attendance procedure: Location of attendance materials such as tardy and absence slips: Procedure for getting work to students returning from absences: Instructional activity for students during attendance:	Leaving the room: Using classroom resources (e.g., computers): Getting assistance: Working with peers: Submitting work: Expectations on format of assignment, allowable resources, late work, extra credit: Recording assignments: What to do if teacher is occupied by a visitor:	Signal for clean-up time: Expectations for the room's condition upon students' leaving:

Figure 9.12   *Observing classroom management.*

Management Area	Observation Notes

Ambience
1. This classroom feels like a _____.
2. What things does the teacher actually do and say to create the tone?
3. What are the big ideas about teaching and learning that seem to be conveyed by the classroom ambience?
4. **Community:** How does the environment establish the norms of shared governance and concern?
5. How does the tone establish
   a. Emotional safety?
   b. Intellectual stimulation?
   c. Social interaction and responsibility?
   d. School as a meaningful and pleasant experience?	

Physical Space
6. Observe how the teacher has structured the *physical layout* of the room.
   • Floor space
   • Wall space
   • Instruction station
   • Special-interest areas
   • Other spaces
7. Observe how the teacher has arranged *instructional materials and resources,* including computers.
8. How does the environment promote *physical safety?*
9. **Productivity:** How does the environment allow for
   a. A balance and variety of activities?
   b. All students to see and hear the teacher?
   c. All students to focus on instruction?	

10. **Efficiency:** How does the environment allow for ease in 　a. The teacher reaching each student? 　b. Students reaching each other? 　c. The teacher and students reaching materials and other 　　areas of the room?	
Time 11. Find the classroom schedule. How does *allocated time* encourage learning? 12. What evidence is there that students are experiencing *success* during **engaged time**? 13. How does the teacher use *noninstructional routines* effectively? List some routines you observed to be particularly effective. 14. If you observe *instruction,* check 　a. Pacing 　b. Transitions 　c. Provision of assistance 　d. Provisions for students who finish early	
Overall 15. List two or more things you learned about classroom management by observing this teacher and classroom.	

Parting Words

Your painstaking efforts to maintain a pleasant and productive learning environment will not always result in a happy citizenry living in educational paradise. Sometimes a negative tone can arise if the teacher struggles with discipline, if the students begin to treat each other with disrespect, or if the class fails to establish a sense of group purpose. Chapter 10 provides additional suggestions for keeping the atmosphere positive, for talking through issues to encourage respect, for building community, and for managing students as a group. If you notice that your classroom is beginning to feel unproductive or unpleasant, try running through some of these steps:

1. *Get a sense of perspective.* What are you trying to accomplish with your students? What is interfering with your class's attempts to build a productive environment? A trusted outside observer may be able to offer a fresh view.
2. *Rebuild a sense of community.* Try a classroom meeting during which you set new goals as a class.

Choose some high-interest activities and perhaps some positive consequences that reward students for working as a group. Allow students to make the space their own.

3. *Reestablish your expectations for student behavior.* Open your eyes wide and remind your students that you care so much about them that you cannot allow them to treat each other or their classroom in harmful ways. Clearly outline the kinds of behaviors you need to see and, if necessary, employ logical consequences to help students with their behavior.
4. *Change something.* Add quiet music. Rearrange the desks. Record yourself and listen to your tone. Rework your routines. Flip the schedule. Laugh at the nuisances that would otherwise drive you to distraction. Have lunch with your students.
5. *Never give up.*

Opportunities to Practice

1. Analyze a teacher's management plan using the observation sheet given in Figure 9.12. You have three choices:

   • Analyze a lesson clip in the My Lab School collection.

   • Observe an experienced teacher's room environment and classroom management. At the end of the observation jot down a few great ideas that are consistent with your own thinking about management. Incorporate them into your own plan.

   • If you are already teaching, ask a colleague or mentor to observe your own management, or video record a lesson and analyze the recording.

2. Read a professional journal article on classroom management. What is the author's implied stance toward education? Are the strategies consistent with what you know about good teaching?

3. Alfie Kohn (1996) is critical of schools' overreliance on punishment and rewards and the illusion of choice it presents for students. To what extent do you agree with him? What would it take to change the practices that he sees as inhumane?

4. Start a file for promising classroom management ideas. Encourage a share session with peers. Observe more classrooms for ideas on management. Remember that every strategy you consider needs to measure up to the tough standard of your stance toward education and must encourage student learning in humane ways. Plenty of management strategies around today fall short of those criteria.

Web Sites

http://www.educationworld.com/a_curr/archives/
     classmanagement.shtml
Educator's World: Classroom management. The site includes a large variety of tips from different sources. Check out the New Teacher Advisor for tips on job interviews and dealing with difficult people. Try the Tech Integration section.

http://www.middleweb.com
Middleweb: Exploring Middle School Reform. This site addresses management and other issues for teachers of the middle years. For classroom management topics, go to "The First Days of Middle School." The free weekly e-newsletter is very good, and the teacher blogs give a realistic picture of living and learning with middle school students.

http://www.nea.org
National Education Association. Under "Tools and Ideas," try "Classroom Management" and "It Works for Me."

http://newmanagement.com
New Management. Rick Morris's Web site. Morris is known for his positive, practical management strategies

that emphasize meeting the basic needs of power, love, fun, freedom, and safety. This site gives articles and tips, but it also sells Morris's products.

http://www.proteacher.com
Pro Teacher. Click on Classroom management. Lots of resources and ideas from practicing teachers are included. Primarily elementary level.

http://www.4teachers.org/
4teachers.org supports teaching with technology. Try the classroom architect tool to arrange your classroom (http://classroom.4teachers.org/). Ad heavy. Another classroom mapping tool—this one 3d—is at the American Federation of Teachers Web site (http://www.aft.org/yourwork/tools4teachers/classmgt/interactives/arrangetool/activity.cfm)

http://www2.scholastic.com/
Scholastic's site. Go to Tools under Teaching resources for a classroom set up tool and a to-do list maker for your students.

Classroom Discipline: Encouraging Appropriate Behavior

10

Before You Begin Reading

Think back through your elementary and secondary schooling experiences. Recall a teacher who was known as being a successful classroom disciplinarian.

1. What was the teacher's reputation?

2. What was your relationship with the teacher like? What about other students' relationship with the teacher?

3. What motivated students' behavior in the teacher's room?

4. How did the teacher prevent misbehavior?

5. How did the teacher respond to misbehavior?

6. What "key(s)" to successful classroom discipline did that teacher seem to hold?

(Note: If you prefer, analyze a teacher who was not successful with classroom discipline. You can learn from that experience, too.)

"True discipline does not exist in the muteness of those who have been silenced but in the stirrings of those who have been challenged, in the doubt of those who have been prodded, and in the hopes of those who have been awakened"

—Paulo Freire (1998, p. 86)

True discipline is self-discipline. Competent, resilient individuals are socially adept with positive relationships and optimistic views about their lives. They strive for self-improvement and possess life skills such as the ability to take initiative and solve problems (Henderson & Milstein, 2003). Running a close second to the family as the most powerful influence on the development of competent children and adolescents is the school

(Henderson & Milstein, 2003; Kaiser & Rasminsky, 2009). This chapter supports you in helping students develop into positive, self-controlled, contributors to their world. Each of its eight sections includes theory, research, and practical tools for student discipline.

1. Classroom Discipline as One Piece of the Puzzle
2. Physician, Heal Thyself: Discipline Starts with You
3. The Goal Is Self-Discipline
4. The Key: A Structured, Consistent, Supportive Environment
5. Relationships as Central
6. Prevention, Not Reaction
7. A Systems Approach
8. Your Own Classroom Discipline Plan

Classroom Discipline as One Piece of the Puzzle

Your efforts to help students develop discipline occur within a much larger puzzle of teaching and learning. First, classroom discipline is connected to all of your other classroom efforts: planning, instruction, and management. When students are deeply engaged in a rich curriculum and meaningful learning, for instance, it is far easier for them to make productive choices about their own behavior. Second, classroom discipline occurs in the larger schoolwide context. Effective schoolwide discipline programs provide caring relationships among adults and students, promote prosocial behavior, and work toward shared values (Frieberg & Lamb, 2009; Osher, Bear, Sprague, & Doyle, 2010). Your classroom practices should support—and be supported by—the school plan. Third, inclusive and responsive teachers are aware of the larger sociocultural context, including its inequities. For example, Black students—and secondarily Latinos and American Indian students—are overselected and oversanctioned in the discipline system, excluding them from instruction at far greater rates than are white and Asian students (Gregory, Skiba, & Noguera, 2010; Yang, 2009). Disproportionate disciplinary actions may contribute to achievement gaps by reducing students' opportunity to learn. Inclusive and responsive teachers examine their own discipline efforts to address such deleterious practices. Finally, classroom discipline is a powerful mechanism for effecting our vision of who our students need to be as we hand them the world. Each of our efforts to support student discipline should be guided by our vision of who the students will become as competent, resilient adults.

Physician, Heal Thyself: Discipline Starts with You

In all they do, inclusive and responsive teachers treat self-understanding as necessary. In the realm of discipline, self-understanding helps teachers understand their own motivations, limitations, and biases. For instance, teachers in one study *overestimated* students' intelligence when they perceived the students as interesting, independent, competent, and assertive and *underestimated* intelligence when the students seemed anxious, immature, and insecure (Alvidrez & Weinstein, 1999). Disability status can affect teacher perceptions too. In Cook's (2004) study and in several similar ones, general education teachers reported feeling less attached to their students with disabilities and rejected them at higher rates than they did their other students. Students who are less attached or are rejected get less positive attention and feedback from their teachers.

And so it is crucial that we examine our own biases and perspectives. When we make our *implicit* understandings of ourselves *explicit*, we increase the odds that our efforts to encourage self-discipline will be principled and proactive: Knowing yourself will help you know—and guide—your students. This section addresses the following points:

- How understanding yourself helps you as a disciplinarian
- Finding emotional control in an emotional endeavor
- Choosing your authority base

How Understanding Yourself Helps You as a Disciplinarian

The end goal of this chapter is for you to form your own classroom discipline plan; without a well-reasoned plan, teachers are likely to be "theoretically blind" and thus be thwarted as proactive disciplinarians (Riley, Lewis, & Brew, 2010, p. 957). Before you are a teacher, you are a person, and for your discipline plan to be workable, it needs to not only reflect your vision as a teacher but your personal perceptions of what's possible and desirable. We all have things that please us or that push our buttons based on our own temperaments and upbringings. Each of us seeks out people who behave in certain ways and avoids others. These personal biases and preferences color the way we see our students and how we interact with them. Try the Inclusive and Responsive Teacher Tip to explore a few things about yourself that might influence you as a classroom disciplinarian.

Finding Emotional Control in an Emotional Endeavor

Teaching can bring a rainbow of emotions. Helping students learn and grow often results in great joy; failing to do so can result in despair. When teachers are socially and emotionally competent, they set a productive tone, encourage supportive relationships, guide students toward self-control, and serve as role models for pro-social behavior (Jennings & Greenberg, 2010). And when teachers act aggressively by angrily yelling or using sarcasm or humiliation they negatively affect students' engagement, behavior, and self-regulation (Riley, Lewis, & Brew, 2010; Sutton, Mudrey-Camino, & Knight, 2009). Not surprisingly, the aspect of teaching that is most likely to evoke negative emotions such as anger is preventing and responding to student misbehavior (Sutton, Mudrey-Camino, & Knight, 2009). Thus, finding and maintaining emotional control is vital for every classroom teacher.

Fortunately, all emotions contain a cognitive component; we need not be ruled by our feelings. Instead, we can choose our emotional reactions to classroom events. Maintaining healthy emotions involves two kinds of regulation: *up regulating* (increasing) positive emotions and *down regulating* (decreasing) negative emotions in the classroom. Teachers use a variety of strategies to up regulate their positive emotions. Last year my student teachers were all about dancing . . . anytime, anyplace. (Don't make me get out the video.) A few common strategies for increasing positive emotions include:

- Focusing on a student's positive qualities
- Listening to upbeat music
- Talking with colleagues
- Using humor
- Using mental exercises such as positive guided imagery

Inclusive and Responsive Teacher Tip

IT'S ALL ABOUT YOU

Try these questions to think about some personal factors that may influence your interactions with students.

1. Name the top three traits you value in a friend. How do you interact with people who *don't* display those traits?
2. What sort of K–12 student were you? What did you think about the people who were *not* your sort of student? What do you value in student behaviors and attitudes now?
3. What did the people who reared you do well? What do you treasure from the lessons they taught you? What are your "I'll do it differently" memories?
4. What sorts of behaviors or attitudes annoy you? How do you respond?
5. No one is perfect. What trait or behavior are you striving to improve in yourself?

Teaching Tip

GETTING CALM

If a conversation with a student begins to get tense, imagine the student's parent standing beside the student. This can help you get calm and choose your words carefully.

Teachers report that down regulating negative emotions in favor of emotional control is perhaps more difficult—though equally important. Our job as adults and as professionals is to model emotional control. Anger is a natural human emotion, but we need to have our emotions in check when addressing students' behavior. And dealing with students who are particularly defiant takes the utmost in emotional maturity (Hall & Hall, 2003).

When angry, I suggest that you step back physically, temporally, and emotionally. You may, for instance, discover that your class showed no mercy in antagonizing the music teacher. You are furious that they could act that way, and you are embarrassed that their behavior may reflect on you. Instead of yelling, though, you lower your voice and say, "I am shocked and angry to hear about this. In fact, I am so angry that I cannot discuss this with you right now. When my head is clearer, we can discuss this situation."

Stepping back leaves you as the boss of you. When we are angry, other people are in control of us (F. Jones, 2000). Strength, according to Jones, comes from calm. By quieting your body through strategies like relaxed breathing, you calm yourself and those around you. Rick Morris offers us the Teaching Tip to help us get and stay calm.

Choosing Your Authority Base

One final way that discipline begins with you is that you choose the kind of authority base you will establish in your classroom. Teachers establish themselves as authorities using different combinations of power (French & Raven, 1959):

- *Expert power:* The group perceives the teacher as having superior knowledge about the content, about teaching, and about individual needs.
- *Referent power:* The group likes and respects the teacher because she is perceived as ethical and concerned about her students.
- *Legitimate power:* The teacher has the right to make certain decisions by the sheer power of her official role as teacher.
- *Reward power:* The teacher has power because she can distribute rewards, including tangible items such as candy and privileges and social awards such as praise and attention.
- *Coercive power:* The teacher has power because she can punish.

Reward power and coercive power predominate in many classrooms, probably because they are often effective for immediate control of student behavior. Examples include "pull your card" systems, table points, candy as a reward, and detention as a punishment. Unfortunately, teachers who establish no firmer authority base than the use of rewards and punishments run a strong risk of having their power collapse. Additionally, rewards and punishments are only temporarily effective and can interfere with the development of self-control (Kohn, 1996; Marshall, 2005).

Instead, teachers should establish more lasting and mutually respectful authority based on their expert and referent power (Savage, 1999). Because both of these kinds of power depend on students' perceptions of you—as an expert and as a concerned, trustworthy adult—you can begin to earn students' respect by demonstrating your knowledge and care. Other kinds of power can be used judiciously as supplements, especially in your early years as a teacher. Secondary teachers work with students who may be more likely to challenge authority the Teaching Tip, Working with big kids.

Teaching Tip

WORKING WITH BIG KIDS

- *Be genuine.* Emphasize, within your own style and as appropriate for the teacher role, caring and supportive relationships. Many secondary students (particularly boys, it seems) are relational learners; who you are matters to them (Raider-Roth et al., 2008; Reichert & Hawley, 2010).
- *Decide right now it isn't about control.* It isn't about physical intimidation either. When you let go of the mistaken goal of control, you have one fewer obstacle to overcome in helping students choose self-control.
- *Work on your teacher presence.* You need to exude self-confidence and communicate that there is no place you'd rather be than with your students.
- *Don't take it personally.* Some of your students may come to you already mistrusting authority (Payne, 2008). Show them that the system can be fair and that you will be respectful.
- *Plan ahead.* Know your limits. Some students will push until you deliver some consequence. Find out your school's plan for different levels of infraction—but don't overuse it.
- *Watch for counter-control.* Secondary students are savvy enough to turn around behaviorist systems to control the teacher. Emphasize instead authentic relationships and rational decision making.
- *Take it from a pro.* Spend time in the presence of a teacher who has a great classroom environment without relying on rewards and punishments. Watch and learn.

The Goal Is Self-Discipline

Pythagoras warned, "No man is free who cannot command himself." Self-control, though, is not innate. We encourage its development through socialization (Good & Brophy, 2000). Indeed, 2500 years after Pythagoras's warning, we teachers are guided by the goal of helping students move from impulsive, self-centered beings to self-directed, autonomous individuals (Gootman, 2001). Teachers agree that self-control and cooperation are important skills (Lane, Pierson, & Givner, 2003), and research suggests that person-centered approaches to discipline—that is, ones that emphasize shared respect and responsibility—are most effective for developing self-control and a number of other positive outcomes (Freiberg & Lamb, 2009).

Children today are tyrants. They contradict their parents, gobble their food, and tyrannize their teachers.

—*Socrates (circa 450 BCE)*

Despite its importance, teachers find it difficult to provide as many opportunities for self-direction as they'd like (Lewis & Burman, 2008). Also, in some students' perceptions, teachers become more coercive—not less—in their responses to student misbehavior (Lewis, 2001). I encourage you to view discipline as an opportunity to gain independence and responsibility. Luckily, many avenues are available to us as we help our students grow toward self-control. Our options fall into two categories:

- Establishing a climate that promotes independence
- Addressing behavior in ways that encourage self-control.

Establishing a Climate that Promotes Independence

Your instruction and physical environment should provide safe opportunities for students to think for themselves and to make meaningful choices. Try these three tools for establishing such a climate:

1. Choices
2. Respect decisions
3. Natural and logical consequences

1. Choices Choice is empowering; it engenders ownership and reduces resistance (Marshall, 2005). Within safe and acceptable limits, you and I can provide repeated and varied opportunities for students to make meaningful decisions. You can arrange options so that a range of choices is acceptable. For instance, students can choose classroom rules, their literature groups, the topics they pursue, their workspaces, and classroom jobs. The more mature the student, the broader the range and number of choices he may be able to handle. When students have the opportunity to make meaningful choices, they see that they are capable of making good decisions and that you respect their ability to do so (Coloroso, 1994).

2. Respect decisions   Once students make choices, we should respect their decisions. We should make it a point to override their choices only if they show themselves unable to follow through or if the consequence of their decisions would be harmful. Students' decisions may not match our own, but unless the consequences are dangerous, students should be allowed to experience them.

3. Natural and logical consequences   People with self-control understand the link between their behaviors and the consequences of their actions. Unfortunately, schools often emphasize rewards and punishments that are not only unrelated to students' behavior but are also delivered by the hands of another, the teacher. Examples include discipline programs that have students copying class rules when they talk out of turn or receiving food for following directions. In programs like these, teachers retain responsibility for delivering the consequences of students' actions, and students may have a harder time establishing authentic motivation for appropriate behavior.

To help students build internal controls and take responsibility for their actions, you can arrange classroom conditions so that they face the natural consequences of their behavior. Natural consequences (Dreikurs, 1968) flow from the behavior and are not arranged by another. For instance, when a student talks while directions are given, he misses the opportunity to gather appropriate materials for his photography project.

When it would be unsafe or unfeasible for students to experience natural consequences, we should provide a consequence that is at least logical. A logical consequence for Sheila's breaking Jaime's pencil out of anger, for instance, is that she supply Jaime with another pencil. Charney (2002) suggests three kinds of logical consequences:

- *Reparations:* When a student or group breaks or loses something, it must be replaced or repaired. The situation must be fixed.
- *Breach of contract and loss of trust:* When a student or group acts in a manner that contradicts the rules of the group, rights are temporarily lost.
- *Time-outs for inappropriate participation:* When a student or group does not participate in a manner consistent with expectations for the situation, the student(s) or group is removed from the situation until better choices are made.

When students live with the consequences of their choices, they come to see that the best discipline is not enforced by an authority but comes from within: They build self-control. You can also nurture self-control in the ways you respond to misbehavior.

Addressing Behavior in Ways that Encourage Self-Control

The following five tools can help you respond to behavior in ways that support self-control:

1. Talk it through and reflect
2. Self-correction
3. Avoid power struggles
4. Anger shields
5. Conflict resolution

1. Talk it through and reflect   Wise teachers do more than put an end to misbehavior: They use misbehavior as an opportunity to teach about better choices. For example, when Tyler accidently swings a baseball bat dangerously close to a friend's face, his teacher responds by moving forward to stop the bat and then asks: "Tyler, look how close that bat came to Dan's face. What could happen if you do not look where you swing?" The teacher uses reflective questions (Marshall, 2005) to guide Tyler to consider the potential harm

Here is your chance to support this student in developing self-control. What will you do?

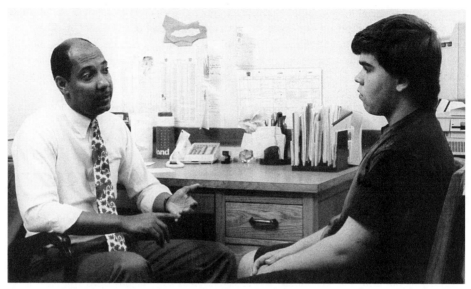

Source: Scott Cunningham/Merrill.

of his impulsive bat swinging, listening openly to his honest answer, and then discussing appropriate alternatives. By guiding Tyler to consider hurtful outcomes, his teacher helps him to forge the links between behavior and its consequences. Dan's face is safe not just for today but for tomorrow as well.

Talking it through can be difficult when you feel rushed. It takes time to teach students about good behavior. Although you may not have included behavior as a daily objective, no doubt it has a place in your long-range goals, and your time investment will most likely be a good one. Talking it through can also be difficult when you feel irritated because you *just want those monsters to stop it.* There are indeed times when belaboring an incident of misbehavior serves only to prolong it. Talk it through when there is a reasonable chance that students have not considered the potential effects of their actions. Otherwise, address the misbehavior as briefly as possible and move on.

Talking it through is useful because it (1) models the expectation that rational people use words to sort things out, (2) tightens the link between behavior and consequence without actually allowing for dangerous consequences, and (3) works to prevent similar misbehavior in the future. Talking it through can help students see their mistakes not as crimes but as opportunities to do better.

2. Self-correction   Your goal is that students control themselves, so whenever possible, allow students themselves to find solutions to their problems and to select appropriate behaviors. When faced with the typical barrage of tattling during rug time ("Teacher! She is bothering me!"), a primary-grade teacher I know tells the offended child, "I am sure you can find a quieter place to sit." The student almost invariably moves quietly to another, less provocative spot on the rug, and his talking friends receive a hint about their own behavior.

As another example, ninth-grade Doug holds a lively conversation during independent work time. His teacher approaches him for a quiet talk: "Doug, the time to chat has passed. Can you find something more productive to do, or would you like me to help you find an alternative?" Doug shrugs, "I guess I will read my novel." As Doug pulls out his book, the teacher responds with an emphasis on the positive: "Good choice! I was pretty sure you would have a good idea!" The teacher joins another group but follows through by glancing at Doug to ensure that his nose is buried in his book. Allowing students to correct their own behavior provides practice—with a safety net—in controlling their own destiny.

You need not correct every incidence of misbehavior you notice. First, sometimes drawing unnecessary attention to a fleeting or relatively minor transgression can interrupt instruction and increase the likelihood that the misbehavior will reoccur. Ignoring some misbehaviors can extinguish them. One caution, though: If you elect to ignore a misbehavior, prepare to ignore it repeatedly. If you eventually respond to misbehavior that you initially ignored, you may unwittingly reinforce it (Obenchain & Taylor, 2005). Second, students can serve as a powerful influence on each other's behavior. A cold rebuff from a peer can do more to direct a poking student's behavior than can your admonitions to remember the rules against poking. If students solve problems on their own, pat yourself on the back and resist the urge to intervene.

3. Avoid power struggles   Independent people have power over their fate in important ways. K–12 students have less power than adults—especially in the classroom setting—and growing toward self-determination can mean questing for more power. When a student outwardly defies you and provokes your anger, you are probably engaged in a power struggle. Power struggles rarely end with satisfactory results, mainly because the student is right: You cannot *make* her do anything. Avoid power struggles in three ways:

- *Diffuse the situation.* Use humor, greater physical distance, or a caring voice to allow the anger to dissipate: "I can see that you are angry. It may be better if we talked about this in 5 minutes. I will be back in a few moments to talk." Usually increasing your physical and emotional distance from the student helps to diffuse the student's anger and allows you to approach the situation more calmly. If a student seems angry or belligerent, you can also use a quiet, concerned question that takes him off guard (Khalsa, 2007): "Are you okay?" "Did I do something that upset you?"
- *Let the student save face.* Offer an out so that the student can comply with your request without submitting entirely to your authority. If a student's sole choice is to do as you say, she can only lose face in front of her peers. As Linda attempts to draw her teacher into a power struggle, for instance, her teacher calmly says, "You may get out your book, or, if you have a better idea, I am listening." Still angry, Linda replies, "Yeah! I want to do nothing!" Her teacher's wise response is to accept the student's alternative, even if it is only vaguely appropriate. "All right. Sometimes I want to do nothing, too. That is a fine choice for the next few minutes. I will be happy when you are finished with that and can join us in math. I miss you when you are gone." The teacher has allowed Linda some control, has provided her with an out so that she can join the math group with at least the appearance of her own free will, and she has reinforced the notion that Linda is a likable person with a contribution to make.
- *Give the student the power.* A student in a power struggle may need to make one more comment after your request for quiet, or feed the hamster one more pellet after you ask him to stop. By allowing those "one mores," you convey that students do indeed have some power over *what* they do *when*. Usually a student's behavior will stop with a "one more" (Schneider, 1997). Only if it continues will you need to address the behavior again.

    You may also elect to abdicate your desire to control the student's behavior entirely: "I certainly cannot force you to use appropriate language, but I must insist on it in my room. You will need to use street language elsewhere." When the student realizes that you are comfortable with your own power—and its limits—he will almost certainly have a lesser need to grab for available power.

4. Anger shields   Expect that, at times, your students will be angry or hurt. Irate parents, similarly, may at times use hostile language with you. Although negative feelings are unavoidable, you and your class deserve to be protected from angry outbursts. You can shield using comments such as "I know you are hurt, but I care too much about our class to let you say unkind things. You need to find another way to handle these feelings. I can make some suggestions if you get stuck." I know a junior high teacher who teaches her students to say "Cancel!" to reject a hurtful message. We've extended the verbal message at my house to include a hand signal (letter C) so that we can shield ourselves with a simple gesture.

    Anger shields teach students that everyone deserves dignity and respect; show students that although we cannot entirely control our environments, we *can* control how we will respond. It's one way to encourage students to draw on their inner resources to handle their negative emotions.

5. Conflict resolution U.S. schools are basically safe places (Mayer & Furlong, 2010), and horribly violent events such as suicides and homicides are far more common for K–12 students *away* from school than *in school* (Borum, Cornell, Modzeleski, & Jimerson, 2010). Still, less violent conflict, such as bullying, is a concern the world over (Swearer, Espelage, Vaillancourt, & Hymel, 2010). In the common conception of bullying, there is an imbalance of power, and the perpetrator purposefully and repeatedly uses physical aggression (e.g., hitting, pushing, or spitting) or social aggression (e.g., making fun, malicious gossip, exclusion from social groups) against the victim. Cyber bullying—where the aggressor uses the Internet to victimize a peer—can be especially terrifying to students given their perceptions of the aggressor's anonymity (Mishna, Saini, & Solomon, 2009). Indeed, digital citizenship is now a priority for schools (Ribble, Bailey, & Ross, 2004). See the 21st Century Teaching and Learning Tip.

Student researchers have recently uncovered a different student perspective on bullying (Thomson & Gunter, 2008). This student perspective includes behaviors such as name calling, isolation, and physical hassling perpetrated not by a single individual upon another but by one cultural subgroup upon others. Bullying tends to peak during the middle school/junior high years. Therefore, teachers in those grades may have a particular responsibility, but students in all grades clearly need adult support in solving conflicts in appropriate ways.

Many students perceive that their teachers do not recognize or act upon bullying incidents. Your job is always to help students build lifelong skills that will assist them in positive interactions throughout their lives. Begin by not tolerating hateful acts. Stop your students from using hate speech, and intervene in acts of bullying. Check with your school for policies regarding bullying; schools rightly treat it very seriously. See the 21st Century Teaching and Learning Tip for some online support to address bullying.

21st Century Teaching and Learning Tip

DIGITAL CITIZENSHIP

The International Society for Technology Education's (2007) National Education Technology Standards emphasize digital citizenship. Digital citizens practice safe, legal, and responsible use of ICT. They display positive attitudes and personal responsibility for using technology to collaborate and learn, and they exhibit leadership with ICT. Each district has an acceptable use policy that students and parents are required to sign. Locate the policy and discover what it tells you about questions such as:

- When and how are students allowed to use cell phones?
- When and how are students allowed to use digital recording devices (such as cell phone, still and video cameras)?
- What policies govern Internet use at school?
- How can we counteract the negative and violent messages that students sometimes encounter in cyberspace? What role should the school system play in teachers' and students' social networking practices?
- What are your responsibilities for preventing students from sending or posting potentially troublesome electronic communications? From violating copyright law?

21st Century Teaching and Learning Tip

NO BULLYING

Try these Web sites on bullying. Many have resources written for students, families, and educators to prevent and intervene when students are involved in bullying.

- Bullying.org (http://www.bullying.org/)
- Stop Bullying Now (http://www.stopbullyingnow.hrsa.gov/kids/)
- Bully Prevention in Positive Behavior Support (http://www.pbis.org/common/pbisresources/tools/pbsbullyprevention.pdf)

Teaching Tip

CONFLICT RESOLUTION

1. Set the rules for a cooperative context (example: no name calling).
2. Listen. Let each person finish without interrupting. Each person states his wants and feelings.
3. Find common ground. Agree on the facts and the issues important to each.
4. Brainstorm solutions.
5. Negotiate proposed solutions.
6. Agree. Listen as each person states the plan aloud.

Many programs assist schools and teachers in preventing violence. However, efforts that focus only on punishment—such as zero tolerance policies—seem to be falling short of their prevention intention (Casella, 2003; Dupper, 2010; Rice, 2009). Instead, teaching students the skills to resolve conflicts peacefully serves a number of long-range purposes (Johnson & Johnson, 2004): It provides them a set of skills they can use to resolve a lifetime of inevitable conflicts, it enhances their moral and social development, and it provides them with a mechanism to change the world. The Teaching Tip presents a general set of skills you can teach your students to resolve conflict.

The Key: A Structured, Consistent, Supportive Environment

Years of parenting research translated into the schooling arena provides very clear directions for classroom teachers: The environments that support development best are *authoritative* ones (Gregory & Cornell, 2009; Walker, 2008; 2009). Figure 10.1 shows the intersections of two dimensions of caring for young people: *control* (low and high) and *nurturance* (low and high). In authoritative classrooms, both control and nurturance are high; the classrooms are well structured and provide plentiful acceptance and support. Students understand that there are limits to their behavior and that expectations for success are high—but so is teachers' support of their efforts (Henderson & Milstein, 2003; van Tartwijk, den Brok, Veldman, & Wubbels, 2009). Nurturing teachers believe in their students' capacity for success, engage in trusting and caring relationships, and provide a positive climate for exploration and learning. Authoritative teachers encourage students to take academic risks and provide safety nets for when students fail. Students in authoritative classrooms are more likely to internalize achievement goals and open up to adult influence (Walker, 2009).

The authoritative environment you create includes a structured, predictable, and focused setting (Chapter 9), and it includes the supportive social emotional climate you set with your relationships and interactions with students. These six tools can help.

Figure 10.1 *Authoritative teachers provide controlled and nurturing environments.*

		CONTROL	
		Low	**High**
NURTURANCE	**Low**	Neglectful	Authoritarian
	High	Permissive	**Authoritative (Optimal)**

1. Structure

In authoritative classrooms and schools, each aspect of the learning environment is structured. Ensure that your physical layout is orderly and fits the academic tasks. Structure classroom time schedules to show that every minute is precious; maximize academic learning time. Keep your behavioral and academic expectations high, clear, and predictable. Further, ensure that students perceive that you monitor them carefully, intervene to protect their safety and best interests, and provide feedback that helps them meet high expectations.

2. High Expectations

Authoritative teachers convey their belief in every student's capacity for success. Remember the warm demanders from Chapter 4? I have many positive memories of teachers who "warmly demanded" my sons' best. For example, when Zach was "sagging" (wearing his pants far lower than his boxers), I appreciated his history teacher telling him to pull his pants up, and keep them up. He did. When Alex admitted to too many hours of X-box, his English teacher told him to turn off the video games and get back in the habit of reading for pleasure. Alex read voraciously that year and ended up as an English major in college. I appreciated it when teachers continued to demand the best from my children, even when we got tired at home.

It seems obvious that we believe that all of our students can learn, right? Of course! However, in the recent Met Life Survey, teachers who worked in schools with higher percentages of low-income families were less likely to believe that their students could succeed or that they were motivated to succeed (MetLife, 2010). Here are some strategies for conveying high expectations for all your students:

- Convey a sense of urgency and excitement about what students need to learn. Knowledge is power. "Education is the tool that gives a child life choices. A teacher who cares enough to make sure a student knows how to survive school and gives that student the necessary skills is providing a gift that will keep affecting lives from one generation to the next" (Payne, 2008, p. 52).
- Use grade-level content standards as a minimum (not maximum) expectation.
- Share grading criteria in advance. Describe how assignments and projects contribute to the final grade.
- Share (or develop with students) grading rubrics and teach students to self-assess.
- Share outstanding samples created by other, similar students.
- Focus on students' individual strengths and build from them. Be a mentor.
- Focus on personal improvement, helping students track their progress over time.
- Use the same praise or "success messages" for all students to protect against unconsciously different expectations. Students can choose these success messages.
- Encourage students to do their best. When their work falls short, help them analyze it and warmly insist on improvement.
- Include family members to build, convey, and enforce shared high expectations. Remember that parenting is difficult; it helps to work as a team.

3. Support

Authoritative teachers help their students meet high expectations. If your students are missing tools, figure out a way to see that they get them. If students lack prerequisite skills, work out a plan for students to pick up those skills, perhaps through tutoring or through a software program. If your students need services beyond the typical program, advocate for them to receive those services. In short, as an inclusive, responsive, and authoritative teacher, you set high expectations and then *do whatever it takes* to help students achieve. Authoritative teachers don't, however, hover; they choose the minimal level of intervention necessary to ensure student success without interfering with student independence.

4. Caring Communication

Effective schools foster a caring climate, personalization, and supportive relationships (Henderson & Milstein, 2003; Osher et al., 2010). Caring communication is necessary in these respectful environments (Gootman, 2008). Teachers' responsibility is to both model caring communication and to teach students the skills necessary to communicate in caring ways. Three such skills include (1) recognizing and labeling feelings—students' own and others; (2) communicating feelings without hurting others; and (3) listening to each other, showing interest, and hearing the speaker's complete message.

5. Clear Limits

Clear classroom limits set the boundaries of permissible behavior. Setting limits is sometimes difficult for new teachers, who tend to be concerned that their students like them. However, one of the kindest things you can do for your students is to provide a stable environment with reasonable limits and to forbid travel beyond those limits. Everyone needs limits; students will push until they find your boundaries. When they find those boundaries, they can turn their attention to other matters. Do them—and yourself—a favor and make your limits clear at the outset.

Students make better choices about their behavior when they know what is expected of them. School and classroom rules are an important way to teach students what we expect. One school, for instance, adopted an elegant set of five rules that provide direction for behaviors in a variety of settings at school: be kind, be safe, be cooperative, be respectful, and be peaceful (Lewis, Sugai, & Colvin, 1998). Note that these are all positively stated. Develop a similar set of classroom rules, either with the students' help or on your own. See the Teaching Tip for suggestions on developing classroom rules.

You also need to establish clear expectations for special circumstances. Before a field trip, for instance, teach your students approximately three specific behaviors you expect to see. A primary teacher might hold up three fingers, one for each expectation, and state in positive and clear terms his expectations for student behavior during the trip: "First, you need to stay with your buddy. Second, you need to keep your hands to yourself. Third, you need to stay where you can see an adult at all times." Then the teacher checks for understanding of his rules: "Let's see how many know the first special rule for today. I see 10 hands up. I will wait for another 10. . . . Good. Say it aloud." He reteaches until he is certain that all students know what he expects. Days with substitute teachers, assemblies, and sports activities are other situations when clearly stated expectations are critical.

Teaching Tip

RULES ON RULES

- Keep your list of rules down to about four or five in number.
- State each rule in positive terms. For instance, "Raise your hand before speaking" is more helpful than "Do not shout out."
- Be certain that students accept the rules as useful and reasonable. Even adolescents, who are prone to challenge authority and assert autonomy, are willing to follow rules if they seem reasonable and fair (Gregory & Cornell, 2009).
- If you choose to have the class develop the rules through group discussion, check that their rules are reasonable and address major areas of concern for classroom behavior (when to talk, when to move around, and how to treat each other and belongings).
- Think about how to operationalize rules. For instance, some teachers operationalize their rules for classroom talk with a color system: "red" for silence, no one out of her seat; "yellow" for whispers in small groups; and "green" for regular conversational level.
- If you elect to include explicit consequences for following and breaking the rules, be sure that they are logical and humane.

6. Consistency

Perhaps even more difficult than setting limits is following through to reinforce those limits. Reinforce limits by responding consistently to students' requests and behavior. Your consistent responses will help students see that their environment is predictable and that they can rely on stable expectations. *They can trust you to say what you mean . . . and mean what you say.* When you show them that you mean what you say, you convey to students that you care enough about them to keep your promises. If you are inconsistent, students will learn that they can do as they please and that they cannot trust you. Given the principle of intermittent reinforcement, a rule that is enforced inconsistently is worse than no rule at all; it makes negative behaviors very difficult to extinguish (Obenchain & Taylor, 2005). "No" must mean "No" every single time. This is a tough one, but your efforts will pay off.

Relationships as Central

One of the clearest conclusions from the research on classroom discipline and student success is the centrality of positive relationships. "Teaching is about building relationships—knowing your students, sharing ideas and life events" (Frieberg & Lamb, 2009, p. 102). In fact, the best predictor for healthy outcomes for youth is supportive relationships with adults like teachers (Henderson & Milstein, 2003; Kaiser & Rasminsky, 2009). Respectful, caring relationships provide support, bolster resiliency, prevent misbehavior, reinforce students' self-worth, encourage students to take necessary academic risks, enhance the academic experience, and build lifelong commitments to learning and citizenship (Davis, 2003; Doyle, 2009; Gregory & Cornell, 2009; Henderson & Milstein, 2003; Payne, 2008; Zuckerman, 2007).

Therefore, relationships are vital, and vigilance in accepting all of our students as valuable humans is essential; students must feel that we respect them as people, are concerned about their needs, and understand their perspectives. Earlier chapters (3, 4, and 9) focused on the basics of forging relationships; this chapter focuses on strategies for maintaining those relationships by treating students with dignity and respect. I suggest that you make it a rule for yourself: Treat all students with dignity and respect.

Caring relationships are based on mutual respect.

Thinkstock

By fostering respect and dignity, we offer hope. Make your classroom a refuge where students receive the same consideration as would respected adults, through both the environment you create and the ways you elect to respond to students' behavior. Here are eleven tips to help you do so by establishing a respectful climate and by responding respectfully to behavior.

The secret in education lies in respecting the student.

—Ralph Waldo Emerson

Establishing a Climate of Dignity and Respect

You want students to know that every person in your classroom is important. Show students that you know and value their perspectives (Wormeli, 2001). Learn about the things they care about and remember to see the world from the eyes of someone their age. Use a warm and respectful voice (Kohn, 1999). In all you do, maintain an environment that exemplifies respect for self and others.

1. Celebrate and suffer   Demonstrate respect for your students' thoughts and experiences by sharing their successes and their slips. When students express emotions, especially sadness or despair, it is tempting for teachers to rush in, quickly analyze the situation, tell students how they should be feeling, fix things, and move on. You need not provide explanations or analyses for every event that causes emotion for your students (Schneider, 1997). A quiet, sad smile, a thumbs-up, or a round of applause may be a terrific way to show students that you understand their positions. The use of such empathic resonance can help your students feel less alone and that you respect their experiences (Kottler & Kottler, 2007).

2. Active listening   You can show that you value students' words and ideas by practicing active listening (Gordon, 1974). In active listening, the teacher summarizes or reflects the speaker's message. For instance, a teacher may begin his reply to a frustrated student, "You seem to be saying that this homework was hard for you." A question stem such as "Are you saying that . . . ?" can also help to ensure clear communication. Active listening shows students that you value their ideas enough to be certain that you understand them correctly. It allows you to demonstrate that you believe communication involves two parties, each deserving to be heard. Gootman (2001) gives six tips for caring listening:

1. *Show interest.* Show interest and pay attention when students speak. Hold your body still and give your full attention.
2. *Hear them out.* Wait until students are finished speaking before saying anything.
3. *Separate your feelings from their feelings.* Respond to the issue, not the emotion.
4. *Look for nonverbal cues.* Body language can help you find the true meaning of the message.
5. *Put student feelings into words.* Try to interpret the message and emotions by rephrasing what you think you have heard.
6. *Don't argue with students' feelings.* Accept students' rights to feel as they do rather than suggesting that they should feel different emotions.

Gootman's tips can be equally effective for helping students listen to their peers.

3. Peer listening   Silent but accepted norms teach students that they need to listen raptly to the teacher but not so carefully to each other. Students need to be encouraged to listen to each other. In a typical scenario, the class chatters over Ray as he shares his ideas. The teacher implores, "Stop, Ray, I can't hear you." When the class quiets down, the teacher repeats Ray's words: "Ray was saying . . ." In this scenario, the teacher is the traffic cop who controls the conversation. Let's rewrite the scenario so that it encourages more respectful and caring interactions: The class chatters, but this time the teacher suggests, "Ray, let's wait just a second. Some of your peers can't hear you yet and I know they're interested." The class quiets down, and the teacher urges: "Ray, why don't you repeat the last thing you said now that you have all ears on you." Now the teacher sends the message that she expects students to listen to each other. She doesn't repeat Ray's words but directly encourages students to listen to each other.

4. Model and teach   Ray's scenario also highlights the importance of directly teaching students to treat others with dignity. Take advantage of the power of modeling to show learners what fairness and dignity look and feel like. When modeling is insufficient, draw students' attention to respectful treatment. If they treat someone disrespectfully, quietly and calmly point out the natural consequences of what they have done and help them find more dignified alternatives. For example, when students use harsh words to tease, tell them firmly that harsh words can hurt and are not allowed in your classroom. Then give them some acceptable alternatives to teasing.

Responding to Behavior

How you choose to respond to inappropriate behavior can teach lessons that last a lifetime. As you shape students' behavior, Curwin and Mendler (2001) advise you to protect students' dignity by thinking about your own: How would you respond if a teacher used this strategy with you? Your words carry tremendous power . . . to humiliate or help. Be certain that you redirect inappropriate behavior without embarrassing learners.

5. Address the behavior   When you praise or provide correction, address students' actions and not their character. Focus on what they do, not who they are. For instance, when your class has listened attentively to a guest speaker, it is more effective to praise specific behaviors ("You all watched and listened with such respect!") than to address students' value as people ("You are so good!"). When you need to correct misbehavior, do not apply words such as lazy, thoughtless, or bad to the students. Instead, provide feedback on what students did that was wrong: "You talked while the guest speaker was talking" instead of "You are so rude!" Say "You left the room a mess" instead of "You are so messy!" Then give the natural consequences attached to their behavior. When you address behavior and not character, you send the message that students are worthy people, even when they err. Teach them to do the same for each other.

6. Private correction   In the instances when most of the class is fine but one student needs redirection, make it a point to speak with her in private. While the others work, approach the student's desk for a calm conversation about her behavior. If you can continue providing adequate supervision, you may elect to hold your conversation in the hall or outside the door. This approach allows the rest of the class to continue without interruption and saves the student from public humiliation. Private communications also lessen the chance that students will respond defensively to your correction to save face.

7. Hints   When some or all of the class needs redirection, it's typical in middle-class culture to start with the lowest level of intervention possible: the hint. You calmly remind students what they should be doing ("Calculators should be put away now. Everyone is finding page 83."). Often no greater intervention is required, and you have shown students that you trust them to follow directions with only a gentle reminder (Zuckerman, 2007). Recall that some cultures are more accustomed to explicit redirections than to hints. You may need to teach "hints" as a strategy.

8. I-messages   Gordon (1974) suggests that students are often unaware of the effects of their actions on others. Teachers can use *I*-statements to state their emotions without anger or blame and without belittling the student. An *I*-statement has three parts:

1. Statement of the problem ("When people sharpen their pencils while I talk . . .")
2. Specific effect of the problem (". . . other students cannot hear me, . . .")
3. Statement of the teacher's feelings (". . . and I am frustrated to have to stop and wait.")

Once a teacher uses an *I*-statement, the teacher and students can work on the problem together. *I*-statements express respect by encouraging students to pay attention to their effects on others, allow the teacher to state emotions without humiliating, and convey the teacher's trust that students can address a problem.

9. Strength refreshers   When students are corrected by their teachers, they may lose perspective that a single mistake is just that: a *single* mistake. You can reaffirm your faith in students' basic goodness by starting your correction with a strength refresher (Schneider, 1997). Remind the student of how he typically behaves and point out that this mistake was atypical for him. For instance, when you discover that Roger spit water during a passing period, you pull him aside for a conversation: "Roger, I was surprised to hear that you spit. You usually do a super job of helping us make sure that our school is a safe and clean place." Because you demonstrate your faith in Roger's usual behavior, he will probably feel less guarded about explaining the incident to you and more eager to correct his behavior.

10. Laughter   Despite your supportive atmosphere and respectful interactions, there are times when students will manage to push your buttons. Some students seem to *live* to get a reaction. If you are able to retain your sense of humor, you can use laughter to diffuse tense situations and maintain dignity—the students' and your own (Kottler, 2002).

When using humor to address behavior, be certain not to direct your humor at students (Frymier, Wanzer, & Wojtaszczyk, 2008). Humor is highly individual, and it is cultural. At least until you have a thorough understanding of your students and a cohesive group spirit, use jokes that are directed at yourself or at situations outside the students. The point is to respond playfully to situations that might otherwise erupt into power struggles or other unproductive interactions.

11. Apologies   Finally, when despite your best attempts you offend a student's dignity, apologize. You may occasionally speak before you think and hurt feelings. Consider using a calm, apologetic message: "That did not sound at all as I had intended. I apologize if I hurt your feelings. Next time I will choose my words more carefully." You will not lessen your authority by admitting a mistake. You will probably, in fact, gain authority by displaying your willingness to disclose and correct an error: You are fair. You model the humility that you hope students will also display. You demonstrate how humans (teachers!) make a mistake, learn from it, and go on.

Prevention, Not Reaction

Some misbehavior occurs because it is human nature to press the limits, to test the predictability of our environments. However, much classroom misbehavior can be prevented. When teachers emphasize proactive, preventive discipline, students' engagement rates are higher and teacher stress levels are lower (Clunies-Ross, Little, & Kienhuis, 2008; Osher et al., 2010; Sutton et al., 2009). Five strategies can help you prevent much misbehavior:

1. Meaningful curriculum and high engagement
2. Motivation and development
3. Anticipation
4. Positive approach
5. Strong presence and nonverbal communication

1. Meaningful Curriculum and High Engagement

When students are engaged in relevant and interesting learning experiences, they are often too busy to misbehave (Miller & Hall, 2009; Stichter et al., 2009). Good news! Student engagement is in your hands. To engage students, you need to maximize learning time, vary your instructional strategies, demand active participation, and help students find meaning in their work. Ask yourself: Do students see the purpose in the content? How well does school capture issues seen as vital to the students? Is the lesson structured to require every student to engage?

Check your curriculum to ensure that the content is appropriate and that you are using rich instruction that accommodates students' diverse needs. Although some topics may not spark immediate student enthusiasm, if you remember to COME IN (Chapter 6), you

Inclusive and Responsive Teaching Tip

BRIDGING THE STUDENTS' WORLDS AND THE SCHOOL'S WORLD

Actively pursue strategies that help *you* incorporate students' worlds into your classroom and help *them* see the importance of what school has to offer.

- *Listen to the issues students discuss and incorporate them into your instruction.* Some educators suggest that students' issues should be placed firmly at the center of the curriculum through thematic planning. Or, more immediately, a teacher might overhear his students discussing an impending threat of a pandemic flu. He plans science lessons that address the history, procedures, and sociopolitical and ethical issues pertaining to vaccination.
- *Use a student survey before you plan a unit to find out what students would like to know about the topic.* A survey may begin, "Students study the American Revolution in many

grades, but sometimes they don't find out what they would really like to know. What do you still not know about that war?" An in-class discussion can serve the same purpose: "Let's make a list of the things we wish we knew . . ."

- *Incorporate students' interests in sports, music, and other aspects of culture into the topics you select and the methods you use to study them.* For example, students may analyze lyrics of rap music for examples of poetic devices.
- *Begin every lesson with an opener.* Openers pique students' curiosity and connect their interests and knowledge with the content of the lesson. A mathematics lesson on exponents might start with a great video clip (http://micro.magnet.fsu.edu/primer/java/scienceopticsu/powersof10/), for instance.
- *State the purpose of your lessons.* Tell students how this information or skill will be useful. Or, have them tell you. "You'll need this for the test" or ". . . for next year" tend not to be convincing reasons for many students.

increase the chances of engaging students and thus forestall misbehavior. Remember to employ every-student-responds techniques (Figure 6.6). Also try watching a recording of yourself teaching. Is your instruction as engaging as you had hoped? If not, think about when you as a student misbehaved. The Inclusive and Responsive Teaching Tip shows you how to prevent misbehavior by bridging worlds.

2. Motivation and Development

Study your specific learners and then align your expectations to their physical and emotional development. For instance, kindergartners should be expected to sit for only about 10 minutes before the activity changes. Despite the fact that high school students can sit for hour-long periods, as a general rule, it is useful to allow students of all ages to spend about 2 minutes actively processing information for every 10 minutes they spend listening. That means after you provide 10 minutes of information, they need a chance to discuss it. Try some of the "tell each other" strategies (Figure 6.6) to help students process information.

Also match your activities and expectations to factors such as the time of day and year. It is human to be sleepy after lunch and antsy before the last bell rings. Primary teachers are especially good at using games such as Simon Says or Copy My Clap Pattern to refocus students' attention. Secondary teachers can provide high-interest activities when students' energy or attention may be likely to wane. Changing physical location or position gives students a break and allows them to refocus (recall the strategies for including physical movement, page 135—Chapter 6).

You can also prevent misbehavior and encourage learning by attending to motivation theory. Research suggests that many elements that affect student motivation, shown in Figure 10.2, can be directly influenced by the teacher (Turner, Meyer, Midgley, & Patrick, 2003). If a student gives up upon viewing a whole sheet of tedious grammar exercises, the teacher may rip the sheet in half to affect the student's *perception of effort and probability of success.* Another teacher works hard to return students' essays shortly after they submit them. He knows *immediate feedback* can increase motivation.

When students lack the enthusiasm to stay focused, try tweaking one of the factors of motivation from this figure. For example, try supporting student motivation by using vivid lessons and creating suspense (Wormeli, 2001). Although motivation to learn is ultimately in the hands of the students, there are many ways you can tweak *your own* behavior to affect students' motivation.

Figure 10.2 *Factors of motivation.*

- *Needs and interests.* Motivation increases when physical, psychological, and social needs are met. Examples include feelings of safety from physical and psychological harm and students' perceptions that they are treated fairly.
- *Level of concern.* Motivation is optimized when there is some tension about completing a task but not enough to provoke acute anxiety.
- *Perception of required effort.* Motivation increases when individuals perceive that the amount of effort required to complete a task is reasonable.
- *Probability of success.* Motivation increases when individuals perceive that there is a good chance they will succeed.
- *Knowledge of results.* Motivation increases when individuals have specific, immediate information about the result of their efforts.

3. Anticipation

You can prevent misbehavior, too, by anticipating and thus avoiding trouble spots. You know that your students are a curious bunch, so if you leave a bowl of mealworms for your science lesson on the front table while you attempt to teach a social studies lesson, you invite misbehavior. By placing the mealworms out of sight, you help students focus their attention on the lesson at hand. Similarly, if you have passed out pointy compasses for your third-period geometry lesson, collect the compasses as students move into the next phase of the lesson. Removing distractions is a sure bet for preventing misbehavior.

Anticipation is key for preventing individual students from escalating in their misbehaviors as well. If you've spent time in classrooms, you can probably conjure an image of a student who displayed a minor misbehavior that quickly became something larger and more troublesome. Often deescalating explosive behaviors involves stopping behaviors before they start. For instance, teachers should know the triggers for particular misbehaviors, pay attention to students' apparent anxiety levels, and teach academic survival skills (Shukla-Mehta & Albin, 2003). Teachers can anticipate difficulties by refusing to engage and by intervening early. It's a matter of planning. See Figure 10.3 for some other trouble spots that can be avoided with careful planning.

Figure 10.3   *Anticipating and avoiding trouble.*

Students are more likely to misbehave when . . .

1. . . . they think you can't see them. So . . .
   - When you stand and talk with an individual, keep your back to the wall and position yourself where you can see the class.
   - Write on an overhead projector or use a document camera rather than the board, especially if you are left-handed.
   - Make occasional eye contact with the students farthest from you as you work with individuals.
2. . . . they are allowed to disengage without clear expectations. So . . .
   - Teach your directions through direct instruction.
   - Plan your transitions between lessons. Think through each aspect of the transition. Make your directions very clear, and minimize the time spent switching activities.
   - Have all your materials ready to go. Lay them out at different stations for quick distribution and collection, as appropriate.
   - Prepare a student to take over if you need to speak with an adult or have another interruption during class. Practice the routine.

Your ability to anticipate common trouble spots will improve with experience. You can begin by planning instruction and your room environment with an eye toward setting students up for success. Teachers with low rates of misbehavior spend time in the beginning of the year explicitly teaching appropriate procedures and behavior. Charney (2002) spends the first six weeks of the school year teaching students to monitor their own behavior and use the items in the room safely through her own version of the three *R*s:

- *Reinforcing:* Commenting on the positive behaviors students demonstrate ("I notice that you are solving that problem together.").
- *Reminding:* Asking students to state the expectations for behavior ("Remind me, where do we put the calculators when we are finished?").
- *Redirecting:* Pointing students toward more appropriate behavior ("Rulers are for measuring.").

You will also use your knowledge of your particular students to anticipate possible misbehaviors. Once you learn that your students go off task quickly during transition times, for instance, plan an appropriate response. When you have a few quiet minutes at home, rehearse your calm, productive responses to those behaviors: What will you do and say the next time students chat during a transition time? Having a response ready often helps to forestall problems. If you have a student who particularly struggles with substitute teachers, work with him to create a plan for your anticipated absence to attend a conference tomorrow.

4. Positive Approach

We all prefer to be in happy places; people do better when they feel better (Marshall, 2005). Figure 10.4 shares some strategies that can help to establish a positive learning environment—and thus prevent misbehavior—from the first day you meet your students.

Because classrooms are crowded and hurried, it is very easy to focus on those students determined to derail our lessons. However, when we emphasize misbehavior, we contribute to a negative tone and provide attention for the wrong bunch of behaviors. Instead of criticizing the students who are facing the wrong way during your **read-aloud,** glance around the group. You will probably notice that more than half are listening raptly. Concentrate on those students. Smile warmly and say, "More than half of you are eagerly listening! I really appreciate that!" Then wait and praise as the other class members give their attention.

Remember, though, that false praise is probably worse than no praise at all; keep your praise genuine. Keep in mind, too, that students' reactions to public praise can vary by age level and by individual. Use the Inclusive and Responsive Teaching Tip to employ praise students prefer.

Figure 10.4   *Establishing a positive environment from day one.*

---

1. *Learn students' names immediately (yes, during the first day).* It is an immediate way to show your respect for them as people. Take 10 quick minutes to go up and down the rows or through the tables, repeating students' names as you memorize them. All who learn at least three new names are winners.

2. *Convey your high expectations and enthusiasm for teaching and learning right away.* Examples include enthusiastic messages about being glad for your time together, stories about you as a person to help show that you expect to connect with students as people, and previews of the exciting things students will learn and do in your class. Help students begin to get to know each other.

3. *Teach your classroom rules or have students develop them in a community.* Keep the number brief and state the rules in positive terms.

4. *Provide for learning and for student choice on the first day.* Ask students what they want to learn about certain subjects, either through private journal entries or via a class chart. Teach at least one real lesson on your first day and prime your students to share what they learned when they go home that night.

5. *Immediately establish routines and effective management to prevent misbehavior.* Teach students your procedures and rules regarding pencil sharpening, leaving their seats, using the restroom, submitting finished work, and other routines right away.

Inclusive and Responsive Teaching Tip

PICK YOUR PRAISE PLATFORM

Blanket, generic praise is rarely helpful and can manipulate or mislead. When given, performance praise needs to be specific and name the performance's admirable attributes. It also needs to be delivered in a manner that is appreciated by students. Students' reactions to teacher praise can vary from highly negative to highly positive (Brophy, 1981). Ask students to record on a card or survey how they like to receive their praise: Privately or publicly. Keep those preferences at hand as you comment on student performance.

In public and private, praise good behavior specifically and in a way that stresses logical consequences: "Thanks for cleaning up, Friends! Now we have lots more time left for other things!" That way you reinforce the notion that students' motivation to behave is not simply to please you, it is to keep the environment productive and enjoyable for all.

5. Strong Presence and Nonverbal Communication

Many efforts to discipline are communicated not through teachers' words but through their strong presence, or bearing. Teachers with strong presence carry themselves with confidence and appear capable and relaxed. Importantly for high school teachers, big teacher presence has nothing to do with physical size; it's not to be confused with the intimidation potential that comes with mass or height. Instead, teacher presence is a set of messages you send to students that you care about them, feel confident in your own abilities, are aware of their actions, and can be trusted to help them make good choices. To communicate a strong teacher presence, dress in a manner that conveys respect for your students and yourself. Stand up straight. Relax. Uncross your arms and keep your hands loosely at your sides. Use eye contact and facial expressions to support your verbal messages. (Remember, though, that your direct gaze may not be returned by students who do not share your cultural norms for conveying respect.)

You'll use nonverbal communication on the move, too, to prevent misbehavior. Without saying a word, Fred Jones (2000) suggests, you can travel purposefully throughout the room, sending the message that you mean business through your direct gaze and relaxed bearing, and by moving your body (turning it, moving it closer to students, and staying long enough to convey your message and ensure compliance, and then moving away).

Indeed, effective classroom managers consistently prevent misbehavior by placing themselves where the action is, monitoring carefully, and using eye contact to direct student behavior (Miller & Hall, 2009). Be careful, too, your nonverbal communication sends respectful messages. Payne (2008) notes that high school students who felt disrespected by teachers referred not to verbal aggression but to nonverbal messages that they perceived as discourteous. The following three strategies might expand your communications repertoire:

- *Gestures.* Like a symphony conductor, use your gestures to make requests for behavior. Pointing is rude, but you can lower both hands, palms down, to indicate a need for lower volume. A hand in front of you, palm forward, can support your message to Angela that she stop talking, as can a quiet shake of your head. Nod when she quiets down. Practice in the mirror to develop "the look" that redirects behavior without a word.
- *Physical proximity.* Some teachers are stuck like glue to the front of the room—but not you. Move throughout the room so that your physical presence is felt by all. Teach in different parts of the room. When you see two students begin to wander **off task,** move physically closer to them but continue teaching. Often your presence alone will bring them back to attention. If not, try tapping a single finger on their desks. Only when these efforts fail do you need to send a verbal message.
- *Withitness.* An effective teacher knows what is happening in every area of the classroom. Kounin's (1977) term *withitness* describes the childhood conclusion that teachers have eyes on the backs of their heads: Teachers need to be aware of all their students' actions all of the time. Position yourself so that you can see all students and

monitor carefully. For instance, position your equipment such as a document camera or projection panel so that you can face the group rather than turning your back on them.

In sum, you have tremendous power to set students up for success by thinking proactively about discipline. Through careful planning, you can stop many unproductive behaviors before they start.

A Systems Approach

Maintaining a productive learning environment and helping students develop self-control requires you to think about your classroom as a system. In a system, elements exist not in isolation but in interaction with each other and serve a purpose together; systems develop patterns of behavior and respond in characteristic ways to outside forces (Guillaume, 1991; Meadows, 2008). Using systems thinking allows us to look for causal connections and changes over time in the face of complexity. Figure 10.5 gives habits of a systems thinker.

Figure 10.5   *Habits of a systems thinker.*

Source: Reprinted with permission-Waters Foundation, Waters Foundation (2007). Habits of a systems thinker. Systems Thinking in Schools. Retrieved from http://www.watersfoundation.org/index.cfm?fuseaction=search.habits

21st Century Teaching and Learning Tip

HELPING YOUR STUDENTS BECOME SYSTEMS THINKERS

- Yours 21st-century students will need systems thinking skills to face many of the societal and environmental issues ahead. Systems thinkers work to see the big picture, look for change over time, change perspectives to understand, think about consequences—including unintended ones, and use habits of inquiry to understand the world (Waters Foundation, 2007).
- Get some background on systems thinking at Facing the Future (http://www.facingthefuture.org/GlobalIssuesResources/ GlobalIssueResources/SystemsThinking/tabid/251/Default.aspx#Elementary_School_Resources) and Systems Thinking in Schools (http://www.watersfoundation.org/index.cfm?fuseaction=materials.main).
- Many graphic organizers help students learn to analyze systems, look for interconnections, and think about change over time. Search for terms such as "Behavior Over Time Graphs," "Stock/Flow Maps," and "Causal Loop Diagrams."

In approaching classroom discipline using systems thinking, we consider issues in context. We think about students in relation to other classroom elements and larger systems. To positively affect student behavior, we identify relevant variables, think about causal links, assess feedback in the system, and use an inquiry frame of mind to ask "What might happen if . . . ?"

A prevalent systems approach for responding to misbehavior is **functional behavior analysis** or functional behavior assessment. Widely used for persistent or disruptive misbehavior, this approach allows teachers to take a nonpunitive approach to helping students improve their behavior. In behavior analysis, we view a negative behavior as serving some useful function or purpose for the student. By analyzing the behavior, we can develop a more specific and thus appropriate plan for changing it.

The Inclusive and Responsive Teaching Tip includes an overall approach employed in behavior analysis (based on Danforth & Smith, 2005; Jackson & Panyan, 2002; Ryan, Halsey, & Matthews, 2003). Comprehensive resources can be found on the Internet by searching "functional behavior analysis" and "functional behavior assessment." Behavioral analysis is effective with many students, but not necessarily all. Hall and Hall (2003) point out that oppositional students may not be receptive to behaviorist approaches to change their actions. Always consider your specific students when you consider a discipline strategy.

Systems thinking also requires you to respond quickly and on different levels to different numbers of issues. Your ability to integrate these different demands for maintaining classroom discipline will increase with experience, especially if you remain vigilant about growth. For now, you can begin to address behavior in multifaceted ways by thinking about (1) group size, (2) overlapping, (3) intensity of response, (4) motivation for misbehavior, and (5) redirecting behavior.

Group Size

Although you will work with individuals daily, much of your time will be spent in working with large groups. Students behave differently in groups than they do as individuals,

Inclusive and Responsive Teaching Tip

BEHAVIOR ANALYSIS

1. What is the problem behavior?
2. When does it occur?
3. What happens right before and after the behavior?
4. How does the student benefit from this behavior? (Does it help the student avoid something? Gain something else?)
5. What have others tried that has worked to change the behavior?
6. What will you try?
7. (Later) Did your plan work?

and each group tends to develop its own personality. Also, despite the public's fears of sensational classroom misbehavior the most common misbehaviors are talking out of turn and general off-task behavior such as bugging other students (Clunies-Ross et al., 2008; Jones, 2000).

For these reasons, you need to develop strategies that will maintain the group's focus. Figure 10.6 suggests some common techniques for managing group behaviors. Note that the tips are not punitive. Instead, they focus on positive, clear communication of expectations, careful monitoring, and specific feedback. Pick the tips that are consistent with your own convictions and with what you know about your students.

Overlapping

In a systems approach, you will also need to handle more than one issue at a time. To maximize the time your class spends on learning, you need to overlap your tasks. In overlapping, you address discipline issues while you continue to teach. For instance, as you respond to a student's content question, you can also move closer to two others who are embroiled in a pencil fight. While listening to a student read, you can also glance around the rest of the room to ensure that all are on task. You may need to give a "teacher look" and a shake

---

Figure 10.6   *Tips for maintaining group focus.*

---

1. Use a signal to gain students' attention. Don't talk while they talk.
   - Make a clear request: "Attention up here, please. Let's come back together."
   - Follow through: "I'll know you're ready when your eyes are on me and your pencils are down." Or: "Thanks Miguel, I see you're ready. . . . Thanks Pat."
   - "Clap once if you can hear me. Clap twice. Clap once . . ."
   - Just wait.
   - Raise a hand and teach students that when they see your raised hand, they need to stop talking and raise their own hand. Follow through.
   - Flash the classroom lights off then on.
   - Use a noise signal, such as a squeaker toy.
   - Lead a clapping pattern; students who are listening join in until all are with you.
   - Hold up a stopwatch and click to measure how many seconds it takes.
   - Try "Give me five" (Wong, 1998). When you say, "Give me five," students go through five steps: eyes on you, be quiet, be still, empty their hands, and listen.

2. Monitor carefully—especially the back and side edges of the room—and provide feedback on students' behavior.
   - Use hints to maintain on-task behavior: "Your group should be on the second job by now."
   - Allow for self-monitoring: "Check your noise level. Are you using quiet voices?"
   - Play soothing music quietly: "If you can't hear the music, your group needs to quiet down."
   - Use a sound monitoring device that beeps when the noise reaches a certain level.

3. Provide feedback on students' behavior as a group.
   - Use verbal statements: "Groups Two and Three, you're working especially well right now. Thanks." Or: "We are able to accomplish so much when you work this well together. Way to go!"
   - Use table points or class points that add up to time on a desired activity or other reward such as a frozen juice bar or a popcorn party. (Check school policy on food.)
   - Use your stopwatch to award extra seconds for a desired activity when students minimize wasted time.

4. Be fair to individuals when you deal with the larger group. Use strategies that don't penalize all students for the behavior of a few. Conversely, if everyone is talking, do not single out one or two students for consequences. If students perceive you as unfair, your expert and referent power erode.

of the head to a student who begins to fold paper airplanes while you work with another group. Through overlapping, you can prevent misbehavior by providing meaningful learning activities, nonverbal communication, and **proximity control** all at once.

Intensity of Response

Your responses to student behavior will vary by level of intensity. Canter (1976) recommends that teachers use assertive requests and that teachers match the response's level of intensity to the seriousness of students' behavior. You may start with a hint: "Everyone should be working now." If students need more support than is provided by your hint, you can use one of these increasingly intense responses:

1. Question about behavior: "What should you be doing right now?" Follow up: "Do you need help in getting started?"
2. Statement of direction using student's name: "Ivy, put away the magazine."
3. Use of eye contact and serious facial expression to match the tone and message: "Ivy, put away the magazine" while you look at her, your eyebrows raised.
4. Use of a gesture in addition to eye contact, serious facial expression, and assertive message: "Ivy, put away the magazine" as you look intently at her and gesture closing the magazine.

When student misbehavior is severely disruptive, more intense responses are appropriate. Many teachers arrange for a "time-out buddy," a fellow respected teacher who can provide a place for students to cool down if they need to be removed from the classroom. If you use time-outs, be certain to send the message that the time-out is a chance to cool down, not to suffer humiliation. Also be certain that you have a system to ensure that students arrive swiftly at the time-out room and that they return promptly. Remember that you have a legal responsibility to provide adequate supervision for every student, so be certain that students are supervised even when removed from the group. Also remember that time away from the group decreases a student's opportunity to learn.

There may be a time when students' misbehavior may take the form of physical fighting. Immediate and considered actions will be necessary. *A plan* for addressing student fights is suggested in the Teacher Tip (Fields, 2004; Moriarty, 2009).

Teaching Tip

ADDRESSING STUDENT FIGHTS

1. Right now—Check policies: What are your legal responsibilities?
2. Next—Create a plan: What will you do? What are your resources?
3. If a confrontation breaks out:

- Try diffusing it with humor or by redirecting the students' emotions. Use verbal interactions to minimize the problem if possible (e.g., suggest that together you solve the problem another way. Increase students' personal space to help them regain emotional control. Ask "dumb" questions (those to which you might know the answer) to get students talking; but don't ask "why."
- Identify yourself as a teacher and, at some point, in a low-key fashion, get the names of the students.
- Give a loud, clear verbal command. Make it specific: "Sit here!"
- Make a decision: Is it safe to intervene?
- If it isn't safe: Get help while still protecting students.
- If it is safe: Intervene without becoming an aggressor. Try wrapping around from behind. Never, though, restrain a student who wants to run. Some sources say teachers should never physically intervene, in part to protect their own physical safety. This is especially the case if you are not trained. Again, check local policies.
- Afterward, carefully document the confrontation.

Another approach that varies level of intervention, this time beyond the classroom level, is response to intervention. Introduced in Chapter 4 as an inclusive and responsive teaching strategy for instructional purposes, response to intervention is also used for supporting appropriate behavior, as shown in Figure 4.4. The principle is the same: Students receive support and intervention based on assessed level of need, and their progress is carefully monitored to adjust interventions. For behavior, the lowest level of intervention—the classroom level, Tier 1—is sufficient for most students to make appropriate behavior choices. The classroom environment, expectations, and consequences are sufficient to support their behavior. For a smaller percentage of students, regular classroom and schoolwide expectations and supports are insufficient; these targeted Tier 2 students' interventions include a higher level of intervention that might include social skill groups, counseling, or mentoring. If Tier 2 interventions are insufficient, very small numbers of students may require even more individualized support through Tier 3 interventions such as a behavior improvement plan. In terms of discipline, response to intervention is often used in conjunction with **positive behavior support** strategies (Sandomierski, Kincaid, & Algozzine, 2007).

Motivation for Misbehavior

A student's persistent misbehavior usually has a cause; when you and the student can identify the cause, you can work together on more acceptable alternatives, thus preventing recurrence and fostering self-control.

Dreikurs, Grunwald, and Pepper (1982) identify four mistaken goals that students pursue. Figure 10.7 describes each of these four goals and suggests reactions that can help you signal the identity of those goals. Dreikurs and colleagues suggest that after you identify the student's goal, you disclose it to the student through questions such as "Could it be that you would like more attention?" Your first impulse to respond to each of these mistaken goals (as suggested in the third column in Figure 10.7) is probably the wrong one. More productive alternatives are given in the fourth column. The key is to respond in a calm and thoughtful manner that helps the student identify his mistaken goal and choose more acceptable avenues for recognition.

An appealing alternative to the Golden Rule, the Platinum Rule, can be of use as you help students move beyond their mistaken goals. The Platinum Rule admonishes us to treat others the way they would like to be treated. If, for instance, students need attention, then we can see to it that they receive attention, albeit for positive decisions they make. If students crave power, we can shape our classrooms to ensure that they have some meaningful control over what they do at school.

Short-Term and Long-Term Redirection

To work toward your overarching goal of student self-control, you will need to enlist strategies that address discipline issues in short- and long-term time spans. Short-term solutions focus on preventing misbehavior or stopping undesirable behavior and replacing it with less harmful alternatives. Short-term solutions are the tools you use immediately and from which you expect quick results. Long-term solutions keep in mind the larger system and broader view of your hopes for students. Long-term tools take longer to implement, and results may build incrementally over time. You will no doubt need to use more than one kind of each strategy to fully address discipline issues, and you will no doubt need to alter your approach as you examine its consequences and effectiveness.

Your fifth-grade student Melanie provides an example. She rarely completes her work during class and has not yet submitted a homework assignment. She shrugs when you lecture her on responsibility and the importance of practice. Frustrated by her apparent indifference, you are determined to help. You begin with a problem-solving conference (e.g., Charney, 2002) to assess Melanie's perspective and interests and to invite her cooperation on working together. You devise a plan, taking the notes shown in Figure 10.8. Notice that your plan includes a multifaceted approach to help Melanie succeed: You will

Figure 10.7 *Identifying and responding to mistaken goals.*

Goal	Description	What It Looks Like	How You Might Respond
Attention seeking	In attempting to gain recognition and acceptance, students behave in socially inappropriate ways.	The teacher's first reaction is to yell. The student stops the misbehavior when corrected but starts again soon.	• Persistently ignore misbehavior. • Hold a personal conference to determine how many times the student will be allowed to exhibit the misbehavior. • Monitor and provide feedback based on the conference. • Provide attention for positive actions.
Power seeking	Students revert to unacceptable means—outwardly refusing their teachers' requests—to gain a sense of power.	The teacher's first reaction is to feel challenged. The student's reaction is defiance.	• Refuse to engage in a struggle, perhaps by instead offering a sympathetic response. • Remove the student or the audience from the situation. • Find authentic ways to allow the student to exercise power.
Revenge seeking	Students who feel that they have been wronged seek to get even.	The teacher's first reaction is to feel hurt or defeated. The student is abusive or complains of unfair treatment.	• Change the student's relationship with the teacher and peers. • Foster respect. • Help student gain social skills. • Refuse to retaliate; use matter-of-fact messages about the behavior.
Display of inadequacy	Students who feel incompetent resist help so that they can avoid even trying.	The teacher's first reaction is frustration to the point of giving up. The student does nothing.	• Never give up on the student. • Keep risks low and celebrate small successes.

modify your curriculum, check with other specialists, include Melanie's family as part of the education team, and restructure your classroom interactions to encourage Melanie's success. In addition to these long-range approaches, also notice that the plan uses short-term strategies: an extrinsic reinforcer (art time as a reward for Melanie's time on task). Although you may be opposed in general to using extrinsic reinforcers, you decide that Melanie needs some immediate success and that the rewards can be dropped later as her successes begin to snowball.

By working on the apathy issue in many ways—with tools you can use tomorrow and tools that will be implemented over the year—you increase the probability of success. You may find that certain aspects of your plan are more effective than others as you work with Melanie, and thus you will drop the least effective tools.

Figure 10.8   *Devising a plan with short- and long-term strategies for redirecting student behavior.*

Short-Term Suggestions	Long-Term Ideas
√ *Conference with Melanie to determine the cause for her not completing work (a la Dreikurs).*	√ *Check curriculum: Differentiate instruction by providing individual projects that tap into her interests. Use read-alouds that inspired her last year (e.g., Baudelaire books).*
√ *Call her father and get his perspective.*	√ *Work on elements of motivation: Break assignments into smaller pieces to increase probability of success and decrease perception of effort required.*
√ *Develop a contract with rewards that she finds appealing (art or science time).*	
√ *Find high-interest, low-vocabulary books.*	√ *Reorganize cooperative learning groups and begin to shift reasonable leadership responsibilities to Melanie.*
√ *Start homework sheet where she writes her assignments each day, and her dad signs nightly.*	√ *Use her parents' input about Melanie's out-of-school expertise (e.g., rugby) to build connections in the classroom.*
√ *Check cumulative record folder to determine if Melanie has any identified learning difficulties.*	
√ *Find a software program that uses reading through science (her interest).*	

The point is to address discipline issues along several dimensions: prevention and response, curriculum and management, group and individual focus, and cause and immediate redirection. It may sound overwhelming, but you will likely find that a few tools can serve many purposes for different learners.

Novice teachers tend to have similar struggles in establishing discipline. Therefore, Figure 10.9 restates a number of the chapter's tools that may be helpful in boosting you over some of the hurdles new teachers typically face as they establish and maintain a positive

Figure 10.9   *Discipline boosts for new teachers.*

Direct→Check→Feedback
- Use clear, positive language to *direct* students' behavior.
- *Check* to see whether students comply. Wait and watch.
- Give specific *feedback* on students' efforts to comply.
- Redirect as necessary.

Keep It Positive
- Focus on what students do well.
- Focus on students when they deserve attention for making good choices.
- Be genuine and specific in your praise.
- Be fair. Smile. Laugh.

Make Your Presence Felt
- Move around the room to teach and monitor.
- Move closer to students who are beginning to stray.
- Monitor students carefully and subtly let them know that you are aware of their actions.
- Carry yourself with confidence.

Avoid Overreliance on Rewards and Punishments
- Point systems, card systems, token economies, and marble jars can all support a positive classroom environment, but be certain that *you*—not the marble jar, not the principal—are the authority in your classroom.
- Focus on logical consequences and self-control.

learning environment. You may wish to review Figure 10.9 during tough days, especially those when your principal or supervisor sits in.

Your Own Classroom Discipline Plan

Your classroom management and discipline program needs to be coherent, consistent, positive, and proactive (Miller & Hall, 2009). This chapter offers a number of tools that may be useful for you in fostering student self-control. Other books, Web sites, and experienced teachers will also propose a number of appealing tips. However, you're the boss of you. Your own discipline plan is based on your philosophy, personality, and preferences in addition to the research. That plan needs to consider your particular students and their families and reflect your genuine appreciation for your students as individuals.

Figure 10.10 provides a planning sheet for your discipline plan. You can begin by once again perusing your stance toward education regarding questions such as, who do I hope my students will be as adults? What should their character be? Then jot down characteristics of your students—the range of their background experiences and their age and developmental levels are examples of characteristics that may be relevant.

Next, consider your own needs, likes, and dislikes (Charles, 1992). Draw from each of these responses to develop your own rules for establishing and maintaining classroom discipline (see Figure 10.11). Remember that "rules" are not the rules that govern the students; rather they are the rules that govern *you:* What are the principles by which you will select your actions when it comes to encouraging discipline? For example, two rules this chapter suggested are: *Treat students with dignity and respect* and *prevent misbehavior.* Then, flesh out your plan by listing tools—specific strategies—that can help you bring each of your rules to life.

Expect your list of tools to grow with your experience. You will receive many discipline suggestions and tools. Before incorporating any tool into your discipline plan, however, be certain that the tool is consistent with the rules that guide your efforts to discipline. If you cannot apply the *tool* to a *rule,* the tip is probably not consistent with your stance on discipline. Stick with the tools that are in concert with what you believe to be good for students. Expect, too, that you will pursue feedback and reflect regularly on your plan. Does it overemphasize compliance? Rewards and punishments? Does it preserve human dignity?

Also consider your other team members. Your plan needs to respond to the cultural, developmental, linguistic, and personal qualities of your students. Families are experts on their children; no one knows them better. How can you appropriately tap into families' knowledge in order to learn about students and to support their growth? How will you work effectively with parents as team members to support student development? Which specialists can provide assistance? What support can you expect from your site administrators and fellow teachers? Capitalize early on the contributions each of these parties can make to the well-being of your class; do not wait until students misbehave to devise a support system. Finally, try out your discipline program. Revise the aspects that are inhumane, ineffective, or unwieldy. The Teaching Tip shares the management and discipline lessons learned by Brittany Even as she completed her first year of classroom teaching.

REMEMBER THE LAW

1. Teachers are prohibited from
   - humiliating students.
   - physically punishing students, except under strict guidelines for corporal punishment (where allowed).
   - using academic penalties for behavioral offenses.
2. Students have rights to due process.

Refresher from Figure 1.2.

Figure 10.10 *My personal discipline program.*

This I believe . . . *(List major points from your stance toward education.)*

My students . . . *(List characteristics of your specific students or of students in general.)*

I need* . . .

I like* . . .

I dislike* . . .

*Avoid statements about static student characteristics here.

My Rules and Some Tools
(Not classroom rules, but principles that guide my approach to discipline.)

My Rule:

Some Tools:

    Establishing an environment

    Preventing misbehavior

    Responding to behavior

My Rule:

Some Tools:

    Establishing an environment

    Preventing misbehavior

    Responding to behavior

My Rule:

Some Tools:

    Establishing an environment

    Preventing misbehavior

    Responding to behavior

My plan for involving families and other team members to help students develop self-control

Figure 10.11   *Formalize your own set of rules . . .*

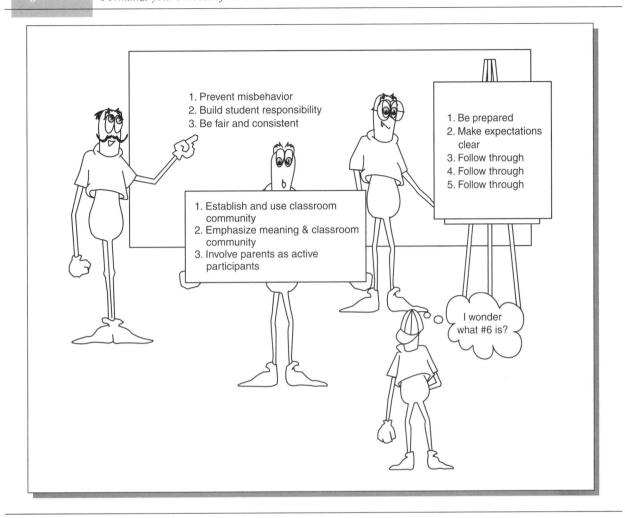

Teaching Tip

TEACHER TO TEACHER: BRITTANY'S ADVICE FOR MANAGEMENT AND DISCIPLINE

- Building a good relationship with the students really motivated them . . . and me.
- Set up your classroom community on Day 1. If you do that, and every student has some responsibility, your job becomes a lot easier.
- Be organized and let the students in on the organization process.
- Always follow through with what you say or have written.
- I found that students were more successful when I let them experience first and then offer my guidance.
- Write down everything! I found myself creating a new list of everything I need to change for next year.

Brittany Even

▪▪

Parting Words

Many, many teachers succeed at establishing fair and productive classrooms, and you can, too. Think about one of these pieces of advice if you feel disheartened about the challenge of helping your students develop self-discipline:

- A bad day is often followed by a good one.
- Classroom discipline is said to be a series of little victories. You and your students build good discipline over time, one interaction at a time. One mistake does not mean you have lost them forever.
- Remember that much of what happens in your classroom is under your control. When students misbehave as a group, ask yourself, "What can *I* do to provide a better environment, help them build skills for self-control, or prevent misbehavior?" Do something.
- If your system does not work, change it.

Teachers who are self-confident about student discipline tend to respond to problematic behavior in ways that are more positive and more consistent with the teachers' overall approach, their stance. Teachers who believe they *can* make a difference in students' behavior and handle discipline situations . . . *do* (Rimm-Kaufman & Sawyer, 2004).

*I*f your horse dies, dismount.

—*U.S. Cavalry Manual
from World War I*

Opportunities to Practice

1. Start with the students. Try one or both of these strategies to build a discipline plan that is responsive to your learners:

   a. Determine students' preferences for how teachers should discipline, perhaps through a questionnaire or an informal interview with questions such as, "What do good teachers do?" "What advice do you have for new teachers?"

   b. Culture makes a difference too. Spend some time learning about your actual students' experiences and about general patterns for their cultural or ethnic groups. Two sources to get you started are Banks (1997) and Grant (1995). The Internet can also provide information. Use the cultural group's name as a search term.

2. Because authentic authority affects classroom discipline, make a plan to build bridges to your students. Make a list of some ideas that can help you connect with your students. Share the list with an experienced colleague to double-check that your strategies are appropriate and, while friendly, maintain your professional standing. Get your students' opinions, too.

3. Observe an experienced teacher in action.

   a. How does the room environment encourage positive behavior?

   b. How does the curriculum prevent misbehavior?

   c. List some strategies the teacher uses to provide feedback to students on their behavior, noting which messages are positive, neutral, or negative.

   d. List some strategies the teacher uses to allow students to monitor and correct their own behavior.

   e. What evidence do you see that the teacher understands and is responsive to students' perspectives?

   f. What else do you notice about the teacher's discipline system?

4. Pick any tool from this chapter. Try it out, either in your classroom or elsewhere when the occasion arises. How did it feel to you as a teacher? To the other party? Remember that there are always effects—usually both intended and unintended. What effects did this tool have in this circumstance?

5. Arrange for a friend to mock interview you for a teaching position, focusing on your approach to discipline. Use your discipline plan (Figure 10.10) as support for the points you make. Your friend could devise difficult scenarios for you to respond to as part of the interview. (Caution: This exercise is harder than it sounds.)

6. Develop a one-page handout of your discipline program that you can share with students, families your master teacher, and other interested parties. You may wish to begin with a credo, or statement of beliefs. (Note: This one-page handout and artifacts such as notes home and photographs of students productively engaged are highly appropriate entries for your professional portfolio.) Invite input, especially from students' families. Try an e-version like a Wordle (www.wordle.net) or a Glogster (http://edu.glogster.com/) if you like.

7. Choose and respond to one of these critical incidents. Use the rules and tools in this chapter or your own to describe the problem and suggest a plan.

   a. Josh, a ninth-grader, walks into fifth period 2 minutes late. His arms are full of books, papers, and notebooks all awaiting a chance to spill to the ground. He gives the teacher a sheepish smile and announces, "Sorry I'm late. My backpack broke at lunch." On the way to his seat, he trips on Brittney's desk. The class bursts out in laughter. Josh's face turns red, and he alone stoops to gather his spilled belongings.

b. Susana, a first-grade teacher, drags into the lounge at lunch. "What is it, Susana?" asks Brent, a fellow teacher. Susana replies: "I am fed up with my students' constant tattling: 'Teacher, he looked at me.' 'Teacher,

she says I copied her.' 'Teacher, she took Dylan's eraser and then put it back when she saw me.' I need this tattling to stop!"

c. Joseph is a new fifth-grade teacher. He is feeling successful about how his students are treating each other, but their constant talking is wearing him down. When he tells them to quiet down, they do, but within three minutes the noise level is back to being too high. He feels like he is nagging with his constant reminders.

 Web Sites

http://www.behavioradvisor.com
Dr. Mac's Amazing Behavior Management Advice Site. This site has many positive, useful ideas for a range of issues.

http://www.gentleteaching.com/
Gentle Teaching International. Gentle teaching is an approach to human interactions that focuses on the values of helping individuals feel safe, valued, and engaged.

http://iris.peabody.vanderbilt.edu/resources.html
Behavior: IRIS Center (Ideas and Research for Inclusive Settings). Includes activities, information, and modules for fostering positive behavior for students in inclusive settings. See materials related to other topics (such as Diversity and Management) as well.

http://www.pbis.org
Positive Behavior Interventions and Support. Rich resources for families and teachers of students at all ages.

Check the online library for links to resources and implementation examples.

http://www.teachervision.com/lesson-plans/lesson-2943.html
Teacher Vision. "How to Manage Disruptive Behavior in Inclusive Classrooms" provides ten questions and answers for analyzing behavior in inclusive classrooms. Click on "Classroom Management" for behavior management tips.

http://www.disciplinehelp.com/teacher/
The "You Can Handle Them All" site gives discipline tips, including suggestions for addressing 117 misbehaviors related to the categories of attention, power, revenge, and self-confidence. Recommend the site to families as well.

Also search terms such as "classroom discipline blog," "positive classroom discipline," and "discipline plans."

Growing in Your Profession

11

Before You Begin Reading

*A*deunt etiam optima: *The best is yet to be.*

Obtaining a teaching credential is a very early—and happy!—stage in your professional development. Good teachers never finish growing. The National Board for Professional Teaching Standards' core propositions on teaching (2002) state that accomplished teachers reflect on their practice to continuously improve. They work effectively with families, communities, and other professionals to shape student success and the world of education. You have already begun your professional journey; it is your job, starting today and for the rest of your career, to continue that journey by reflecting critically on your work, growing in your competence, and engaging deeply as a member of the educational community. Through its three sections, this chapter encourages you to stretch professionally by

- Engaging in the professional community
- Using professional ethics as your guide
- Providing some advice from the heart

Engaging in the Professional Community

Your students' success depends in part on your willingness and ability to engage with others in sharing, implementing, and refining professional knowledge. In addition to interacting with students, you will be deeply involved in the life of your school through activities such as student data review, committee work, and curriculum development. Three aspects of engagement you may think about right now include becoming an effective staff member, growing from feedback on your teaching, and pursuing professional development.

Becoming an Effective Staff Member

Success in your job as a teacher extends far beyond your classroom door. From the first day you step on campus, you will want to demonstrate your willingness and ability to listen, learn, and function well as a staff member. Get to know each of the many staff members and volunteers who spend their days at school. Talk with the janitor and office personnel. Find the specialists. Smile and say hello to the family members on site. Learn about your administrators' priorities. Each of these people contributes to school life and learning.

Your colleagues will probably welcome you with plenty of informal support. Many experienced peers at your site will likely offer assistance to the new teacher on the block. They may advise you as you stand near the photocopy machine or tear off butcher paper for your bulletin boards. Some may even offer more intense help in topics such as arranging your room, working with discipline challenges, getting to know the site, or planning your curriculum.

*T*he brighter you are, the more you have to learn.

—*Don Herold*

Some of your less experienced colleagues will also serve as a source of support because of the benefits that can be derived from being new together. The Teaching Tip gives some suggestions from Brittany Even as she completed her first year in the classroom (you met Brittany in Chapter 10). Her words are encouraging because, despite the fact that they allude to the challenges of teaching (teaching looks easy . . . from the outside!), they also communicate that there are many actions you can take to build your own success. I particularly appreciate Tip Number 9: *Take risks. Take a chance*. Figure 11.1 depicts the impressive ocean mural that Brittany's students created. She reports that she wasn't sure if she was up to the challenge but that it turned out to be the most memorable learning experience of the year.

When on-site experienced colleagues give advice or offer to help, your response can be essential to your growth as a professional and for your easy adjustment to the school culture. Experienced teachers emphatically state that the fastest way for a novice to be shunned by a school staff is to act as if she knows it all and has nothing to learn. As you respond to

Teaching Tip

TEACHER TO TEACHER: BRITTANY'S ADVICE FOR THE EARLY DAYS

1. Be prepared for *anything*.
2. Be open to the criticism from your fellow colleagues.
3. Be ready to communicate with parents and do not take things personally.
4. Find a teacher at the new school to help you get accustomed to the expectations and routines.
5. If you don't know . . . *ask*.
6. Vent to a safe person when you have a bad day.
7. Do not dwell on mistakes, just move forward and learn from them.
8. Don't let your bad day affect your teaching. That only takes away from students' learning experience.
9. Take risks. Take a chance.
10. Finally, have a goal and a plan for the future.

Figure 11.1   *Take a risk! Brittany's class's ocean mural.*

The students integrated research skills, science, writing, and art to create with 30-foot-long mural. They took a risk . . . and reaped the rewards. (approximately 9 ft × 30 ft).
Britany Even

well-meaning attempts to help, remember that you bring the enthusiasm of a "new kid," no matter your age. You may be finishing an intense teacher preparation program, so you may not feel that you need every piece of advice that comes your way. Nevertheless, be gracious. You have the gift of enthusiasm; others bring the gift of experience. Find the gem of usefulness—even if it is merely the willingness to help—that each person brings to you. Offer your own advice sparingly. Establish from your first day on site that you are eager to learn and that you respect the wisdom of experienced teachers and staff. Listen.

Conversely, you may find yourself in a lonely situation with no offers of help. In this case, be the first to shake a hand, smile, and say hello. Introduce yourself and make it clear that you are thrilled about being part of the team. Find another inexperienced friend or a teacher at the same grade level or in the same subject area who is willing to talk shop. Join networks for support that are not site-based.

It can be tempting to join in lounge conversations as a way to establish yourself as a member of the group. Sometimes lounge talk, unfortunately, degenerates into negative conversations about students, family members, or school personnel. It will be important for you to avoid such conversations for a number of reasons. Poisonous people can sap your energy and deflect your focus from where it should be. Also, it is unkind and of questionable ethics to speak ill of others. It reflects poorly on you as a professional. Additionally, complaining can serve to make you feel like a victim rather than like the competent professional you are (Kottler, 2002).

When negative conversations come up, you may try changing the subject, or as, Kottler recommends, focusing on one or two *positive* qualities of your students or others. Six out of ten teachers recently surveyed reported being "very satisfied" with teaching as a career (MetLife, 2010). These highly satisfied teachers have stronger beliefs in their students and are more confident in their ability to help students succeed. Go sit by them in the lounge. Keep company with teachers who maintain a positive outlook; they will feed your soul.

In addition to informal opportunities to integrate into the school staff, you will also engage in a shared journey with your colleagues in support of student learning. Whereas in days past, teachers often experienced their profession as an isolating one, teachers today are less likely to report a sense of isolation because they work as members of many overlapping teams. Chances are you will be working in teams such as:

- Grade-level teams or department teams for curricular planning
- Professional learning communities to review student assessment data and adjust instruction
- Student study teams or student intervention teams to assist students in succeeding in behavior and academic work
- Committees to plan school events or adopt curricula, resources, or materials
- School site council for program and budget review
- School intervention team for response to intervention implementation
- Individualized education program teams that plan and review annual progress for each student with an IEP or other plan

These teams will be comprised of a variety of personnel such as family members, peers, administrators, subject matter coaches (e.g., literacy and mathematics), psychologists, therapists, aides, specialists, and community members. With each member holding varied expertise and perspectives, maximizing teams' effectiveness will require you to stretch your people skills and strive to be an effective team member. What does it mean to be an effective team member? I reviewed guiding documents in education (such as the NBPTS core convictions, state teaching standards, and 21st Century Teaching and Learning Skills) and ideas in fields such as industry and sports to develop a list of the characteristics that appear to be widely accepted as qualities of effective team members. Effective team members are goal directed, open, flexible, competent, and committed to learning. Figure 11.2 presents these qualities more fully.

Growing from Feedback on Your Teaching

In many states, new teachers receive assistance and feedback on their teaching through formally assigned mentors, or **support providers,** often through **induction programs** that provide comprehensive support systems. In 2007, thirty-three states had induction programs

Figure 11.2   *Qualities of effective team members.*

To Be an Effective Team Member:

1. *Commit to the team.* Get to know the other team members as people and as professionals, and work on improving relationships within the team. Build trust among members over time.

2. *Commit to shared goals.* Ensure that the team's goals are clear and shared by all members. Keep goals the focus of the team's work, and be sure to welcome change toward those goals. Check progress toward the goals frequently.

3. *Respect other team members.* Begin with an appreciation that perspectives will necessarily be diverse; hold the mindset that diversity brings strength. Realize the limits of your own knowledge and experience. See members for their strengths and value their contributions openly.

4. *Be open and flexible.* Be receptive to new ideas in general and to the ideas of other team members. Be ready to compromise and to shift your thinking for the good of the group's goal. Be flexible in assuming different roles; lead or follow as the context and task at hand demand.

5. *Contribute.* Be action oriented. Be ready to take on a task to work toward the goal. Encourage others to do so too. Be dependable.

6. *Communicate.* Listen. Communicate openly but respectfully. Use a variety of modes of communication and communicate for different purposes and in different contexts. Conflict is normal; help your team build strategies to address it productively.

7. *Be competent and be a learner.* Use a variety of thinking skills to accomplish the goals: problem solving, reasoning, systems thinking, and decision making. Know your stuff. Do your homework. Reflect on your knowledge and performance and work on continual improvement.

8. *Be positive.* Share a sense of optimism and enthusiasm. Support other teammates.

(Kaufman, 2007). Mentors or support providers often conduct observations (perhaps formal or informal, but separate from the personnel evaluation process), offer assistance, and help shape professional development activities based on the needs of new teachers.

New teachers report very clearly that the support of a trusted colleague who is officially assigned to help out is a key factor in the new teachers' satisfaction and success. Further, states such as California are finding that teachers stay in the profession at higher rates when induction programs are in place (Reed, Rueben, & Barbour, 2006) and students can experience higher achievement (Sawchuk, 2010). Find out what types of mentoring and induction support are offered in your state and district and determine the extent to which you can provide input into the selection of your mentor.

In addition to informal assistance and observations, you will receive structured feedback on your teaching. Some feedback on your teaching will be formal, based on an administrator's or other official's evaluation of your teaching. In formal instances, structured observation sessions often begin with a brief preobservation conference at which you may be given the opportunity to direct the observation. The observer may ask what you would like her to focus on. Have an answer ready. If no immediate need comes to mind, consider using one of the principles of instruction: COME IN (you could even provide Figure 6.8 with elements of your choice circled). After the lesson, you will probably have a postobservation conference. The observer may begin by asking for your analysis of the lesson. Be frank and specific in assessing the strengths and weaknesses of your teaching. Then brace yourself for the evidence or advice from the observer.

It can be difficult to accept criticism about something so close to your heart as your teaching. The worst thing to do when you receive suggestions is to take a defensive posture and state immediately why those suggestions do not apply to you or will not work. The observer knows something about teaching or he could not be in the position to offer advice in this format. One of the best things to do when you receive advice (even if you hate it) is to smile, establish eye contact, and say thank you. Then you can add something sincere to show that you understand the point of the suggestions. Honest examples, in order of decreasing enthusiasm, include the following:

- "Thanks. Those are great ideas! No *wonder* they pay you the big bucks!"
- "Thanks. That just might work! I will try it tomorrow."
- "Thanks. You have given me lots of things to think about!"
- "Thanks. I appreciate your ideas. I will need to think about some ways to make them work for my situation."
- "Thanks. Tell me more about how I could make that suggestion work in my room."

Your postobservation conference will probably be helpful and positive. However, if you have limped through a painful postobservation session, you can go home and nurse your wounded pride. Probably in just a few hours (or days) you will find some kernel of wisdom or helpfulness in the words that stung initially. The point is not to be false in your reaction to criticism but to realize that every teacher has room to grow and that once you can get over a possible negative initial reaction, you can appreciate a fresh insight into teaching.

Sometimes advice on your teaching may not be offered, even though you eagerly ask for it. For instance, you may have a formal lesson observation for which the evaluator gives nonspecific feedback: "Wonderful lesson! Great job!" Be ready with some pointed questions that require the sharing of evidence collected by the observer. For instance, you could ask the observer whether your instruction engaged all of the students, or whether the observer noted any evidence that students were mastering the content. (Again, provide Figure 6.8 or your credo of education. Ask the evaluator to gather relevant evidence.)

You may at times need assistance of a more dire nature. For example, you may have a student who is particularly troubled or you may be struggling to meet the needs of a specific group of students. Being a classroom teacher means being part of a team, so be certain that you ask for help. Talk with your principal, mentor, or supervisor about your needs, stating them in a professional, clear way at the appropriate place and time. Do not place blame or suggest that you are not responsible for difficult situations ("I was given the roughest class!"). Your aim is to help your students learn, and you are exactly the person who is responsible for them. Have alternatives ready if you are faced with unfair or difficult practices or procedures. Be assertive and positive, with an effort to serve as part of the solution, not part of the problem. Get your needs met without sacrificing others' rights or dignity. Use *I*-statements (presented in Chapter 10). Convey your sense of self-trust that you have the ability to make a difference and your sense of eagerness to learn. Finally, remember that learning to teach is a developmental affair. The kinds of concerns you have, the sophistication of your thinking and your strategies, and the realm of your influence will almost certainly shift as you grow with experience.

Pursuing Professional Development

According to Wiggins and McTighe (2006), we teachers grow when we find personal meaning in our work, when we reflect, and when we question ourselves within a supportive environment. Many teachers find that informal and formal opportunities to talk about teaching in its daily context contribute invaluably to their growth. Formal opportunities to pursue professional learning also propel teacher learning. Your school and district will require professional development; you should also be proactive about pursuing professional development that meets your own personal and professional goals (Shanklin, 2009). The Responsive and Inclusive Teaching Tip gives some advice for setting future inclusive teaching goals.

As you select professional development experiences, a number of criteria are important. First, select experiences that are likely to have the greatest effect on both you and your students. This sort of development tends to:

- Focus on student learning
- Focus on building your knowledge of the content and how to teach it
- Include hands-on, active learning that can transform your teaching
- Occur in a collaborative context that links standards, curriculum and assessment
- Be sustained over time (Darling-Hammond & Richardson, 2009).

Second, focus on the experiences that best meet your long-term goals (check your work at the beginning of the chapter). Here are some professional development options that might fit those goals.

Attending Workshops   Workshops have the benefit of requiring a relatively low time and financial investment, and you can target workshops that meet your specific interests. Unless there is follow through, though, they may make little long-term difference in your practice. To maximize a workshop's benefits, try attending with a team, join a network on the topic, or try peer observations as you implement some of the ideas.

Membership in Professional Organizations   This text has shared many professional organizations, included subject-based organizations (such as National Council of Teachers of English) and ones with other foci (such as the National Association for

---

Responsive and Inclusive Teaching Tip

CONTINUING THE PURSUIT OF RESPONSIVE AND INCLUSIVE TEACHING

Nieto (2009) urges us to continue to strive—and thrive—as inclusive and responsive teachers by taking three action steps for professional development:

1. *Learn about ourselves.* Professional learning is fueled by continuous reassessment of who we are.

2. *Learn about our students.* Pursuit of students' worlds through activities like home visits helps us understand their perspectives and realities.

3. *Develop allies.* Making friends who share our hopes and concerns allows us to face the uncertainties of teaching and provides a collaborative setting that fuels growth.

Multicultural Education). Joining professional organizations gives you a voice in the profession beyond the local level, it provides you with opportunities to network, and it provides rich professional resources. To make the most of your membership, you may want to get actively involved with the organization's conferences and local efforts. Joining the organization's state or regional chapter is a strong mechanism for sustained involvement.

Observations and Travel   We teachers learn so much by watching each other in action. Try joining a **Lesson Study** or **action research** group or complete informal observations of peers at your site. Traveling a bit farther down the road (e.g., to another site or district) or engaging in more distant educational trips (such as study trips to other countries) can offer the benefits of increasing your cultural competence. To maximize learning from observations and travel, be sure to have a clear focus in mind (What are you looking for? What do you hope to learn?) and schedule time to talk with the "natives" about the meaning behind what you observe.

Advanced Certification and Study   Pursuing advanced credentials, certificates, or degrees opens your options in the profession and often leads to advancement on the pay scale. Examples include adding National Boards Certification, a master's degree, or a specialized credential. To choose an appropriate program, look first at your goals: Where are your passions? Are you excited about technology? Staff development? Also check labor force predictions. For instance, with a looming shortage of up to a million teachers—with math and science positions being the hardest to fill (Gonzales, 2010)—many elementary level teachers are pursuing additional secondary level certification in mathematics and science.

Online education is an increasingly popular choice. About one-quarter of students enrolled in higher education were taking at least one online course in 2008 (Kern, 2010), and that population is predicted to continue to increase sharply. If you haven't taken an online course yet and are considering doing so, ask yourself how motivated you are. Students who are most successful in online environments tend to be highly self-motivated and organized. Many quizzes are available to help you determine the likelihood that online learning is a good fit for you (See the 21st Century Teaching and Learning Tip.) If you select an online option for a certificate or degree, ask these questions:

1. Is the university accredited by a respected accrediting body?
2. What is the reputation not just of the university but of the program in your specific field of interest? Is the program accredited?
3. If it's important to you, is there an on-site location? (Some students prefer hybrid instruction of face-to-face and online.)
4. What is the quality of the faculty, and are they trained in online instruction? (Kern, 1010).

E-Development   The 21st century provides new opportunities for teacher learning. Whereas in previous centuries teaching was largely a private affair, new media push us to make it public through online professional communities and social networking (Lieberman & Marce, 2010). Online communities for teachers reduce isolation (Hramiak, 2010) and provide opportunities for professional support, guidance, and inspiration

21st Century Teaching and Learning Tip

ASSESS THE FIT

Use an online survey to determine whether online learning is for you. Search "is online learning for me?"

(Duncan-Howell, 2010). Teacher blogs can hold the benefits of allowing for group dialog (Killeavy & Moloney, 2010), reflection on practice and knowledge transformation (Sun, 2010). Teachers are also connecting online through microblogging (Twitter). One or more of these e-networking tools may fit your interests and style. You might pick one you haven't tried yet and get started by:

- *Following a blog for teachers.* There are hundreds. Find one by searching "top teacher blogs" or using a more specific search term ("art teacher blogs").
- *Writing your own blog.* Use a free tool like Word Press (wordpress.com) or Blogger (blogger.com).
- *Subscribing to a Twitter community for education.* Search "twitter for teachers."
- *Tweeting.* Plenty of quick start tutorials are available online.
- *Joining a social network for teachers.* Classroom 2.0 is an example.

Using Professional Ethics as Your Guide

Ethics and **morals** are the often tacit rules that govern how people should treat each other. According to Goodlad (1990), the entire enterprise of education is a moral one; the primary purposes of schools, providing access to knowledge and enculturating the young, are moral callings. Further, teachers are part of a system. When you enter this profession, you accept its code of ethics (Soltis, 1986). You take on the obligation to act in the best interest of your students, including commitments such as protecting them and taking responsibility to help them learn. These are weighty responsibilities. Further, teaching is fraught with tensions and dilemmas that require you to act as a moral agent (Buzzelli & Johnston, 2001; Kidder & Born, 1998–1999). Finally, you have entered a career in which professionals are typically held to a higher moral standard than the general public. In each of your dealings, be certain that professional ethics inform your choices about how to act and what to say.

> *T*he test of the morality of a society is what it does for its children.
>
> —*Dietrich Bonhoeffer*

Using professional ethics as your guide means that you must advocate for the students and advocate for yourself. Advocating for the students means that you

1. Ensure students' physical and emotional safety. Be certain that you carefully monitor the students and make reasonable efforts to protect them from bodily and psychological harm. Learn to recognize symptoms of stress and distress in students (Kottler & Kottler, 2007).
2. Know students' legal rights and your responsibilities. Protect students' right to privacy. Do not discuss them casually in the lounge.
3. Report suspected abuse. Your role is not to gather evidence to erase doubt. You are legally bound to report *suspected* abuse. Do not rationalize to save yourself—or the family—the pain and trouble.
4. Work to secure appropriate services if you suspect that students' needs are going unmet. Be certain that you watch both male and female students and students of color to assess their potential for gifted programs and check for your own biases when you recommend counseling or other services.
5. Build meaningful partnerships with families and others who are experts. Commit to working as part of a team in the best interests of the students.
6. Begin with the attitude that you *can* serve as a positive influence on students' lives. If you do not know an answer, you can—and will—find one. Teachers with high degrees of **self-efficacy** tend to be more effective than ones who do not believe they can effect change.
7. Think about the long-term consequences of your actions, and consider your choices from a variety of perspectives.
8. Being a professional is more than being an employee. Do everything you need to do to help students learn.
9. Even if it feels like everyone else has, never give up.

Advocating for yourself means that you

1. Know your responsibilities, rights, and benefits. Read your contract. Understand how to obtain legal representation if you need it.
2. Plan for your future. See the Teaching Tip for ensuring your own financial well-being.
3. Are careful about being alone with students and using physical contact. Check local policies for the conditions under which it is acceptable to touch a student. Find out what to do if a student touches you in a way that makes you uncomfortable.
4. Are a model digital citizen. Make very cautious decisions about e-mail communications and your participation in social media such as social networking sites. Assume that nothing you post to the Web is private. Explore further aspects of digital citizenship at digitalcitizenship.net.
5. Are a team player. Find the good in each staff member. Steer clear of those who whine or complain; instead associate with these who view the profession with a positive outlook.
6. Volunteer for a committee or two that benefits the school. Do not sign up for every committee in your eagerness, though, because your students (and your personal life) will be shortchanged. Say "yes" to the commitments that you can accomplish well.
7. Strike a balance in your life. Your family—and your students—will benefit from your being well-rounded. See the Teaching Tip for some ideas for coping with stress.
8. Choose your battles. Not every insult to your sensibilities is worth a fight to the death.
9. Are on time. Stay as late as necessary to do a good job.
10. Eat something healthy once in awhile and get some sleep.
11. Have confidence in your ability to teach and to improve. Teachers who believe that they can learn, grow, and make a difference . . . do.

21st Century Teaching and Learning Tip

FINANCIAL LITERACY FOR TEACHERS: TEACHER RETIREMENT PLANS

Dan Otter, who has taught students in elementary school (including my son), middle school, and college around the nation, has been helping teachers and students become financially literate since the inception of his 403Bwise Web site a decade ago. Here's a financial literacy primer from Dan.

Financial literacy is the ability to "use knowledge and skills to manage one's financial resources effectively for lifetime financial security" (Jump$tart Coalition for Personal Financial Literacy, 2007). It is a critical 21st-century skill not only for students, but also for teachers. Understanding the workings of teacher retirement plans at the beginning of one's career can pay enormous benefits in the future.

Teachers typically have two types of retirement plans available to them: a state-run pension plan, and a self-directed 403(b) supplemental retirement plan. Pension plans are also known as defined benefit (DB) plans because the benefit paid out to the teacher in retirement is "defined" by a formula that includes years of service and salary. For information on the workings of your pension plan, including how to make retirement payout projections, visit your pension's Web site. If an Internet search does not turn up the appropriate Web address, consult your employer.

The 403(b) plan is also known as a defined contribution (DC) plan because the benefit in retirement is "defined" by how much the individual contributes to the plan. Although participation in a pension plan is typically automatic upon employment with all investment decisions made by the operators of the plan, a teacher must both choose to participate in a 403(b) plan, and make all investment decisions. Wisely choosing and allocating investments is no small task. For complete information on the workings of the 403(b), including how to choose and allocate investments, see the Web site www.403bwise.com.

Dan Otter

Teaching Tip

COPING WITH STRESS

When you feel stressed . . .

1. Remind yourself aloud that you have the skills to handle this. You've handled plenty of stressful situations.
2. Decide whether this issue is inside your circle of influence. If it isn't, let it go. Confine your worries to the things you can do something about.
3. Choose your reaction. You can't change what people do; you can only choose your own response.
4. Close your eyes and breathe. Three times. Deeply. In through your nose, out through your mouth. Then roll your head forward, left then right.
5. Listen to music that makes you happy.
6. Go for a walk. Or do something else that totally changes your physical and mental location.
7. Think long-term. How much will this matter in a year? In 10 years?
8. Tell yourself what you have learned for next time.
9. Laugh.

Some Advice from the Heart

You are entrusted with one of the greatest privileges I know: shaping young lives in the classroom. My deepest hope for you is that you will approach each day in the classroom with passion and with the burning desire to do one thing better than you did yesterday. My final words of advice for you come from me as a *world citizen* who trusts you to bring up the next generation as an informed, compassionate group, as a *teacher* who expects you to lead students to discover the power and beauty of knowledge, and as a *parent* who speaks for others in believing that every day, when we release to your care our cherished children, you will provide a safe and loving atmosphere where their minds and spirits will be uplifted. My final suggestions are these:

> *R*espect for the fragility of an individual life is still the first mark of the educated man.
>
> —*Norman Cousins*

1. *Listen to your students.* Teaching is more than telling. When one of my sons was very young, I needled his teacher at back-to-school night to hear some wonderful words about my precious son (remember, parents are ego involved). Her comment? "I am surprised he cannot cut." That teacher, it turns out, said many helpful, positive things about my child over the course of the school year. But at this early moment, I felt like I had been punched in the stomach. My son's teacher did not know that he sat on the couch at age 3 and sang "Nobody knows the troubles I've seen." She did not know that he asked about volcanoes on Mars. She knew he could not cut. She knew him in terms of what he could not yet do, in terms of his deficits. Please think about your students as people. Believe in them as knowers and learners. Listen to their stories. Entertain their questions. Even five-year-olds have lived a lifetime before meeting you.

2. *Be careful with the praise you give.* When you compliment a student, be genuine and specific. Your ultimate goal is not to shore students up with a steady stream of shallow and false praise. You are not the ultimate authority. You probably do not want your students to grow dependent on you—or anyone else—for judgments of their self-worth. Self-esteem should be based instead on students' own assessments of their work and abilities, on their own ability to judge a job done well. Help them recognize good work. Teach them to value themselves for who they are and what they can accomplish.

3. *Do not waste people's time.* You may be new. You may be learning. No doubt you will be better next year. But remember that this year is likely the only chance at tenth (or second or any) grade that your students will ever have. I can promise that some days in the classroom will feel like survival. If you begin to experience entire weeks during which you are searching for activities to keep students occupied, you are wasting people's time. Do not try to justify the educational benefits of a steady diet of word searches. You need to do better. Get some rest and start planning meaningful learning experiences.

   4. *Stay only as long as you are effective.* Classroom teaching is not for everyone, and in many cases it is not forever. It is difficult to teach. Even expert teachers have bad days . . . and bad years. If you ever hate your job each morning, you need to change your life. You can change what you do in your classroom. You can change grade levels or school assignments. You can remain in education but leave the classroom. Or you can take your own set of skills and use them in a different field. It is not a disgrace to leave teaching. You will do everyone a service if you leave when it is time to go. There are many ways for each of us to contribute to the world.

   5. *Pull from inner resources.* My personal experience with classroom teaching is that it can bring tremendous emotional highs—watching a student learn can inspire awe—and

Figure 11.3   *Quotes that have helped me learn about teaching.*

(My apologies to those whose words I've misremembered over time.)
"Now that you have a child, you know how much I love you."
   —LuAnn Munns Berthel, my mother, who taught me in one sentence how deeply
     one can love.

"They're only children."
   —attributed to Gordon Guillaume, my father-in-law, by Beverly Guillaume, his
     wife. These words remind me that the job of a child, apparently, is sometimes
     purely to annoy.

"If you are committed to improving, you probably will."
   —Cheryl Bloom, my master teacher, who taught me to keep working at
     classroom discipline.

"'Stop worrying so much about *teachers'* questions, and start worrying about
students' questions."
   —a rough paraphrase of five years with James T. Dillon, who taught me to listen.

"Interesting people do more than teach."
   —Carol Barnes, who taught me that well-educated people have a variety of
     interests in their lives.

"Assume that people are doing the best they can."
   —Jodi Elmore, my student teacher, who reminds me that I should approach
     people with the understanding that most of us just keep trying to do the best
     we can using what we have.

"What you focus on will grow."
   —Ernie Mendes, who reminds me to see people in terms of their strengths rather
     than in terms of their shortcomings.

Here's a lighter set I've composed to capture my own foibles.
Murphy's Laws for Teachers
   1. Things take about two to three times longer than the time you have (or than
      you expected).
   2. The lesson right before (or right after) the one your supervisor (or principal)
      observes is great.
   3. Typos in memos to families are much easier to spot right after you send the
      papers home.
   4. Someone will throw up before winter break.

lows. There may be times when even those who love you the most cannot pick you up after a tough day in the classroom. Instead, you will need to draw on your inner resources to reconsider your motivations and refresh your resolve to have a better day tomorrow. One of the devices I use when I need to encourage myself is a collection of quotes from people in my life who have helped me learn about teaching. Some of the deposits in my quote bank are shown in Figure 11.3. Try creating your own collection of quotes to provide some advice when you are in need.

6. *Look for the best.* Each person you encounter has something to add to your professional life. The students each offer their own funny idiosyncrasies and their fresh, rough-and-tumble view of the world. Your staff members have been in your place and have learned from it. Finally, *you* have something to contribute to the world through your teaching. Look for the best you have to offer and nurture it. Good wishes to you.

No bubble is so iridescent or floats longer than that blown by the successful teacher.

—Sir William Osler

Opportunities to Practice

1. Interview a trusted, respected colleague for some advice on professional development. Share your work from the chapter-opening exercise and ask for insights.

2. Commit to one formal professional growth opportunity right now:

   a. Subscribe to one professional journal.

   b. Conduct research on an issue faced by one or more of your students.

   c. Attend a workshop.

   d. Join a professional organization or network.

   e. Take a field trip to another classroom on your site (or beyond).

   f. Write a reflection on your practice. Share it with your students.

   g. Explore a Web site that your students are excited about. Find out why they find it engaging. Discovering what makes students happy (instant feedback? E-tokens?) can help you understand their needs and think about how to incorporate some of those things into your teaching.

3. Develop your own quotation collection.

4. How will you know whether you are improving in your teaching? Make a list of things you will accept as evidence that you are sharpening your professional skills. Consider using the self-analysis tool found in Figure 1.6 to reanalyze your practice.

Web Sites

http://www.ascd.org
Association for Supervision and Curriculum Development. Go to "Publications" for blogs and try "Research a Topic" for current information on a number of important issues. A number of professional development courses are available online. Some resources are for members only.

http://www.bartleby.com/100/
Bartlett's Familiar Quotations, 10th ed. Also try Creative Quotations (http://www.creativequotations.com). Sites

like these can help you locate quotations to enhance your lessons and provide a professional boost.

http://www.nationjob.com/education
Nation Job Network. This is the Education Jobs page.

http://www.pta.org
The National Teacher Parent Association. Includes information on issues, news, and resources.

Glossary

Accommodations Changes to classroom resources, instruction, or conditions that allow students to learn or to show what they know despite specific areas of need such as physical or learning disabilities. Accommodations do not change the learning expectations to which students are held.

Accountability The idea that educators and schools should be held responsible for student mastery of the curriculum.

Achievement gaps Marked and sustained discrepancies in the academic progress (typically measured by standardized tests) among the scores of certain subgroups of the student population.

Action research Research conducted by practitioners to explore problems or issues in their own contexts. Data collection and analysis are less formal than in published research, and the focus is not on generalizability but on impact in the local setting.

Active participation Strategies employed by the teacher during a lesson to ensure that every student overtly engages in and responds to the lesson.

Adaptive testing Computer-based testing where the level of difficulty adjusts to the examinees' answers.

Adequate Yearly Progress A requirement of the Elementary and Secondary Education Act (ESEA) that stipulates that every school and every subgroup of the school's population must raise performance toward proficiency by a certain percentage each year.

Analytical trait rubric An assessment tool that allows the reader to rate components of a performance separately, using criteria that are specific to each component.

Asperger's syndrome A developmental disorder typified by repetitive behaviors and impaired social interactions.

Assistive technology A wide range of built items (noncomputer-based) and computer-based hardware and software that aid people with physical disabilities in functioning, learning, and communicating.

Audience response systems A digital technology wherein each audience member (student) has a remote control or other input device and uses it to vote on topics or answer questions from the teacher. Each response is tabulated, and results are depicted as a projected image, often through a graph. Results can be stored and printed. Virtual systems allow students to provide input through their own handheld devices such as smart phones or netbooks.

Backward planning An approach to curricular planning that begins with the end product: the envisioned student performance. With this clear vision of what students should be able to do as a result of instruction, teachers plan instructional events. Specifying performance through rubrics created with students is often a component of backward planning.

Behavior (portion of objective) That portion of the objective that specifies, in observable terms, what the student will be able to do as a result of instruction. The expected student performance.

Behavioral intervention plan (BIP) As mandated by IDEA, students with behaviors that impede their learning or the learning of others—as a manifestation of their disability—must receive a functional behavioral analysis and plan to address their behaviors in positive ways.

"Big idea" approach An approach to unit planning in which the teacher begins with a focus on the major ideas or generalizations related to the content and then selects activities designed to help students develop those big ideas.

Bilingual education programs Programs that teach the native language and target language as subject areas and use both languages as modes of communication. They are based on the conviction that students will learn content more quickly and have additional linguistic skills if they are taught in their native language alongside the target language. Use of the native language typically drops off as use of the target language increases.

Blueprints Documents that specify the content represented in a test and give information related to the format such as the number of each type of selection-type and constructed-response items.

Caretaker speech Talk that has the purpose of clear communication. It focuses on immediate concerns rather than abstract or distant ideas and is adjusted syntactically to the current linguistic abilities of the listener. Caretaker speech is one way to provide comprehensible input for English learners.

Classroom meeting A gathering in which all classroom participants have the opportunity to provide input to the agenda and the meeting itself. Classroom meetings can serve a number of purposes such as event planning, open discussion, and problem solving. The teacher facilitates, but students play an active leadership role.

Concept map A graphic organizer that is hierarchically organized, presenting a major concept or idea and revealing the connections among the concept and its subconcepts.

Conditions (portion of objective) The portion of the objective that specifies relevant aspects of the environment such as the materials, time, or resorces that will be available (or not) to students as they demonstrate mastery of the objective.

Constructed response An assessment item that requires students to compose an answer rather than selecting one.

Content standards Statements of the subject matter teachers are to teach and students are to master. Developed at different levels (national, state, and local), standards describe outcomes that students should demonstrate in given curricular areas throughout the grades.

Criteria (portion of objective) The portion of the objective that specifies how well a student is to perform. Criteria provide the standard against which the student performance will be assessed. Criteria are often stated in terms of speed, accuracy, or quality.

Criterion-referenced Assessments that compare students' performance to an external standard rather than to the performance of their peers.

Critical attributes Those characteristics that define an object, organism, or phenomenon.

Curricular integration The combination of two or more traditional content areas in a manner that reveals the connectedness of the subject matter. There are many approaches to curricular integration.

Curriculum That which students are expected to learn at school and that which they actually learn there.

Curriculum compacting An instructional approach undertaken with the aim of teaching only the content students have not previously mastered. The typical sequence is as follows: identification of learning goals, assessment of student progress related to those goals, provision of instruction to meet nonmastered learning goals.

Deductive strategies Instructional approaches that move from general rules or principles to specific examples of those principles. Teachers present content directly, and students engage in a carefully sequenced set of activities to ensure mastery.

Democratic classrooms Classrooms where teacher and students share power and responsibility more equally than is the case in traditional classrooms. Shared decision making through democratic processes is an emphasis.

Differentiated instruction An approach to instruction that provides a range of resources and activities designed to meet students' varying assessed needs and interests. Differentiated tasks should be engaging and challenging and should allow students to work in a variety of instructional formats. Instruction can be differentiated for *content* so that students learn different things, *process* so that they go about learning differently, or *product* so that they select among different ways to show their learning.

Digital divide Persistent gaps in access to digital technologies among certain subgroups of the population.

Digital natives Prensky's (2001) term, used to refer to individuals who have grown up with ubiquitous access to digital technologies. Their counterparts are digital immigrants, who learn technologies later in life.

Direct instruction A deductive approach to instruction where the teacher states the major idea or skill early in the lesson and then systematically and explicitly leads students to mastery of the objective.

Directed lesson A lesson in which the teacher maintains careful control of the content, presents it explicitly to the students, and allows them to practice during the lesson as they work toward and demonstrate mastery of the lesson's objective.

Document camera An image capture device that allows the operator to enlarge and project the image of a two-dimensional object (such as a photograph or sheet of text) or a three-dimensional object for an audience.

Dominant culture In a region, the group of people whose ways of thinking and behaving are predominant. Factors such as historical precedence, population size, and social status influence which culture is dominant in an area at any point in time.

Emotional intelligence A person's ability to understand his own emotions and the emotions of others and to use this understanding in deciding how to act appropriately.

English learners Students who are in the process of mastering English in addition to one or more other languages, including the home language. Also deemed English language learners.

Error pattern analysis An approach to data analysis that examines students' work to determine whether students are making consistent mistakes and what misunderstandings those mistakes represent.

Essential question A conceptual or overarching question that fans curiosity and frames study throughout an instructional unit. It should be phrased to capture major, enduring ideas related to the content.

Ethics Values related to human conduct in terms of what is right and wrong.

Explicit curriculum The content (knowledge, skills, and attitudes) that schools set out to teach. It is often contained in the adopted texts and other materials as well as in the daily activities selected by teachers and schools.

Fair use An aspect of U.S. copyright law that allows for limited use of copyrighted materials without requiring permission for use.

Flexible groupings Patterns of organizing students into different groups for instruction. The size of the groupings can range from individuals to the entire class. Groupings are adjusted to address students' current needs and the goals and activities. Thus, rather than remaining in static groups, students in flexible groups are often regrouped based on ongoing assessment.

Formative assessment Assessment of student learning that yields results used to shape future instruction.

Free appropriate public education A federal right of all U.S. students including those with disabilities. This right guarantees that each student's education is paid for by the public (not the student or family) and that the education is suited to the needs of the student.

Functional behavior analysis An approach to changing students' misbehavior by assessing its causes, planning an intervention that addresses that cause, trying the intervention, and assessing its effect.

Funds of knowledge The bodies of knowledge, social networks, and cultural resources found in students' homes and surrounding communities.

General education General education classrooms are those in which students with no identified special needs are placed. Smaller numbers of students receiving special services are also typically found within general education classrooms, but general education teachers are not required to hold special certification. Instead, they work as part of a team with special educators to provide appropriate instruction for students with identified needs.

Gifted   A student classified as gifted has been identified as possessing demonstrated or potential high ability in specific academic and other performance areas.

Gifted and Talented Education   Programs designed to meet the needs of students identified as academically gifted or otherwise talented. Such programs vary widely across districts and states and offer services through a wide variety of structures such as self-contained classrooms, gifted clusters, and resource programs.

Grade Equivalent (GE) score   A norm referenced score that gives the grade level and month (e.g. 7.1) of the typical person who earned a given raw score.

Graphic organizers   Visual presentations of information. The displays are organized to reveal important aspects of or patterns in the information. Graphic organizers can be developed by teachers and students at any phase during the instructional cycle.

Handheld device   A mobile, pocket-size computing device such as a personal digital assistant or a smart phone.

High-stakes test   A student or teacher assessment where the consequences are perceived to be very important to one or more groups of stakeholders. For students, grade retention and graduation are examples of high-stakes decisions that can result from their test scores.

Highly qualified teachers   As stipulated by the No Child Left Behind act, highly qualified teachers (a) have demonstrated competence in each core subject area they teach, (b) hold at least a bachelor's degree, and (c) are fully licensed by the state.

Holistic rubric   An assessment tool that allows the reader to give an overall rating to a performance. Performances are rated as being consistent with particular levels of overall quality.

Home schooling   The practice of educating students outside the school context, most notably within the home. Home schooling became legal in all U.S. states in 1993 and is a growing trend.

Implicit curriculum   The lessons students learn without their teachers having consciously selected or taught them. Students learn the implicit curriculum by drawing inferences about correct ways to think and behave based on their experiences in schools.

Inclusion   A practice of educating students with disabilities—to the maximum extent possible—with their nondisabled peers.

Individualized education program (IEP)   A legally binding document that details the educational plan for a student who is identified as having one or more disabilities. The plan states the student's disability and provides present levels of performance, instructional objectives, assessment plans, and a statement of the least restrictive environment for the student. It is reviewed annually.

Individuals with Disabilities Education Act (IDEA)   Formerly P.L. 94–142, this law requires all states that receive federal education funds to provide individuals with disabilities between the ages of 3 and 21 with a free and appropriate public education designed to meet the student's specific needs and prepare them for independence and employment.

Induction programs   Programs designed to assist new teachers through the induction, or early, years of teaching.

Inductive strategies   Instructional approaches that begin with specific data and help students find a rule or pattern. Discovery learning is an inductive strategy.

Information and Communication Technology   Digital technologies related to processes of how people communicate, generate, store, find, and use information.

Inquiry lesson   An inductive lesson wherein students pursue a question or problem by using scientific processes such as observation, inference, and hypothesis testing to arrive at one or more answers.

Instructional strategies   Ways of arranging parts of a lesson according to particular patterns of student and teacher behaviors to accomplish certain goals. Some examples include inquiry, cooperative learning, and direct instruction.

Interactional   Phenomena wherein parties affect each other through reciprocal action.

Interactive whiteboard   An electronic writing surface typically driven by a computer. It can capture and store the information recorded upon it, and it can be used to control (through touch) computer-generated images displayed on the screen.

Learning centers   Stations designed for small groups of students to focus on particular content or activities. Students may all rotate through a series of centers, or students may work at centers that meet their interests or targeted needs.

Learning styles   A combination of factors that together indicate how a person perceives information, interacts with it, and responds to the learning environment. Several schemes can be used to describe students' preferred learning styles.

Least restrictive environment   Holds that students with disabilities should be educated with their nondisabled peers to the maximum extent possible and should have access to the curriculum, activities, and programs available to nondisabled students. The severity of a student's disability determines the appropriate degree of restrictiveness in the educational environment. Restrictive environments are those that contain only students with disabilities.

Lesson study   A professional development model where teachers work in small groups to plan a lesson. They observe each other teach the lesson and then, later, reflect on the lesson and revise it. Lesson study originated in Japan and is used increasingly in the United States.

Linguistic   Of or pertaining to language.

Literature circles   Essentially book clubs for students. Typically, students select from a variety of works (often fiction but increasingly nonfiction as well) and meet in small groups with assigned roles to study and appreciate their selected texts.

Local assessments Measures used with the intent of gathering information about student performance at the classroom, school, or district level. The purpose is not to compare student performance with that of students in other places, but to gather specific information related to local curricular and instructional efforts and student learning within the immediate context.

Metacognition Thinking about thinking. Understanding of one's own thinking.

Mentors Individuals who support the growth and development of less experienced peers, often in a partner relationship. Mentors can be formally assigned and complete a prescribed set of tasks, or they can work informally with their protegees and offer less structured support.

Modifications Changes to classroom resources, instruction, or conditions to allow students to learn or show what they know despite areas of need such as physical or learning disabilities. Modifications substantially alter the learning expectations to which students are held.

Monitor To actively observe students for specified purposes, often to ensure that they are safe and engaged in learning activities.

Morals Principles of right and wrong in relation to human conduct.

Multimedia projects Computer-based projects that combine different media such as sound, text, animation, and images to create an integrated product.

Multiple embodiments Varied examples of a single concept. Embodiments should be selected to portray the critical attributes of the concept.

Multiple measures A variety of assessment strategies used as part of a system to obtain a valid portrait of student performance and growth.

Mutual accommodation The notion that both the teacher and the students must actively work to learn about the members of the classroom community and the content. Through mutual accommodation, learning is not the sole responsibility of the student; the teacher must take an active role in learning about students and increasing her professional knowledge and skills to foster learning effectively.

National Assessment of Educational Progress (NAEP) Conducted for more than 40 years, the NAEP is a test that provides information about how U.S. students achieve in various subject areas. Representative samples of students in private and public schools from all fifty U.S. states are assessed in grades 4, 8, and 12. Long-term trend data and data by state, subject area, and student subgroups are available. Data are not reported for individual students or schools.

National Board certification An advanced level of certification available to teachers across the nation. This optional certification process compares a teacher's practices to a set of standards through performance-based assessments such as portfolios, video-recorded lessons, and student work samples. It also includes a written examination. Many states offer financial compensation

for the application process and some sort of incentive for certified teachers.

National Board for Professional Teaching Standards (NBPTS) An independent, nonprofit, and nonpartisan organization comprised of teachers and other educational leaders. The NBPTS's core conviction is that the key to improving student learning is to strengthen teaching. The NBPTS developed performance-based assessments of teacher performance in relation to sets of professional teaching standards. See also *National Board certification.*

No Child Left Behind Act of 2001 Federal legislation that revises the Elementary and Secondary Education Act, first enacted in 1965 and modified at several other points in history. The act is designed to fuel gains in student achievement and hold states and schools more accountable for student progress. Students in low-performing schools are a special focus. The legislation increases the role of the federal government in education and is currently being modified for reauthorization.

Norm-referenced Assessments or scores that compare one student's performance with that of others.

Null curriculum The content that is not explicitly taught in schools. One example from many places in the United States, some may argue, is physical fitness in terms of whole-body wellness and skills. General patterns for the null curriculum exist based on factors such as geographical region, local values, and historical context. The null curriculum is also a product of an individual's idiosyncratic experiences in school.

Off task A description of the behaviors students exhibit when they are engaged in activities other than those specified by the lesson objective or the task at hand.

On task A description of the behaviors students exhibit when they are actively engaged in activities related to the task at hand or the lesson objective.

Opportunity gap Persistent discrepancies in the educational experiences afforded certain subgroups in the U.S. student population.

Pacing guide A document that specifies the content to be addressed in a certain sequence for a given period of time, such as for the day, week, month, or term.

Percentile The score below which a given percentage of the scores in a distribution fall. For example, 75 percent of the scores in a sample fall below the 75th percentile.

Positive behavior support An approach, often school- or districtwide to supporting student behavior based on prevention, data analysis, positive interventions, and progress monitoring.

Praxis A series of Educational Testing Service tests for beginning teachers designed to measure academic skills (Praxis I, taken to enter a teacher education program), subject-matter knowledge (Praxis II, taken to demonstrate competence in the subject matter related to the prospective credential area), and classroom performance (Praxis III, completed for licensure).

Pre-assessments Measures used before instruction begins to determine students' current knowledge, attitudes, or skills. Pre-assessment results help teachers plan learning experiences that most closely address students' needs.

Primacy effect   The tendency for humans to remember the first stimuli or information to which they are exposed in a given situation.

Problem-based learning   An instructional model where students work collaboratively to address ill-defined, complex, realistic problems of interest to them. Teachers serve as facilitators, and technology usually figures prominently.

Progress monitoring   Assessment efforts that allow teachers and students to analyze students' growth toward the learning goals. Formally, progress monitoring plots in a line graph students' rate of progress with the rate required in order to meet learning goals. Instruction is adjusted to ensure that students' rate is sufficient to meet goals.

Proximity control   Based on the fact that students who are physically farthest from the teacher tend to misbehave, proximity control has teachers moving closer to students to prevent and redirect misbehavior.

Read-aloud   The portion of the day in which teachers read text to the class, often for the primary purposes of fostering appreciation for the work and enjoyment in the act of reading. Can also refer to the selected text itself.

Realia   Real-life materials that can support students' understanding of the content. Examples include actual objects such as coins, tools, and articles of clothing.

Recency effect   The tendency for humans to remember the last stimuli or information to which they are exposed in a given situation.

Reliable   An instrument is reliable if it delivers consistent results. Reliable instruments yield similar results with different scorers and when given under varied conditions.

Response to intervention (RTI)   An educational approach that focuses on collecting data on student progress, providing a systematic instructional intervention, and then frequently assessing changes in student progress. Currently RTI can be used in place of or in addition to traditional means for determining specific learning disabilities.

Reteach   Efforts taken by a teacher to present content to students who did not master it as a result of an earlier presentation.

Routine   A repeatable set of behavioral steps to accomplish recurring events, such as taking roll.

Rubrics   Sets of guidelines that specify the relevant criteria for a student product and indicate levels of performance.

Scaffold   Social interactions whereby experts use supportive environments and behaviors to support novices' efforts to increase their skill or knowledge (Vygotsky, 1978).

School accountability   The notion that schools should be held responsible for student achievement, usually determined by student test scores. Accountability typically is defined through rewards or punishments at varying levels, including, for example, financial incentives for high student performance or the takeover of schools that fail to demonstrate growth in student achievement.

School Accountability Report Card (SARC)   Mandated by No Child Left Behind, the report card is a document that must be made publicly available each year. It must specify, in understandable language, student performance at three levels (basic, proficient, and advanced), and must show achievement data by student subgroup. The report card must also must disclose if the school has been identified as needing improvement or other action.

Scope and sequence   A section in teacher's editions of classroom texts that specifies the content that is addressed in the text (scope) and suggests plans for laying out the content over time (sequence). It is typically presented in the form of a chart that displays not only the grade level addressed in the text, but also its connection to the content of the text of other grade levels as well.

Selection-type item   A test item where the respondent chooses the answer from among those given. True/false, matching, and multiple-choice items are examples. The contrast is constructed-response items.

Self-efficacy   One's own judgments of one's abilities to produce desired results, to succeed, or to control one's circumstances.

Semantic   Of or pertaining to meaning.

Service learning   Projects through which students continue their own learning of some content or topic by providing assistance related to the topic to individuals, groups, or organizations.

Sheltered instruction   Instruction that "shelters" the linguistic demands of a lesson while simultaneously seeking to ensure that English learners master the content of the lesson. Sheltered instruction includes both discrete strategies such as teaching key vocabulary terms as well as general approaches such as building classroom environments where students feel safe to communicate.

Simulation   An instructional strategy wherein students undergo a series of activities designed to replicate a real-life situation, the conditions faced within that situation, and the decision-making processes required to succeed in that situation.

Social action   Planned efforts by individuals or groups to address social issues they hold as important.

Social media   Use of easily accessible web and mobile device applications that employ user-generated content in order to increase interaction and allow users to share information quickly and easily. Examples include wikis, blogs, microblogs, podcasts, and photo or videosharing.

Social network service   A Web-based service that connects users with similar interests and allows them to interact over the Internet through tools such as instant messaging and e-mail.

Social Reconstructionism   A branch of educational thought that views schools as active agents to improve society. Schools, in this view, serve as transformers rather than as transmitters of the status quo. Notable proponents include George S. Counts and Harold Rugg.

Sociocultural   An adjective that describes factors pertaining to both the social and cultural aspects of a phenomenon. Sociocultural elements describe those ways of behaving and living that are developed by people in groups and transmitted to future generations.

Socioeconomic status   Some measure of a person's or group's income level and social class.

Specific learning disabilities   Disabilities possessed by individuals who have adequate cognitive functioning in general and the ability to learn some things easily. Specific learning disabilities can relate to basic psychological processes involved in learning and using mathematics or in understanding and using spoken or written language.

Speech or language disorders   Disorders related to the transfer of knowledge or information such as ideas and feelings. Speech disorders are specifically related to the verbal components of the communication process.

Standards-based instruction   Teaching to a set of outcomes prescribed through local, state, or national content standards. Standards-based instruction may offer benefits such as uniformly high expectations for all students and close alignment among materials, instruction, and assessment. Potential drawbacks include a narrowing of the curriculum to what is prescribed in the standards and curriculum and lessons that are less responsive to local students and community needs.

Student achievement   Student knowledge and skills, often as measured by test scores. Some people are concerned that achievement is currently construed too narrowly and should be more broadly conceived of through a variety of goals pertaining to student growth and how it is measured.

Student-led conferences   In contrast to traditional teacher-led conferences with families, student-led conferences ask students to take the leadership role in sharing and evaluating their work and articulating their growth. Student-led conferences seek to engage students, parents, and teachers in dialogue about student learning by shifting the power away from the teacher, who acts as a facilitator at the conference, and more equally into the hands of the student and family members.

Student Information System   A software application for managing student data such as special education plans, attendance, and grades.

Student performance standards   Explicit statements of the educational outcomes students are to attain. Typically student performance standards specify the content, behavior, and level at which students are expected to perform.

Summative   Measures that serve the primary purpose of reporting students' postinstructional performance.

Support provider   An experienced colleague who is formally assigned to assist a new teacher throughout the induction (or early) years in the teaching profession.

Teachable moment   An often unexpected opportunity for the teacher and students to explore an event or idea that arises from daily life or classroom events.

Teacher's editions   The teachers' versions of classroom texts. Teacher's editions typically include many kinds of assistance for teachers, including the answers to exercises, suggested lesson sequences, prompts for using the materials with students, and suggestions for reteaching or extending the material presented in the text.

Textbook adoptions   The processes by which schools commit to using particular text series. Typically, state boards of education approve works from among competing publishers, and districts select from among the approved texts those they feel are most appropriate for their local setting. The adoption cycle allows schools to obtain current materials for a variety of subject areas after a set number of years.

Thematic instruction   An approach that organizes curriculum around themes that cut across traditional subject areas rather than using the subjects themselves as the organizing principle.

Think aloud   A strategy in which one describes one's thought processes while carrying out a target activity. The point is to help students sense the critical attributes of the target activity and the important decisions requried by it.

Tracking   A practice of arranging students into stable, relatively homogeneous groups based on perceived ability or demonstrated achievement. Research on tracking suggest that it frequently does not improve achievement for students in the lower tracks, as these students often receive lower-quality instruction. Conversely, many teachers feel that tracking helps them meet students' needs better by reducing the range of performance in their classes.

Trade books   Commercial books, often sold in bookstores.

Unit   A collection of lessons that address a common goal or topic.

Unschooling   An approach to education wherein learning is based on students' interests and goals rather than upon a set curriculum. Unschooling is often considered one form of home schooling, with adults providing resources and guiding students to access them as their needs and interests dictate.

Valid   A measure is valid to the extent to which it measures what it is intended to measure.

Web 2.0   Uses of the Web that encourage interaction, collaboration, and creativity. This is in contrast with the original, read-only nature of the Web.

Word cloud   A visual display of the words or tags on an Internet site or in some set of text. It is used to describe the content of the site. The importance or prevalence of terms can be shown using color or font size.

References

Aarons, D. I. (2009). Test scores for students with disabilities found on rise. *Education Week, 29*(13), 13.

Abedi, J., & Herman, J. (2010). Assessing English language learners' opportunity to learn mathematics: Issues and limitations. *Teachers College Record, 112*(3), 723–746.

Adams, G. L., & Engelmann, S. (1996). *Research on direct instruction: 25 years beyond DISTAR*. Seattle, WA: Educational Achievement Systems.

Adams, J. (12 May 1780). Letter to his wife Abigail Adams. Retrieved from http://www.creativequotations.com.

Adams, M., Bell, L. A., & Griffin, P., Eds. (2007). *Teaching for diversity and social justice* (2nd ed.). New York: Routledge.

Ainsworth, L, & Viegut, D. (2006). *Common formative assessments: How to connect standards-based instruction and assessment*. Thousand Oaks, CA: Corwin.

Akiba, M., LeTendre, G. K., & Scribner, J. P. (2010). Teacher quality, opportunity gap, and national achievement in 46 countries. *Educational Researcher, 36*(7), 369–387.

Albert, L. (1996). *Cooperative discipline*. Circle Pines, MN: American Guidance Service.

Alexander, K., & Alexander, M. D. (2005). *American public school law* (6th ed.). Belmont, CA: Wadsworth.

Allchin, D. (2005). "Hands-off" dissection? *American Biology Teacher, 67*, 369–373.

Allen, D., Ort, S., & Schmidt, J. (2009). Supporting classroom assessment practice: Lessons from a small high school. *Theory into Practice, 48*(1), 72–80.

Allen, J. B., Ed. (1999). *Class actions: Teaching for social justice in elementary and middle school*. New York: Teachers College Press.

Allen, R. (2003). The democratic aims of service learning. *Educational Leadership, 60*(6), 51–54.

Alvidrez, J., & Weinstein, R. (1999). Early teacher perceptions and later student academic achievement. *Journal of Educational Psychology, 91*, 731–746.

American Association of School Librarians (2007). Standards for the 21st Century Learner. Retrieved from http://www.ala.org/ala/mgrps/divs/aasl/guidelinesandstandards/learningstandards/AASL_Learning_Standards_2007.pdf

Amrein, A. L., & Berliner, D. C. (2002). High-stakes testing and student learning. *Policy Analysis Archives, 10*(18). Retrieved from http://epaa.asu.edu/ojs/article/viewFile/297/423

Amrein, A. L., & Berliner, D. C. (2003). The effects of high-stakes testing on student motivation and learning. *Educational Leadership, 60*(5), 32–38.

Anderson, K. (2007). Tips for teaching: Differentiating instruction to include all students. *Preventing School Failure, 51*(3), 49–54.

Anderson, L. W. (2005). Objectives, evaluation, and the improvement of education. *Studies in Educational Evaluation, 31*(2–3), 102–113.

Anderson, L. W. (Ed.), Krathwohl, D. R. (Ed.), Airasian, P. W., Cruikshank, K. A., Mayer, R. E., Pintrich, P. R., Raths, J., & Wittrock, M. C. (2001). *A taxonomy for learning, teaching, and assessing: A revision of Bloom's Taxonomy of Educational Objectives*. Boston: Allyn & Bacon.

Annenberg Institute for School Reform. (2004). Professional learning communities: Professional development strategies that improve instruction. Retrieved from http://www.annenberginstitute.org/images/ProfLearning.pdf.

Arter, J. A., & McTighe, J. (2001). *Scoring rubrics in the classroom: Using performance criteria for assessing and improving student performance*. Thousand Oaks, CA: Corwin Press.

Ashlock, R. B. (2005). *Error patterns in computation. Using error patterns to improve instruction* (9th ed.). Upper Saddle River, NJ: Merrill/Prentice Hall.

Au, W. (2007). High-stakes testing and curricular control: A qualitative metasynthesis. *Educational Researcher, 36*(5), 258–267.

Audet, R. H., & Jordan, L. K. (Eds.). (2005). *Integrating inquiry across the curriculum*. Thousand Oaks, CA: Corwin.

Baeder, A. (2010). Stepping into students' worlds. *Educational Leadership, 67*(5), 56–60.

Baglieri, S., & Knopf, J. (2004). Normalizing difference in inclusive teaching. *Journal of Learning Disabilities, 37*(6), 525–529.

Bailey, J. M., & Guskey, T. R. (2001). *Implementing student-led conferences*. Thousand Oaks, CA: Corwin Press.

Baker, S., Gersten, R., & Lee, D. S. (2002). A synthesis of empirical research on teaching mathematics to low-achieving students. *The Elementary School Journal, 103*(1), 51–73.

Banks, J. (1997). *Teaching strategies for ethnic studies* (6th ed.). Needham Heights, MA: Allyn & Bacon.

Banks, J. (2009). Human rights, diversity, and citizenship education. *Educational Forum, 73*(2), 100–110.

Banks, J. A. (2005). Multicultural education: Characteristics and goals. In J. A. Banks and C. A. M. Banks (Eds.), *Multicultural education: Issues and perspectives* (5th ed., pp. 3–30). Hoboken, NJ: Wiley.

Banks, J. A. (2008). Diversity, group identity, and citizenship education in a global age. *Educational Researcher, 37*(3), 129–139.

Barron, A. E., Hogarty, K. Y., Kromrey, J. D., & Lenkway, P. (1999). An examination of the relationships between student conduct and the number of computers per student in Florida schools. *Journal of Research on Computing in Education, 32*(1), 98–107.

Bartolome, L. I. (1994). Beyond the methods fetish: Toward a humanizing pedagogy. *Harvard Educational Review, 64*(2), 173–194.

Becker, R. R. (2000). The critical role of students' questions in literacy development. *Educational Forum, 64,* 261–271.

Bellamy, T., & Goodlad, J. (2008). Continuity and change: On the pursuit of a democratic public mission for our schools. *Phi Delta Kappan, 89,* 565–571.

Bennett, C. I. (1995). *Comprehensive multicultural education: Theory and practice* (3rd ed.). Boston: Allyn & Bacon.

Benson, B., & Barnett, S. (2005). *Student-led conferencing using showcase portfolios.* (2nd ed.). Thousand Oaks, CA: Corwin Press.

Benzel, K. N. (Ed.). (1997). *Western landscaping book.* Menlo Park, CA: Sunset Books.

Berends, M., & Peñaloza, O. (2010). Increasing racial isolation and test score gaps in mathematics: A 30-year perspective. *Teachers College Record, 112,* 978–1007.

Berliner, D. (1984). The half-full glass: A review of research on teaching. In Hosford, Philip L., Ed. *Using What We Know About Teaching.* Reston, VA: Association for Supervision and Curriculum Development, pp. 51–84.

Berliner, D. (2004). Describing the behavior and documenting the accomplishments of expert teachers. *Bulletin of Science Technology and Society, 24*(3), 200–212.

Berliner, D. (2006). Our impoverished view of educational research. *Teachers College Record, 108,* 949–995.

Berliner, D. (2009). MCLB (Much Curriculum Left Behind): A U.S. calamity in the making. *The Educational Forum, 73*(4), 284–296.

Beveridge, T. (2010). No Child Left Behind and fine arts classes. *Arts Education Policy Review, 111*(1), 4–7.

Bilingual Education Act of 1994, Public Law No. 103–382. Section 7102.

Bingham, G., Holbrook, T., & Meyers, L. (2010). Using self-assessments in elementary classrooms. *Phi Delta Kappan, 91*(5), 59–61.

Black, P., & Wiliam, D. (1998). Assessment and classroom learning. *Assessment in Education: Principles, Policy & Practice, 5*(1), 7–74.

Black, S. (2001). Ask me a question. How teachers use inquiry in the classroom. *American School Board Journal, 188*(5), 43–45.

Black, S. (2010). Never say no. *American School Board Journal, 197*(5), 39–40.

Blanchett, W. (2006). Disproportionate representation of African American students in special education: Acknowledging the role of white privilege and racism. *Educational Researcher, 35*(6), 24–28.

Bloom, B., Englehart, M., Hill, W., Furst, E., & Krathwohl, D. (1956). *Taxonomy of educational objectives: The classification of education goals. Handbook I: Cognitive domain.* New York: Longman Green.

Blosser, P. E. (1990). Using questions in science classrooms. Research matters—to the science teacher. No. 9001. National Association of Research in Science Teaching. Retrieved from http://www.narst.org/publications/research/question.cfm.

Bohn, C. M., Roehrig, A. D., & Pressley, M. (2004). The first days of school in the classrooms of two more effective and four less effective primary-grade teachers. *The Elementary School Journal, 104,* 269–287.

Bomer, R., & Bomer, K. (2001). For *a better world: Reading and writing for social action.* Portsmouth, NH: Heinemann.

Bondy, E., & Ross, D. (2008). The teacher as warm demander. *Educational Leadership, 66*(1), 54–58.

Bondy, E., Ross, D., Gallingane, C., & Hambacher, E. (2007). Creating environments of success and resilience. *Urban Education, 42,* 326–348.

Booher-Jennings, J. (2006). Rationing education in an era of accountability. *Phi Delta Kappan, 87,* 756–761.

Borman, G., & Dowling, M., (2010). Schools and inequality: A multilevel analysis of Coleman's equality of educational opportunity data. *Teachers College Record, 112,* 1201–1246.

Borum, R., Cornell, D., Modzeleski, W., & Jimerson, S. (2010). What can be done about school shootings? A review of the evidence. *Educational Researcher, 39*(1), 27–37.

Bowen, C. W. (2000). A quantitative literature review of cooperative learning effects on high school and college chemistry achievement. *Journal of Chemical Education, 77*(1), 116–119.

Bowman, R. (2007). How can students be motivated: A misplaced question? *Clearing House, 81*(2), 81–86.

Brand, S., Dunn, R., & Greb, F. (2002). Learning styles of students with attention deficit hyperactivity disorder: Who are they and how can we teach them? *Clearing House, 75,* 268–273.

Bransford, J. (2000). *How people learn: Brain, mind, experience, and school.* Washington, DC: National Academy Press.

Brenner, D., & Hiebert, E. (2010). If I follow the teachers' editions, isn't that enough? Analyzing reading volume in six core reading programs. *The Elementary School Journal 110*(3), 347–363.

Brigham, F., & Brigham, M. (2010). Preventive instruction. *American School Board Journal, 197*(6), 32–33.

Bright, R. M. (2006). Literacy backpacks in teacher education: Launching support for home and school literacy. *Journal of Reading Education, 31*(2), 24–34.

Broderick, A., Mehta-Parekh, H., & Reid, D. (2005). Differentiating instruction for disabled students in inclusive classrooms. *Theory into Practice, 44*(3), 194–202.

Bromley, K., Irwin-De Vitis, L., & Modlo, M. (1995). *Graphic organizers: Visual strategies for active learning.* New York: Scholastic.

Brookhart, S., Moss, C., & Long, B. (2008). Formative assessment that empowers. Educational *Leadership, 66*(3), 52–57.

Brophy, J. (1981). Teacher praise: A functional analysis. *Review of Educational Research, 51,* 5–32.

Brophy, J. (1997). Effective instruction. In H. J. Walberg & G. D. Haertel (Eds.), *Psychology and educational practice* (pp. 212–232). Berkeley, CA: McCutchan.

Brophy, J. (2010). Classroom management as socializing students into clearly articulated roles. *Journal of Classroom Interaction, 45*(1), 41–45.

Brown, D. (2004). Urban teachers' professed classroom management strategies: Reflections of culturally responsive teaching. *Urban Education, 39,* 266–289.

Brown, M. R. (2007). Educating all students: Creating culturally responsive teachers, classrooms, and schools. *Intervention in School and Clinic, 43,* 57–62.

Brozo, W. G. (2009). Response to intervention or responsive instruction? Challenges and possibilities of response to intervention for adolescent literacy. *Journal of Adolescent & Adult Literacy, 53,* 277–281.

Bruer, J. T. (1997). Education and the brain: A bridge too far. *Educational Researcher, 26*(8), 4–26.

Bruner, J. (1960). *The process of education.* Boston: Harvard University Press.

Bruner, J. (1986). *Actual minds, possible worlds.* Cambridge, MA: Harvard University Press.

Bruner, J. B., Goodnow, J. J., & Austin, G. A. (1960). *A study of thinking.* New York: John Wiley & Sons.

Bumgardner, S. (2010). The equitable distribution of high-quality teachers. *District Administration, 46*(2), 45–47.

Burniske, R. W. (2008). *Literacy in the digital age* (2nd ed.). Thousand Oaks, CA: Corwin Press.

Burris, C. (2010). Detracking for success. *Principal Leadership, 10*(5), 30–34.

Butler, L. (2009). A step-by-step guide to response to intervention. *Principal, 89*(1), 46–50.

Buzzelli, C., & Johnston, B. (2001). Authority, power, and morality in classroom discourse. *Teaching and Teacher Education, 17*, 873–884.

Byrd-Blake, M., Afolayan, M. O., Hunt, J. W., Fabunmi, M., Pryor, B. W., & Leander, R. (2010). Morale of teachers in high poverty schools: A post-NCLB mixed methods analysis. *Education and Urban Society, 42*(4), 450–472.

Caine, G., & Caine, R. N. (2001). *The brain, education, and the competitive edge.* Lantham, MD: Scarecrow Press.

Caine, R. N., & Caine, G. (1994). *Making connections: Teaching and the human brain.* Menlo Park, CA: Addison-Wesley.

Caine, R. N., Caine, G., McClintic, C. L., & Klimek, K. J. (2005). *12 brain/mind learning principles in action.* Thousand Oaks, CA: Corwin.

Caldwell, J. S., & Ford, M. P. (2002). *Where have all the bluebirds gone? How to soar with flexible grouping.* Portsmouth, NH: Heinemann.

California Department of Education & California Association for the Gifted. (1994). *Differentiating the core curriculum and instruction to provide advanced learning opportunities.* Sacramento: California Department of Education. Retrieved from http://eric.ed.gov/ERICDocs/data/ericdocs2/content_storage_01/0000000b/80/23/2c/b9.pdf.

California Department of Education. (2005). *Physical education model content standards for California public schools kindergarten through grade twelve.* Sacramento: California Department of Education.

Campbell, P. B., & Storo, J. N. (1994). Girls are . . . Boys are . . . : Myths, stereotypes & gender differences. Office of Educational Research and Improvement, U.S. Department of Education. Retrieved from http://www.campbell-kibler.com/Stereo.pdf.

Canter, L. (1976). *Assertive discipline: A take-charge approach for today's educator.* Seal Beach, CA: Canter & Associates.

Caram, C., & Davis, P. (2005). Inviting student engagement with questioning. *Kappa Delta Pi Record, 42*(1), 18–23.

Casella, R. (2003). Zero tolerance policy in schools: Rationale, consequences, and alternatives. *Teachers College Record, 105*, 872–892.

Cavanaugh, S. (2006, November 16). Technology helps teachers home in on student needs. *Education Week, 26*(12), 10–11. Retrieved from http://www.edweek.org/ew/articles/2006/11/15/12calculators.h26.html.

Cazden, C. (1986). Classroom discourse. In M. Wittrock (Ed.), *Handbook of research on teaching* (3rd ed., pp. 432–462). New York: Macmillan.

Center for Applied Special Technology (CAST). (2010). UDL guidelines version 1.0. Retrieved from http://www.udlcenter.org/aboutudl/udlguidelines.

Center for Media Literacy. (2007). Media literacy: A definition . . . and more. http://www.medialit.org/reading_room/rr2def.php.

Center for Research on Education, Diversity & Excellence. (2002). The five standards for effective pedagogy. Retrieved from http://crede.berkeley.edu/standards/standards.html.

Center for the Study of Mathematics Curriculum. (2006). The intended mathematics curriculum as represented in state-level curriculum standards: Consensus or confusion? Executive summary. Retrieved from http://www.mathcurriculumcenter.org/st_std_exec_sum.pdf.

Center on Education Policy. (2006). From the capital to the classroom: Year 4 of the No Child Left Behind Act. Retrieved from http://www.ecs.org/html/Document.asp?chouseid=6851.

Center on Education Policy. (2010). *How many schools have not made adequate yearly progress under the No Child Left Behind Act?* Retrieved from http://www.cep-dc.org/index.cfm?fuseaction=document_ext.showDocumentByID&nodeID=1&DocumentID=303.

Centers for Disease Control and Prevention. (2004) Youth risk behavior surveillance—United States, 2003. MMWR Surveillance Summaries [Introduction] 2004; 53(SS02), pp 1–96. Retrieved from www.cdc.gov/mmwr/preview/mmwrhtml/ss5302a1.htm.

Central Intelligence Agency. (2010). *The world factbook.* Retrieved from https://www.cia.gov/library/publications/the-world-factbook/geos/us.html.

Charles, C. M. (1992). *Building classroom discipline* (4th ed.). White Plains, NY: Longman.

Charney, R. S. (2002). *Teaching children to care: Classroom management for ethical and academic growth, K–8.* Greenfield, MA: Northeast Foundation for Children.

Child Labor Public Education Project. (n.d.). Child labor in U.S. history. http://www.continuetolearn.uiowa.edu/laborctr/child_labor/.

Chin, C., & Brown, D. E. (2000). Learning in science: A comparison of deep and surface approaches. *Journal of Research in Science Teaching, 37*(2), 109–138.

Chorzempa, B. F., & Graham, S. (2006). Primary-grade teachers' use of within–class ability grouping in reading. *Journal of Educational Psychology, 98*, 529–541.

Civic Enterprises. (2008). One *dream, two realities: Perspectives on America's high schools.* Retrieved from http://www.civicenterprises.net/pdfs/onedream.pdf.

Clunies-Ross, P., Little, E., & Kienhuis, M. (2008). Self-reported and actual use of proactive and reactive classroom management strategies and their relationship with teacher stress and student behaviour. *Educational Psychology, 28*, 693–710.

Cochran-Smith, M. (2003). The unforgiving complexity of teaching: Avoiding simplicity in the age of accountability. *Journal of Teacher Education, 54*(1), 3–5.

Coffield, F., Moseley, D., Hall, E., & Ecclestone, K. (2004). *Learning styles and pedagogy in post-16 learning. A systematic and critical review.* London: Learning and Skills Research Centre. Retrieved from https://crm .lsnlearning.org.uk/user/order.aspx?code=041543.

Cole, R. W. (Ed.). (1995). *Educating everybody's children: Diverse teaching strategies for diverse learners. What research and practice say about improving achievement.* Alexandria, VA: Association for Supervision and Curriculum Development.

Coles, G. (July 2000). "Direct, explicit, and systematic"—bad reading science. *Language Arts, 77,* 543–545.

Colombo, M., & Colombo, P. (2007). Using blogs to improve differentiated instruction. *Education Digest, 73*(4), 10–14.

Coloroso, B. (1994). *Kids are worth it! Giving your child the gift of inner discipline.* New York: William Morrow.

Common Core State Standards Initiative. (2010). English Language Arts Standards » Writing » Grade 5. Retrieved from http://www.corestandards.org/the-standards/english-language-arts-standards/writing/grade-5/.

Cook, B. G. (2004). Inclusive teachers' attitudes toward their students with disabilities: A replication and extension. *The Elementary School Journal, 104*(4), 307–320.

Cooper, S. (2009). Preservice teachers' analysis of children's work to make instructional decisions. *School Science and Mathematics, 109*(6), 355–362.

Corbin, C. (2008). *Unleashing the potential of the teenage brain: 10 powerful ideas.* Thousand Oaks, CA: Corwin.

Cortes, C. E. (2000). *The children are watching: How the media teach about diversity.* New York: Teachers College Press.

Costa, A., & Kallick, B. (Eds.). (2000). *Assessing and reporting on habits of mind.* Alexandria, VA: Association for Supervision and Curriculum Development.

Costa, J., Caldeira, H., Gallastegui, J. R., & Otero, J. (2000). An analysis of question asking on scientific texts explaining natural phenomena. *Journal of Research in Science Teaching, 37,* 602–614.

Cotton, K. (2001). Close-up #5: Classroom questioning School Improvement Research Series (SIRS): Research you can use. Northwest Regional Educational Laboratory Retrieved from http://educationnorthwest.org/webfm_send/569.

Cozzul, M. C., Freeze, R., Lutfiyya, Z. M., & Van Walleghem, J. (2004). The roles of nondisabled peers in promoting the social competence of students with intellectual disabilities in inclusive classrooms. *Exceptionality Education Canada, 14*(1), 23–41.

Croninger, R., Rice, J., Rathbun, A., & Nishio, M. (2007). Teacher qualifications and early learning: Effects of certification, degree, and experience on first-grade student achievement. *Economics of Education Review, 26*(3), 312–324.

Csikszentmihalyi, M., & Csikszentmihalyi, I. S. (Eds.). (2006). *A life worth living: Contributions to positive psychology.* Oxford: Oxford University Press.

Cuban, L. (2006). The laptop revolution has no clothes. *Education Week, 26*(8), 29.

Cuban, L. (2010). *How long does it take to become a "good" teacher?* Retrieved from http://larrycuban.wordpress.com/ 2010/04/20/how-long-does-it-take-to-become-a-good-teacher/.

Cummins, J. (1981). The role of primary language development in promoting educational success for language minority students. In California State Department of Education (Ed.), *Schooling and language minority students: A theoretical framework* (pp. 3–49). Los Angeles: National Dissemination and Assessment Center. (ERIC Document Reproduction Service No. 249 773)

Cummins, J. (2007). Pedagogies for the poor? Realigning reading instruction for low-income students with scientifically based reading research. *Educational Researcher, 36,* 564–572.

Cunningham, C. A., & Billingsley, M. (2003). *Curriculum webs: A practical guide to weaving the web into teaching and learning.* Boston: Allyn & Bacon.

Curwin, R., & Mendler, A. N. (2001). *Discipline with dignity.* Upper Saddle River, NJ: Merrill/Prentice Hall.

Danforth, S., & Smith, T. J. (2005). *Engaging troubling students: A constructivist approach.* Thousand Oaks, CA: Corwin.

Daniels, H. (2002). *Literature circles: Voice and choice in book clubs and reading groups* (2nd ed.). Portland, ME: Stenhouse.

Danielson, C. (1996). *Enhancing professional practice: A framework for teaching.* Alexandria, VA: Association for Supervision and Curriculum Development.

Darling-Hammond, L. (2000). Teacher quality and student achievement: A review of state policy evidence. *Educational Policy Analysis Archives, 8*(1). Retrieved from http://epaa.asu.edu/epaa/v8n1/.

Darling-Hammond, L. (2007). Third annual "Brown" lecture in education research—the flat earth and education: How America's commitment to equity will determine our future. *Educational Researcher, 36*(6), 318–334.

Darling-Hammond, L. (2009). America's commitment to equity will determine our future. *Phi Delta Kappan 91*(4), 8–14.

Darling-Hammond, L., French, J., & Garcia-Lopez, S. (Eds.). (2002). *Learning to teach for social justice.* New York: Teachers College Press.

Darling-Hammond, L., & Friedlaender, D. (2008). Creating excellent and equitable schools. *Educational Leadership, 65*(8), 14–21.

Darling-Hammond, L., & McCloskey, L. (2008). Assessment for learning around the world: What would it mean to be internationally competitive? *Phi Delta Kappan, 90*(4), 263–272.

Darling-Hammond, L, & Richardson, N. (2009). Teacher learning: What matters? *Educational Leadership, 66*(5), 46–53.

Davidman, L., & Davidman, P. T. (1997). *Teaching with a multicultural perspective: A practical guide.* New York: Longman.

Davis, H. (2003). Conceptualizing the role and influence of student-teacher relationships on children's social and cognitive development. *Educational Psychologist, 38*(4), 207–234.

DeBell, M., & Chapman, C. (2006). *Computer and Internet use by students in 2003.* (NCES 2006-065). U.S. Department of Education. Washington, DC: National Center for Education Statistics.

De Welde, K., Laursen, S., & Thiry, H. (n.d.). *Women in science, technology, engineering and math (STEM).* Retrieved from http://www.socwomen.org/socactivism/ stem_fact_sheet.pdf.

Deddeh, H., Main, E., & Fulkerson, S. (2010). Eight steps to meaningful grading. *Phi Delta Kappan, 91*(7), 53–58.

Delpit, L. (1995). *Other people's children: Cultural conflict in the classroom.* New York: New Press.

Delpit, L. (2006). Lessons from teachers. *Journal of Teacher Education, 57*(3), 220–231.

Demski, J. (2010). A quicker clicker. *THE Journal, 37*(3), 17–18.

Dillon, J. T. (1987). Unpublished course syllabus for Education 139: Curriculum and Instruction, University of California at Riverside.

Dillon, J. T. (1988a). The remedial status of student questioning. *Journal of Curriculum Studies, 20,* 197–210.

Dillon, J. T. (1988b). *Questioning and teaching: A manual of practice.* New York: Teachers College Press.

Dillon, J. T. (1990). *The practice of questioning.* London: Routledge.

Din, F. S. (2000). Use direct instruction to improve reading skills quickly. *Rural Educator, 21*(3), 1–4.

Dorrell, L. D., & Busch, A. (2000). Censorship in schools: The impact of conservative Christian pressure. *Quest, 28*(3), 24–26.

Douglas, K. (2009). Sharpening our focus in measuring classroom instruction. *Educational Researcher, 38*(7), 518–521.

Downing, J. E., & Eichinger, J. (2003). Creating learning opportunities for students with severe disabilities in inclusive classrooms. *Teaching Exceptional Children, 36*(1), 26–31.

Doyle, W. (1986). Classroom organization and management. In M. Wittrock (Ed.), *Handbook of research on teaching* (3rd ed., pp. 392–431). New York: Macmillan.

Doyle, W. (2009). Situated practice: A reflection on person-centered classroom management. *Theory into Practice, 48*(2), 156–159.

Dreikurs, R. (1968). *Psychology in the classroom* (2nd ed.). New York: Harper & Row.

Dreikurs, R., Grunwald, B., & Pepper, F. (1982). *Maintaining sanity in the classroom: Classroom management techniques* (3rd ed.). New York: Harper & Row.

Driscoll, M. P. (2002). *How people learn (and what technology might have to do with it).* ERIC Digest. (ERK Document Reproduction Service No. ED470032 2002-10-00)

Driver, R. (1981). Pupils' alternative frameworks in science. *European Journal of Science Education, 3,* 93–101.

Driver, R. (1989a). Changing conceptions. In P. Adey (Ed.), *Adolescent development and school science.* London: Falmer.

Driver, R. (1989b). Students' conceptions and the learning of science. *International Journal of Science Education, 11,* 481–490.

Druck, K., & Kaplowitz, M. (2005). Preventing classroom violence. *Education Digest: Essential Readings Condensed for Quick Review, 71*(2), 40–43.

Duckworth, E. R. (1996). *The having of wonderful ideas and other essays on teaching and learning* (2nd ed.). New York: Teachers College Press.

Duffy, D. G. (1998, June). Teaching and the balancing of round stones. *Phi Delta Kappan, 79,* 777–780.

Duncan-Howell, J. (2010). Teachers making connections: Online communities as a source of professional learning. *British Journal of Educational Technology, 41*(2), 324–340.

Dunn, M. A. (2000). Closing the book on social studies: Four classroom teachers go beyond the text. *Social Studies, 91*(3), 132–136.

Dupper, D. (2010). Does the punishment fit the crime? The impact of zero tolerance discipline on at-risk youths. *Children & Schools, 32*(2), 67–69.

Dutro, E. (2009). Children writing "hard times": Lived experiences of poverty and the class-privileged assumptions of a mandated curriculum. *Language Arts, 87*(2), 89–98.

Dutro, E., Kazemi, E., Balf, R., & Lin, Y. (2008). "What are you and where are you from?": Race, identity, and the vicissitudes of cultural relevance, *Urban Education, 43,* 269–300.

Dyson, L. (2010). Unanticipated effects of children with learning disabilities on their families. *Learning Disability Quarterly, 33*(1), 43–55.

Echevarria, J., & Graves, A. (1998). *Sheltered content instruction: Teaching English-language learners with diverse abilities.* Boston: Allyn & Bacon.

Echevarria, J., Vogt, M. E., & Short, D. (2004). *Making content comprehensible for English language learners: The SIOP model* (2nd ed.). Boston: Allyn & Bacon.

Economist. (Fall 2009) *Did you know? Version 4.0.* Retrieved from http://www.youtube.com/watch?v=C2jDOkzrVew.

Edgoose, J. (2010). Hope in the unexpected: How can teachers still make a difference in the world? *Teachers College Record, 112*(2), 386–406.

Education Commission of the States. (2000). *Every student a citizen: Creating the democratic self (executive summary).* Denver, CO: Education Commission of the States. Retrieved from http://www.ecs.org/clearinghouse/16/77/1677.pdf.

Educational Testing Service. (2002). Pathwise/Praxis III domains. Retrieved from http://www.ets.org.

Education Week. (4 May 2006). The information edge: Using data to accelerate achievement. *Education Week, 25*(35), 8–9. Retrieved from http://www.edweek.org/ew/articles/2006/05/04/35intro.h25.html.

Edwards, J., & Fraser, K. (1983). Concept maps as reflectors of conceptual understanding. *Research in Science Education, 13,* 19–26.

Eeds, M., & Wells, D. (1989). Grand conversations: An exploration of meaning construction in literature study groups. *Research in the Teaching of English, 23*(1), 4–29.

Effrat, A., & Schimmel, D. (2003). Walking the democratic talk: Introduction to the special issue on collaborative rule making as preparation for democratic citizenship. *American Secondary Education, 31*(3), 3–15.

Eisner, E. (1979). *The educational imagination: On the design and evaluation of school programs* (3rd ed., pp. 87–107). Upper Saddle River, NJ: Merrill/Prentice Hall.

Eisner, E. (2006). The satisfactions of teaching. *Educational Leadership, 63*(6), 44–46.

Ellis, A. K. (1998). *Teaching and learning elementary social studies* (6th ed.). Boston: Allyn & Bacon.

Elmore, R. F. (1979–1980). Backward mapping: Implementation research and policy decisions. *Political Science Quarterly, 94,* 601–616.

Elsaleh, I. (2010). Teachers' interactions with curriculum materials in mathematics. *School Science and Mathematics, 110*(4), 177–179.

Emmer, E., Evertson, C., & Anderson, L. (1980). Effective classroom management at the beginning of the school year. *Elementary School Journal, 80,* 219–231.

Emmer, E. T., Evertson, C., & Worsham, M. E. (2002). *Classroom management for secondary teachers* (6th ed.). Boston: Allyn & Bacon.

Epstein, J. (2002). *School, family, and community partnerships: Your handbook for action* (2nd ed.). Thousand Oaks, CA: Corwin Press.

Epstein, J. (2005). Developing and sustaining research-based programs of school, family, and community partnerships: Summary of five years of NNPS research. National Network of Partnership Schools. Retrieved from http://www.csos.jhu .edu/p2000/pdf/Research%20Summary.pdf.

Epstein, J. (2008). Improving family and community involvement in secondary schools. *Education Digest, 73*(6), 9–12.

Epstein, J., & Salinas, K. (2004). Partnering with families and communities. *Educational Leadership, 61*(8), 12–18.

Erden, F., & Wolfgang, C. H. (2004). An exploration of the differences in prekindergarten, kindergarten, and first grade teachers' beliefs related to discipline when dealing with male and female students. *Early Child Development and Care, 174*(1), 3–11.

Erikson, E. (1968). *Identity: Youth and crisis.* New York: W. W. Norton.

Evertson, C., & Emmer, E. (1982). Effective classroom management at the beginning of the school year in junior high classes. *Journal of Educational Psychology, 74,* 485–498.

Fairlie, R. W., London, R. A., Rosner, M., & Pastor, M. (2006). *Crossing the divide: Immigrant youth and digital disparity in California.* University of California, Santa Cruz: Center for Justice, Tolerance, and Community. Retrieved from http://cjtc.ucsc.edu/docs/digital.pdf.

Faltis, C. (2001). *Joinfostering: Teaching and learning in multilingual classrooms* (3rd ed.). Upper Saddle River, NJ: Merrill/Prentice Hall.

Farris, P. J., Werderich, D. E., Nelson, P. A., & Fuhler, C. J. (2009). Male call: Fifth-grade boys' reading preferences. *The Reading Teacher, 63*(3), 180–188.

Federation of American Scientists. (2006). Harnessing the power of video games for learning: Summit on educational games. Retrieved from http://www.fas.org/gamesummit/ Resources/Summit%20on%20Educational%20Games.pdf.

Fenstermacher, G., & Richardson, V. (2005). On making determinations of quality in teaching. *Teachers College Record, 107*(1), 186–213.

Fields, L. (2004). Handling student fights. *The Clearinghouse, 77*(3), 108–110.

Fillmore, L. W. (1982) Instructional language as linguistic input: Second language learning in classrooms. In L. C. Wilkinson (Ed.), *Communicating in the classroom* (pp. 283–296). New York: Academic Press.

Finkel, D. L. (2000). *Teaching with your mouth shut.* Portsmouth, NH: Boynton/Cook.

Fischer, L., Schimmel, D., & Kelly, C. (1999). *Teachers and the law* (5th ed.). New York: Longman.

Flowers, C. P., Hancock, D. R., & Joyner, R. E. (2000). Effects of instructional strategies and conceptual levels on students' motivation and achievement in a technology course. *Journal of Research and Development in Education, 33*(3), 187–194.

Ford, D. (2005). Welcoming all students to room 202: Creating culturally responsive classrooms. *Gifted Child Today, 28*(4), 28–30.

Ford, D. (2010). Culturally responsive classrooms: Affirming culturally different gifted students. *Gifted Child Today, 33*(1), 50–53.

Ford, D. Y. & Kea, C. D. (2009). Creating culturally responsive instruction: For students' sake and teachers' sake. *Focus on Exceptional Children, 41*(9), 1–18.

Fordham Foundation. (2006). How well are states educating our neediest children? The Thomas F. Fordham Foundation. Retrieved from http://www.edexcellence.net/doc/ TFR06FULLREPORT.PDF.

Fordham Institute. (2008). High achieving students in the era of No Child Left Behind. Retrieved from http://www .fordhamfoundation.org/doc/20080618_high_achievers.pdf.

Frank, C. (1999). *Ethnographic eyes: A teacher's guide to classroom observation.* Portsmouth, NH: Heineman.

Frederickson, N., Warren, L., & Turner, J. (2005). "Circle of friends"—an exploration of impact over time. *Educational Psychology in Practice, 21*(3), 197–217.

Freiberg, H. (1996). From tourists to citizens in the classroom. *Educational Leadership, 54,* 32–36.

Freiberg, H., Connell, M., & Lorentz, J. (2001). Effects of consistency management on student mathematics achievement in seven Chapter 1 elementary schools. *Journal of Education for Students Placed at Risk, 6*(3), 249–270.

Freiberg, H., Huzinec, C., & Templeton, S. (2009). Classroom management—a pathway to student achievement: A study of fourteen inner-city elementary schools. *Elementary School Journal, 110*(1), 63–80.

Freiberg, H., & Lamb, S. (2009). Dimensions of person-centered classroom management. *Theory into Practice, 48*(2), 99–105.

Freire, P. (1998). *Pedagogy of freedom.* Lanham, MD: Rowman & Littlefield Publishers.

French, J. R. P., & Raven, B. (1959). Bases of social power. In D. Cartwright (Ed.), *Studies in social power.* Ann Arbor, MI: University of Michigan.

Frey, N., & Fisher, D. (2009). Using common formative assessments as a source of professional development in an urban American elementary school. *Teaching & Teacher Education, 25*(5), 674–680.

Frey, N., Fisher, D., & Moore, K. (2005). *Designing responsive curriculum: Planning lessons that work.* Lanham, MD: Rowman & Littlefield Education.

Frye, B., & Vogt, H. (2010). The causes of underrepresentation of African American children in gifted programs and the need to address this problem through more culturally responsive teaching practices in teacher education programs. *Black History Bulletin, 73*(1), 11–17.

Frymier, A., Wanzer, M., & Wojtaszczyk, A. (2008). Assessing students' perceptions of inappropriate and appropriate teacher humor. *Communication Education, 57*(2), 266–288.

Fuchs, D., & Fuchs, L. S. (2005). Responsiveness-to-interventions: A blueprint for practitioners, policymakers, and parents. *Teaching Exceptional Children, 38*(1), 57–61.

Fuchs, L., Fuchs, D., & Compton, D. (2010). Rethinking response to intervention at middle and high school. *The School Psychology Review, 39*(1), 22–28.

Fuhrman, S., & Lazerson, M. (Eds.). (2005). *The public schools.* Oxford, NY: Oxford University Press.

Gagne, R. (1985). *The conditions of learning* (4th ed.). New York: Holt, Rinehart & Winston.

Gagnon, G. W., Jr., & Collay, M. (2001). *Designing for learning: Six elements in constructivist classrooms.* Thousand Oaks, CA: Corwin Press.

Gardner, H. (1983). *Frames of mind: The theory of multiple intelligences.* New York: Basic Books.

Gardner, H. (1993). *Multiple intelligences: The theory in practice.* New York: Basic books.

Gardner, H. (1999). *Intelligence reframed: Multiple intelligences for the 21st century.* New York: Basic Books.

Gardner, H. (2006). *Multiple intelligences: New horizons.* New York: Basic Books.

Gardner, J. E., Wissick, C. A., Schweder, W., & Canter, L. S. (2003). Enhancing interdisciplinary instruction in general and special education. *Remedial & Special Education, 24*(3), 161–172.

Garrett, J. L. (2006). Educating the whole child. *Kappa Delta Pi Record, 42*(4), 154–155.

Gartner. (7 April 2010). Gartner says more than 50 percent of pcs purchased for users under the age of 15 will have touchscreens by 2015. Gartner Newsroom. Retrieved from http://www.gartner.com/it/page.jsp?id=1336913.

Gatto, J. T. (1992). *Dumbing us down: The hidden curriculum of compulsory schooling.* Philadelphia: New Society Publishers.

Gatto, J. T. (2001). *The underground history of American education: A schoolteacher's intimate investigation into the problem of modern schooling.* New York: Oxford Village Press.

Gaudin, S. (19 November 2009). Intel: Chips in brains will control computers by 2020. *Computerworld.* Retrieved from http://www.computerworld.com/s/article/9141180/Intel_Chips_in_brains_will_control_computers_by_2020.

Gay, G. (2000). *Culturally responsive teaching: Theory, research, & practice.* New York: Teachers College Press.

Gay, G. (2002). Preparing for culturally responsive teaching. *Journal of Teacher Education, 53*(2), 106–116.

Gega, P. C., & Peters, J. M. (2002). *Science in elementary education* (9th ed.). Upper Saddle River, NJ: Merrill/Prentice Hall.

George, C. (2010). Effects of response cards on performance and participation in social studies for middle school students with emotional and behavioral disorders. *Behavioral Disorders, 35* (3), 200–213.

Gersten, R., Baker, S. K., Shanahan, T., Linan-Thompson, S., Collins, P., & Scarcella, R. (2007). Effective literacy and English language instruction for English learners in the elementary grades: A practice guide (NCEE 2007–4011). Washington, DC: National Center for Education Evaluation and Regional Assistance, Institute of Education Sciences, U.S. Department of Education. Retrieved from http://ies.ed.gov/ncee/wwc/publications/practiceguides.

Ginsberg, M. (2007). Lessons at the kitchen table. *Educational Leadership, 64*(6), 56–61.

Glasgow, N. A. (1997). *New curriculum for new times: A guide to student–centered, problem-based learning.* Thousand Oaks, CA: Corwin Press.

Glasser, W. (1986). *Control theory in the classroom.* New York: Harper & Row.

Glickman, C. (2009). Educating for citizenship. *Education Digest, 74*(8), 50–56.

GLSEN. (2009). The experiences of lesbian, gay, bisexual and transgender middle school students (GLSEN Research Brief). New York: Gay, Lesbian and Straight Education Network. Retrieved from http://www.glsen.org/binary-data/GLSEN_ATTACHMENTS/file/000/001/1475-1.pdf.

Goldstein, L. (2005). Becoming a teacher as a hero's journey: Using metaphor in preservice teacher education. *Teacher Education Quarterly, 32*(1), 7–24.

Goleman, D. (1995). *Emotional intelligence.* New York: Bantam Books.

Goleman, D. (1998). *Working with emotional intelligence.* New York: Bantam Books.

Gonzales, M. A. (January 2010). NEA applauds President Obama's focus on increasing math and science teacher corps: National initiative goes hand in hand with NEA work to fill STEM teacher shortage. National Education Association. Retrieved from http://www.nea.org/home/37542.htm.

Gonzalez, N., Andrade, R., Civil, M., & Moll, L. (2001). Bridging funds of distributed knowledge: Creating zones of practices in mathematics. *Journal of Education for Students Placed at Risk (JESPAR), 6*(1–2), 115–132.

Gonzalez, N., Moll, L. C., & Amanti, C. (Eds.). (2005). *Funds of knowledge: Theorizing practices in households, communities, and classrooms.* Malwah, NJ: Lawrence Erlbaum.

Good, T. L., & Brophy, J. E. (1987). *Looking in classrooms* (4th ed.). New York: Harper & Row.

Good, T. L., & Brophy, J. E. (2000). *Looking in classrooms* (8th ed.). New York: Longman.

Goodlad, J. (1984). *A place called school.* New York: McGraw-Hill.

Goodlad, J. I. (1990). The occupation of teaching in schools. In J. I. Goodlad, R. Soder, & K. A. Sirotnik (Eds.), *The moral dimensions of teaching.* San Francisco: Jossey-Bass.

Goodlad, J. I. (1997). *In praise of education.* New York: Teachers College Press.

Goodlad, J. (2004). Fulfilling the public purpose of schooling: Educating the young in support of democracy may be leadership's highest calling. *School Administrator, 61*(5), 14–17.

Gootman, M. E. (2001). *The caring teacher's guide to discipline: Helping young students learn self-control, responsibility, and respect* (2nd ed.). Thousand Oaks, CA: Corwin Press.

Gootman, M. (2008). *The caring teacher's guide to discipline: helping students learn self-control, responsibility, and respect, K-6* (3rd ed.). Thousand Oaks, CA: Corwin Press.

Gordon, T. (1974). *Teacher effectiveness training.* New York: David McKay.

Grant, C. A. (Ed.). (1995). *Educating for diversity: An anthology of multicultural voices.* Boston: Allyn & Bacon.

Grant, C. A., & Sleeter, C. E. (1998). *Turning on learning: Five approaches for multicultural teaching plans for race, class, gender, and disability* (2nd ed.). Upper Saddle River, NJ: Merrill/Prentice Hall.

Green, T. D., & Brown, A. (2002). *Multimedia projects in the classroom: A guide to development and evaluation.* Thousand Oaks, CA: Corwin.

Greene, J. P., & Winters, M. A. (2006). Leaving boys behind: Public high school. Civic Report No. 48. *Manhattan Institute for Policy Research.* Retrieved from http://litigationindustry.com/html/cr_48.htm.

Gregory, A., & Cornell, D. (2009). "Tolerating" adolescent needs: Moving beyond zero tolerance policies in high school. *Theory into Practice, 48*(2), 106–113.

Gregory, A., Skiba, R., & Noguera, P. (2010). The achievement gap and the discipline gap: Two sides of the same coin? *Educational Researcher, 39*(1), 59–68.

Gregory, G. H., & Kuzmich, L. (2004). *Data driven differentiation in the standard-based classroom.* Thousand Oaks, CA: Corwin.

Griffin, P., & Ouelett, M. (2003). From silence to safety and beyond: Historical trends in addressing lesbian, gay, bisexual, transgender issues in K–12 schools. *Equity & Excellence in Education, 36*(2), 106–114.

Griffiths, A., VanDerHeyden, A., Parson, L., & Burns, M. (2006). Practical applications of response-to-intervention research. *Assessment for Effective Intervention, 32*, 50–57.

Gronlund, N. E. (2004). *Writing instructional objectives for teaching and assessment* (7th ed.). Upper Saddle River, NJ: Merrill/Prentice Hall.

Guillaume, A. M. (1991). *Teachers' pedagogy and their perceptions of classroom complexity.* Unpublished doctoral dissertation, University of California.

Guillaume, A. M., Yopp, R., & Twardos, K. (2006). Helping new teachers: Forging family links. Presentation at the State BTSA and Intern Directors' Meeting, Sacramento, CA.

Guillaume, A. M., Yopp, R. H., & Yopp, H. K. (1996). Accessible science. *Journal of Educational Issues for Language Minority Students, 17*, 67–85.

Guillaume, A. M., Yopp, R. H., & Yopp, H. K. (2007). *50 strategies for active teaching: Engaging K–12 learners in the classroom.* Upper Saddle River, NJ: Merrill/Prentice Hall.

Guskey, T. (2002). Computerized gradebooks and the myth of objectivity. *Phi Delta Kappan, 83*, 775–780.

Haar, J., Hall, G., Schoepp, P. & Smith, D. H. (2002). How teachers teach to students with different learning styles. *Clearing House, 75*(3), 142–145.

Hadhazy, A. (14 March 2010). Beyond the mouse: 5 ways we'll interface with future computers *TechNewsDaily.* Retrieved from http://www.technewsdaily.com/beyond-the-mouse-5-ways-well-interface-with-future-computers-0308/6.

Hall, P. S., & Hall, N. D. (2003). *Educating oppositional and defiant children.* Alexandria, VA: Association for Supervision and Curriculum Development.

Hall, T., & Stegila, A. (2003). *Peer mediated instruction and intervention.* Wakefield, MA: National Center on Accessing the General Curriculum. Retrieved from http://www.cast.org/publications/ncac/ncac_peermii.html.

Hamm, M., & Adams, D. (2002). Collaborative inquiry: Working toward shared goals. *Kappa Delta Pi Record, 38*(3), 115–118.

Hargreaves, M., Shorrocks-Taylor, D., Swinnerton, B., Tait, K., & Threlfall, J. (2004). Computer or paper? That is the question: Does the medium in which assessment questions are presented affect children's performance in mathematics? *Educational Research, 46*(1), 29–42.

Harms, W., & DePencier, I. (1996). Dewey creates a new kind of school: Chapter one. *100 Years of Learning at the University of Chicago Laboratory Schools.* Retrieved from http://www.ucls.uchicago.edu/data/files/gallery/HistoryBookDownloadsGallery/chapter1_3.pdf.

Harrison, G., Andrews, J., & Saklofske, D. (2003). Current perspectives on cognitive and learning styles. *Education Canada, 43*(2), 44–47.

Harrow, A. (1969). *A taxonomy of the psychomotor domain: A guide for developing behavioral objectives.* New York: David McKay.

Hattie, J., & Timperley, H. (2007). The power of feedback. *Review of Educational Research, 77*(1), 81–112.

Hebert, E. A. (2001). *The power of portfolios: What children can teach us about learning and assessment.* San Francisco: Jossey-Bass.

Helsing, D. (2007). Regarding uncertainty in teachers and teaching. *Teaching & Teacher Education, 23*, 1317–1333.

Henderson, A. T., Mapp, K. L, Johnson, V. R., & Davies, D. (2007). *Beyond the bake sale: The essential guide to family-school partnerships.* New York: The New Press.

Henderson, M. T., & Mapp, K. L. (2002). *A new wave of evidence: The impact of school, family, and community connections on student achievement.* Austin, TX: National Center for Family & Community Connections with Schools and Southwest Educational Development Laboratory. Retrieved from http://www.sedl.org/connections/resources/evidence.pdf.

Henderson, N., & Milstein, M. (2003). *Resiliency in schools: Making it happen for students and educators.* Thousand Oaks, CA: Corwin Press.

Herman, J. L., Osmundson, E., Ayala, C., Schneider, S. & Timms, S. M. (2006). *The nature and impact of teachers' formative assessment practices.* CSE Report 703. Los Angeles: CRESST/University of California.

Hill, J. D., & Flynn, K. M. (2006). *Classroom instruction that works with English language learners.* Alexandria, VA: Association for Supervision and Curriculum Development.

Hobbs, R. (2006). Non-optimal uses of video in the classroom. *Learning, Media & Technology, 31*(1), 35–50.

Hoffman, M. (1979). Development of moral thought, feeling, and behavior. *American Psychologist, 34*, 958–968.

Hohlfeld, T. N., Ritzhaupt, A. D., Barron, A. E. & Kemker, K. (2008). Examining the digital divide in K-12 public schools: Four-year trends for supporting ICT literacy in Florida. *Computers & Education, 51*(4), 1648–1663.

Holcomb, Lori B. (2009). Results & lessons learned from 1:1 laptop initiatives: A collective review. *TechTrends: Linking Research & Practice to Improve Learning, 53*(6), 49–55.

Holmes, K., Rutledge, S., & Gauthier, L. (2009). Understanding the cultural-linguistic divide in American classrooms: Language learning strategies for a diverse student population. *Reading Horizons, 49*(4), 285–300.

Holt, J. C. (2004). *Instead of education: Ways to help people do things better.* Boulder, CO: Sentient Publications.

Hoover, R. L., & Kindsvatter, R. (1997). *Democratic discipline: Foundation and practice*. Upper Saddle River, NJ: Merrill/Prentice Hall.

Horgan, D. D. (1995). *Achieving gender equity: Strategies for the classroom*. Boston: Allyn & Bacon.

Horn, C. (2010). Response cards: An effective intervention for students with disabilities. *Education and Training in Autism and Developmental Disabilities, 45*(1), 116–123.

Hramiak, A. (2010). Online learning community development with teachers as a means of enhancing initial teacher training. *Technology, Pedagogy and Education, 19*(1), 47–62.

Hu, W. (28 February 2010). In middle school, charting their course to college and beyond. *New York Times*. Retrieved from http://www.nytimes.com/2010/03/01/education/01schools.html?_r=1.

Huebner, T. (2010). What the research says about differentiated instruction. *Educational Leadership, 67*(5), 79–81.

Hunter, M. (1982). *Mastery teaching*. El Segundo, CA: Instructional Dynamics.

Hurt, J. (2003). *Taming the standards: A commonsense approach to higher student achievement, K–12*. Portsmouth, NH: Heinemann.

International Association for the Evaluation of Educational Achievement (IEA). (2007a) Table 1. Average mathematics scores of fourth- and eighth-grade students, by country: 2007. Trends in International Mathematics and Science Study (TIMSS), 2007. Retrieved from http://nces.ed.gov/timss/table07_1.asp.

International Association for the Evaluation of Educational Achievement (IEA). (2007b) Table 3. Average science scores of fourth- and eighth-grade students, by country: 2007 Trends in International Mathematics and Science Study (TIMSS), 2007. Retrieved from http://nces.ed.gov/timss/table07_3.asp.

International Society for Technology Education. (2007). The ISTE National Education Technology Standards (NET·S) and Performance Indicators for Students. Retrieved from http://www.iste.org/Content/NavigationMenu/NETS/ForStudents/2007Standards/NETS_for_Students_2007_Standards.pdf.

Internet World Statistics. (2010). *United States of America Internet Users as of November 2009*. Retrieved from http://www.internetworldstats.com/america.htm#us.

Irvine, J., & Fraser, J. (1998). Warm demanders. *Education Week, 17*(35), 56–57.

Jackson, L. & Panyan, M. V. (2002). *Positive behavioral support in the classroom*. Baltimore: Paul H. Brookes.

Jackson, P. (1986). *The practice of teaching*. New York: Teachers College Press.

Jacob, E. (1999). *Cooperative learning in context: An educational innovation in everyday classrooms*. Albany: State University of New York Press.

Janzen, J. (2008). Teaching English language learners in the content areas. *Review of Educational Research, 78*(4), 1010–1038.

Jehlen, A. (2000). Science texts flunk the test. *NEA Today, 18*(7), 29.

Jennings, P., & Greenberg, M. (2010). The prosocial classroom: Teacher social and emotional competence in relation to student and classroom outcomes. *Review of Educational Research, 80*(1), 491–525.

Jensen, E. (2000). Brain-based learning: A reality check. *Educational Leadership, 57*(7), 76–80.

Jensen, E. (2005). *Teaching with the brain in mind*. Alexandria, VA: Association for Supervision and Curriculum Development.

Jeynes, W. H. (2005). A meta-analysis of the relation of parental involvement to urban elementary school student academic achievement. *Urban Education, 40*, 237–269.

Jeynes, W. (2010). The salience of the subtle aspects of parental involvement and encouraging that involvement: Implications for school-based programs. *Teachers College Record, 112*, 747–774.

Johnson, D. D., Johnson, B., Farenga, S. J., & Ness, D. (2008). *Stop high-stakes testing: An appeal to America's conscience*. Lanham, MD: Rowman & Littlefield Publishers.

Johnson, D. W., & Johnson, R. T. (1999). *Learning together and alone: Cooperative, competitive, and individualistic learning* (5th ed.). Boston: Allyn & Bacon.

Johnson, D. W., & Johnson, R. T. (2004). Implementing the "Teaching Students to Be Peacemakers Program." *Theory into Practice, 43*(1), 68–79.

Johnson, J. Y., & Hirsch, J. (2010). Are interactive whiteboards worth the investment? No. *Learning and Leading with Technology, 37*(8), 6–7. Reprinted electronically at http://www.iste.org/Content/NavigationMenu/Publications/LL/LLIssues/Volume3720092010/JuneJulyNo8/Are_Interactive_Whiteboards_Worth_the_In.htm.

Johnston, P. (2010). Response to intervention (RTI) in reading: An instructional frame for RTI. *Reading Teacher, 63*(7), 602–604.

Jones, F. (1987). *Positive classroom discipline*. New York: McGraw-Hill.

Jones, F. (2000). *Tools for teaching: Discipline, instruction, motivation*. Santa Cruz, CA: Frederic H. Jones & Associates.

Jones, R. (2000). Textbook troubles. *American School Board Journal, 187*(12), 18–21.

Jump$tart Coalition for Personal Financial Literacy. (2007). *National Standards in K–12 personal Finance Education* (3rd ed.). Accessed from http://www.jumpstart.org/national-standards.html.

Kagan, S. (1994). *Cooperative learning*. San Juan Capistrano, CA: Kagan Cooperative Learning.

Kagan, S. (2000). *Silly sports and goofy games*. San Clemente, CA: Kagan Publishing.

Kagan, S. (spring 2001). Kagan structures: Research and rationale. *Kagan Online Magazine*. Retrieved from http://www.kaganonline.com/free_articles/dr_spencer_kagan/research_rationale.php.

Kajder, S. (2006). *Bringing the outside in: Visual ways to engage reluctant readers*. Portland, ME: Stenhouse.

Kaplan, S. (2003). Advocacy as teaching: The teacher as advocate. *Gifted Child Today, 26*(3).

Karathanos, K. (2009). Exploring U.S. mainstream teachers' perspectives on use of the native language in instruction with English language learner students. *International Journal of Bilingual Education and Bilingualism, 12*(6) 615–633.

Kaufman, J. (2007). Induction programs for new and beginning teachers. ECS State Notes. Teaching Quality/Induction Programs for New Teachers. Education Commission of the States. Retrieved from http://www.ecs.org/clearinghouse/76/65/7665.pdf.

Kaufman, J., Jaser, S., Vaughan, E., Reynolds, J., Donato, J., et al. (2010). Patterns in office referral data by grade, race/ethnicity, and gender. *Journal of Positive Behavior Interventions, 12*, 44–54.

Kaiser, B., & Rasminsky, J. (2009). *Challenging behavior in elementary and middle school.* Upper Saddle River, N.J.: Pearson.

Keller, J. B., & Bichelmeyer, B. A. (2004). What happens when accountability meets technology integration. *TechTrends: Linking Research & Practice to Improve Learning, 48*(3), 17–24.

Kelley, M., & Clausen-Grace, N. (2009). Facilitating engagement by differentiating independent reading. *Reading Teacher, 63*, 313–318.

Kennedy, K. M. (2009). Twitter lessons in 140 characters or less. *Education Week 29*(8). Retrieved from http://www.edweek.org/ew/articles/2009/10/21/08twitter_ep.h29.html.

Kennedy, K., Chan, J., Fok, P., & Yu, W. (2008). Forms of assessment and their potential for enhancing learning: Conceptual and cultural issues. *Educational Research for Policy and Practice, 7*(3), 197–207.

Kern, R. (2010). Maximizing an online education. *U.S. News & World Report, 147*(5), 46–47.

Khalsa, S. S. (2007). *Teaching discipline and self-respect: Effective strategies, anecdotes, and lessons for successful classroom management.* Thousand Oaks, CA: Corwin.

Kidder, R. M., & Born, P. L. (1998–1999, December–January). Resolving ethical dilemmas in the classroom. *Educational Leadership, 56*(4), 38–41.

Killeavy, M., & Moloney, A. (2010). Reflection in a social space: Can blogging support reflective practice for beginning teachers? *Teaching and Teacher Education, 26*, 1070–1076.

King, M. L., Jr. (1947). *The purpose of education.* Excerpted in the Papers of Martin Luther King., The Martin Luther King, Jr. Papers Project, Stanford University. Retrieved from http://www.ncat.edu/~univstud/The%20Purpose%20of%20Education.pdf.

Kingston, P. W., Hubbard, R., Lapp, B., Schroeder P., & Wilson, J. (2003). Why education matters. *Sociology of Education, 76*(1), 53–70.

Kleinfeld, J. (1975). Effective teachers of Eskimo and Indian students. *School Review, 83*(2), 301–344.

Kliebard, H. M. (2002). *Changing course: American curriculum reform in the 20th century.* New York: Teachers College Press.

Knowles, L. (2009). Differentiated instruction in reading: Easier than it looks! *School Library Media Activities Monthly, 25*(5), 26–28.

Koepke, M. F., & Harkins, D. A. (2008). Conflict in the classroom: Gender differences in the teacher-child relationship. *Early Education & Development, 19*, 843–864.

Kohlberg, L. (1963). *Essays on moral development.* San Francisco, CA: Harper & Row.

Kohn, A. (1996). *Beyond discipline: From compliance to community.* Alexandria, VA: American Society of Curriculum and Development.

Kohn, A. (1999, September). Constant frustration and occasional violence. *American School Board Journal, 186*(9), 20–24.

Kohn, A. (2001). Fighting the tests. *Phi Delta Kappan, 82*(5), 348–347.

Kohn, A. (2006a). *Beyond discipline: From compliance to community.* 10th anniversary edition. Alexandria, VA: ASCD.

Kohn, A. (2006b). *The Homework Myth: Why Our Kids Get Too Much of a Bad Thing.* Cambridge, MA: Da Capo Press.

Kosciw, J. G., & Diaz, E. M. (2008). *Involved, Invisible, Ignored: The Experiences of Lesbian, Gay, Bisexual and Transgender Parents and Their Children in Our Nation's K–12 Schools.* Washington, DC: GLSEN. Retrieved from http://www.glsen.org/binary-data/GLSEN_ATTACHMENTS/file/000/001/1104-1.pdf.

Kottler, J. A. (1997). *What's really said in the teacher's lounge: Provocative ideas about cultures and classrooms.* Thousand Oaks, CA: Corwin Press.

Kottler, J. A. (2002). *Students who drive you crazy.* Thousand Oaks, CA: Corwin.

Kottler, J. A., & Kottler, E. (2007). *Counseling skills for teachers.* Thousand Oaks, CA: Corwin.

Kounin, J. (1977). *Discipline and group management in classrooms.* New York: Holt, Rinehart & Winston.

Kounin, J. (1983, November). Classrooms: Individuals or behavioral settings? *Monographs in Teaching and Learning.* Bloomington, IN: Indiana University.

Kovalik, S. J., & Olsen, K. D. (2001). *Exceeding expectations: A user's guide to implementing brain research in the classroom* (3rd ed.). Federal Way, WA: Books for Educators.

Kozol, J. (1991). *Savage inequalities: Children in America's schools.* New York: Crown.

Kozol, J. (2000). An unequal education. *School Library Journal, 46*(5), 46–49.

Kozol, J. (2005). The *Shame of the nation: The restoration of apartheid schooling in America.* New York: Crown Publishers.

Krashen, S. (1997). Why bilingual education? ERIC Digest. Retrieved from http://ericae.net/ericdb/ED403101.htm.

Krashen, S. D. (1981). *Second language acquisition and second language learning.* Pergamon Press. Retrieved from http://sdkrashen.com/SL_Acquisition_and_Learning/index.html.

Krathwohl, D., Bloom, B., & Masia, B. (1964). *Taxonomy of educational objectives: The classification of educational goals. Handbook II: Affective domain.* New York: David McKay.

Kulik, C. C., & Kulik, J. A. (1991). Effectiveness of computer-based instruction: An updated analysis. *Computers in Human Behavior, 7*(1–2), 75–94.

Lachat, M. A. (2004). *Standards-based instruction and assessment for English language learners.* Thousand Oaks, CA: Corwin.

Laczko-Kerr, I., & Berliner, D. C. (2002). The effectiveness of "Teach for America" and other under-certified teachers on student academic achievement: A case of harmful public policy. *Education Policy Analysis Archives, 10*(37). Retrieved from http://epaa.asu.edu/epaa/v10n37.

Laczko-Kerr, I., & Berliner, D. C. (2003). In harm's way: How undercertified teachers hurt their students. *Educational Leadership, 60*(8), 34–39.

Ladson-Billings, G. (2003, March). I used to love science . . . and then I went to school: The challenge of school science in urban schools. Plenary Session at the Annual Meeting of the National Association for Research in Science Teaching, Philadelphia, PA.

Ladson-Billings, G. (2006). From the achievement gap to the education debt: Understanding achievement in U.S. schools. *Educational Researcher, 35*(7), 3–12.

Laitsch, D. (2006). Assessment, high stakes, and alternative visions: Appropriate use of the right tools to leverage improvement. Education Policy Research Unit, EPSL-0611-222-EPRU. Retrieved from http://epsl.asu.edu/epru/documents/EPSL-0611-222-EPRU.pdf.

Lambros, A. (2002). *Problem-based learning in K–8 classrooms.* Thousand Oaks, CA: Corwin.

Lane, K. L., Pierson, M. R., & Givner, C. C. (2003). Teacher expectations of student behavior: Which skills do elementary and secondary teachers deem necessary for success in the classroom? *Education and Treatment of Children, 26*, 413–430.

Lau v. Nichols, 1974, Public Law 414, U.S. 563.

Layton, C. A., & Lock, R. H. (2007). 20 ways to. . . use authentic assessment techniques to fulfill the promise of No Child Left Behind. *Intervention in School and Clinic, 42*(3), 169–173.

Lazarus, W., & Mora, F. (2000). *Online content for low-income and underserved Americans: The digital divide's new frontier. A strategic audit of activities and opportunities.* Santa Monica, CA: Children's Partnership. (ERIC Document Reproduction Service No. ED 440 190)

Lee, J. (2006). *Tracking achievement gaps and assessing the impact of NCLB on the gaps: An in depth look into national and state reading and math outcome trends.* Cambridge, MA: The Civil Rights Project at Harvard University.

Lee, S., Wehmeyer, M., Soukup, J., & Palmer, S. (2010). Impact of curriculum modifications on access to the general education curriculum for students with disabilities. *Exceptional Children, 76*(2), 213–233.

Lenski, S. D. (2001). Intertextual connections during discussions about literature. *Reading Psychology, 22*(4), 313–335.

Levy, T. (2000). Lookout point: The character of their content. *Social Education, 64*(5), 2.

Lewis, C., Perry, R., & Hurd, J. (2004). A deeper look at lesson study. *Educational Leadership, 61*(5), 6–11.

Lewis, J., & Kim, E. (2008). A desire to learn: African American children's positive attitudes toward learning within school cultures of low expectations. *Teachers College Record, 110*, 1304–1329.

Lewis, R. (2001). Classroom discipline and student responsibility: The students' view. *Teaching and Teacher Education, 17*, 307–319.

Lewis, R., & Burman, E. (2008). Providing for student voice in classroom management: Teachers' views. *International Journal of Inclusive Education, 12*(2), 151–167.

Lewis, T., Sugai, G. & Colvin, G. (1998). Reducing problem behavior through a school-wide system of effective behavioral support: Investigation of a school-wide social skills training program and contextual interventions. *School Psychology Review, 27*, 446–459.

Lieberman, A., & Mace, D. (2010). Making practice public: Teacher learning in the 21st century. *Journal of Teacher Education, 61*(1), 77–88.

Lieberman, L. J., James, A. R., & Ludwa, N. (2004). The impact of inclusion in general physical education for all students. *Journal of Physical Education Recreation and Dance, 75*(5), 37–42.

Lincoln, M. (2002). *Conflict resolution communication.* Laham, MD: Scarecrow Education.

Lindqvist, P., & Nordänger, U. K. (2006). Who dares to disconnect in the age of uncertainty? Teachers' recesses and "off-the-clock" work. *Teachers & Teaching: Theory and Practice, 12*, 623–637.

Loewen, J. W. (1996). *Lies my teacher told me: Everything your American history textbook got wrong.* New York: Simon & Schuster.

Lopez, O. S. (2010). The digital learning classroom: Improving English language learners' academic success in mathematics and reading using interactive whiteboard technology. *Computers & Education, 54*, 901–915.

Lou, Y., Abrami, P., Spence, J. C., Poulsen, C., Chambers, B., & d'Apolliana, S. (1996). Within-class grouping: A meta-analysis. *Review of Educational Research, 66*, 423–458.

MacGillivray, L, Ardell, A., & Curwen, M. (2010). Supporting the literacy development of children living in homeless shelters. *Reading Teacher, 63*, 384–392.

MacIver, M. A., & Kemper, E. (2002). The impact of direct instruction on elementary students' reading achievement in an urban school district. *Journal of Education for Students Placed at Risk, 7*(2), 197–220.

Mael, F., Alonso, A., Gibson, D., Rogers, K., & Smith, M. (2005). *Single-sex versus coeducational schooling: A systematic review.* U.S. Department of Education. Retrieved from http://www2.ed.gov/rschstat/eval/other/single-sex/single-sex.pdf.

Mager, R. F. (1997). *Preparing instructional objectives. A critical tool in the development of effective instruction* (3rd ed.). Atlanta: Center for Effective Performance.

Maheady, L., Michielli-Pendl, J., Mallette, B., & Harper, G. F. (2002). A collaborative research project to improve the academic performance of a diverse sixth grade science class. *Teacher Education and Special Education, 25*(1), 55–70.

Maloney, R. S. (2002). Virtual fetal pig dissection as an agent of knowledge acquisition and attitudinal change in female high school biology students. Unpublished doctoral dissertation for New Orleans University. Retrieved from http://louisdl.louislibraries.org/cgi-bin/showfile.exe?CISOROOT=/NOD&CISOPTR=29&filename=30.pdf.

Manning, S. (2006). Recognizing gifted students: A practical guide for teachers. *Kappa Delta Pi Record, 42*(2), 64–68.

Manning, S., Stanford, B., & Reeves, S. (2010). Valuing the advanced learner: Differentiating up. *Clearing House, 83*(4), 145–149.

Markow, D., & Martin, S. (2005). *The MetLife survey of the American teacher, 2004–2005: Transitions and the role of supportive relationships.* Retrieved from http://www.eric.ed.gov/PDFS/ED488837.pdf.

Marlowe, B. A., & Page, M. L. (1998). *Creating and sustaining the constructivist classroom.* Thousand Oaks, CA: Corwin Press.

Marshall, M. (2005). Discipline without stress, punishments, or rewards. *Clearing House, 79*(1), 51–54.

Marx A., Fuhrer U., & Hartig T. (1999). Effects of classroom seating arrangements on children's question-asking. *Learning Environments Research, 2,* 249–263.

Marzano, R. J. (2004). *Building background knowledge for academic achievement.* Alexandria, VA: Association of Supervision and Curriculum Development.

Marzano, R. J. (2007). *The Art and Science of Teaching: A Comprehensive Framework for Effective Instruction.* Alexandria, VA: Association for Supervision and Curriculum Development.

Marzano, R.J. (2009). Teaching with interactive whiteboards. *Educational Leadership, 67*(3), 80–82.

Marzano, R. J., Pickering, D. J., & Pollock, J. E. (2001). *Classroom instruction that works: Research-based strategies for increasing student achievement.* Alexandria, VA: Association for Supervision and Curriculum Development.

Matsumura, L. C., & Pascal, J. (2003). *Teachers' assignments and student work: Opening a window on classroom practice.* CSE Report 602. Los Angeles: CRESST/University of California.

McCarthy, M. M., Cambron-McCabe, N. H., & Thomas, S. B. (1998). *Public school law: Teachers' and students' rights* (4th ed.). Boston: Allyn & Bacon.

McDaniel, T. R. (1979). The teacher's ten commandments: School law in the classroom. *Phi Delta Kappan, 60,* 703–708.

McIntosh, R., Vaughn, S., Schumm, J., Haager D., & Lee, O. (1993). Observations of students with learning disabilities in general education classrooms. *Exceptional Children, 60,* 249–261.

McKay, R. R. (2010). Mexican Americans and repatriation. *The Handbook of Texas Online.* Retrieved from http://www.tshaonline.org/handbook/online/articles/MM/pqmyk.html.

McLeskey, J., Rosenberg, M. S., & Westling, D. L. (2010). *Inclusion: Effective Practices for all Students.* Upper Saddle River, NJ: Pearson.

McMahon-Klosterman, K., & Ganschow, L (1979). Using error pattern analysis. *Exceptional Teacher, 1,* 4–5, 9, 11.

Meadows, D. (2008). *Thinking in systems: A primer.* White River Junction, VT: Chelsea Green Publishing.

Medina-Jerez, W., Clark, D. B., & Medina, A. (2007). Science for ELLs: Rethinking our approach. *The Science Teacher, 74*(3), 52–56.

Meeks, G. (2009). Goodbye interactive whiteboard. *School Planning & Management, 48*(12), 13.

Menken, K. (2008). *English learners left behind: Standardized testing as language policy.* Clevedon, England: Multilingual Matters.

Metiri Group. (2006). Technology in schools: What the research says. Cisco Systems. Retrieved from http://www.cisco.com/web/strategy/docs/education/TechnologyinSchoolsReport.pdf.

MetLife. (2010). *The MetLife survey of the American Teacher: Collaborating for student success.* Retrieved from http://www.metlife.com/assets/cao/contributions/foundation/american-teacher/MetLife_Teacher_Survey_2009.pdf.

Metropolitan Center for Urban Education. (2008). *Culturally responsive classroom management strategies.* Retrieved from http://steinhardt.nyu.edu/scmsAdmin/uploads/005/121/Culturally%20Responsive%20Classroom%20Mgmt%20Strat2.pdf.

Metropolitan Life Insurance Company. (2002). *The Metlife survey of the American teacher. Student life: School, home and community.* New York: Author. Retrieved from http://www.metlife.com/Applications/Corporate/WPS/CDA/PageGenerator/0,1674,P2817,00.html.

Meyer, L. M. (2000). Barriers to meaningful instruction for English learners. *Theory into Practice, 39*(4), 228–236.

Middlecamp, C. H., & Nickel, A. L. (2000). Doing science and asking questions: An interactive exercise. *Journal of Chemical Education, 77*(1), 50–52.

Miller, G. A. (1956). The magical number seven, plus or minus two: Some limits on our capacity for processing information. *Psychological Review, 63,* 81–97.

Miller, G. A., Galanter, E., & Pribram, K. H. (1960). *Plans and the structure of behavior.* New York: Holt, Rinehart & Winston.

Miller, G., & Hall, T. (2009). *Classroom management.* Wakefield, MA: National Center on Accessing the General Curriculum. Retrieved from http://www.cast.org/publications/ncac/ncac_classroom.html.

Miller, T., & Spicer, R. (1998). How safe are our schools? *American Journal of Public Health, 88*(3), 413–418.

Mishna, F., Saini, M., & Solomon, S. (2009). Ongoing and online: Children and youth's perceptions of cyber bullying. *Children & Youth Services Review, 31,* 1222–1228.

Modern Language Association. (2010). *The Modern Language Association language map.* Retrieved from http://www.mla.org/map_main.

Mokhtari, K., Thoma, J., & Edwards, P. (2009). How one elementary school uses data to help raise students' reading achievement. *Reading Teacher, 63*(4), 334–337.

Montgomery, W. (2001). Creating culturally responsive, inclusive classrooms. *Teaching Exceptional Children, 33*(4), 4–9.

Moos, D., & Azevedo, R. (2009). Learning with computer-based learning environments: A literature review of computer self-efficacy. *Review of Educational Research, 79*(2), 576–600.

Moriarty, A. (2009). Managing confrontations safely and effectively. *Kappa Delta Pi Record, 45*(2), 78–83.

Morris, R. (2000). *New management handbook: A step-by-step guide for creating a happier, more productive classroom.* San Diego: New Management.

Mosher, R. S. (2001). Silence, listening, teaching, and the space of what is not. *Language Arts, 78,* 366–370.

Muller, C., Riegle-Crumb, C., Schiller, K., Wilkinson, L., & Frank, K. (2010). Race and academic achievement in racially diverse high schools: Opportunity and stratification. *Teachers College Record, 112,* 1038–1063.

Mulvey, J. (2010). The feminization of schools. *The Education Digest, 75*(8), 35–38.

Munro, D., & Stephenson, J. (2009). The effects of response cards on student and teacher behavior during vocabulary instruction. *Journal of Applied Behavior Analysis, 42*(4), 795–800.

Myles, B. S., & Simpson, R. (2001). Understanding the hidden curriculum: An essential social skill for children and youth with Asperger syndrome. *Intervention in School and Clinic, 36*, 279–286.

National Assessment of Education Progress. (2008a). Mathematics scores increase for 17-year-olds whose parents did not finish high school. Retrieved from http://nationsreportcard.gov/ltt_2008/ltt0007.asp?tab_id=tab2&subtab_id=Tab_1#chart.

National Assessment Educational Program. (2008b). Trend in NAEP reading average scores for 17-year-old students, by gender. Retrieved from http://nationsreportcard.gov/ltt_2008/ltt0008.asp?tab_id=tab3&subtab_id=Tab_1#chart.

National Association of School Psychologists. (2002). Social skills: Promoting positive behavior, academic success, and school safety. Retrieved from http://www.naspcenter.org/factsheets/socialskills_fs.html.

National Board for Professional Teaching Standards. (2002). The five propositions of accomplished teaching. Retrieved from http://www.nbpts.org/the_standards/the_five_core_propositio.

National Center for Education Statistics. (2003). Highlights from the TIMMS 1999 video study of eighth-grade mathematics teaching. Retrieved from http://nces.ed.gov/pubs2003/timssvideo/.

National Center for Education Statistics. (2005). Distance Education Courses for Public Elementary and Secondary School Students: 2002–03. Retrieved from http://nces.ed.gov/surveys/frss/publications/2005010/index.asp?sectionid=2.

National Center for Education Statistics. (2008a). Table 5.3. Percentage of children ages 6–18 whose parents had completed high school, by parent and race/ethnicity: 2007. Retrieved from http://nces.ed.gov/pubs2008/nativetrends/tables/table_5_3.asp.

National Center for Education Statistics. (2008b). Table 23. Percentage of elementary and secondary school children whose parents were involved in school activities, by selected child, parent, and school characteristics: 1999, 2003, and 2007. *Digest of Education Statistics*. Retrieved from http://nces.ed.gov/programs/digest/d09/tables/dt09_023.asp.

National Center for Education Statistics. (2009a). NAEP 2008 trends in academic progress. Retrieved from http://nces.ed.gov/nationsreportcard/pdf/main2008/2009479.pdf.

National Center for Education Statistics. (2009b). Table 18. Number and percentage distribution of family households, by family structure and presence of own children under 18: Selected years, 1970 through 2008. Digest of Education Statistics. Retrieved from http://nces.ed.gov/programs/digest/d09/tables/dt09_018.asp.

National Center for Education Statistics. (2009c). Table 42. Number and percentage of public school students eligible for free or reduced-price lunch, by state: 2000–01, 2004–05, 2005–06, and 2006–07. Digest of Education Statistics. Retrieved from http://nces.ed.gov/programs/digest/d08/tables/dt08_042.asp.

National Center for Education Statistics. (2009d). Table 51. Percentage distribution of students 6 to 21 years old served under Individuals with Disabilities Education Act, Part B, by educational environment and type of disability: Selected years, fall 1989 through fall 2007. Retrieved from http://nces.ed.gov/programs/digest/d09/tables/dt09_051.asp.

National Center for Education Statistics. (2009e). Table 54. Percentage of gifted and talented students in public elementary and secondary schools, by sex, race/ethnicity, and state: 2004 and 2006. Retrieved from http://nces.ed.gov/programs/digest/d09/tables/dt09_054.asp.

National Center for Education Statistics. (2009f). Table 2. Percentage distribution of school teachers, by race/ethnicity, school type, and selected school characteristics: 2007–08. Retrieved from http://nces.ed.gov/pubs2009/2009324/tables/sass0708_2009324_t12n_02.asp

National Center for Education Statistics. (2010a). Educational Technology in Public School Districts: Fall 2008, First Look. Retrieved from http://nces.ed.gov/pubs2010/2010003.pdf.

National Center for Education Statistics. (2010b). Indicator 4: Racial/Ethnic Enrollment in Public Schools. *The Condition of Education*. Retrieved from http://nces.ed.gov/programs/coe/2010/section1/indicator04.asp.

National Center for Education Statistics. (2010c). Indicator 25: Poverty Concentration in Public Schools. *The Condition of Education, 2010*. Retrieved from http://nces.ed.gov/programs/coe/2010/section4/indicator25.asp.

National Center for Education Statistics. (2010d). Indicator 6: Children and youth with disabilities. *The Condition of Education*. Retrieved from http://nces.ed.gov/programs/coe/2010/section1/indicator06.asp.

National Center for Education Statistics. (2010e).What are the characteristics of teachers working in high-poverty schools? *The Condition of Education*. Retrieved from http://nces.ed.gov/programs/coe/2010/analysis/section2b.asp.

National Center for Education Statistics. (2010e). TIMSS 2007 Results. Trends in International Mathematics and Science Study (TIMSS). Retrieved from http://nces.ed.gov/timss/faq.asp#9.

National Center for Education Statistics. (2010g). Table A-5-2. Number and percentage of children ages 5–17 who spoke a language other than English at home and who spoke English with difficulty, by selected characteristics: 2008. Retrieved from http://nces.ed.gov/programs/coe/2010/section1/table-lsm-2.asp

National Center for Education Statistics. (2010h). *Trends in International Mathematics and Science Study*. Retrieved from http://nces.ed.gov/timss/index.asp.

National Comprehensive Center for Teacher Quality. (2009). America's opportunity: Teacher effectiveness and equity in K-12 classrooms. Retrieved from http://www.tqsource.org/publications/2009TQBiennial/2009BiennialReport.pdf.

National Research Council. (1996). *National Science Education Standards*. Washington, DC: National Academy Press.

National Research Council. (2000). *How people learn: Brain, mind, experience, and school*. J. Bransford, A. L. Brown, & R. R. Cocking (Eds.). Washington, DC: National Academies Press.

National Research Council. (2008). *Common standards for K-12 education? Considering the evidence*. Washington DC: The National Academies Press.

Nelson, C. (n.d.). A photo essay on the Great Depression. *Modern American Poetry*. http://www.english.illinois.edu/maps/depression/photoessay.htm.

New York Times. (17 December 1911). Taft to lay first light house stone; New settlement headquarters for the blind will be a six-story structure. *New York Times.* Retrieved from http://query.nytimes.com/mem/archive-free/pdf?res=9F0D E2D91E31E233A25754C1A9649D946096D6CF.

New York Times. (30 July 1915). Miss Holt now aids men blinded in war; Opens a "Lighthouse" in France, to be operated on lines of the one in New York. *New York Times.* Retrieved from http://query.nytimes.com/gst/abstract.html? res=9906E0DF133FE233A25753C3A9619C946496D6CF.

Newmann, V. (1994). *Math journals: Tools for authentic assessment.* San Leandro, CA: Teaching Resource Center.

Nieto, S. (1996). *Affirming diversity: The sociopolitical context of multicultural education* (2nd ed.). White Plains, NY: Longman.

Nieto, S. (2004). *Affirming diversity: The sociopolitical context of multicultural education* (4th ed.). Boston: Allyn & Bacon.

Nieto S. (2009). From surviving to thriving. *Educational Leadership, 66*(5), 8–13.

Noble, T. (2004). Integrating the revised Bloom's taxonomy with multiple intelligences: A planning tool for curriculum differentiation. *Teachers College Record, 106,* 193–211.

Noddings, N. (1995). *Philosophy of education.* Boulder, CO: Westview Press.

Noddings, N. (2010). Differentiate, don't standardize. *Education Week, 29*(17), 29–31.

Northwest Regional Educational Laboratory. (2005). Providing feedback. *Focus on effectiveness: Research based strategies.* Retrieved from http://www.netc.org/focus/strategies/prov.php.

Novak, J. D. (1990). Concept maps and Venn diagrams: Two metacognitive tools for science and mathematics education. *Instructional Science, 19,* 29–52.

Novak, J. D. (1991). Clarify with concept maps: A tool for students and teachers alike. *The Science Teacher, 58*(7), 45–49.

Novak, J. D. (1998). *Learning, creating, and using knowledge: Concept maps as facilitative tools in schools and corporations.* Mahwah, NJ: Lawrence Erlbaum.

Novak, J. D., & Gowin, D. B. (1984). *Learning how to learn.* New York: Cambridge University Press.

Nunley, K. F. (2006). *Differentiating the high school classroom.* Thousand Oaks, CA: Corwin Press.

Nystrand, M., Wu, L., Gamoran, A., Zeiser, S., & Long, D. (2003). Questions in time: Investigating the structure and dynamics of unfolding classroom discourse. *Discourse Processes, 35*(2), 135–198.

O'Shea, M. R. (2005). *From standards to success.* Alexandria, VA: Association for Supervision and Curriculum Development.

O'Toole, J., Burton, B. (2005). Acting against conflict and bullying. The Brisbane Dracon Project 1996–2004—emergent findings and outcomes. *Research in Drama Education, 10,* 269–283.

O'Toole, J., & Dunn, J. (2008). Learning in dramatic and virtual worlds: What do students say about complementarity and future directions? *Journal of Aesthetic Education, 42*(4), 89–104.

Oakes, J. (2005). *Keeping track: How schools structure inequality* (2nd ed.). New Haven, CT: Yale University Press.

Oakes, J., & Rogers, J. (2006). *Learning power: Organizing for education and justice.* New York: Teachers College Press.

Obenchain, K. M., & Abernathy, T. V. (2003). 20 ways to build community and empower students. *School Intervention in School and Clinic, 39*(1), 55–60.

Obenchain, K., & Taylor, S. (2005). Behavior management: Making it work in middle and secondary schools. *The Clearing House, 79*(1), 7–11.

OECD. (2007). PISA 2006: Science competencies for tomorrow's world: Executive summary. Retrieved from http://www.pisa.oecd.org/dataoecd/15/13/39725224.pdf.

OECD. (2010). *OECD Programme for International Student Assessment.* Retrieved from http://www.pisa.oecd.org/pages/0,3417,en_32252351_32235907_1_1_1_1_1,00.html.

Ogle, D., & Correa-Kovtun, A. (2010). Supporting English-language learners and struggling readers in content literacy with the "partner reading and content, too" routine. *Reading Teacher, 63*(7), 532–542.

Ohio Department of Education. (2001). Mathematics academic content standards. Retrieved from http://www.ode.state.oh.us/GD/Templates/Pages/ODE/ODEDetail.aspx?page=3&TopicRelationID=1704&ContentID=801&Content=86689.

Olivos, E. M. (2006). *Power parents: A critical perspective of bicultural parent involvement in public schools.* New York: Peter Lang.

Olson, J. (2008). The crucial role of the teacher. Choosing questions and timing to improve your effect on students' learning. *Science and Children, 46*(2), 45–49.

Orozco, C. E. (2002). Del Rio Isd v. Salvatierra. *Handbook of Texas Online.* Retrieved from http://www.tshaonline.org/handbook/online/articles/DD/jrd2.html.

Orsborn, E., Patrick, H., Dixon, R. S., & Moore, D. W. (1995). The effects of reducing teacher questions and increasing pauses on child talk during morning news. *Journal of Behavioral Education, 5,* 347–357.

Osher, D., Bear, G., Sprague, J., & Doyle, W. (2010). How can we improve school discipline? *Educational Researcher, 39*(1), 48–58.

Owen, M. (2004). The myth of the digital native. *Futurelab: Viewpoint—article.* Retrieved from http://www.futurelab.org.uk/resources/publications-reports-articles/web-articles/Web-Article561.

Pai, Y., Adler, S. A., & Shadiow, L. (2006). *Cultural foundations of education* (4th ed). Upper Saddle River, NJ: Merrill/Prentice Hall.

Paige, R., & Witty, E. (2010). *The Black-white achievement gap: Why closing it is the greatest civil rights issue of our time.* New York: Amacom Books.

Painter, D. (2009). Providing differentiated learning experiences through multigenre projects. *Intervention in School and Clinic, 44*(5), 288–293.

Palardy, G. J., & Rumberger, R. W. (2008). Teacher effectiveness in first grade: The importance of background qualifications, attitudes, and instructional practices for student learning. *Educational Evaluation and Policy Analysis 30,* 111–140.

Palumbo, A., & Sanacore, J. (2007). Classroom management: Help for the beginning secondary school teacher. *Clearing House, 81*(2), 67–70.

Pappas, C. C., Kiefer, B. Z., & Levstik, L. S. (2006). *An integrated language perspective in the elementary schools: An action approach* (4th ed.). Boston: Allyn and Bacon.

Parish, T. B., et al. (2006). *Effects of the implementation of Proposition 227 on the education of English learners, K–12: Findings from a five-year evaluation* (Final report for AB56 and AB 1116, submitted to the California Department of Education). Palo Alto, CA: American Institutes for Research. Summary retrieved from http://www.wested.org/online_pubs/CC-06-06.pdf.

Partnership for 21st Century Skills. (2004). Learning for the 21st century: A report and mile guide for 21st century skills. Retrieved from http://www.21stcenturyskills.org/downloads/P21_Report.pdf.

Partnership for 21st Century Skills. (2009). *P21 framework definitions.* Retrieved from http://www.p21.org/documents/P21_Framework_Definitions.pdf.

Pashler, H., McDaniel, M., Rohrer, D., & Bjork, R. (2008). Learning styles: Concepts and evidence. *Psychological Science in the Public Interest, 9*(3), 105–119.

Pawan, F. (2008). Content-area teachers and scaffolded instruction for English language learners. *Teaching & Teacher Education, 24*(6), 1450–1462.

Pay Scale. (1010). Salary Survey for Country: United States. Retrieved from http://www.payscale.com/research/US/Country=United_States/Salary/by_Gender.

Payne, R. (2008). Nine powerful practices. *Educational Leadership, 65*(7), 48–52.

Pellegrini, A. D., & Bohn, C. M. (2005). The role of recess in children's cognitive performance and school adjustment. *Educational Researcher, 34*(1), 13–19.

Perry, L, & McConney, A. (2010). Does the SES of the school matter? An examination of socioeconomic status and student achievement using PISA 2003. *Teachers College Record, 112*, 1137–1162.

Peterson, M. (2010). Computerized games and simulations in computer-assisted language learning: A meta-analysis of research. *Simulation & Gaming, 41*, 72–93.

Phelps, R. P. (Ed.). (2005). *Defending standardized testing.* Malwah, NJ: Lawrence Erlbaum Associates.

Piaget, J. (1952). *Origins of intelligence in children.* New York: W. W. Norton.

Pisha, B., & Coyne, P. (2001). Smart from the start: The promise of universal design for learning. *Remedial and Special Education, 22*, 197–203.

Pope, N., Green, S., Johnson, R., & Mitchell, M. (2009). Examining teacher ethical dilemmas in classroom assessment. *Teaching & Teacher Education, 25*(5), 778–782.

Popham, W. J. (2008). *Transformative assessment.* Alexandria, VA: Association for Supervision and Curriculum Development.

Popham, W. J., & Baker, E. (1970). *Establishing instructional goals.* Upper Saddle River, NJ: Prentice Hall.

Powell, J. V., Aeby, V. G., Jr., & Carpenter-Aeby, T. (2003). A comparison of student outcomes with and without teacher facilitated computer-based instruction. *Computers & Education, 40*(2), 183–191.

Powers, J. M. (2004). High-stakes accountability and equity: Using evidence from California's Public Schools Accountability Act to address the issues in *Williams v. State of California. American Educational Research Journal, 41*, 763–795.

Prakash, M. S., & Waks, L. J. (1985). Four conceptions of excellence. *Teachers College Record, 87*(1), 79–101.

Predavec, M. (2001). Evaluation of E-Rat, a computer-based rat dissection, in terms of student learning outcomes. *Journal of Biological Education, 35*(2) 75–80.

Prensky, M. (2001). Digital natives, digital immigrants. *On the Horizon, 9*(5). Retrieved from http://www.marcprensky.com/writing/Prensky%20-%20Digital%20Natives,%20Digital%20Immigrants%20-%20Part1.pdf.

Prensky, M. (2005–2006). Listen to the natives. *Educational Leadership, 63*(4), 8–13.

Prison Pay Scale Initiative. (2005). Gender is an important "filter" on who goes to prison. Retrieved from http://www.prisonpolicy.org/graphs/genderinc.html.

Project WILD. (2001). *Project WILD: K–12 curriculum & activity guide.* Houston, TX: Council for Environmental Education.

Pryor, C. R. (2004). Creating a democratic classroom: Three themes for citizen teacher reflection. *Kappa Delta Pi Record, 40*(2), 78–82.

Putman, S., & Kingsley, T. (2009). The atoms family: Using podcasts to enhance the development of science vocabulary. *Reading Teacher, 63*(2), 100–108.

Quiocho, A. M. L., & Daoud, A. M. (2006). Dispelling myths about Latino parent participation in schools. *The Educational Forum, 70*, 255–267.

Rabinowitz, S., & Brandt, T. (2001). Computer-based assessment: Can it deliver on its promise? WestED Knowledge Brief. Retrieved from http://www.wested.org/online_pubs/kn-01-05.pdf.

Raider-Roth, N., Albert, N., Bircann-Barkey, I., Gidseg, E., & Murray, T. (2008). Teaching boys: A relational puzzle. *Teachers College Record, 110*, 443–481.

Randolph, J. (2007). Meta-analysis of the research on response cards: Effects on test achievement, quiz achievement, participation, and off-task behavior. *Journal of Positive Behavior Interventions, 9*(2), 113–128.

Ravitch, D. (2003a). Thin gruel: How the language police drain the life and content from our texts. *American Educator, 27*(2), 6–19.

Ravitch, D. (2003b). Leaving reality out: How textbooks (don't) teach about tyranny. *American Educator, 27*(3), 32–38.

Reed, D., Rueben, K., & Barbour, E. (2006). Retention of new teachers in California. Public Policy Institute of California. Retrieved from http://www.ppic.org/content/pubs/rb/RB_206DRRB.pdf.

Reeves, D. B. (2003). High performance in high poverty schools: 90/90/90 and beyond. Center for Performance Assessment. Retrieved from http://www.sabine.k12.la.us/online/leadershipacademy/high%20performance%2090%2090%2090%20and%20beyond.pdf.

Reichert, M., & Hawley, R. (2010). Reaching boys: An international study of effective teaching practices. *Phi Delta Kappan, 91*(4), 35–39.

Reis, S. M., & Renzulli, J. S. (1995). Curriculum compacting: A systematic procedure for modifying the curriculum for above average ability students. *Gifted Education Communicator, 26*(2). Retrieved from http://www.gifted.uconn.edu/sem/semart08.html.

Resnick, L. (2010). Nested learning systems for the thinking curriculum. *Educational Researcher, 39*(3), 183–197.

Rettig, M. D., McCullough, L. L., Santos, K. E., & Watson, C. R. (2004). *From rigorous standards to student achievement: A practical process.* Larchmont, NY: Eye on Education.

Reynolds, A. (1992). What is competent beginning teaching? A review of the literature. *Review of Educational Research, 62*(1), 1–35.

Ribble, M. S., Bailey, G. D., & Ross, T. W. (2004). Digital citizenship: Addressing appropriate technology behavior. *Learning and Leading with Technology, 32*(1), 6–9, 11.

Riccomini, P. (2005). Identification and remediation of systematic error patterns in subtraction. *Learning Disability Quarterly, 28*(3), 233–242.

Richardson, V., Ed. (2001). *Handbook of research on teaching* (4th ed.). Washington, DC: American Educational Research Association.

Rice, S. (2009). Education for toleration in an era of zero tolerance school policies: A Deweyan analysis. *Educational Studies, 45*, 556–571.

Riley, P., Lewis, R., & Brew, C. (2010). Why did you do that? Teachers explain the use of legal aggression in the classroom. *Teaching and Teacher Education, 26*, 957–964.

Rimm-Kaufman, S. E., & Sawyer, B. E. (2004). Primary-grade teachers' self-efficacy beliefs, attitudes toward teaching, and discipline and teaching practice priorities in relation to the "responsive classroom" approach. *The Elementary School Journal, 104*, 321–341.

Roberts, P. L., & Kellough, R. D. (2008). *A guide for developing interdisciplinary thematic units* (4th ed.). Upper Saddle River, NJ: Merrill/Prentice Hall.

Roberts, S. M., & Pruitt, E. Z. (2003). *Schools as professional learning communities.* Thousand Oaks, CA: Corwin.

Rock, M., Gregg, M., Ellis, E., & Gable, R. (2008). REACH: A framework for differentiating classroom instruction. *Preventing School Failure, 52*(2), 31–47.

Rodriguez-Brown, F. V. (2009). *Home-school connection: Lessons learned in a culturally and linguistically diverse community.* New York: Routledge.

Rogers, B. (Ed.). (2004). *How to manage children's challenging behaviour.* London: Paul Chapman.

Rogers, M. (13 December 2006). *What will replace the laptop?* MSNBC Interactive. Retrieved from http://www.msnbc.msn.com/id/16042808/

Rogers, S., Ludington, J., & Graham, S. (1998). *Motivation and learning.* Evergreen, CO: Peak Learning Systems.

Roller, C. M. (n.d.). *No Child Left Behind: A survey of its impact on IRA members.* Retrieved from http://www.reading.org/Libraries/Reports_and_Standards/NCLB_survey_022005.sflb.ashx.

Rollins, K., Mursky, C., Shah-Coltrane, S., & Johnsen, S. (2009). RTI models for gifted children. *Gifted Child Today, 32*(3), 20–30.

Ronis, D. L. (2008). *Clustering standards in integrated units* (2nd ed.). Thousand Oaks, CA: Corwin Press.

Rose, L. C. (2004). No Child Left Behind: The mathematics of guaranteed failure. *Educational Horizons, 82*(2), 121–130.

Ross, D., Bondy, E., Gallingane, C., & Hambacher, E. (2008). Promoting academic engagement through insistence: Being a warm demander. *Childhood Education, 84*(3), 142–146.

Rowe, M. (1986). Wait-time: Slowing down may be a way of speeding up. *Journal of Teacher Education, 37*(1), 43–50.

Rudolph, A. M. (2006). *Techniques in classroom management: A resource for secondary teachers.* Lanham, MD: Rowman & Littlefield Education.

Rush, S. E. (2006). *Huck Finn's "hidden" lessons: Teaching and learning across the color line.* Lanham, MD: Rowman & Littlefield.

Russell, H. R. (1990). *Ten-minute field trips* (2nd ed.). Washington, DC: National Science Teachers Association.

Ryan, A. L., Halsey, H. N., & Matthews, W. J. (2003). Using functional assessment to promote desirable student behavior in schools. *Teaching Exceptional Children, 35*(4), 8–15.

Sadler, J. E. (1966). *J. A. Comenius and the concept of universal education.* New York: Barnes & Noble.

Safe Schools Coalition of Washington. (1999). *Eighty-three thousand youth: Selected findings of eight population-based studies as they pertain to anti-gay harassment and the safety and well-being of sexual minority students.* Retrieved from http://www.safeschoolscoalition.org/83000youth.pdf.

Salend, S. (2009). Technology-based classroom assessments: Alternatives to testing. *Teaching Exceptional Children, 41*(6), 48–58.

Sandomierski, T., Kincaid, D., & Algozzine, B. (2007). *Response to intervention and positive behavior support: brothers from different mothers or sisters from different misters?* Retrieved from http://www.rti4success.org/images/stories/pdfs/rti_and_positive_behavior_support.pdf

Sangster, M. (2007). Reflecting on pace. *MT: Mathematics Teaching, 204*, 34–36.

Savage, T. V. (1999). *Teaching self-control through management and discipline* (2nd ed.). Boston: Allyn & Bacon.

Savage, T. V., & Armstrong, D. (2000). *Effective teaching in elementary social studies* (4th ed.). Upper Saddle River, NJ: Merrill/Prentice Hall.

Sawchuk, S. (28 June 2010). Teacher induction found to raise student scores. *EdWeek.* Retrieved from http://www.edweek.org/login.html?source=http://www.edweek.org/ew/articles/2010/06/28/36induction.h29.html&destination=http://www.edweek.org/ew/articles/2010/06/28/36induction.h29.html&levelId=2100.

Schifini, A. (1994). Language, literacy, and content instruction: Strategies for teachers. In K. Spangenberg-Urbschat & R. Pritchard (Eds.), *Kids come in all languages: Reading instruction for ESL students* (pp. 158–179). Newark, DE: International Reading Association.

Schmidt, W. H., & Cogan, L. S. (2009). The myth of equal content. *Educational Leadership, 67*(3), 44–47.

Schmidt, W. H., Wang, H. C., & McKnight, C. C. (2005). Curriculum coherence: An examination of U.S. mathematics and science content standards from an international perspective. *Journal of Curriculum Studies, 37*, 525–559.

Schneider, M. F. (1997). *25 of the best parenting techniques ever.* New York: St. Martin's Press.

Schofield, J. W. (2005). The colorblind perspective in school: Causes and consequence. In J. A. Banks & C. A. M. Banks (Eds.), *Multicultural education: Issues and perspectives* (5th ed., pp. 265–288). Hoboken, NJ: Wiley Jossey-Bass.

Schultz, K. (2003). *Listening: A framework for teaching across differences.* New York: Teachers College Press.

Schultz-Zander, R., Buchter, A., & Dalmer, R. (2002). The role of ICT as a promoter of students' cooperation. *Journal of Computer Assisted Learning, 18*, 438–448.

Schussler, D. (2009). Beyond content: How teachers manage classrooms to facilitate intellectual engagement for disengaged students. *Theory into Practice, 48*(2), 114–121.

Scott, C. (2010). The enduring appeal of "learning styles." *Australian Journal of Education, 54*(1), 5–17.

Selfridge, J. (2004). The Resolving Conflict Creatively Program: How we know it works. *Theory into Practice, 43*(1), 59–67.

Shanklin, N. (2009). Being proactive about your professional learning: What's the payoff? *Voices from the Middle, 16*(4), 45–47.

Shaywitz, S. E., Holahan, J. M., Freudenheim, D. A., Fletcher, J. M., Makuch, R. W., & Shaywitz, B. A. (2001). Heterogeneity within the gifted: Higher IQ boys exhibit behaviors resembling boys with learning disabilities. *Gifted Child Quarterly, 45*, 16–23.

Sheehey, P., Ornelles, C., & Noonan, M. (2009). Biculturalization: Developing culturally responsive approaches to family participation. *Intervention in School & Clinic, 45*(2), 132–139.

Sheldon, S. B., & Epstein, J. L. (2005). Involvement counts: Family and community partnerships and mathematics achievement. *Journal of Educational Research, 98*(4), 196–206.

Shukla-Mehta, S. M., & Albin, R. W. (2003). Twelve practical strategies to prevent behavioral escalation in classroom settings. *Preventing School Failure, 47*(4), 156–161.

Shulman, L. S. (1983). Autonomy and obligation: The remote control of teaching. In *Handbook of teaching and policy*, ed. Lee S. Shulman and Gary Sykes. New York: Longman.

Silberman, M. (1996). *Active learning: 101 strategies to teach any subject*. Boston: Allyn & Bacon.

Simonsen, B., Fairbanks, S., Briesch, A., Myers, D., & Sugai, G. (2008). Evidence-based practices in classroom management: Considerations for research to practice. *Education & Treatment of Children, 31*, 351–380.

Skinner, B. F. (1971). *Beyond freedom and dignity*. New York: Knopf.

Slavin, R. E. (1995). *Cooperative learning* (2nd ed.). Boston: Allyn & Bacon.

Slavin, R. E. (1997). *Educational psychology: Theory and practice* (5th ed.). Boston: Allyn & Bacon.

Slavin, R. E. (2003). A reader's guide to scientifically based research. *Educational Leadership, 60*(5), 12–16.

Slavin-Baden, M., & Major, C. H. (2004). *Foundations of problem-based learning*. New York: Society for Research into Higher Education & Open University Press.

Smith, F., Hardman, F., Wall, K., & Mroz, M. (2004). Interactive whole class teaching in the National Literacy and Numercy Strategies. *British Educational Research Journal, 30*, 395–411.

Smutny, J. F. (2003). *Gifted education: Promising practices*. Bloomington, IN: Phi Delta Kappa Educational Foundation.

Solomon, Y., Warrin, J., & Lewis, C. (2002). Helping with homework? Homework as a site of tension for parents and teenagers. *British Education Research Journal, 28*, 603–622.

Soltis, J. F. (1986). Teaching professional ethics. *Journal of Teacher Education, 37*(3), 2–4.

Spencer, B. H., & Guillaume, A. M. (2009). *35 Strategies for Developing Content Area Vocabulary*. Boston, MA: Allyn & Bacon.

Spencer, B., & Guillaume, A. M. (2006). Integrating curriculum through the learning cycle: Content-based reading and vocabulary instruction. *The Reading Teacher, 60*, 206–219.

St. John, E. P., Manset, G., Chung, C. G., & Worthington, K. (2001). *Assessing the rationales for educational reforms: A test of the professional development, comprehensive reform, and direct instruction hypotheses*. Policy Research Report. Bloomington: Indiana University. Education Policy Center. (ERIC Document Reproduction Service No. ED458 641)

Stahl, R. J. (1994). Using "Think-Time" and "Wait-Time" Skillfully in the Classroom. ERIC Digest ED370885 1994-05-00. ERIC Clearinghouse for Social Studies/Social Science Education. Bloomington, IN.

Starnes, B. (2010). On carrots and sticks, joyful teaching, and coming to the light. *Phi Delta Kappan, 91*(8), 74–75.

Steelman, J. D. (2005). Multimedia makes its mark. *Learning & Leading with Technology, 33*(1), 16–19.

Stefanakis, E. H. (2002). *Multiple intelligences and portfolios: A window into the learner's mind*. Portsmouth, NH: Heinemann.

Sternberg, R. J. (1994). Answering questions and questioning answers: Guiding children to intellectual excellence. *Phi Delta Kappan, 76*(2), 136–138.

Sternberg, R. J. (1997a). Successful intelligence: A broader view of who's smart in school and in life. *International Schools Journal, 17*(1), 19–31.

Sternberg, R. J. (1997b). What does it mean to be smart? *Educational Leadership, 54*(6), 20–24.

Stevens, D. D., & Levi, A. J. (2005). *Introduction to rubrics*. Sterling, VA: Sylus.

Stichter, J., Lewis, T., Whittaker, T., Richter, M., & Johnson, N., et al. (2009). Assessing teacher use of opportunities to respond and effective classroom management strategies: Comparisons among high- and low-risk elementary schools. *Journal of Positive Behavior Interventions, 11*(2), 68–81.

Stiggins, R. (2001). *Student-involved classroom assessment* (3rd ed.). Upper Saddle River, NJ: Merrill/Prentice Hall.

Stiggins, R. (2009). Assessment for learning in upper elementary grades. *Phi Delta Kappan, 90*(6), 419–421.

Stronge, J. H. (2002). *Qualities of effective teachers*. Alexandria, VA: ASCD.

Suchman, J. R. (1962). *The elementary school training program in scientific inquiry*. Report to the U.S. Office of Education, Project Title VII, Project 216. Urbana, IL: University of Illinois.

Suicide.org. (n.d). Suicide statistics. Retrieved from http://www.suicide.org/suicide-statistics.html.

Sun, Y. (2010). Developing reflective cyber communities in the blogosphere: A case study in Taiwan higher education. *Teaching in Higher Education, 15*(4), 369–381.

Sunkin, A. (21 June 2010). Schools react to textbook trends. More districts look for online components. *Times-Herald Record*. Retrieved from http://www.recordonline.com/apps/pbcs.dll/article?AID=/20100621/NEWS/6210319.

Sutton, R., Mudrey-Camino, R., & Knight, C. (2009). Teachers' emotion regulation and classroom management. *Theory into Practice, 48*(2), 130–137.

Svihla, V., Vye, N., Brown, M., Phillips, R., Gawel, D., & Bransford, J. (2009). Interactive learning assessments for the 21st century. *Education Canada, 49*(3), 44–47.

Swain, M. (1985). Communicative competence: Some roles of comprehensible input and comprehensible output in its development. In S. Gass & C. Madden (Eds.), *Input in second language acquisition* (pp. 235–253). Rowley, MA: Newbury House.

Swanson, H. L. (2001). Searching for the best model for instructing students with learning disabilities. *Focus on Exceptional Children, 34*(2), 1–15.

Swanson, H. L., & Sachse-Lee, C. (2000, March–April). A meta-analysis of single-subject-design intervention research for students with LD. *Journal of Learning Disabilities, 33*(2), 114–136.

Swearer, S., Espelage, D., Vaillancourt, T., & Hymel, S. (2010). What can be done about school bullying? Linking research to educational practice. *Educational Researcher, 39*(1), 38–47.

Taba, H. (1967). *Teacher's handbook for elementary social studies*. Reading, MA: Addison-Wesley.

Tanaka, J., Wolf, J., Klaiman, C., Koenig, K., & Cockburn, J., et al. (2010). Using computerized games to teach face recognition skills to children with autism spectrum disorder: The let's face it! program. *Journal of Child Psychology & Psychiatry, 51*(8), 944–952.

Tannenbaum, R., & Rosenfeld, M. (1997). *Evaluation criteria of teaching practices: A study of job-relatedness and training needs assessment*. Princeton, NJ: Educational Testing Service. Retrieved from http://www.ets.org/Media/Research/pdf/RR-97-23.pdf.

Tardif, C., Laine, F., Rodriguez, M., & Gepner, B. (2007). Slowing down presentation of facial movements and vocal sounds enhances facial expression recognition and induces facial-vocal imitation in children with autism. *Journal of Autism & Developmental Disorders, 37*(8), 1469–1484.

Tashlik, P. (2010). Changing the national conversation on assessment. *Phi Delta Kappan, 91*(6), 55–59.

Thomas, W. P., & Collier, V. P. (2001). A national study of school effectiveness for language minority students' long-term academic achievement. Center for Research on Education, Diversity and Excellence. Retrieved from http://crede.berkeley.edu/research/llaa/1.1_final.html.

Thomson, P., & Gunter, H. (2008). Researching bullying with students: A lens on everyday life in an 'innovative school.' *International Journal of Inclusive Education, 12*(2), 185–200.

Thorson, S. A. (2003). *Listening to students: Reflections on secondary school classroom management*. Boston: Allyn & Bacon.

Thousand, J. S., Villa, R. A., & Nevin, A. I. (2007). *Differentiating Instruction: Collaborative planning and teaching for universally designed learning*. Thousand Oaks, CA: Corwin Press.

Tobin, K. (1986). Effects of teacher wait time on discourse characteristics in mathematics and language arts classes. *American Educational Research Journal, 23*(2), 191–200.

Tobin, T., Sugai, G., & Colvin, G. (2000). Using discipline referrals to make decisions. *NASSP Bulletin, 84*(616), 106–117.

Tomlinson, C. A. (2001). *How to differentiate instruction in mixed-ability classrooms* (2nd ed.). Alexandria, VA: Association for Supervision and Curriculum Development.

Tomlinson, C. A., Kaplan, S. N., Renzulli, J. S., Purcell, J., Leppien, J., & Burns, D. (2002). *The parallel curriculum: A design to develop high potential and challenge high-ability learners*. Thousand Oaks, CA: Corwin.

Torff, B., & Tirotta, R. (2010). Interactive whiteboards produce small gains in elementary students' self-reported motivation in mathematics. *Computers & Education, 54*, 379–383.

Tse, J., Strulovitch, J., Tagalakis, V., Meng, L., & Fombonne, E. (2007). Social skills training for adolescents with Asperger syndrome and high-functioning autism. *Journal of Autism & Developmental Disorders, 37*(10), 1960–1968.

Tullis, P. (2010). An 'A' in abstractions. *T H E Journal, 37*(3), 26–32.

Turner, J. C., Meyer, D. K., Midgley, C., & Patrick, H. (2003). Teacher discourse and sixth-graders' reported affect and achievement behaviors in two high-mastery/high-performance mathematics classrooms. *The Elementary School Journal, 103*, 357–382.

Tyack, D. (2003). *Seeking common ground: Public schools in a diverse society*. Cambridge: Harvard University.

Tyack, D., & Cuban, L. (1995). *Tinkering toward utopia: A century of public school reform*. Cambridge: Harvard University.

Tyre, P. (2008). *The trouble with boys*. New York: Crown Publishers.

Tyson, K. (2003). Notes from the back of the room: Problems and paradoxes in the schooling of young black students. *Sociology of Education, 76*, 326–343.

U.S. Census Bureau. (2008). Percent of people 5 years and over who speak a language other than English at home. Retrieved from http://factfinder.census.gov/servlet/GCTTable?_bm=y&-geo_id=01000US&-_box_head_nbr=GCT1601&-ds_name=ACS_2008_3YR_G00_&-_lang=en&-mt_name=ACS_2008_3YR_G00_GCT1601_US9T&-format=US-9T.

U.S. Census Bureau. (2009a). *Internet use in the United States: October 2009. Table 1. Reported Internet usage for households, by selected householder characteristics: 2009*. Retrieved from http://www.census.gov/population/www/socdemo/computer/2009.html.

U.S. Census Bureau. (2009b). Income, poverty and health insurance in the United States: 2009 – Highlights. Retrieved from http://www.census.gov/hhes/www/poverty/data/incpovhlth/2009/highlights.html.

U.S. Census Bureau. (2010). School enrollment—Social and economic characteristics of students: October 2008. Retrieved from http://www.census.gov/population/www/socdemo/school/cps2008.html.

U.S. Department of Education, National Center for Education Statistics. (2006a). Internet access in U.S. public schools and classrooms: 1994–2005 (NCES 2007-020). Retrieved http://www.nces.ed.gov/fastfacts/display.asp?id=46.

U.S. Department of Education, National Center for Education Statistics. (2006b). *The condition of education: 2006. Ratings of school violence and crime*. NCES 2006-071. Washington, DC: http://www.eric.ed.gov/PDFS/ED491909.pdf.

U.S. Department of Education, National Center for Education Statistics. Indicators of School Crime and Safety. (2006c) Indicator 11: Bullying at school. Retrieved from http://nces.ed.gov/programs/crimeindicators/crimeindicators2006/ind_11.asp.

U.S. Department of Education. (2003). Meeting the highly qualified teachers challenge: The secretary's second annual report of teacher quality. Retrieved from http://www.ed.gov/about/reports/annual/teachprep/2003title-ii-report.pdf.

U.S. Department of Education. (2010). *Blueprint for reform. The reauthorization of the Elementary and Secondary Education Act*. Retrieved from http://www2.ed.gov/policy/elsec/leg/blueprint/blueprint.pdf.

Underwood, J. (2004). Legal protections gay students must receive. *Education Digest: Essential Readings Condensed for Quick Review*, *70*(4), 16–26.

Underwood, J., & Webb, L. D. (2006). *School law for teachers*. Upper Saddle River, NJ: Merrill/Prentice Hall.

Vacca, J. J. (2007). Incorporating interests and structure to improve participation of a child with autism in a standardized assessment: A case study analysis. *Focus on Autism and Other Developmental Disabilities*, *22*(1), 51–59.

Valencia, R., & Block, M. S. (2002). "Mexican Americans don't value education!": The basics of the myth, mythmaking, and debunking. *Journal of Latinos and Education*, *1*(2), 81–103.

Valli, L., Croninger, R. G., Chambliss, M. J., Graeber, A. O., & Buese, D. (2008). *Test driven: High-stakes accountability in elementary schools*. New York, NY: Teachers College Press.

van Tartwijk, J., den Brok, P., Veldman, I., & Wubbels, T. (2009). Teachers' practical knowledge about classroom management in multicultural classrooms. *Teaching & Teacher Education*, *25*, 453–460.

van Zee, E. H., Iwasyk, M., Kurose, A., Simpson, D., & Wild, J. (2001). Student and teacher questioning during conversations about science. *Journal of Research in Science Teaching*, *38*(2), 59–90.

Vandewater, E. A., Rideout, V. J., Wartella, E. A., Huang, X., Lee, J. H., & Shim, M. (2007). Digital childhood: Electronic media and technology use among infants, toddlers, and preschoolers. *Pediatrics*, *119*(5), 1006–1015. Retrieved from http://pediatrics.aappublications.org/cgi/content/full/119/5/e1006.

Vaughn, S., Cirino, P., Wanzek, J., Wexler, J., Fletcher, J., et al. (2010). Response to intervention for middle school students with reading difficulties: Effects of a primary and secondary intervention. *The School Psychology Review V*, *39*(1), 3–21.

Vaughn, S., Hughes, M. T., Moody, S. W., & Elbaum, B. (2001). Instructional grouping for reading for students with LD: Implications for practice. *Intervention in School and Clinic*, *36*(3), 131–137.

Vincent, T. (2009). *Podcasting for teachers and students*. Retrieved from http://learninginhand.com/storage/podcasting_images/Podcasting_Booklet.pdf

VOYCE. (2008). *Student-led solutions to the nation's dropout crisis*. Retrieved from http://voyceproject.org/sites/default/files/voycereport111308.pdf.

Vygotsky, L. S. (1978). *Mind in society: The development of higher psychological processes*. M. Cole, V. John-Steiner, S. Scribner, & E. Souberman (Eds.). Cambridge, MA: Harvard University Press.

Wahl, L., & Duffield, J. (2005). Using flexible technology to meet the needs of diverse learners. WestEd Knowledge Brief. Retrieved from http://www.wested.org/online_pubs/kn-05-01.pdf.

Wakefield, J. F. (2006, April). Textbook usage in the United States: The case of U.S. history. Paper presented at the International Seminar on Textbooks, Santiago, Chile. Retrieved from http://www.eric.ed.gov/PDFS/ED491579.pdf.

Walker, J. (2008). Looking at teacher practices through the lens of parenting style. *Journal of Experimental Education*, *76*(2), 218–240.

Walker, J. (2009). Authoritative classroom management: How control and nurturance work together. *Theory into Practice*, *48*(2), 122–129.

Walker-Dalhouse, D., Risko, V., Esworthy, C., Grasley, E., & Kaisler, G., et al. (2009). Crossing boundaries and initiating conversations about RTI: Understanding and applying differentiated classroom instruction. *Reading Teacher*, *63*(1), 84–87.

Walsch, J. A., & Sattes, B. D. (2005). *Quality questioning: Research-based practices to engage every learner*. Thousand Oaks, CA: Corwin.

Ware, F. (2006). Warm demander pedagogy: Culturally responsive teaching that supports a culture of achievement for African American students. *Urban Education*, *41*, 427–456.

Warschauer, M., Knobel, M., & Stone, L. (2004). Technology and equity in schooling: Deconstructing the digital divide. *Educational Policy*, *18*, 562–588.

Watanabe, M. (2008). Tracking in the era of high-stakes state accountability reform: Case studies of classroom instruction in North Carolina. *Teachers College Record*, *110*, 489–534.

Waters Foundation (2007). Habits of a systems thinker. Systems Thinking in Schools. Retrieved from http://www.watersfoundation.org/index.cfm?fuseaction=search.habits

Webb, P. T. (2002). Teacher power: The exercise of professional autonomy in an era of strict accountability. *Teacher Development*, *6*(1), 47–62.

Weinstein, C. S., Tomlinson-Clarke, S., Curran, M. (2004). Toward a conception of culturally responsive classroom management, *Journal of Teacher Education*, *55*(1), 25–38.

Wellesley College Center for Research on Women. (1992). *The AAUW report: How schools shortchange girls*. Washington, DC: American Association of University Women Educational Foundation.

Wenglinsky, H. (2000). *How teaching matters: Bringing the classroom back into discussions of teacher quality*. Princeton, NJ: Milken Family Foundation and Educational Testing Service.

Westby, C. (2010). Multiliteracies: The changing world of communication. *Topics in Language Disorders*, *30*(1), 64–71.

Whaples, R. (2005). Child labor in the United States. EH.Net Encyclopedia, edited by Robert Whaples. Retrieved from http://eh.net/encyclopedia/article/whaples.childlabor.

Whitehurst, T., & Howells, A. (2006). "When something is different people fear it": Children's perceptions of an arts-based inclusion project. *Support for Learning*, *21*(1), 40–44.

Wiggins, G., & McTighe, J. (2005). *Understanding by design* (2nd ed). Alexandria, VA: Association for Curriculum and Supervision.

Wiggins, G., & McTighe, J. (2006). Examining the teaching life. *Educational Leadership*, *63*(3), 26–29.

Wilkins, M. M., Wilkins, J. L. M., & Oliver, T. (2006). Differentiating the curriculum for elementary gifted mathematics students. *Teaching Children Mathematics, 13*(1), 6–13.

Williams, R. (2009). Black-white biracial students in American schools: A review of the literature. *Review of Educational Research, 79*, 776–804.

Wimer, J. W., Ridenour, C. S., Thomas, K., & Place, A. W. (2001). Higher order teacher questioning of boys and girls in elementary mathematics classrooms. *Journal of Educational Research, 95*(2), 84–92.

Wisconsin Model Academic Standards. (1998). Retrieved from http://dpi.wi.gov/standards/elaa12.html.

Witzel, B. S., & Mercer, C. D. (2003). Using rewards to teach students with disabilities: Implications for motivation. *Remedial and Special Education, 24*(2), 88–96.

Wolk, R. (2010). Education: The case for making it personal. *Educational Leadership, 67*(7), 16–21.

Wong, H. (1998). *The first days of school.* Mountain View, CA: Harry K. Wong Publications.

Wong Fillmore, L, & Snow, C. (2000). *What teachers need to know about language.* ERIC Clearinghouse on Languages and Linguistics.

Wormeli, R. (2001). *Meet me in the middle: Becoming an accomplished middle-level teacher.* Portland, ME: Stenhouse.

Wormeli, R. (2006). *Fair isn't always equal: Assessing and grading in the differentiated classroom.* Portland, ME: Stenhouse.

Wren, D. (1999). School culture: Exploring the hidden curriculum. *Adolescence, 34*, 593–596.

Yang, K. (2009). Discipline or punish? Some suggestions for school policy and teacher practice. *Language Arts, 87*(1), 49–61.

Young, J. R. (27 November 2009). Teaching with Twitter: Not for the faint of heart. *Chronicle of Higher Education, 56*(14).

Younger, M. R., & Warrington, M. (2006). Would Harry and Hermione have done better in single-sex classes? A review of single-sex teaching in coeducational secondary schools in the United Kingdom. *American Educational Research Journal, 43*, 579–620.

Yu, L., & Rachor, R. (2000). *The two-year evaluation of the three-year direct instruction program in an urban public school system.* (ERIC Document Reproduction Service No. ED 441 831).

Zirkel, P., & Thomas, L. (2010). State laws for RTI: An updated snapshot. *Teaching Exceptional Children, 42*(3), 56–63.

Zuckerman, J. (2007). Classroom management in secondary schools: A study of student teachers' successful strategies. *American Secondary Education, 35*(2), 4–16.

Index